[redacted]

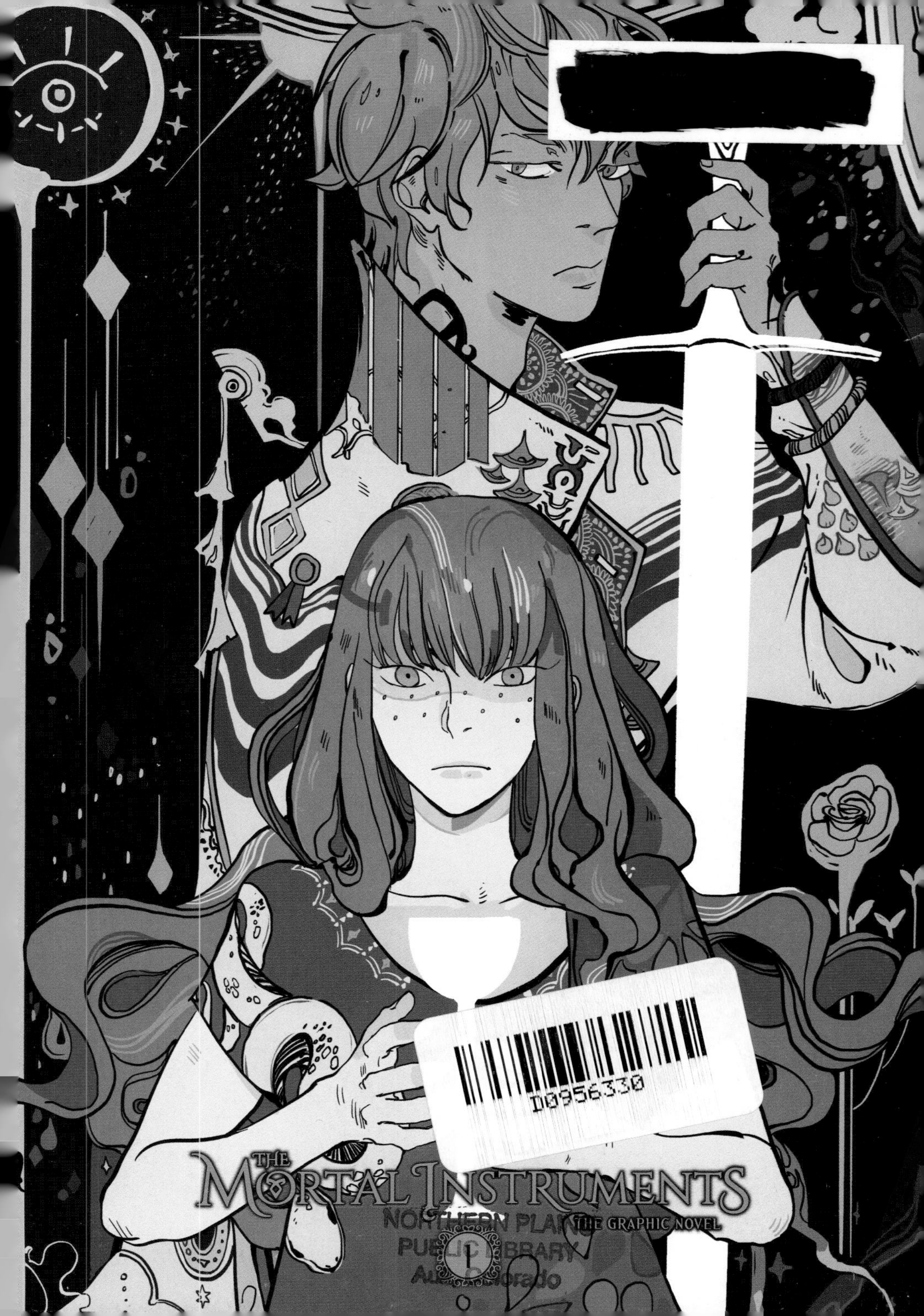
THE MORTAL INSTRUMENTS
THE GRAPHIC NOVEL
1

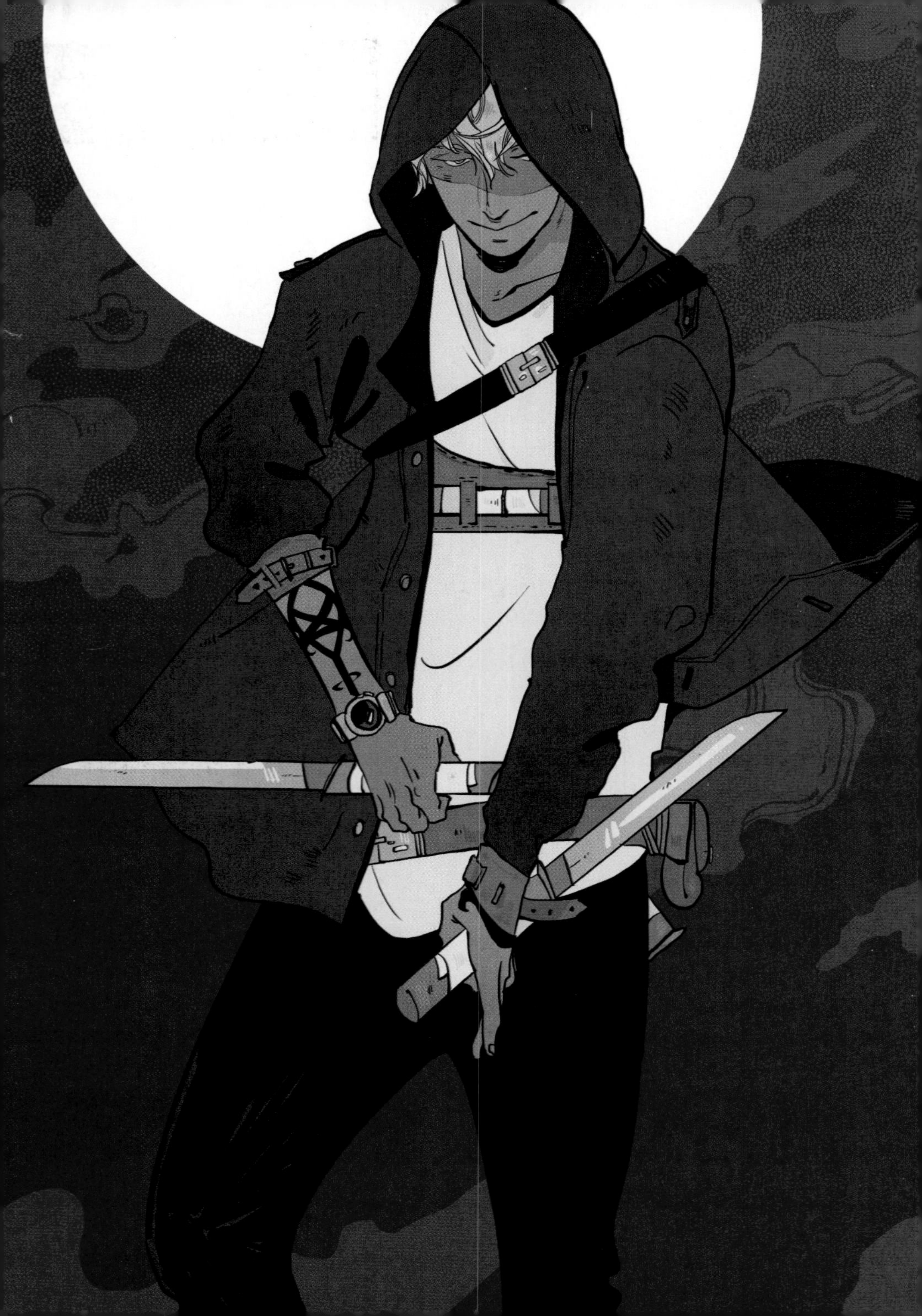

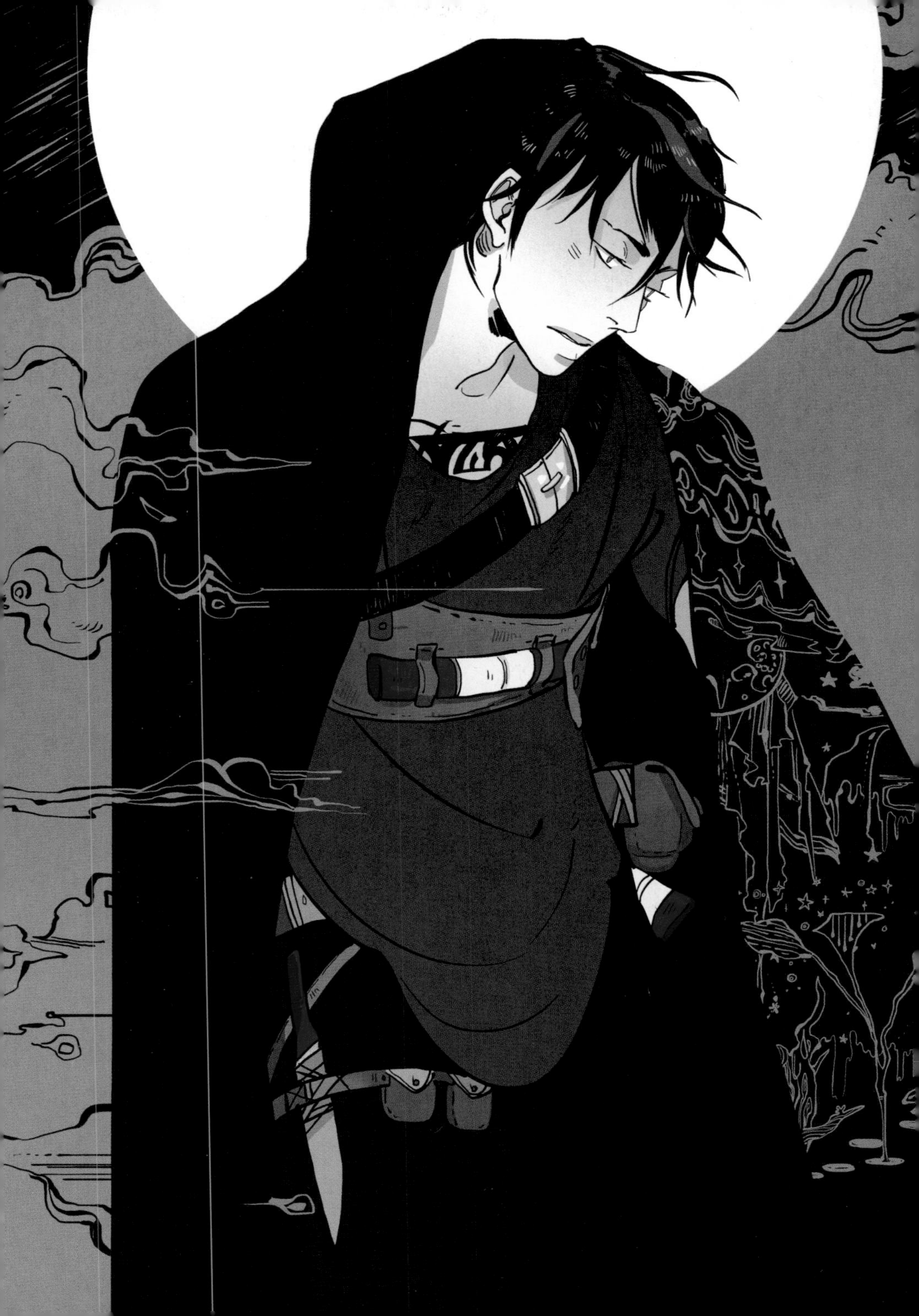

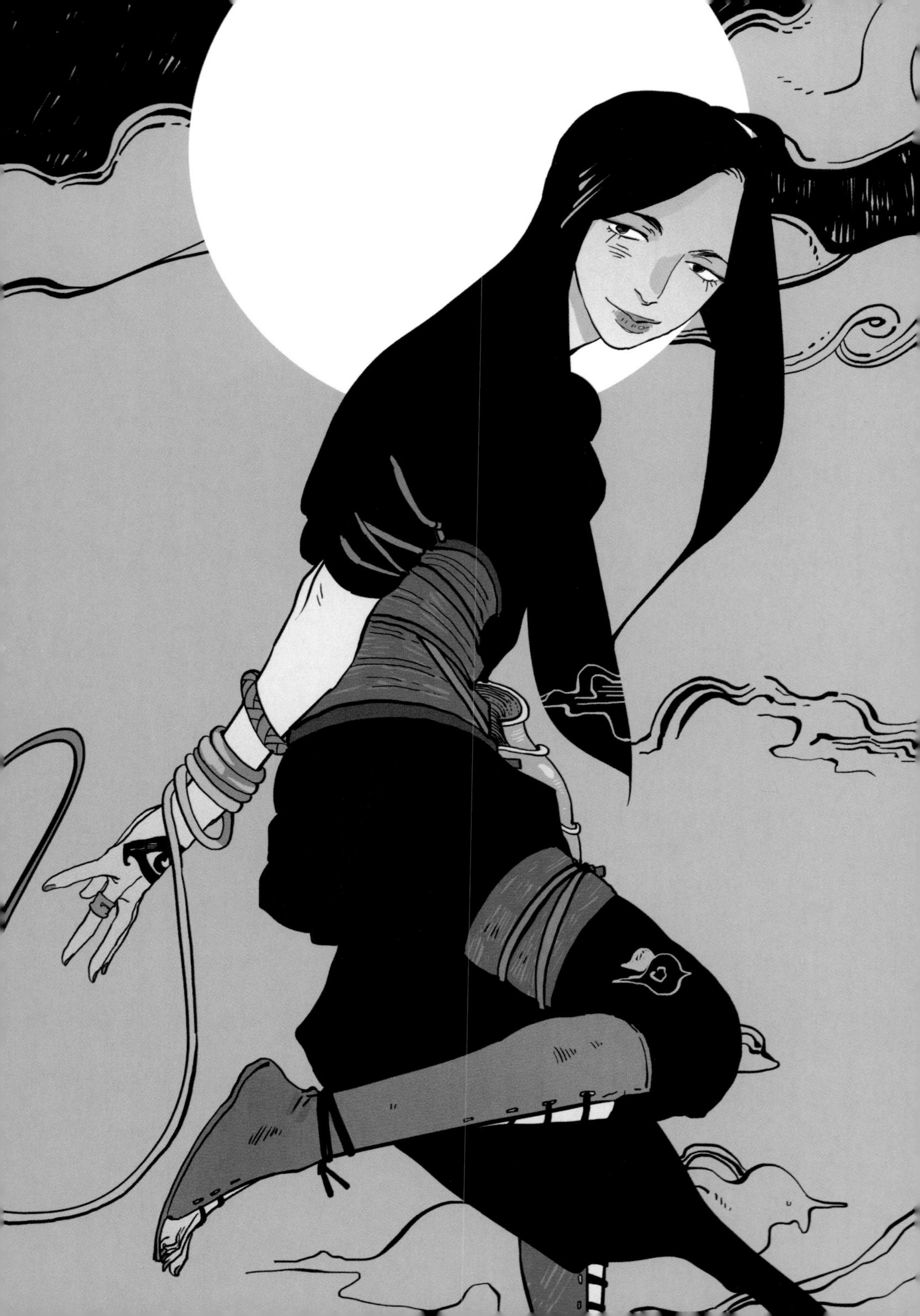

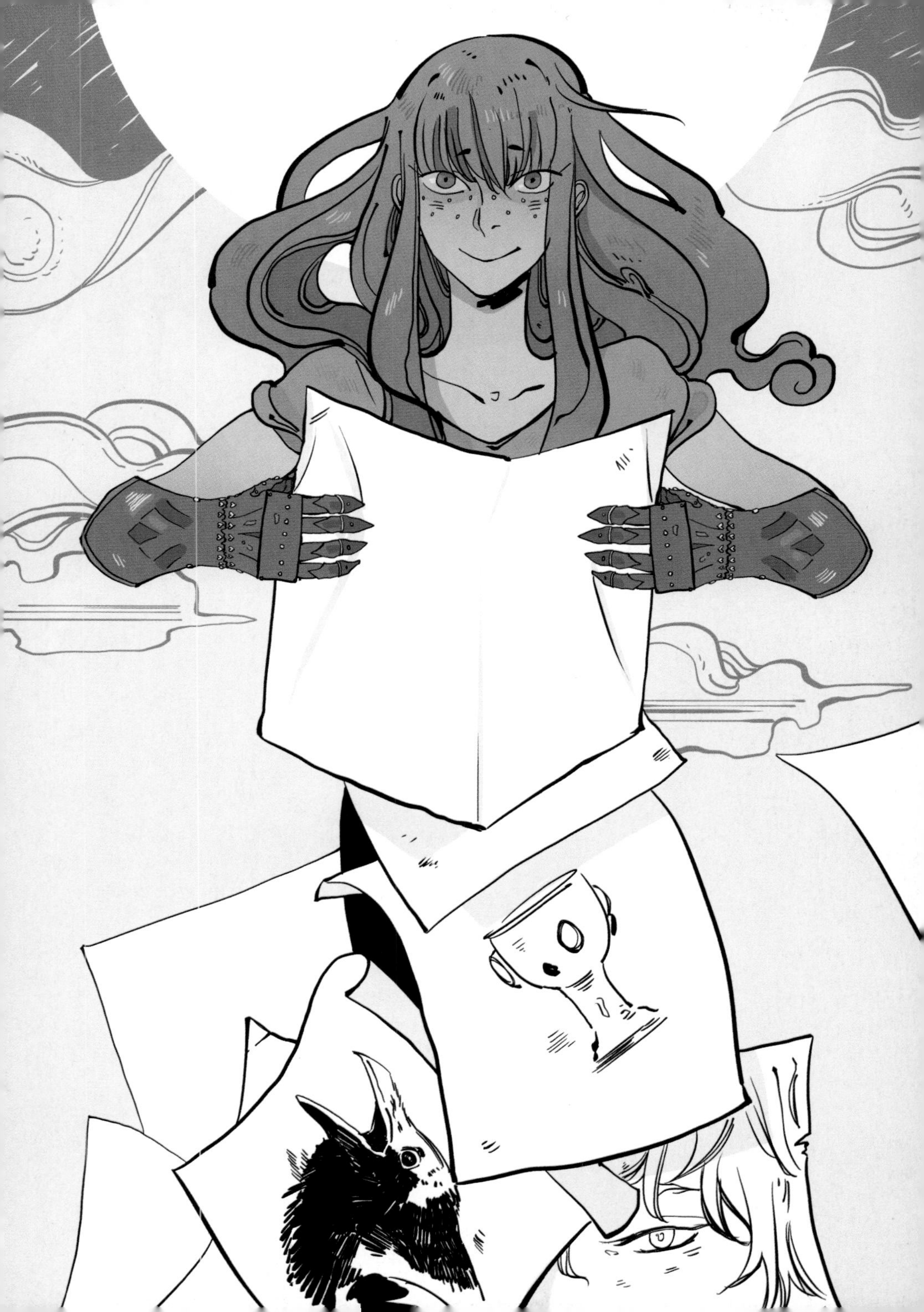

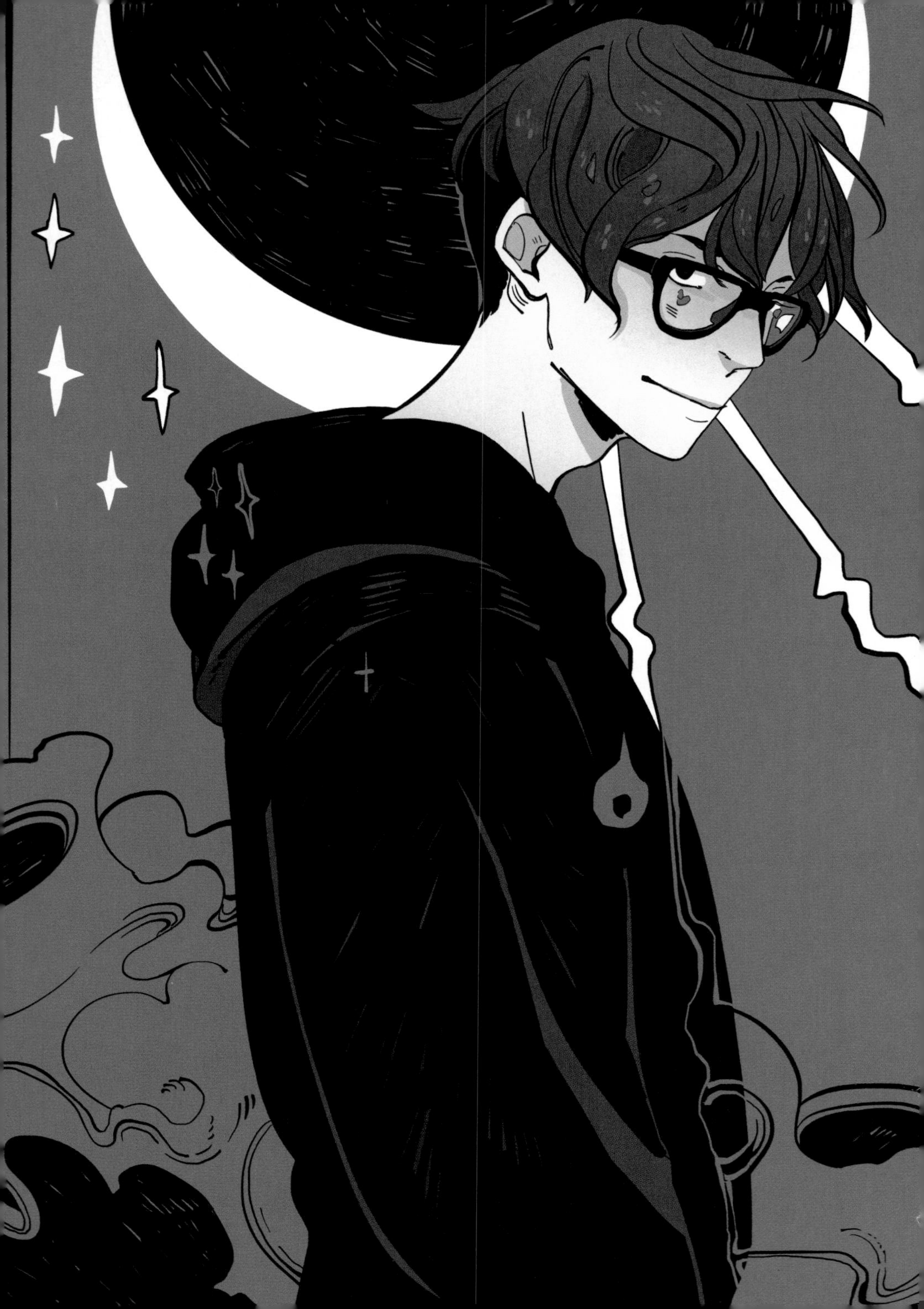

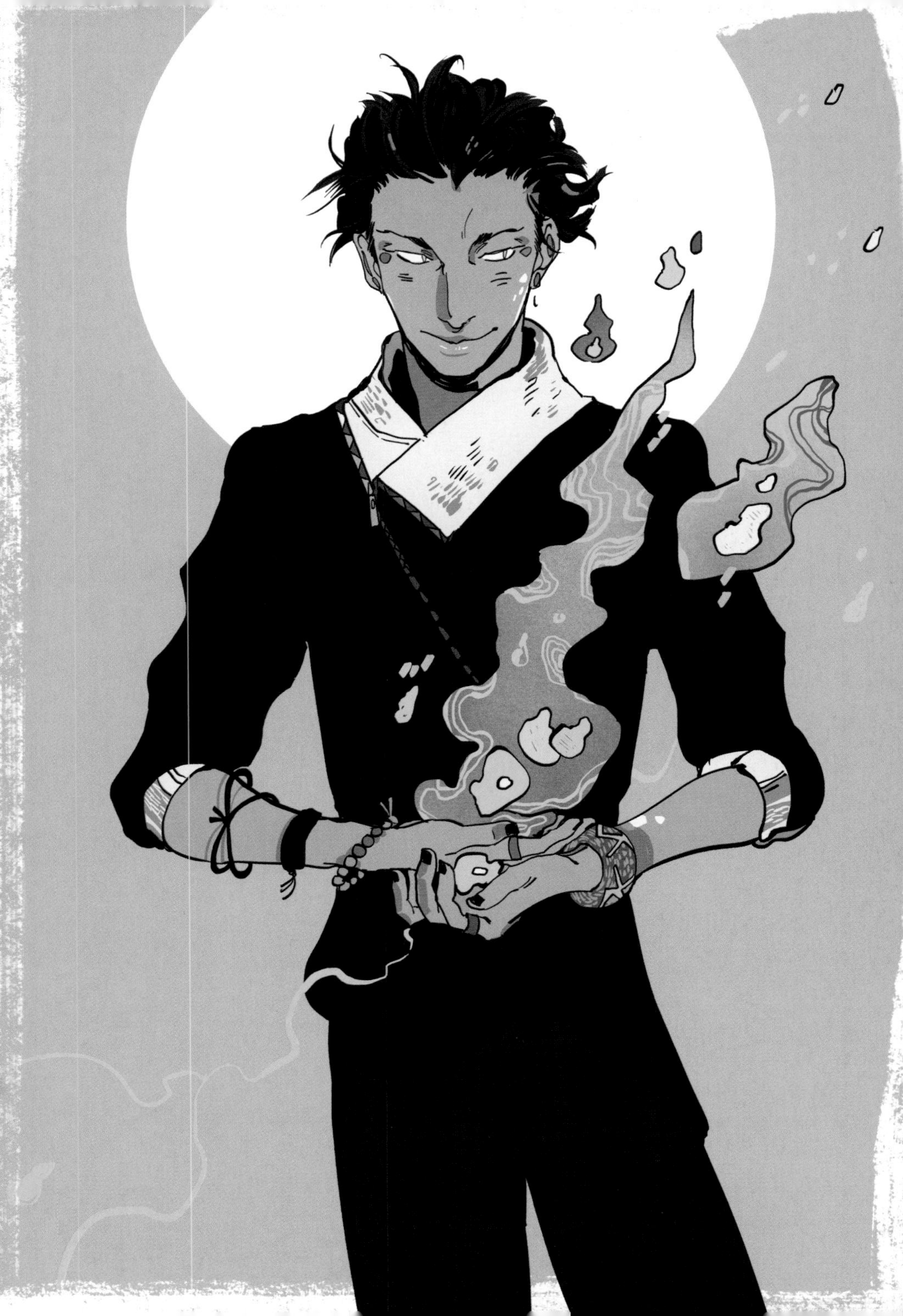

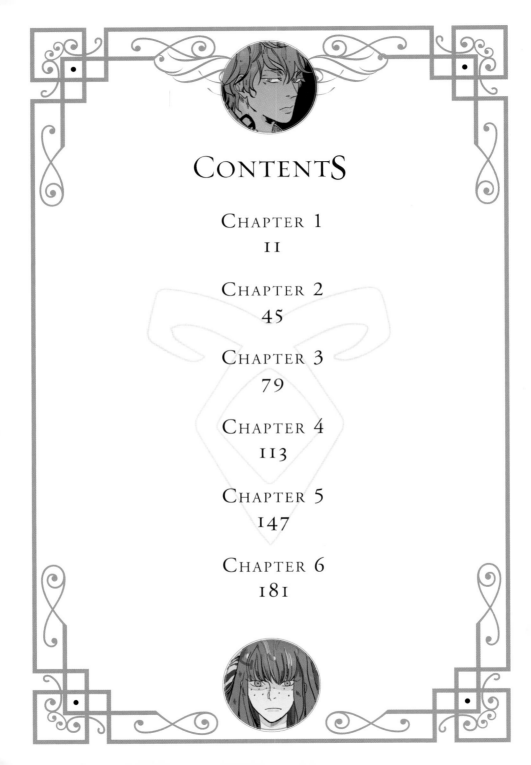

CONTENTS

From Cassandra Clare

I'm delighted to share *The Mortal Instruments* graphic novels with you at last. I've looked forward to this adaptation for years, hoping it would take shape, and I'm thrilled to see Clary and her friends take on new life in a new medium.

As a big fan of graphic novels, film, and television, when I write I tend to have a visual, cinematic vision of the scenes I'm composing. One of the wonderful aspects of graphic novel adaptation is that you get to see your favorite scenes brought to life in a manner that remains very faithful to the way they occur in the source material, while at the same time getting to layer in lots of fun little details, visual clues, and facial expressions that wouldn't otherwise be included.

Cassandra Jean is the perfect person to bring *The Mortal Instruments* to life visually. I first encountered Cassandra's work when I came across her Shadowhunter fan art. I was blown away by how similar her renderings of the characters were to the way I envisioned them in my own mind. Eventually, I hired her to create official Shadowhunter artwork, including a tarot deck and a series of character portraits based on the Victorian language of flowers. At this point, it's getting hard to keep track of all the wonderful Shadow World art she's created, and her illustrations have become a vital and familiar part of the Shadowhunter chronicles. With this project, I love that she gets to return to where it all started... with Clary and Simon, Jace, Isabelle, and Alec, and their fateful evening at the Pandemonium Club.

This graphic adaptation feels especially appropriate, since Clary herself is an artist and avid reader of manga, comics, and other sequential art. I've always aimed to write about people who feel as real as friends, and since so many of my friends love comics and graphic novels, I wrote characters who share those interests. Clary and Simon would love this adaptation. I know I sure do.

THE MORTAL INSTRUMENTS ❶
THE GRAPHIC NOVEL

CASSANDRA CLARE
CASSANDRA JEAN

ART AND ADAPTATION: CASSANDRA JEAN
LETTERING: JUYOUN LEE

Yen Press
1290 Avenue of the Americas
New York, NY 10104

Visit us at yenpress.com
facebook.com/yenpress
twitter.com/yenpress
yenpress.tumblr.com
instagram.com/yenpress

First Yen Press Edition: October 2017

Yen Press is an imprint of Yen Press, LLC.
The Yen Press name and logo are trademarks of Yen Press, LLC.

The publisher is not responsible for websites (or their content) that are not owned by the publisher.

Library of Congress Control Number: 2017945496

ISBNs: 978-0-316-46581-6 (paperback)
978-0-316-47637-9 (ebook)

10 9 8 7 6 5 4 3

WOR

Printed in the United States of America

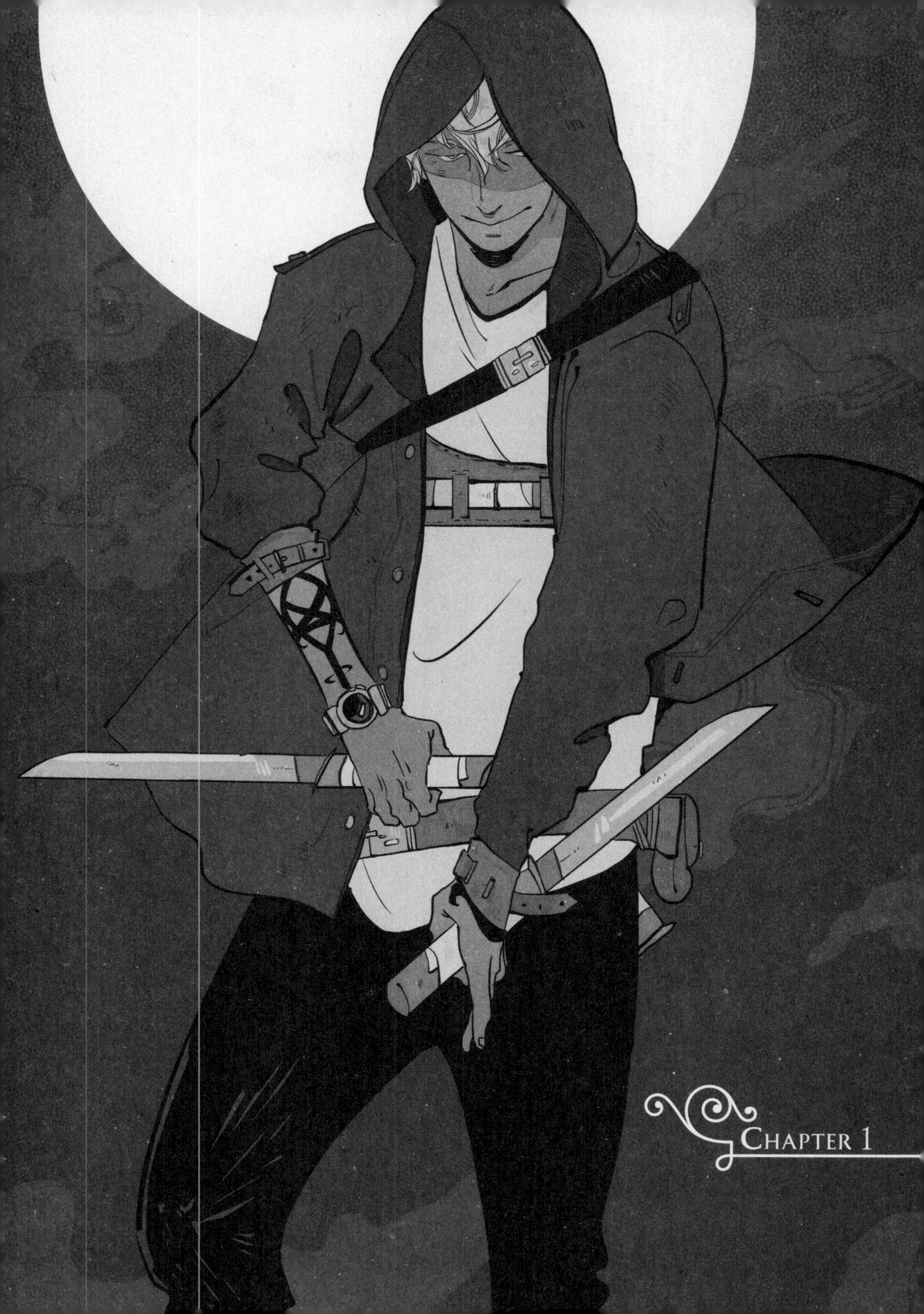

Chapter 1

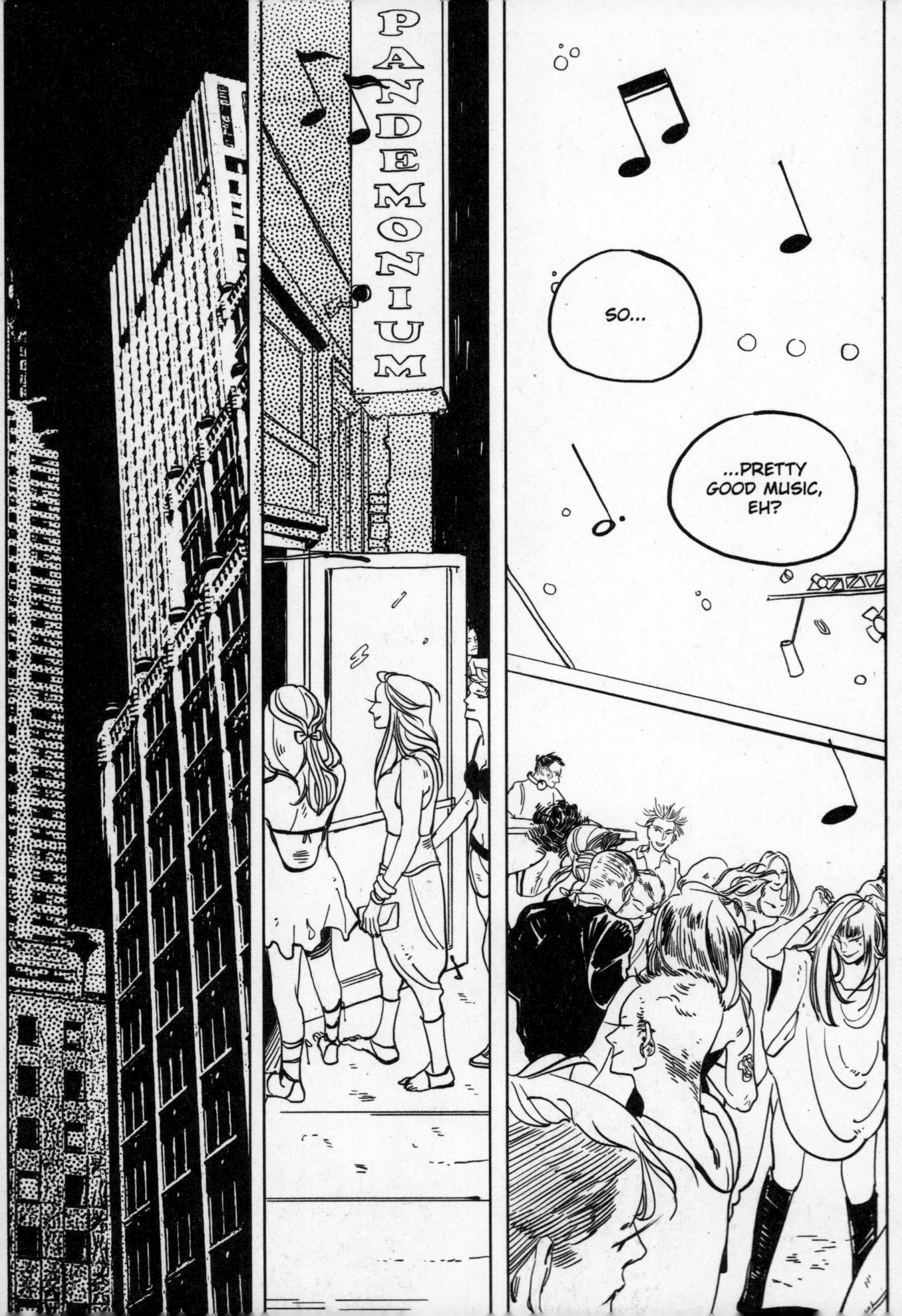
PANDEMONIUM
SO...
...PRETTY GOOD MUSIC, EH?

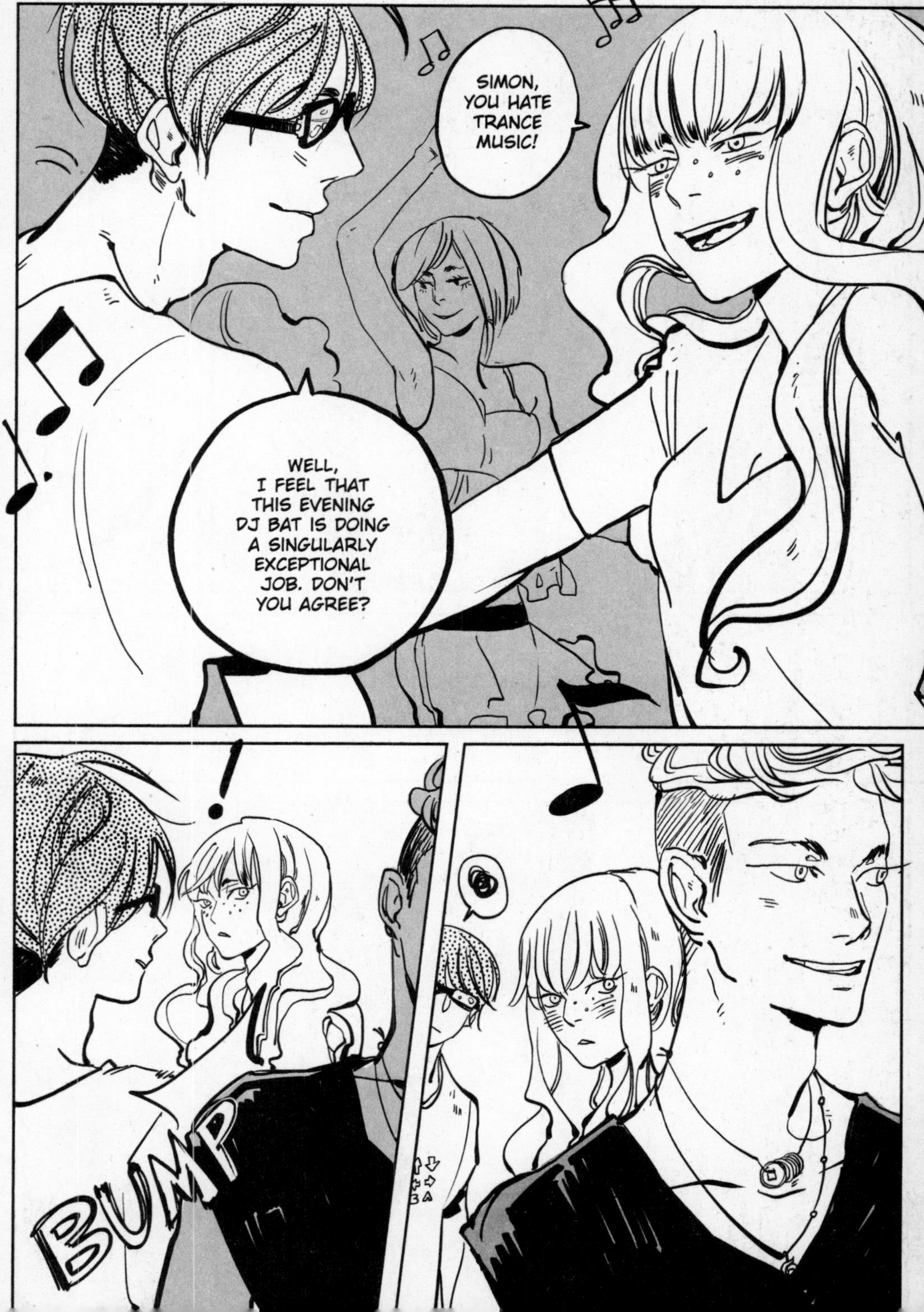
SIMON, YOU HATE TRANCE MUSIC!
WELL, I FEEL THAT THIS EVENING DJ BAT IS DOING A SINGULARLY EXCEPTIONAL JOB. DON'T YOU AGREE?
!
BUMP

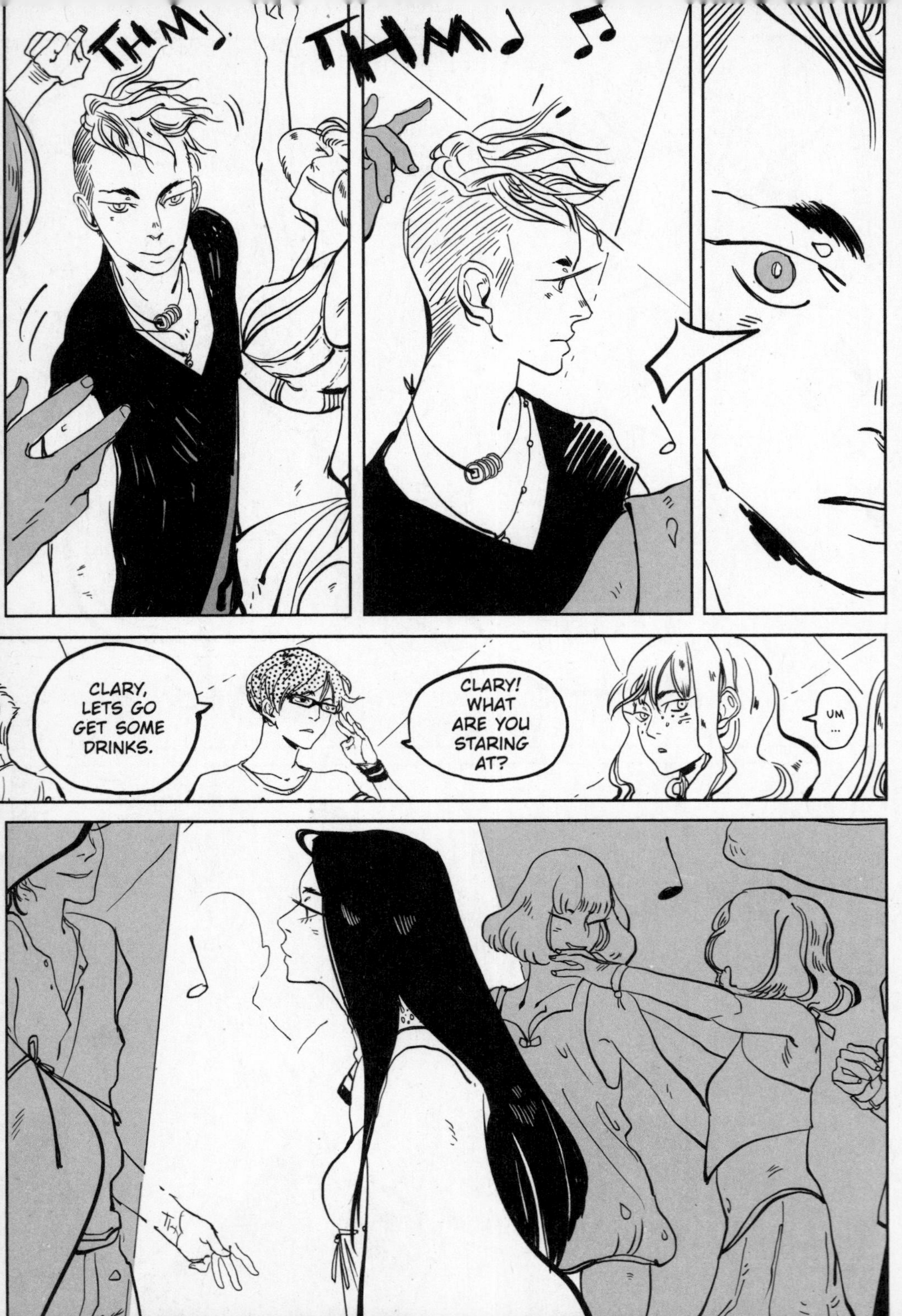
THM♪
THM♪♫
CLARY, LETS GO GET SOME DRINKS.
CLARY! WHAT ARE YOU STARING AT?
UM ...

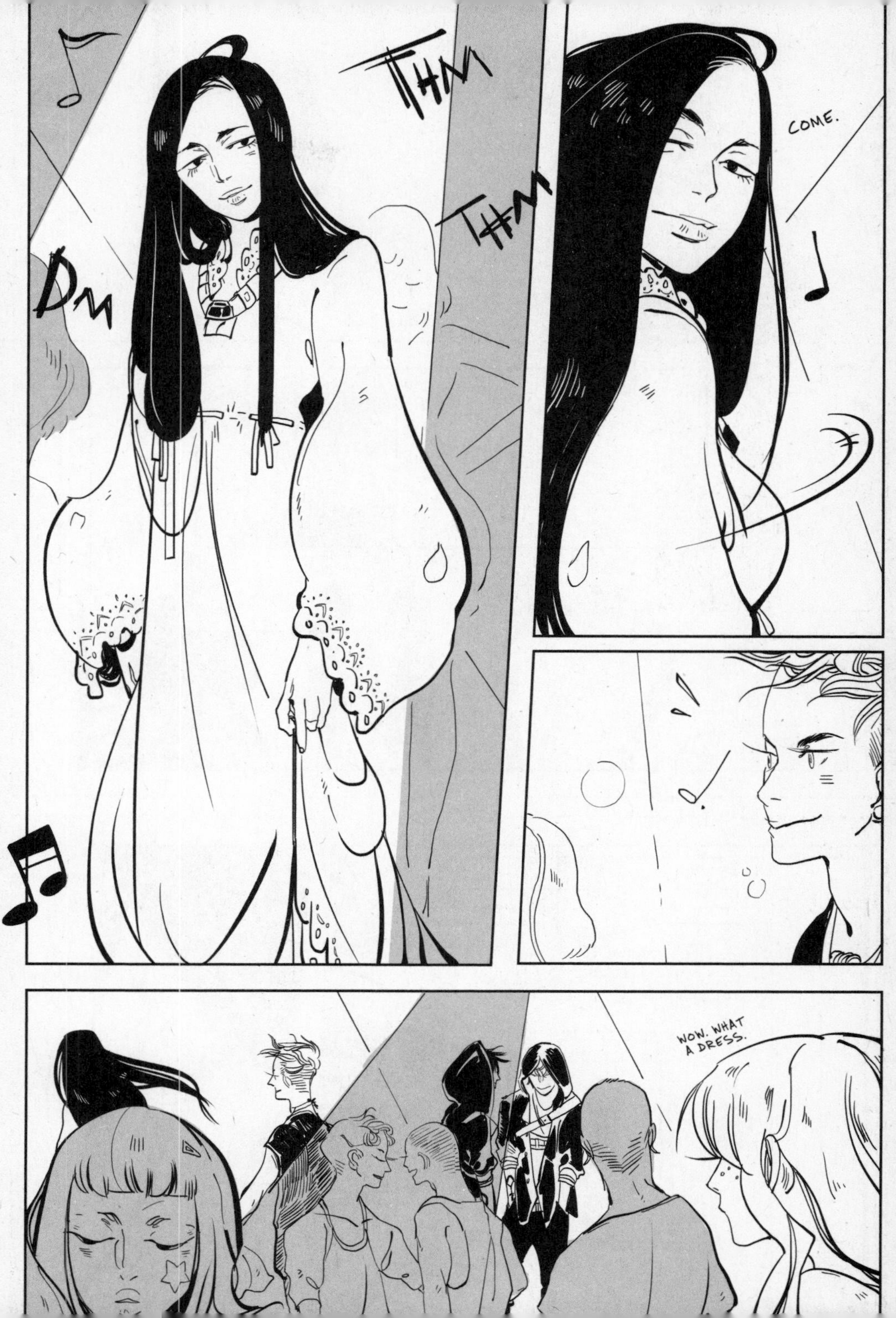

THM
THM
DM
COME.
WOW. WHAT A DRESS.

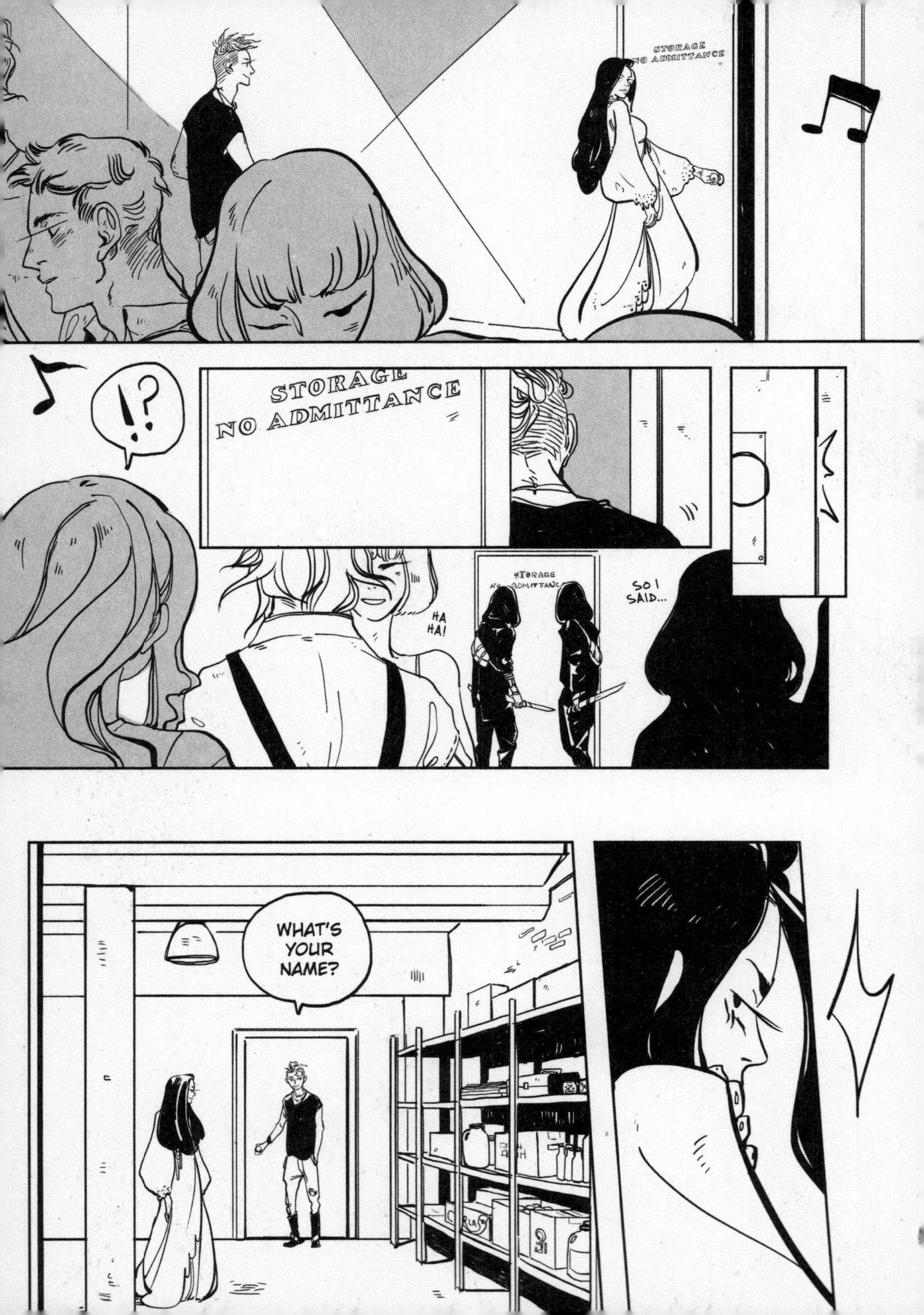
STORAGE
NO ADMITTANCE
!?
STORAGE
NO ADMITTANCE
STORAGE
NO ADMITTANCE
HA HA!
SO I SAID...
WHAT'S YOUR NAME?

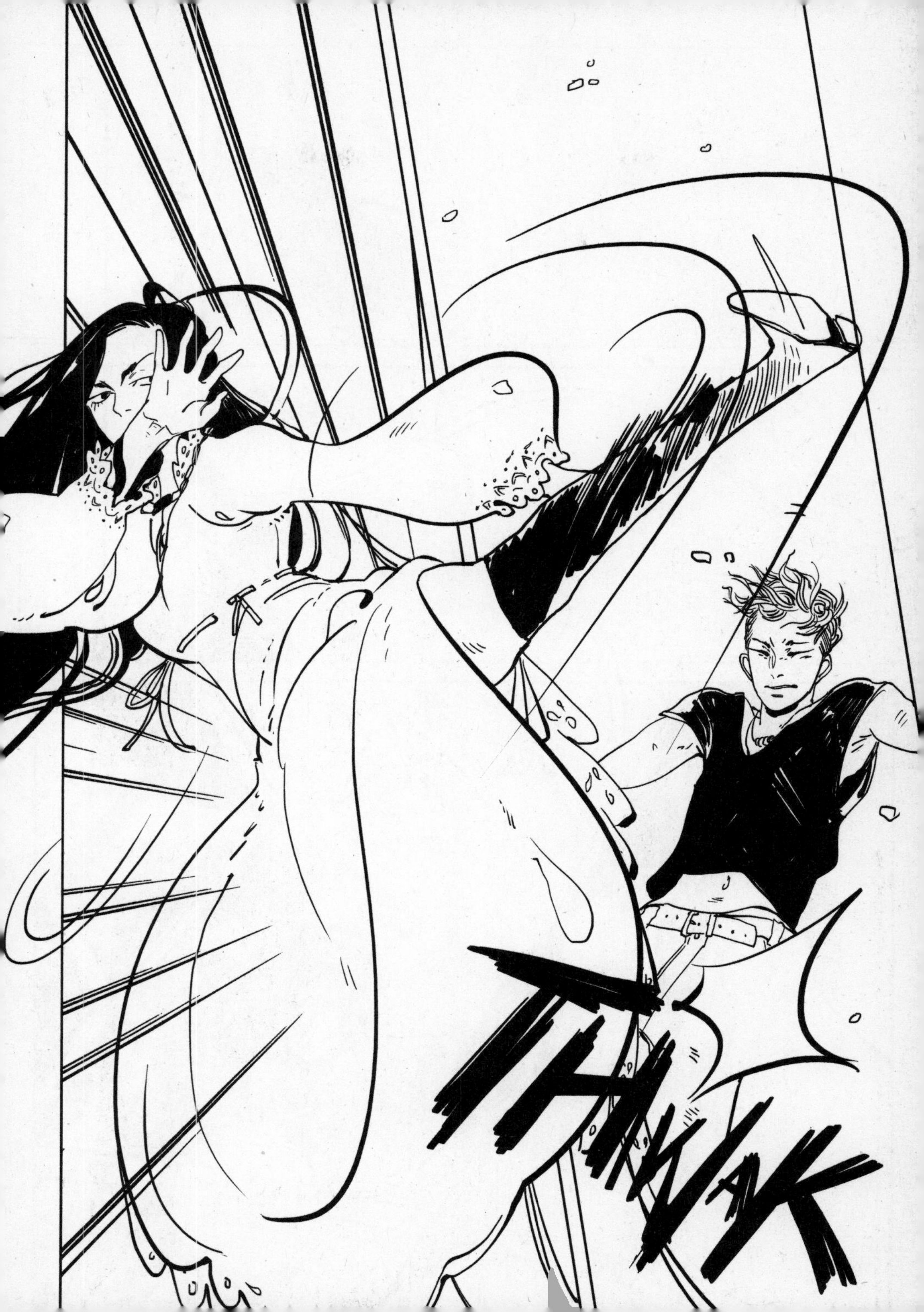
THWAK

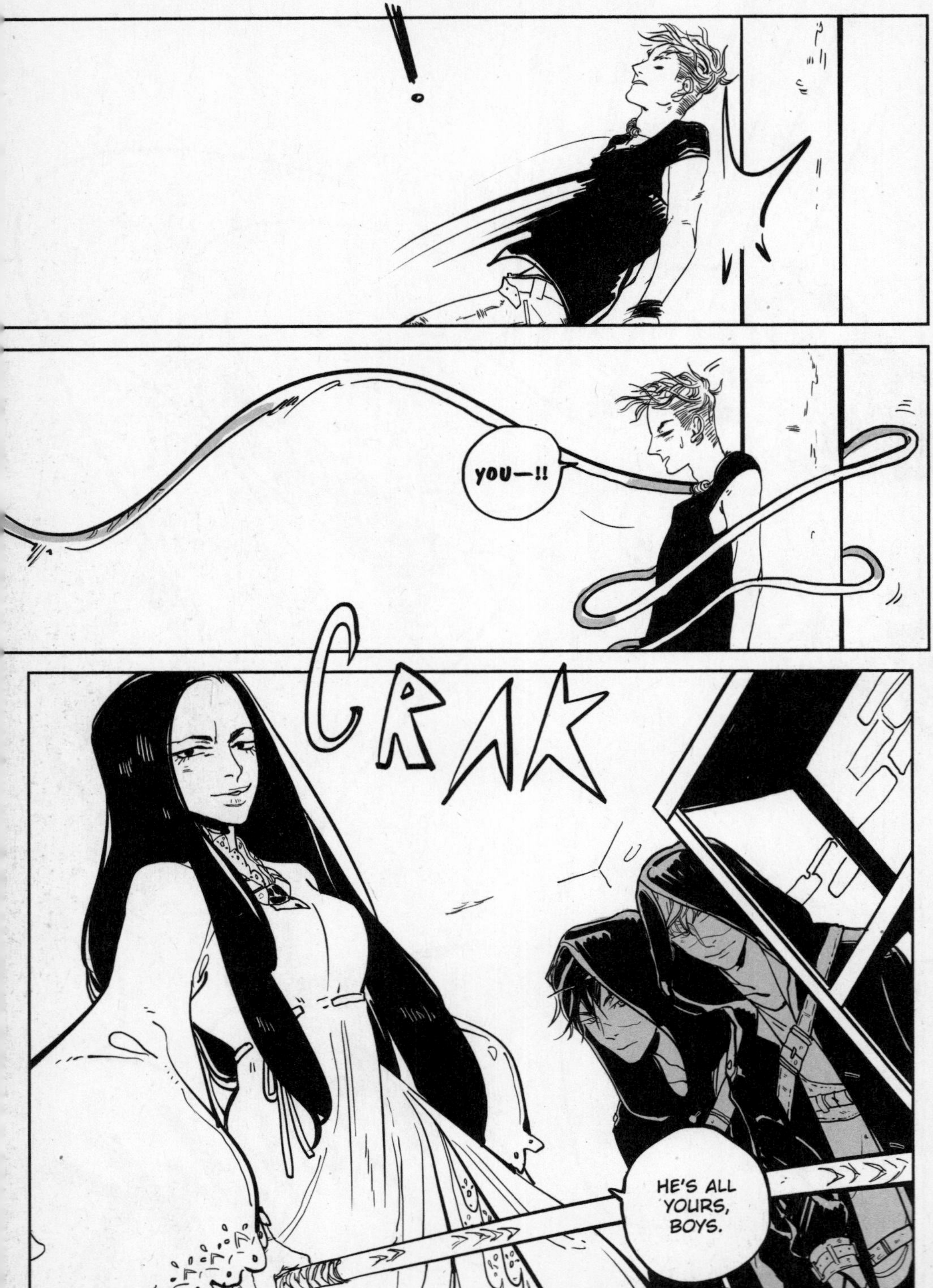
!
YOU—!!
CRAK
HE'S ALL YOURS, BOYS.

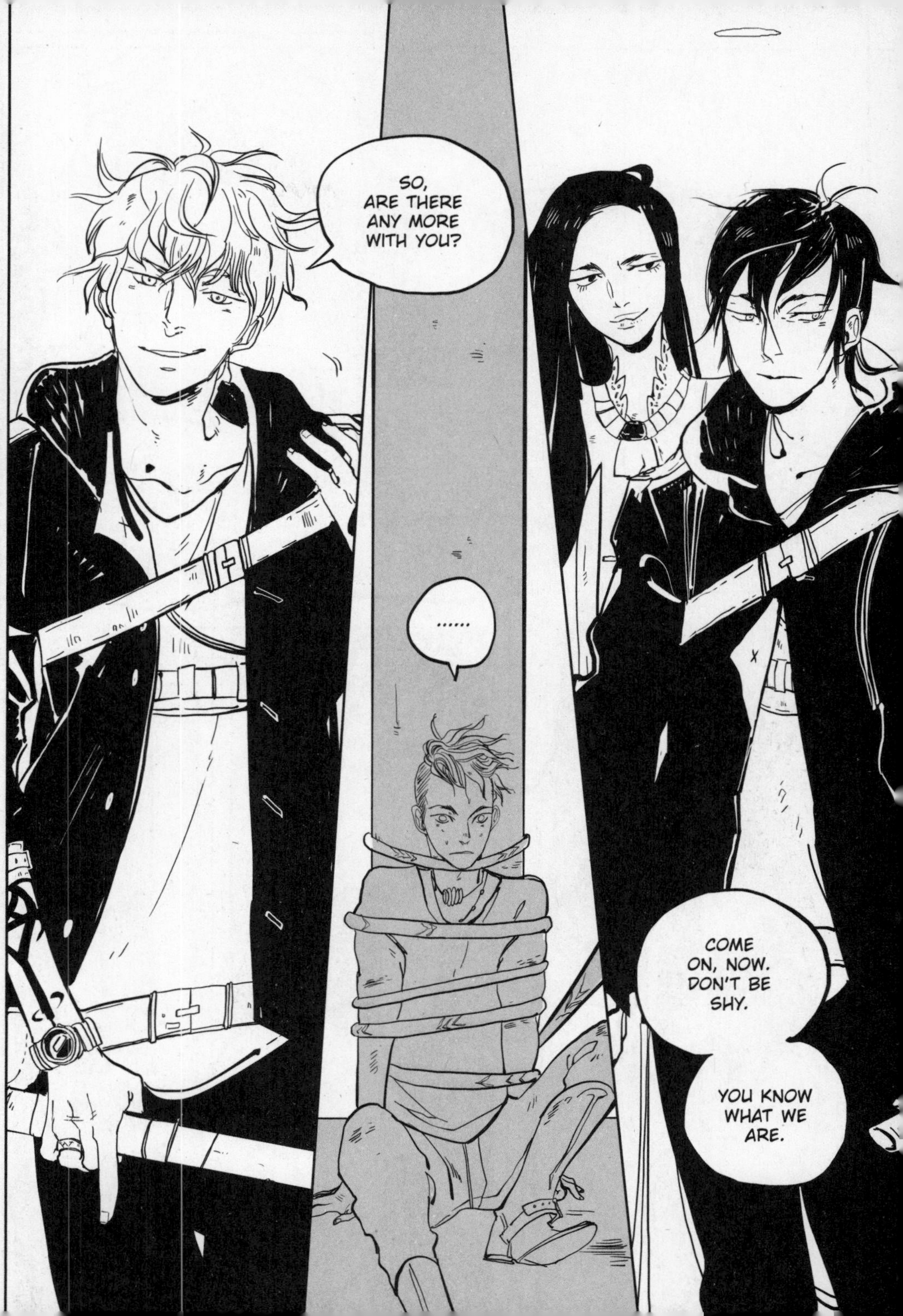
SO, ARE THERE ANY MORE WITH YOU?
......
COME ON, NOW. DON'T BE SHY.
YOU KNOW WHAT WE ARE.

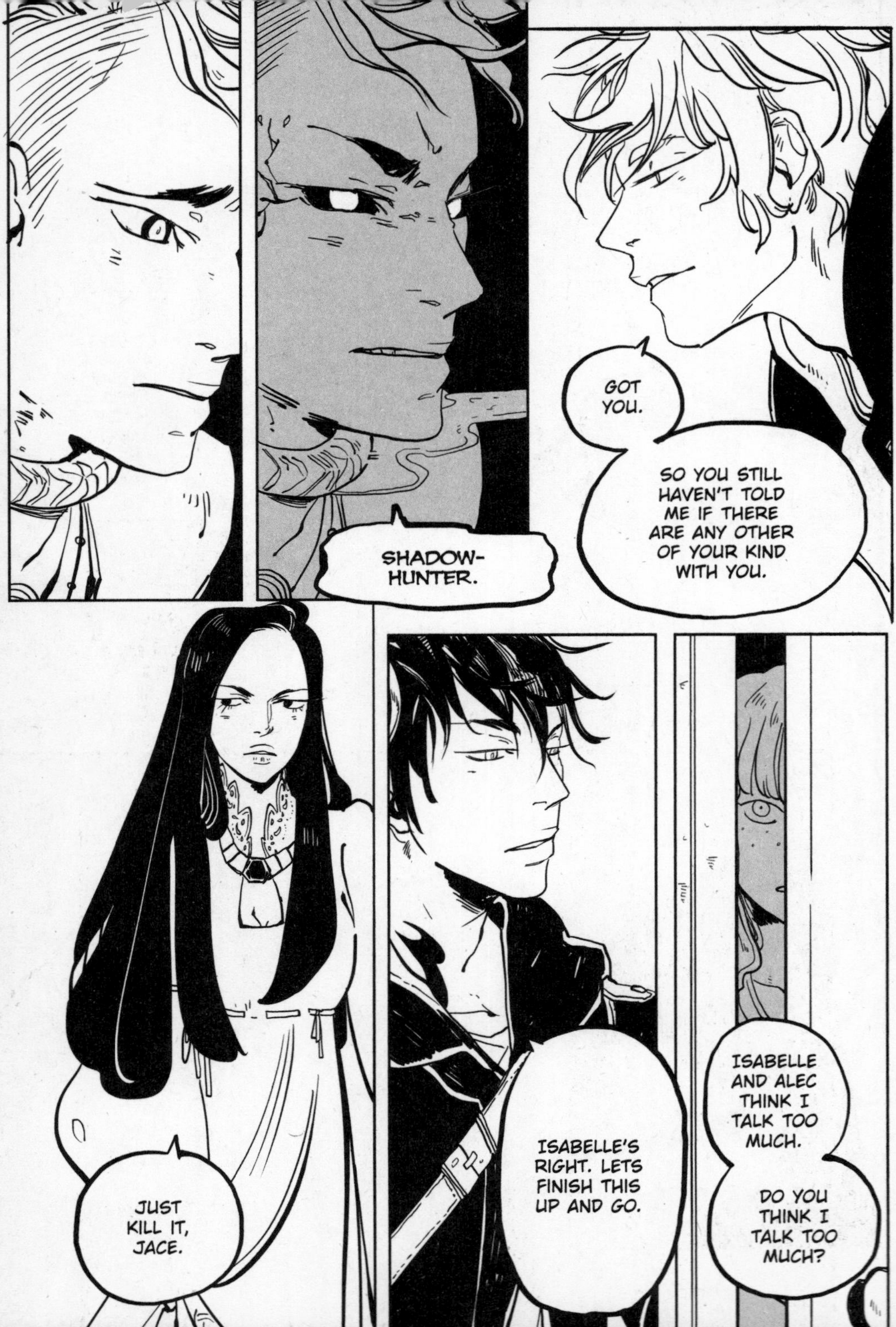
SHADOW-HUNTER.
GOT YOU.
SO YOU STILL HAVEN'T TOLD ME IF THERE ARE ANY OTHER OF YOUR KIND WITH YOU.
JUST KILL IT, JACE.
ISABELLE'S RIGHT. LETS FINISH THIS UP AND GO.
ISABELLE AND ALEC THINK I TALK TOO MUCH.
DO YOU THINK I TALK TOO MUCH?

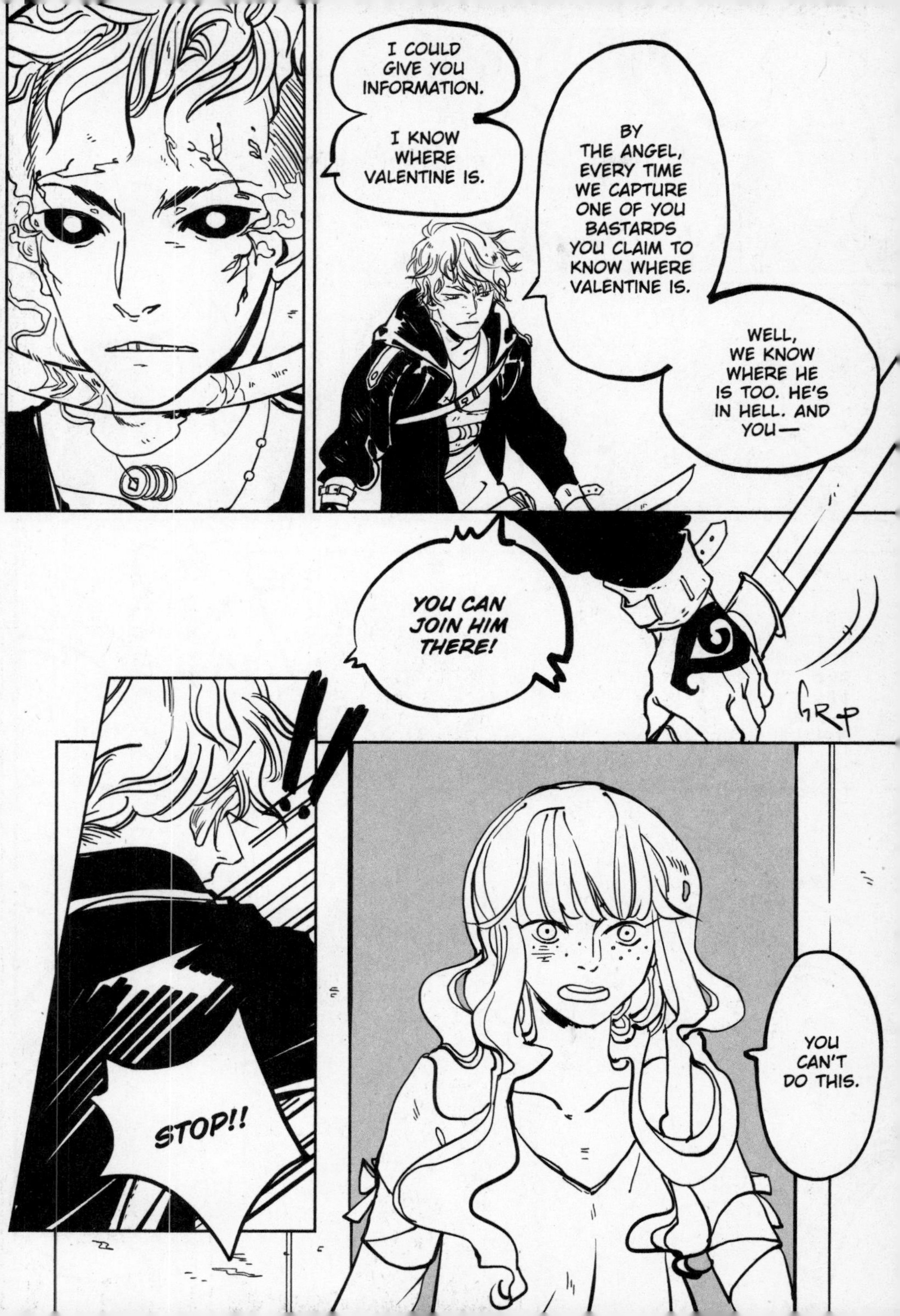
I COULD GIVE YOU INFORMATION.
I KNOW WHERE VALENTINE IS.
BY THE ANGEL, EVERY TIME WE CAPTURE ONE OF YOU BASTARDS YOU CLAIM TO KNOW WHERE VALENTINE IS.
WELL, WE KNOW WHERE HE IS TOO. HE'S IN HELL. AND YOU—
YOU CAN JOIN HIM THERE!
GRIP
!!
STOP!!
YOU CAN'T DO THIS.

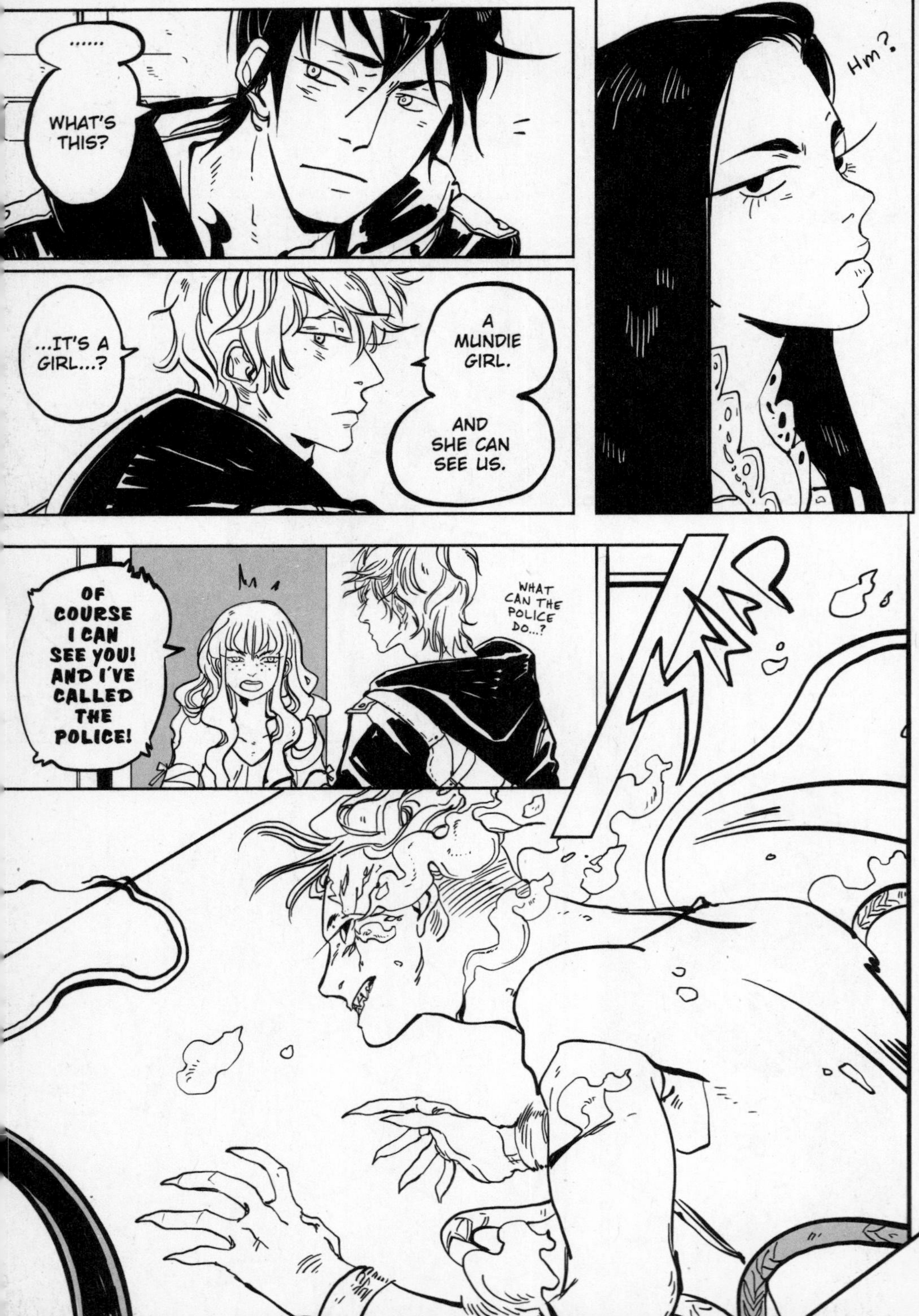
......
WHAT'S THIS?
...IT'S A GIRL...?
A MUNDIE GIRL.
AND SHE CAN SEE US.
Hm?
OF COURSE I CAN SEE YOU! AND I'VE CALLED THE POLICE!
WHAT CAN THE POLICE DO...?
SNAP

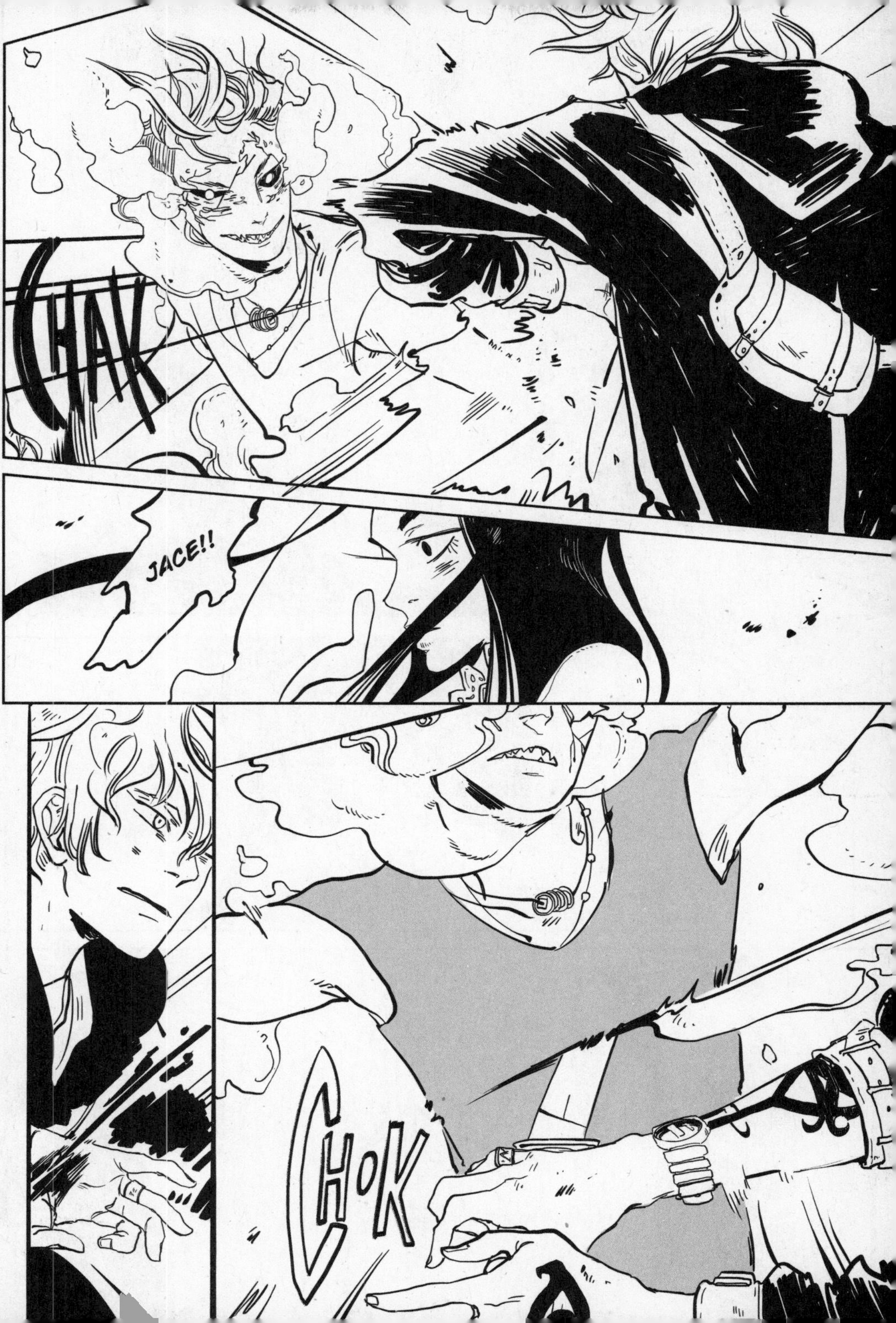
CHAK
JACE!!
CHOK

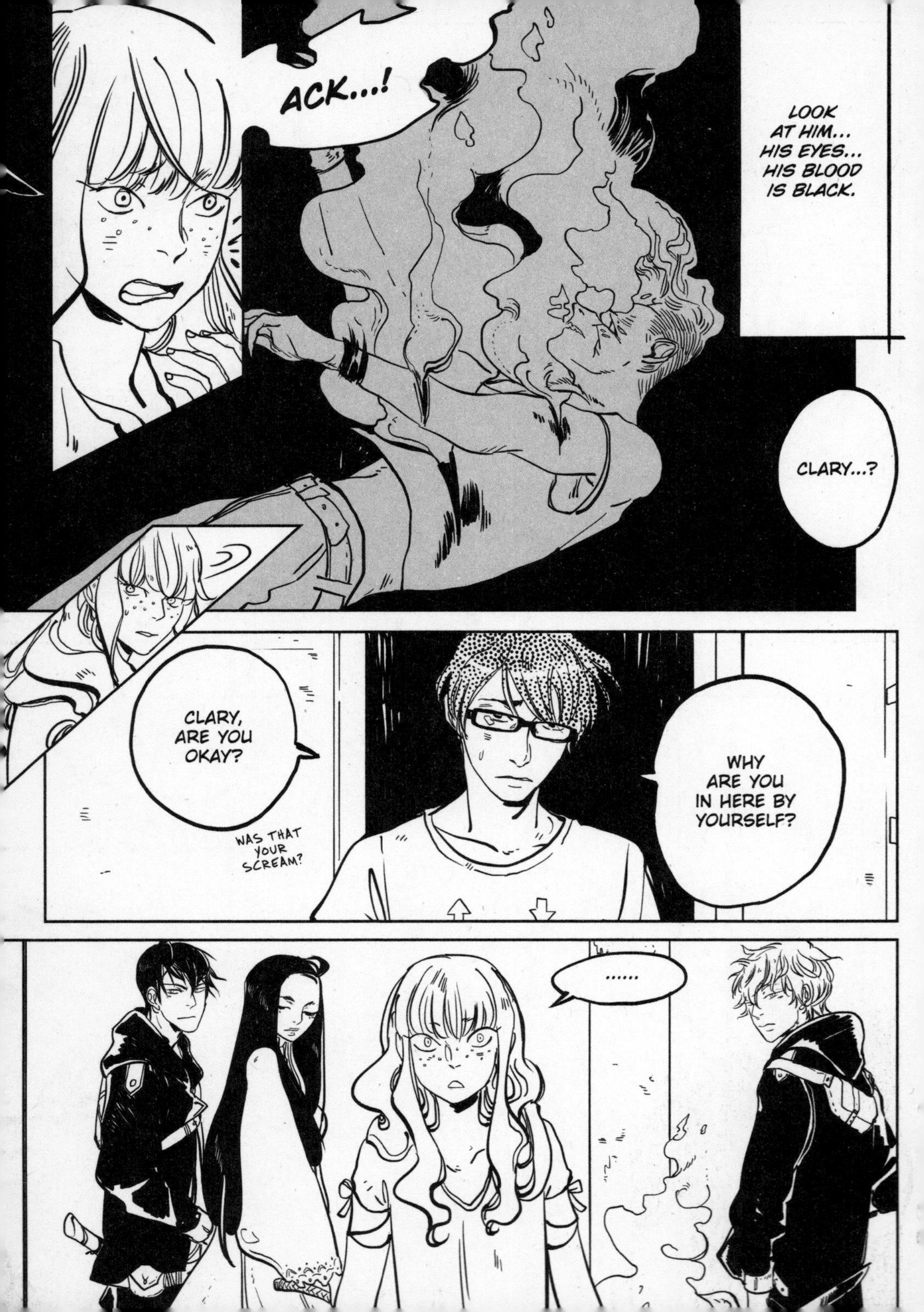
ACK...!
LOOK AT HIM... HIS EYES... HIS BLOOD IS BLACK.
CLARY...?
CLARY, ARE YOU OKAY?
WAS THAT YOUR SCREAM?
WHY ARE YOU IN HERE BY YOURSELF?
......

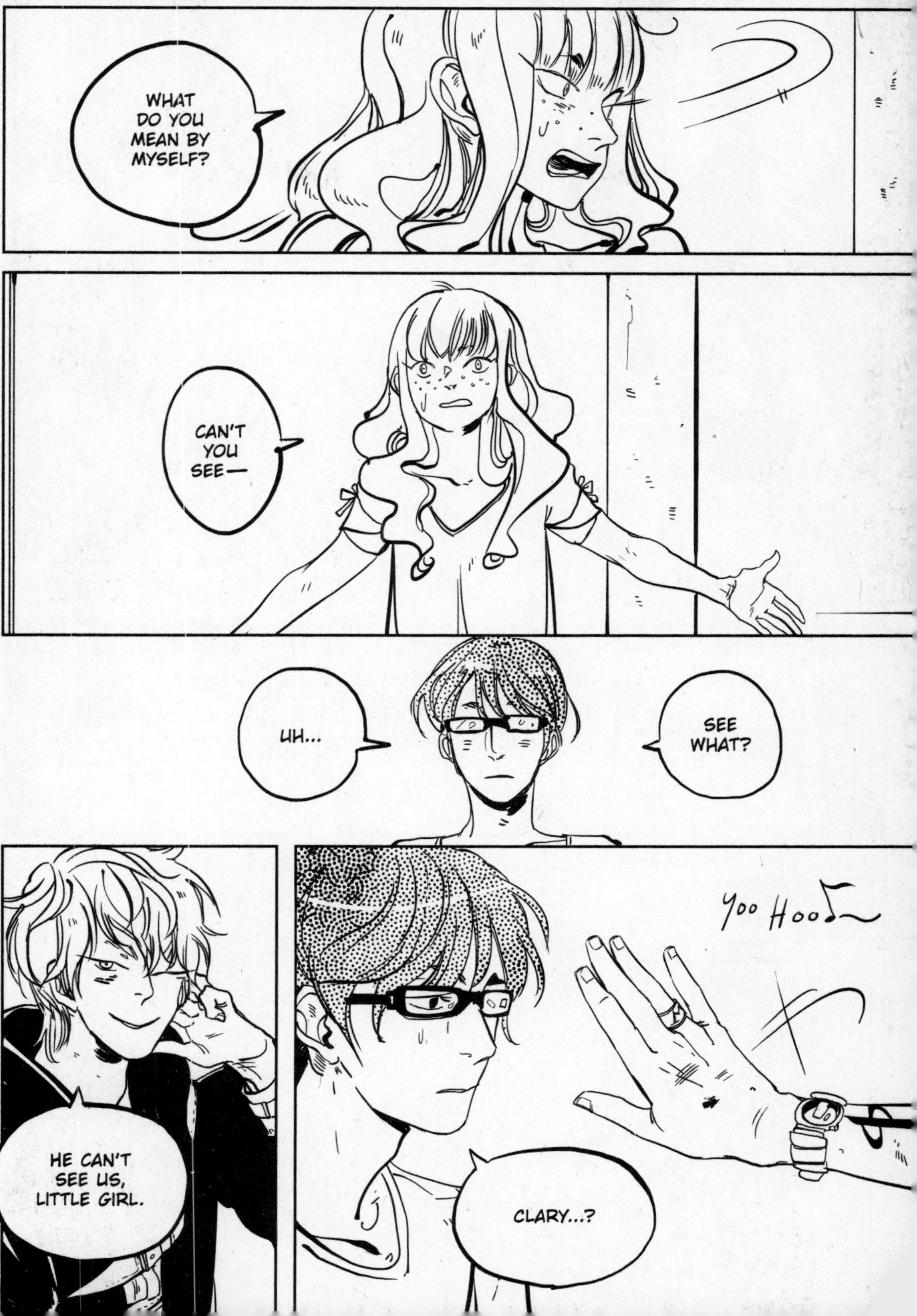
WHAT DO YOU MEAN BY MYSELF?
CAN'T YOU SEE—
UH...
SEE WHAT?
HE CAN'T SEE US, LITTLE GIRL.
YOO HOO~
CLARY...?

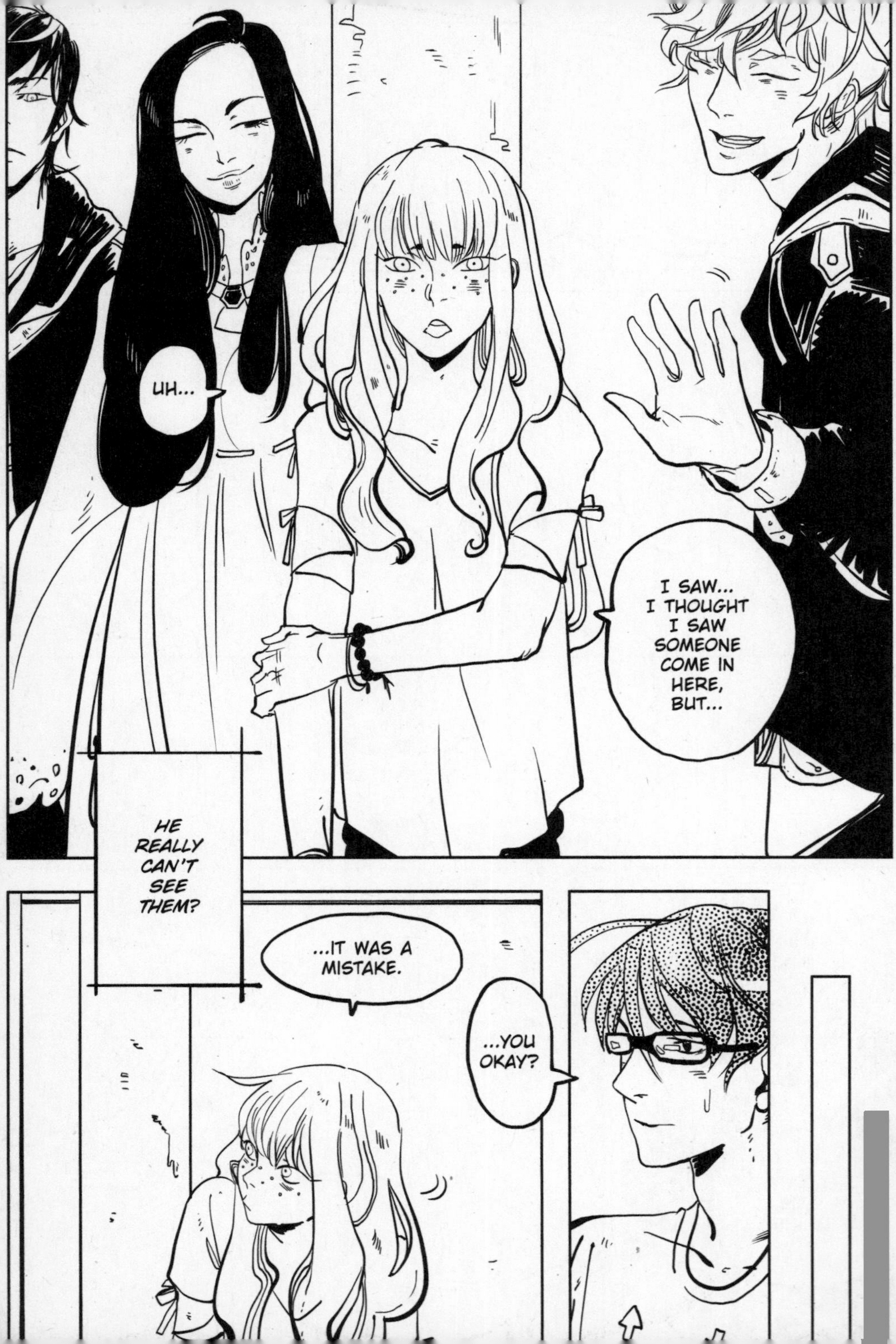
UH...
I SAW... I THOUGHT I SAW SOMEONE COME IN HERE, BUT...
HE REALLY CAN'T SEE THEM?
...IT WAS A MISTAKE.
...YOU OKAY?

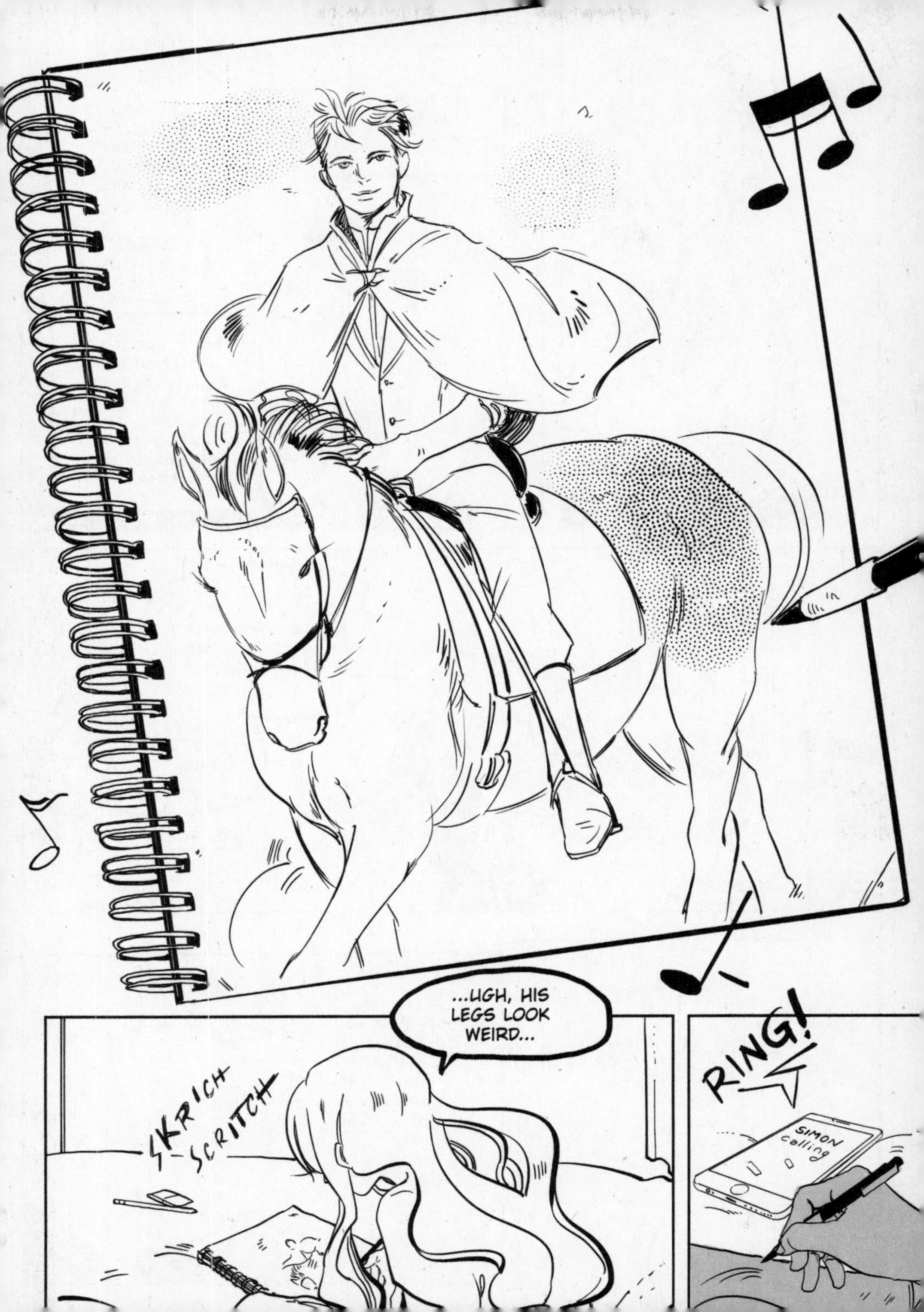
...UGH, HIS LEGS LOOK WEIRD...
SKRICH SCRITCH
RING!
SIMON calling

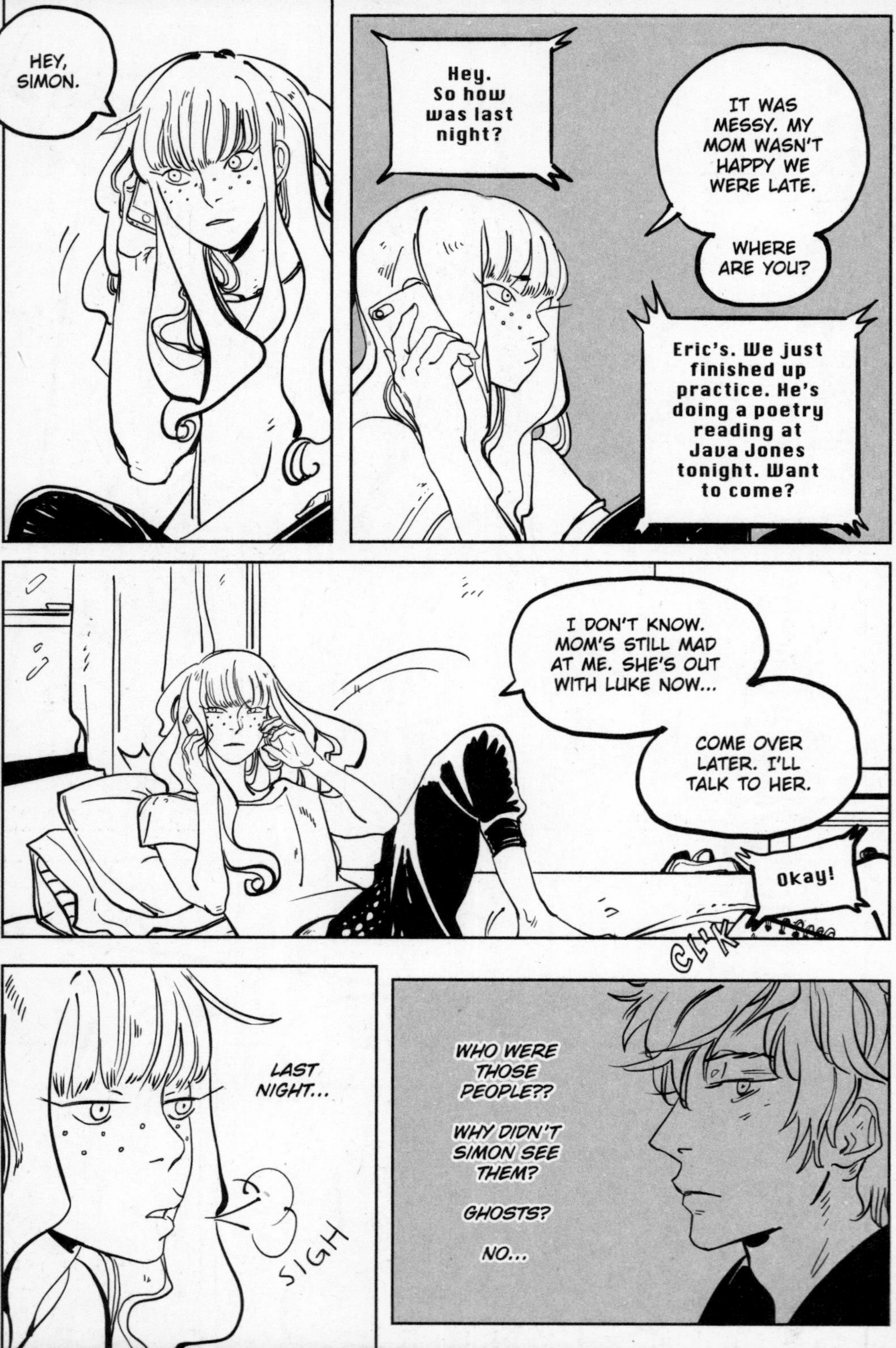
HEY, SIMON.
Hey. So how was last night?
IT WAS MESSY. MY MOM WASN'T HAPPY WE WERE LATE.
WHERE ARE YOU?
Eric's. We just finished up practice. He's doing a poetry reading at Java Jones tonight. Want to come?
I DON'T KNOW. MOM'S STILL MAD AT ME. SHE'S OUT WITH LUKE NOW...
COME OVER LATER. I'LL TALK TO HER.
Okay!
CLIK
LAST NIGHT...
SIGH
WHO WERE THOSE PEOPLE??
WHY DIDN'T SIMON SEE THEM?
GHOSTS?
NO...

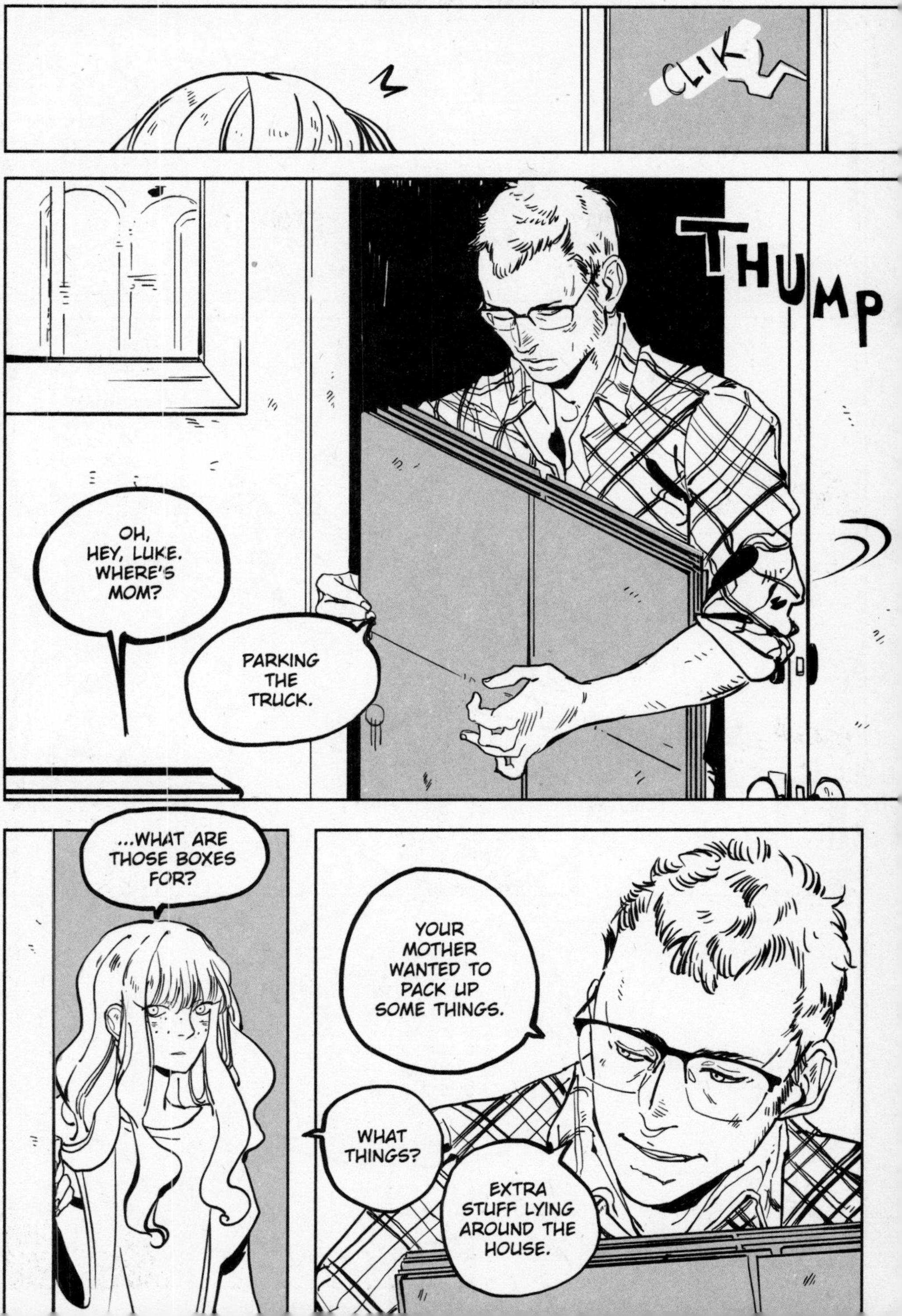
CLIK
THUMP
OH, HEY, LUKE. WHERE'S MOM?
PARKING THE TRUCK.
...WHAT ARE THOSE BOXES FOR?
YOUR MOTHER WANTED TO PACK UP SOME THINGS.
WHAT THINGS?
EXTRA STUFF LYING AROUND THE HOUSE.

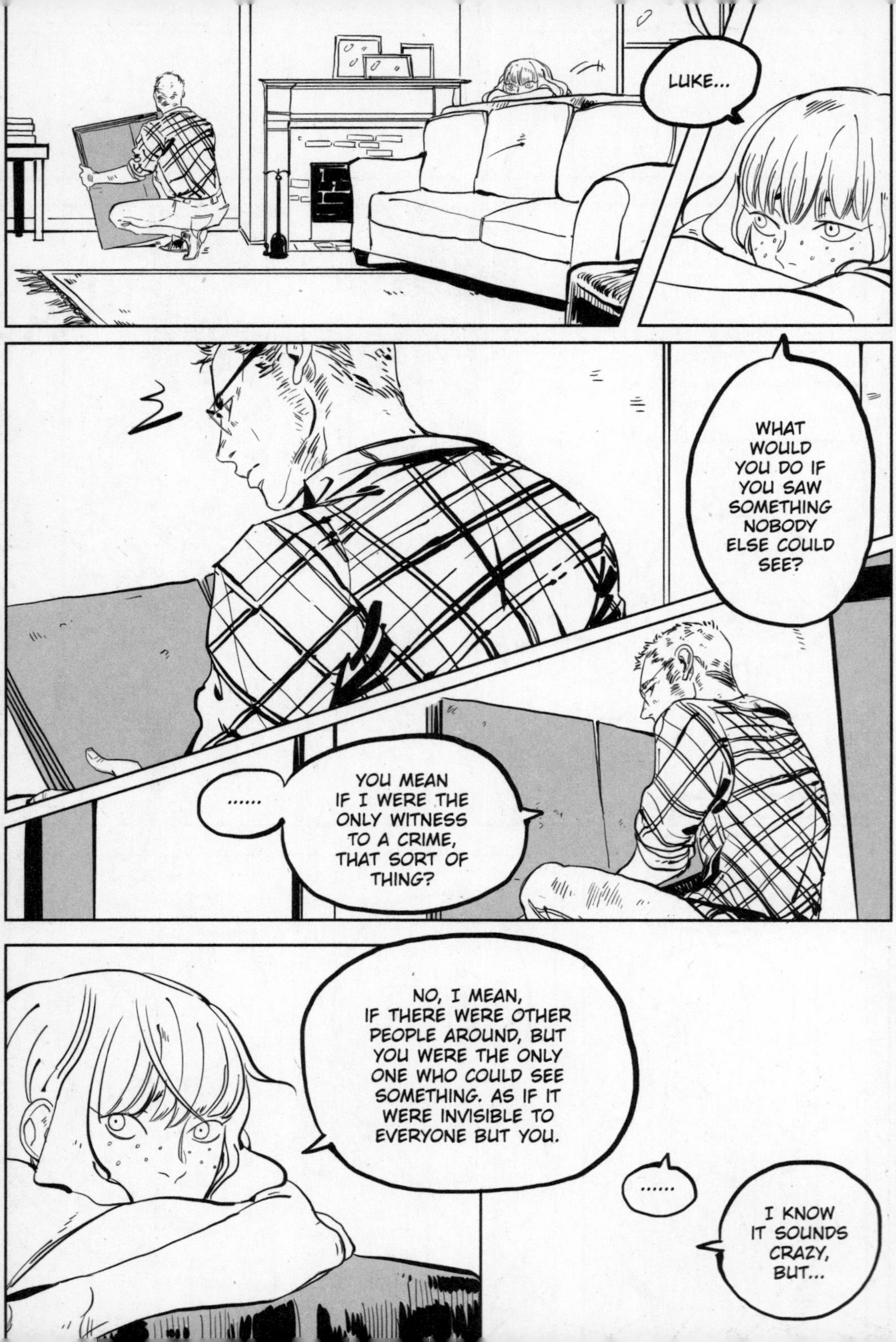
LUKE...
WHAT WOULD YOU DO IF YOU SAW SOMETHING NOBODY ELSE COULD SEE?
......
YOU MEAN IF I WERE THE ONLY WITNESS TO A CRIME, THAT SORT OF THING?
NO, I MEAN, IF THERE WERE OTHER PEOPLE AROUND, BUT YOU WERE THE ONLY ONE WHO COULD SEE SOMETHING. AS IF IT WERE INVISIBLE TO EVERYONE BUT YOU.
......
I KNOW IT SOUNDS CRAZY, BUT...

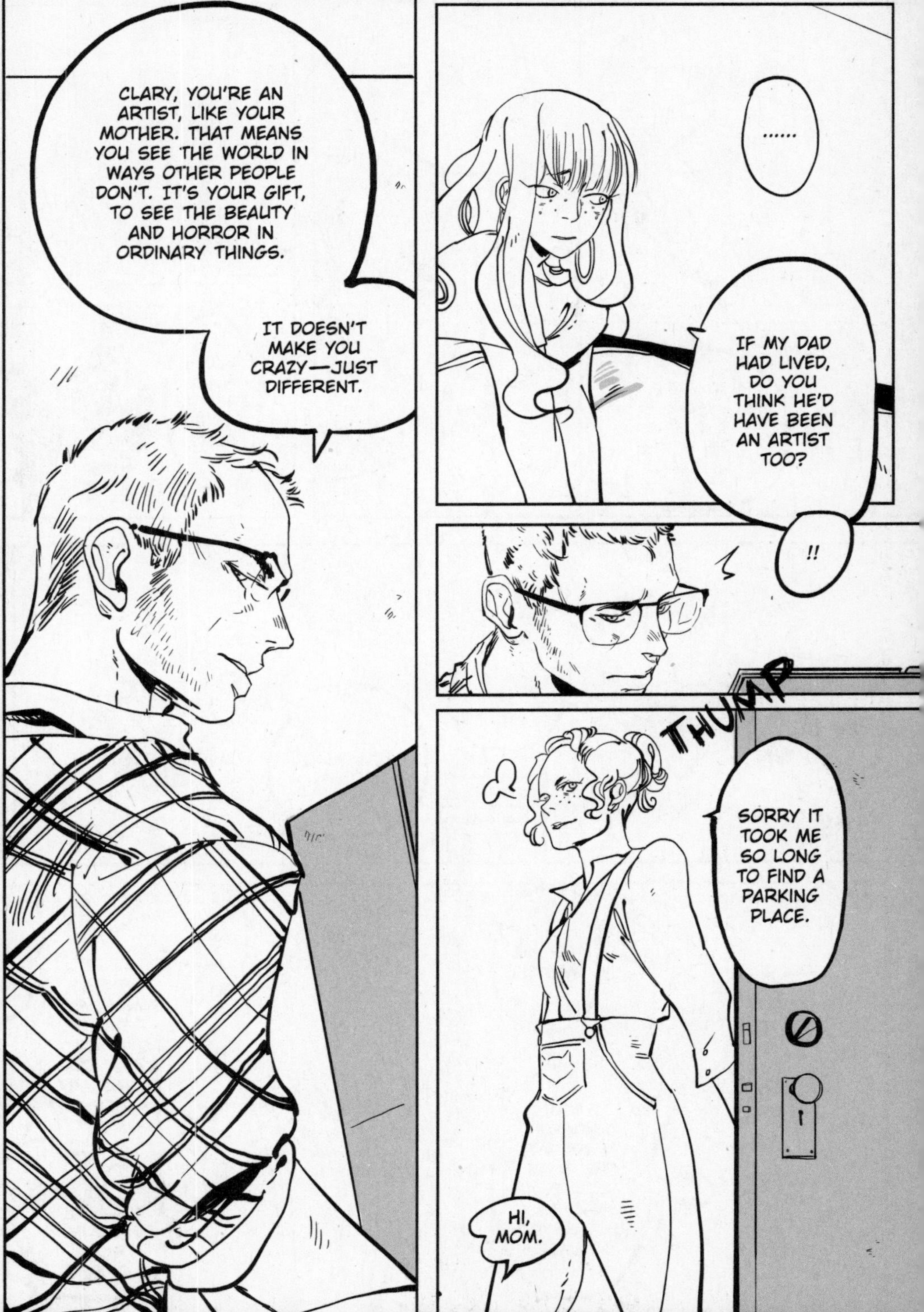
CLARY, YOU'RE AN ARTIST, LIKE YOUR MOTHER. THAT MEANS YOU SEE THE WORLD IN WAYS OTHER PEOPLE DON'T. IT'S YOUR GIFT, TO SEE THE BEAUTY AND HORROR IN ORDINARY THINGS.
IT DOESN'T MAKE YOU CRAZY—JUST DIFFERENT.
......
IF MY DAD HAD LIVED, DO YOU THINK HE'D HAVE BEEN AN ARTIST TOO?
!!
THUMP
SORRY IT TOOK ME SO LONG TO FIND A PARKING PLACE.
HI, MOM.

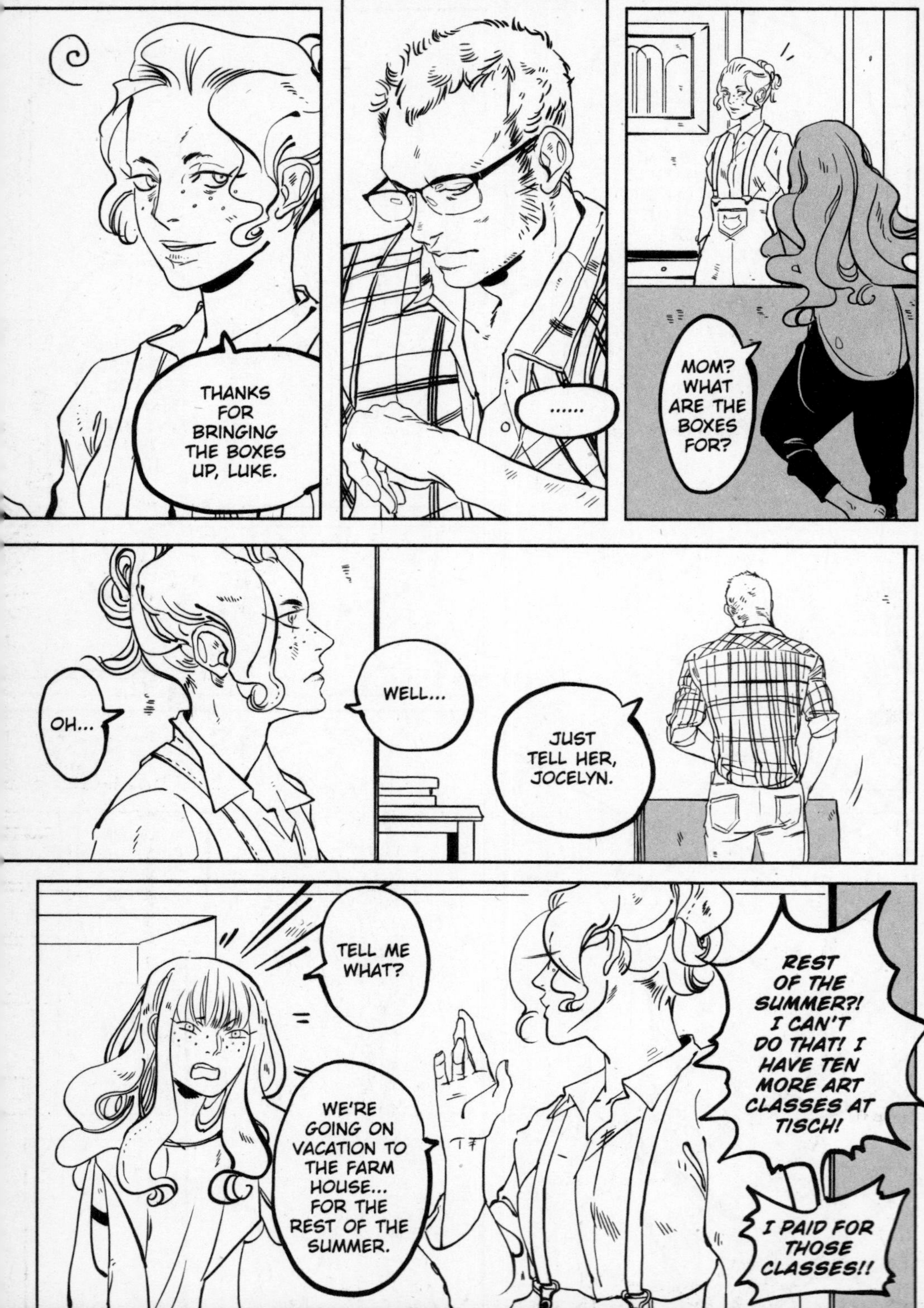
THANKS FOR BRINGING THE BOXES UP, LUKE.
......
MOM? WHAT ARE THE BOXES FOR?
OH...
WELL...
JUST TELL HER, JOCELYN.
TELL ME WHAT?
WE'RE GOING ON VACATION TO THE FARM HOUSE... FOR THE REST OF THE SUMMER.
REST OF THE SUMMER?! I CAN'T DO THAT! I HAVE TEN MORE ART CLASSES AT TISCH!
I PAID FOR THOSE CLASSES!!

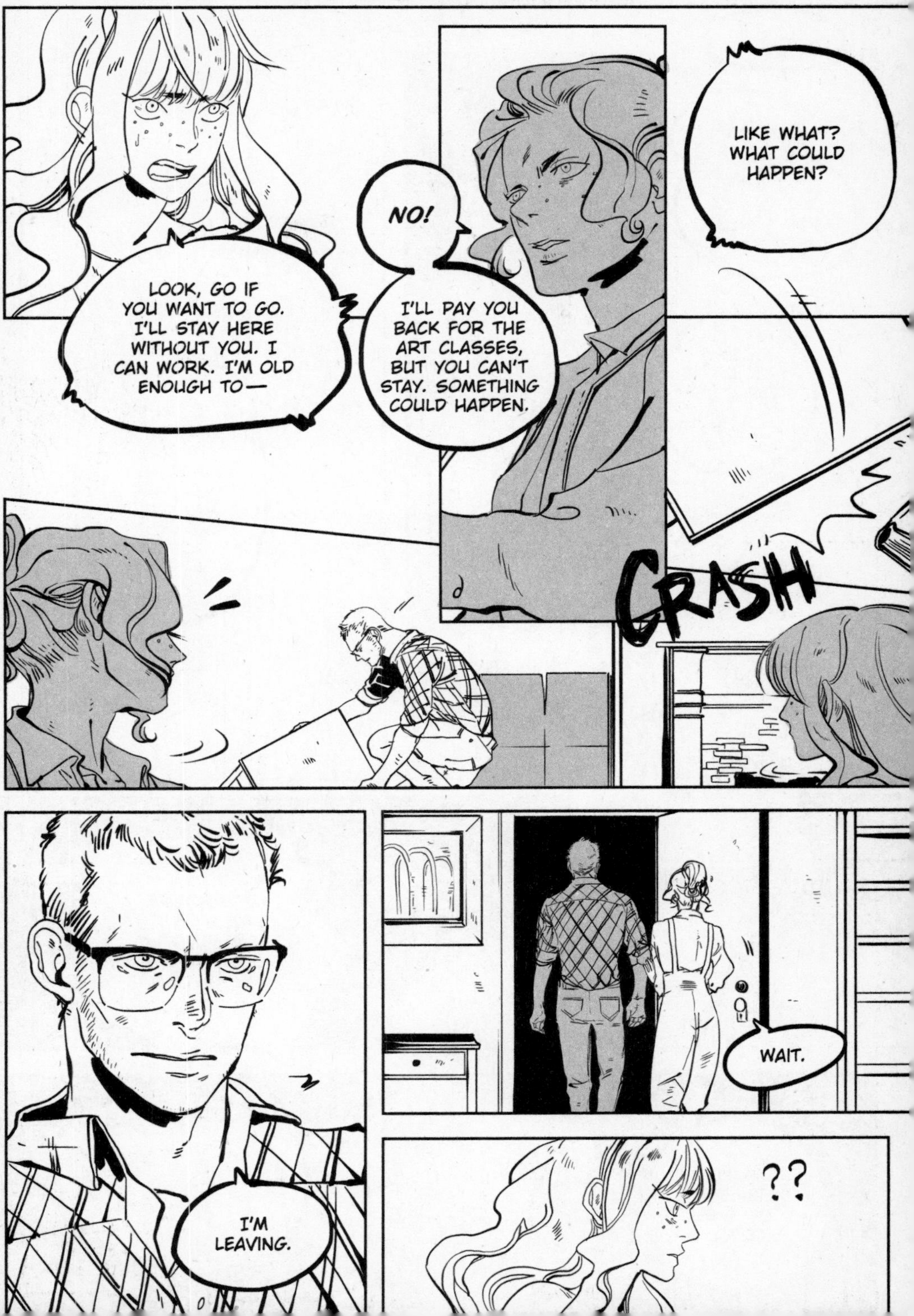
LOOK, GO IF YOU WANT TO GO. I'LL STAY HERE WITHOUT YOU. I CAN WORK. I'M OLD ENOUGH TO—
NO!
I'LL PAY YOU BACK FOR THE ART CLASSES, BUT YOU CAN'T STAY. SOMETHING COULD HAPPEN.
LIKE WHAT? WHAT COULD HAPPEN?
CRASH
I'M LEAVING.
WAIT.
??

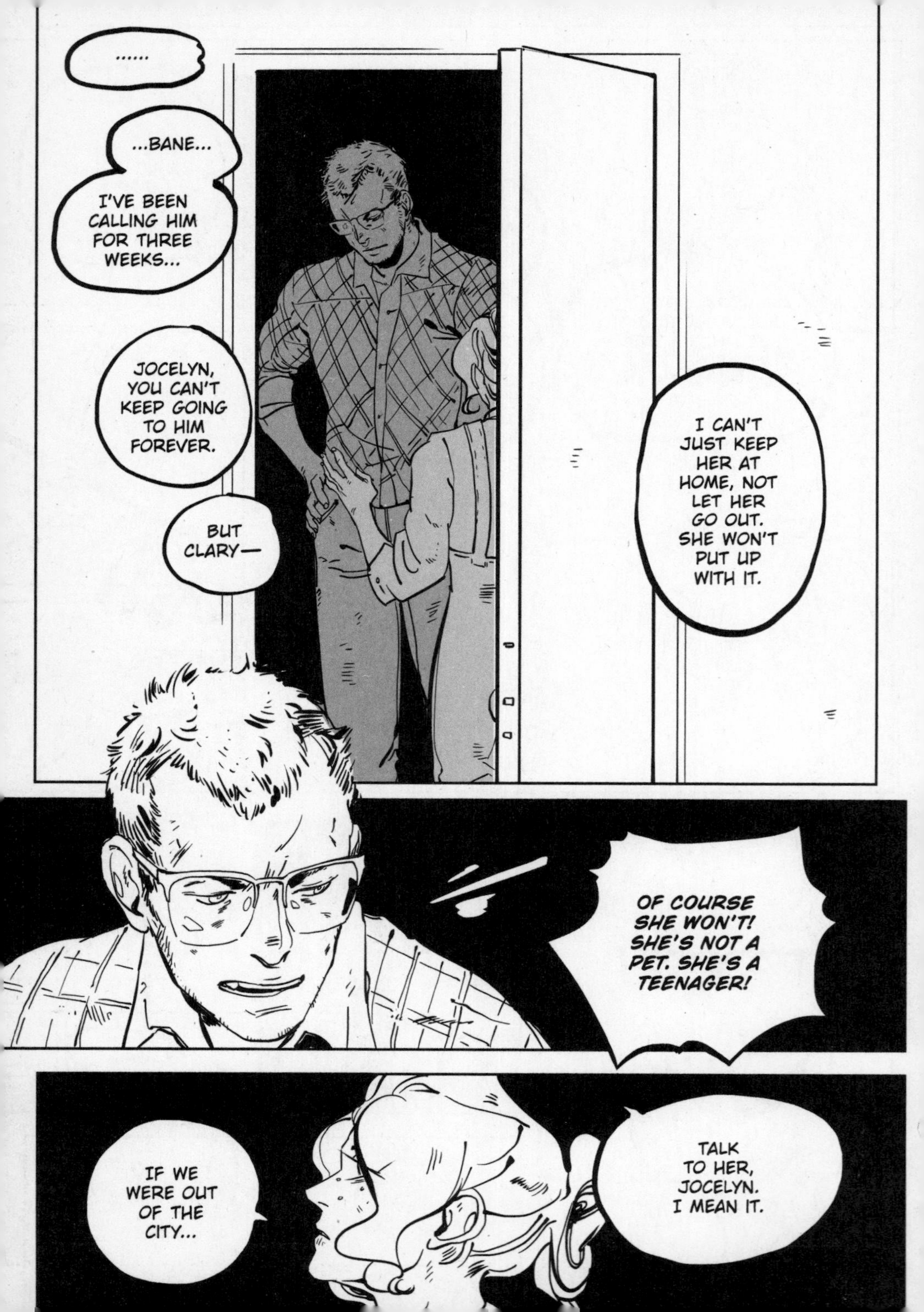

......
...BANE...
I'VE BEEN CALLING HIM FOR THREE WEEKS...
JOCELYN, YOU CAN'T KEEP GOING TO HIM FOREVER.
BUT CLARY—
I CAN'T JUST KEEP HER AT HOME, NOT LET HER GO OUT. SHE WON'T PUT UP WITH IT.
OF COURSE SHE WON'T! SHE'S NOT A PET. SHE'S A TEENAGER!
IF WE WERE OUT OF THE CITY...
TALK TO HER, JOCELYN. I MEAN IT.

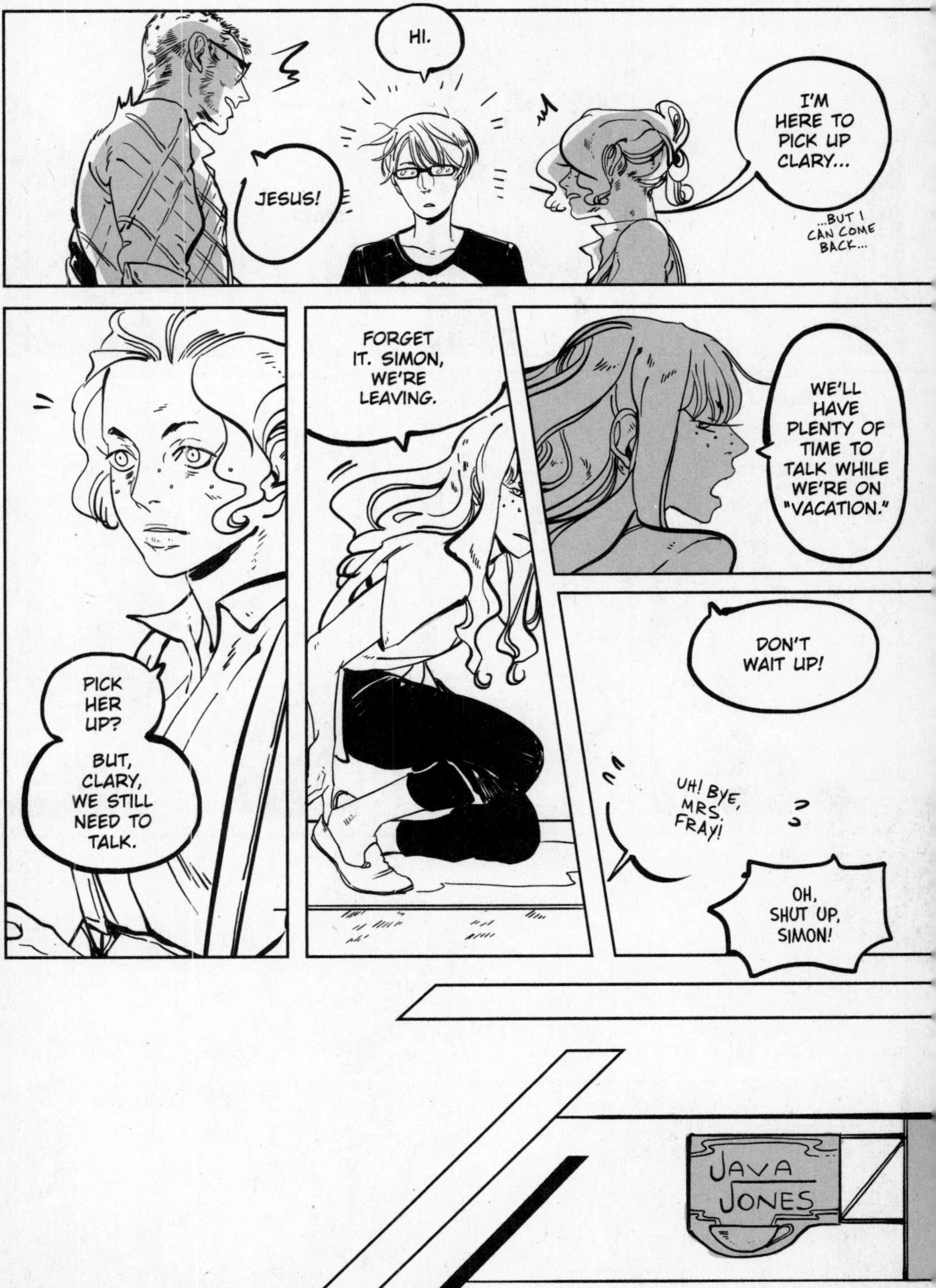
HI.
JESUS!
I'M HERE TO PICK UP CLARY...
...BUT I CAN COME BACK...
PICK HER UP?
BUT, CLARY, WE STILL NEED TO TALK.
FORGET IT. SIMON, WE'RE LEAVING.
WE'LL HAVE PLENTY OF TIME TO TALK WHILE WE'RE ON "VACATION."
DON'T WAIT UP!
UH! BYE, MRS. FRAY!
OH, SHUT UP, SIMON!
JAVA JONES

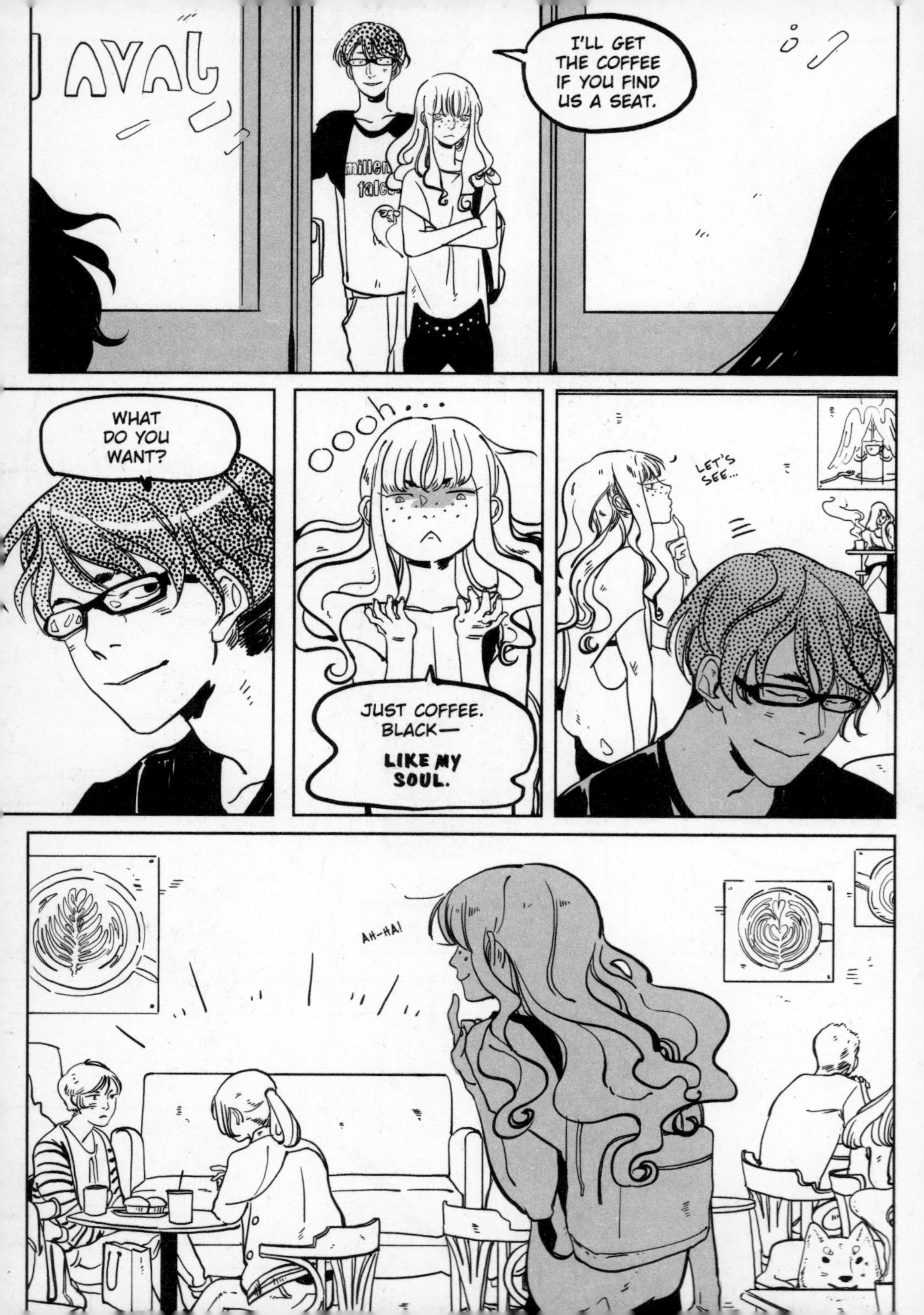
AVAL
I'LL GET THE COFFEE IF YOU FIND US A SEAT.
WHAT DO YOU WANT?
oooh...
JUST COFFEE. BLACK—
LIKE MY SOUL.
LET'S SEE...
AH-HA!

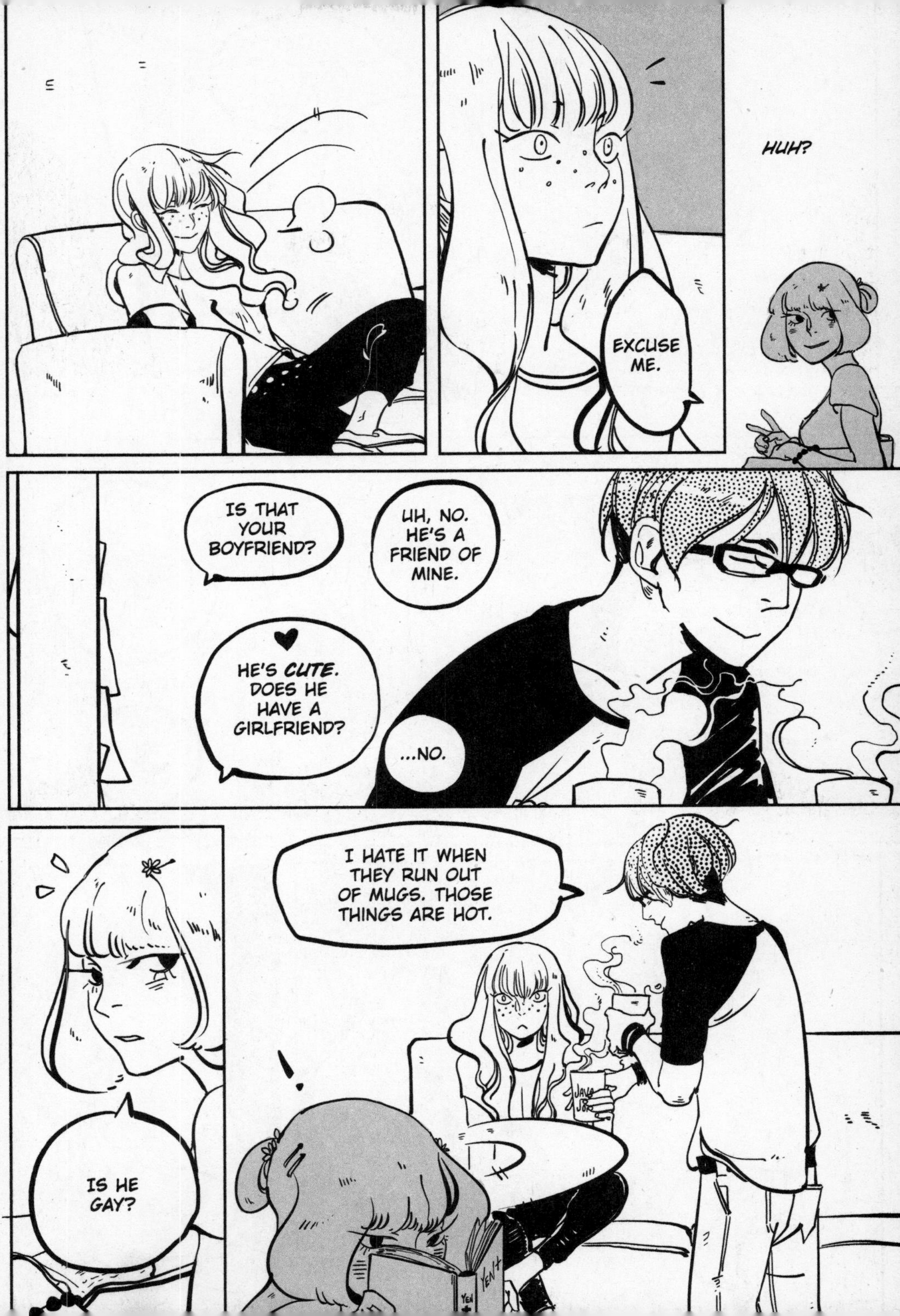
HUH?
EXCUSE ME.
IS THAT YOUR BOYFRIEND?
UH, NO. HE'S A FRIEND OF MINE.
HE'S CUTE. DOES HE HAVE A GIRLFRIEND?
...NO.
IS HE GAY?
I HATE IT WHEN THEY RUN OUT OF MUGS. THOSE THINGS ARE HOT.
JAVA JOE
YEN

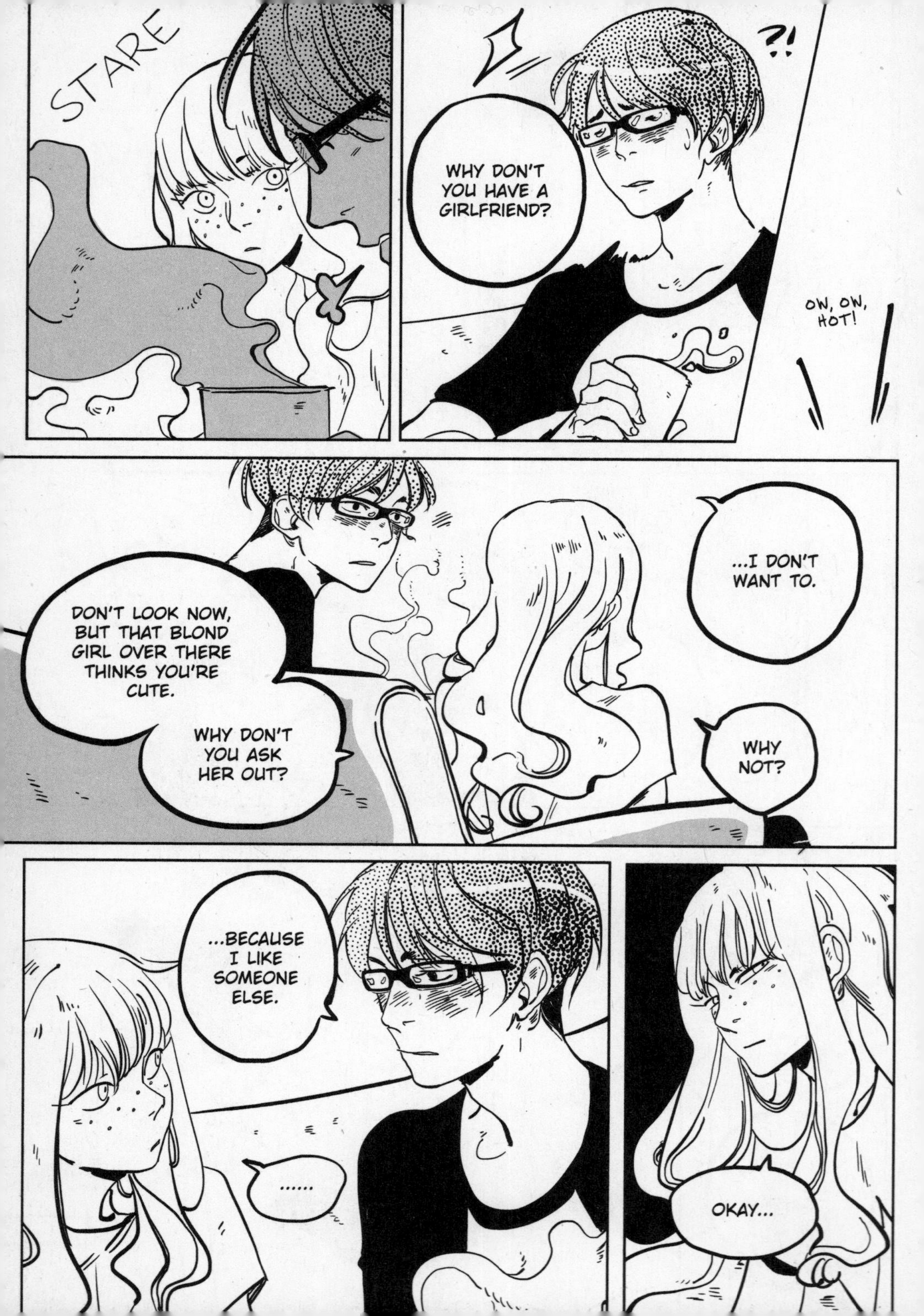
STARE
?!
WHY DON'T YOU HAVE A GIRLFRIEND?
OW, OW, HOT!
DON'T LOOK NOW, BUT THAT BLOND GIRL OVER THERE THINKS YOU'RE CUTE.
WHY DON'T YOU ASK HER OUT?
...I DON'T WANT TO.
WHY NOT?
...BECAUSE I LIKE SOMEONE ELSE.
......
OKAY...

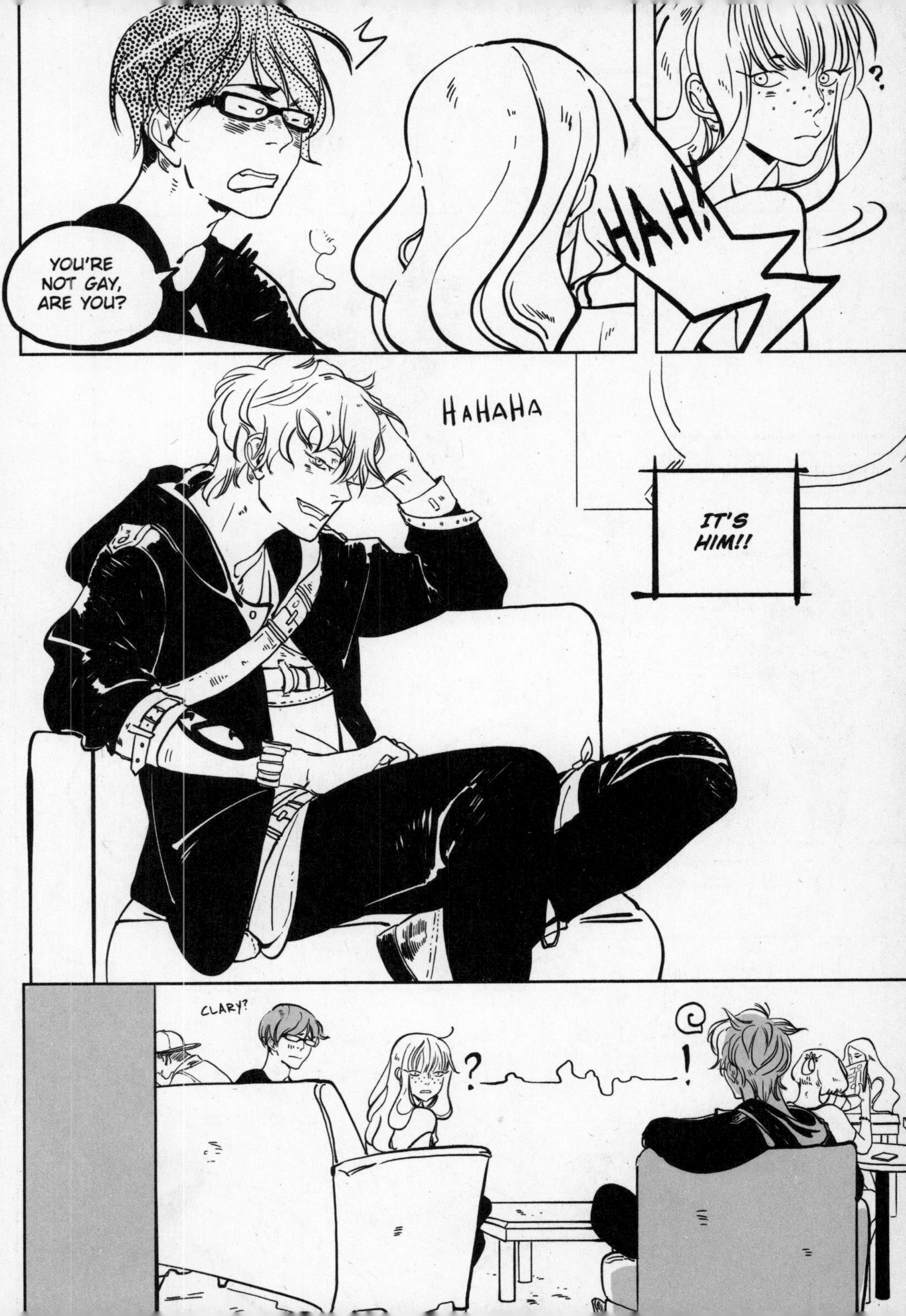

YOU'RE NOT GAY, ARE YOU?
HAH!
HaHaHa
IT'S HIM!!
CLARY?

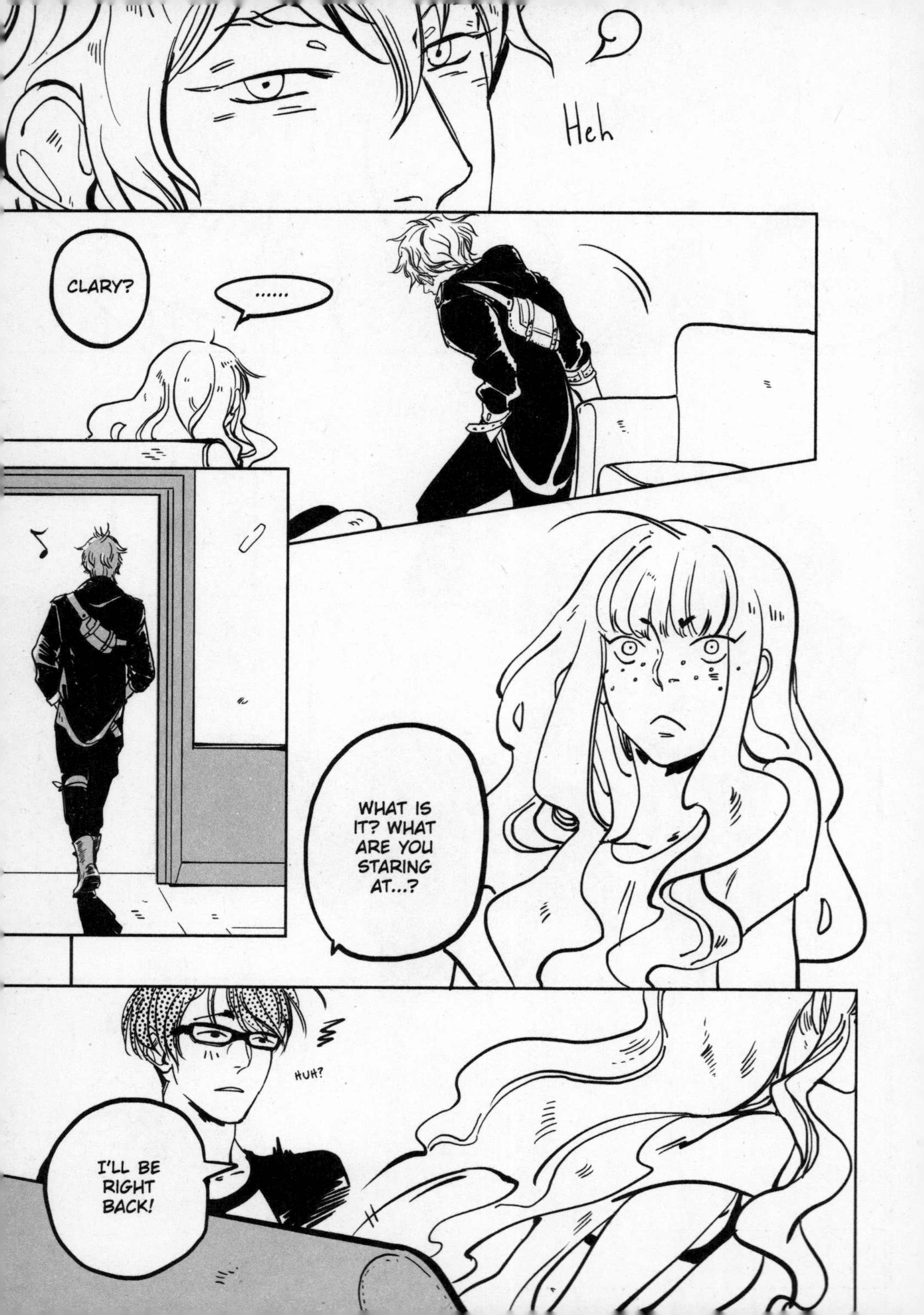
Heh
CLARY?
......
WHAT IS IT? WHAT ARE YOU STARING AT...?
HUH?
I'LL BE RIGHT BACK!

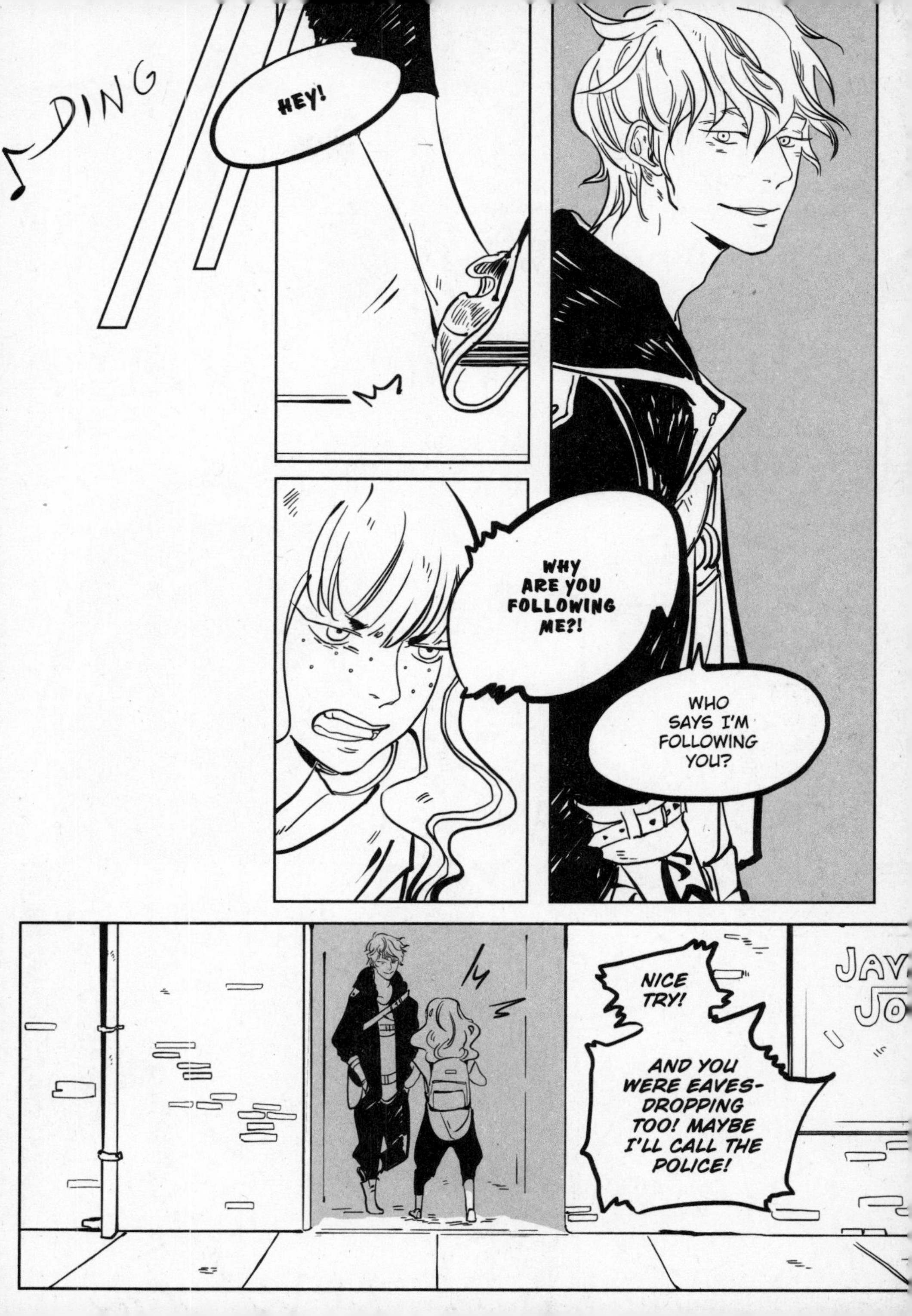
DING
HEY!
WHY ARE YOU FOLLOWING ME?!
WHO SAYS I'M FOLLOWING YOU?
NICE TRY!
AND YOU WERE EAVES-DROPPING TOO! MAYBE I'LL CALL THE POLICE!

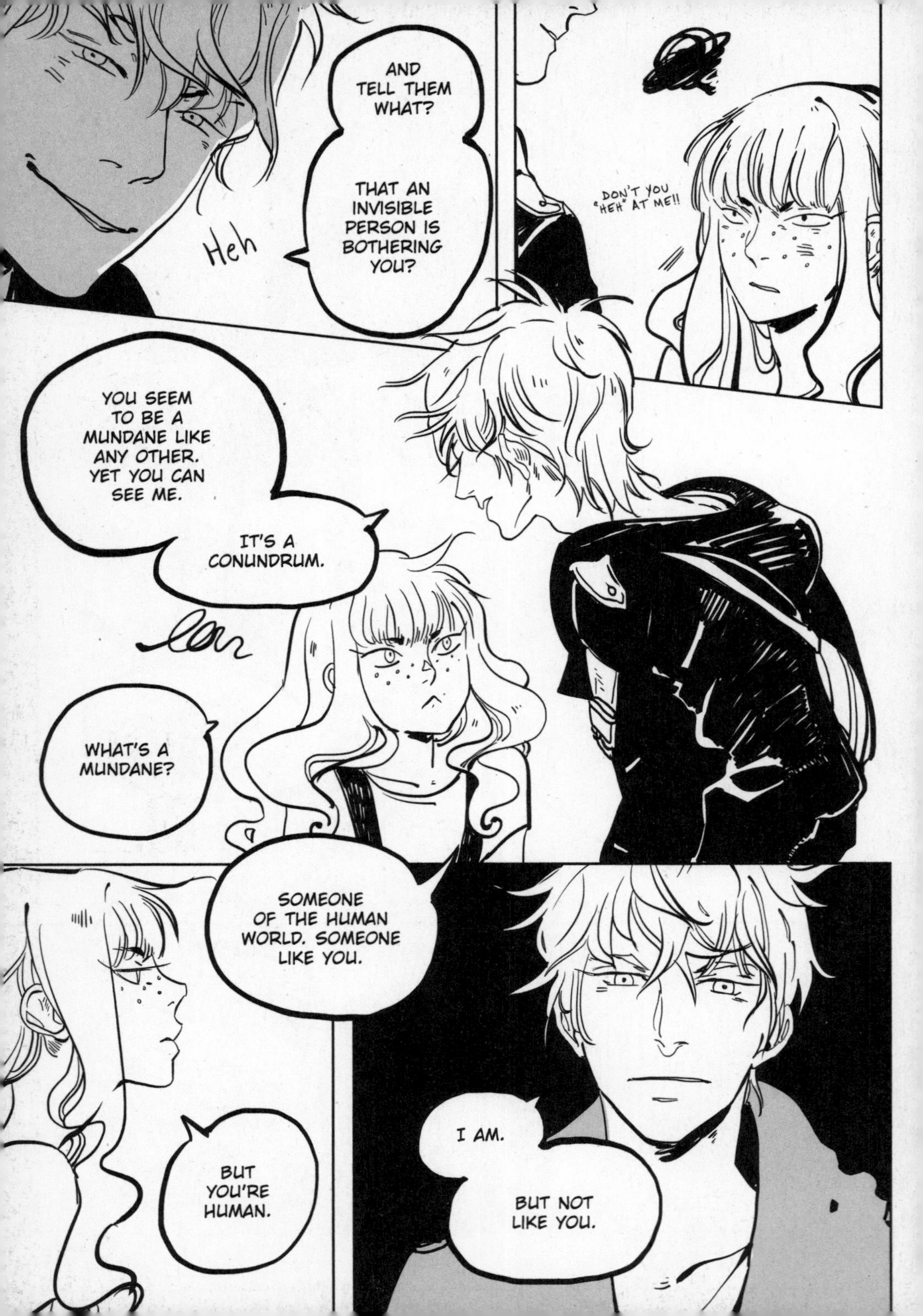
Heh
AND TELL THEM WHAT?
THAT AN INVISIBLE PERSON IS BOTHERING YOU?
DON'T YOU "HEH" AT ME!!
YOU SEEM TO BE A MUNDANE LIKE ANY OTHER. YET YOU CAN SEE ME.
IT'S A CONUNDRUM.
WHAT'S A MUNDANE?
SOMEONE OF THE HUMAN WORLD. SOMEONE LIKE YOU.
BUT YOU'RE HUMAN.
I AM.
BUT NOT LIKE YOU.

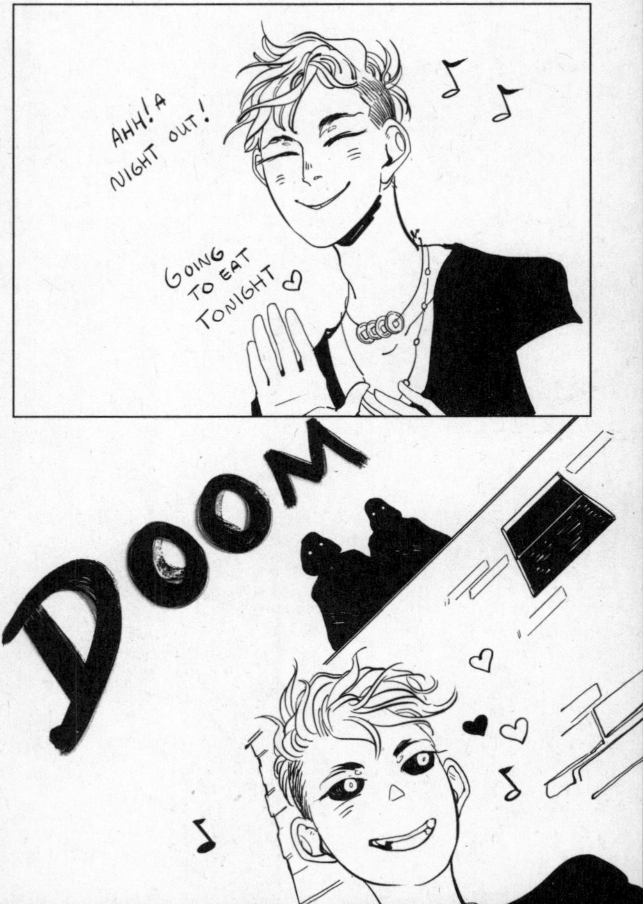
AHH! A NIGHT OUT!
GOING TO EAT TONIGHT ♡
DOOM

THE MORTAL INSTRUMENTS

THE GRAPHIC NOVEL

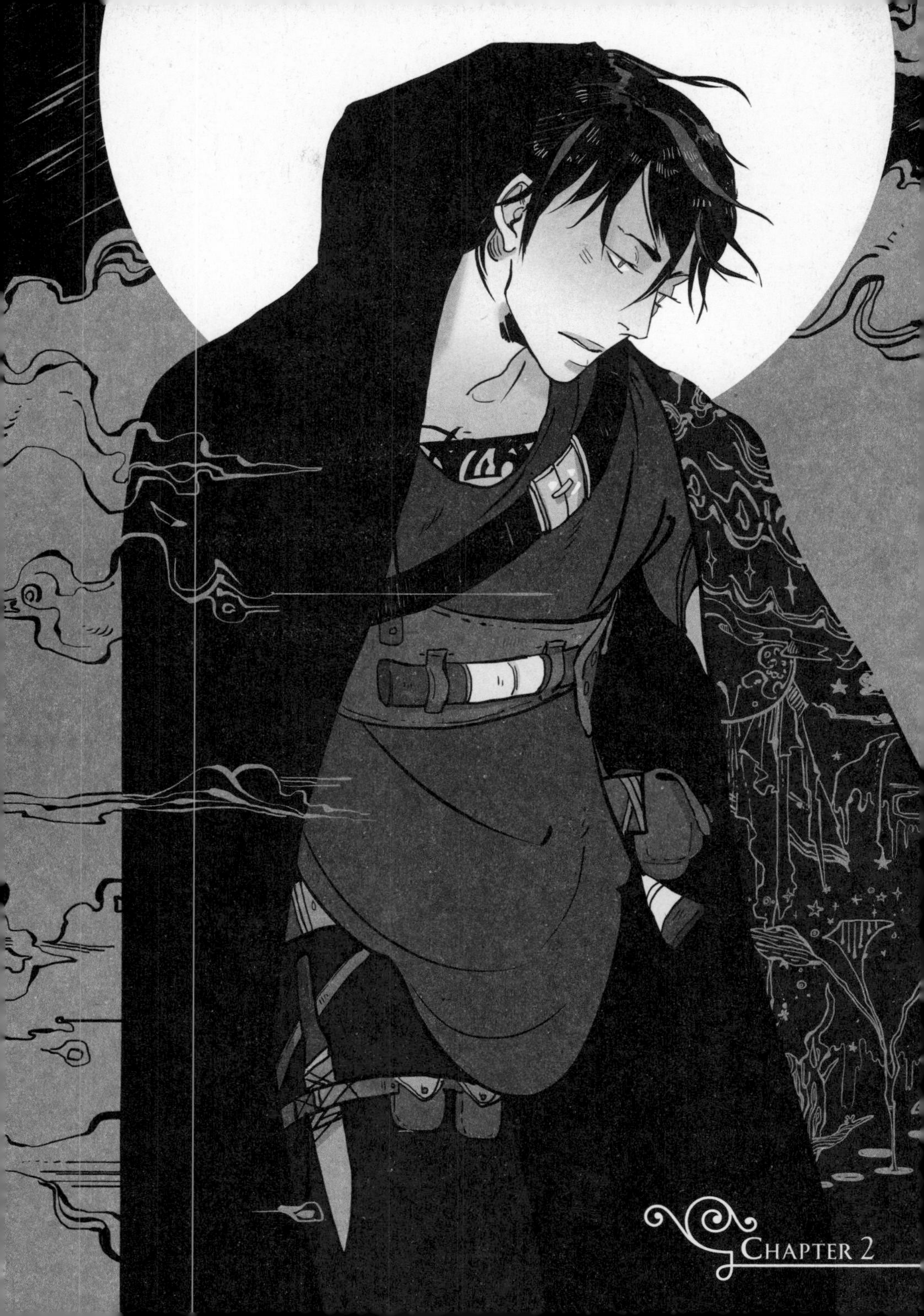

Chapter 2

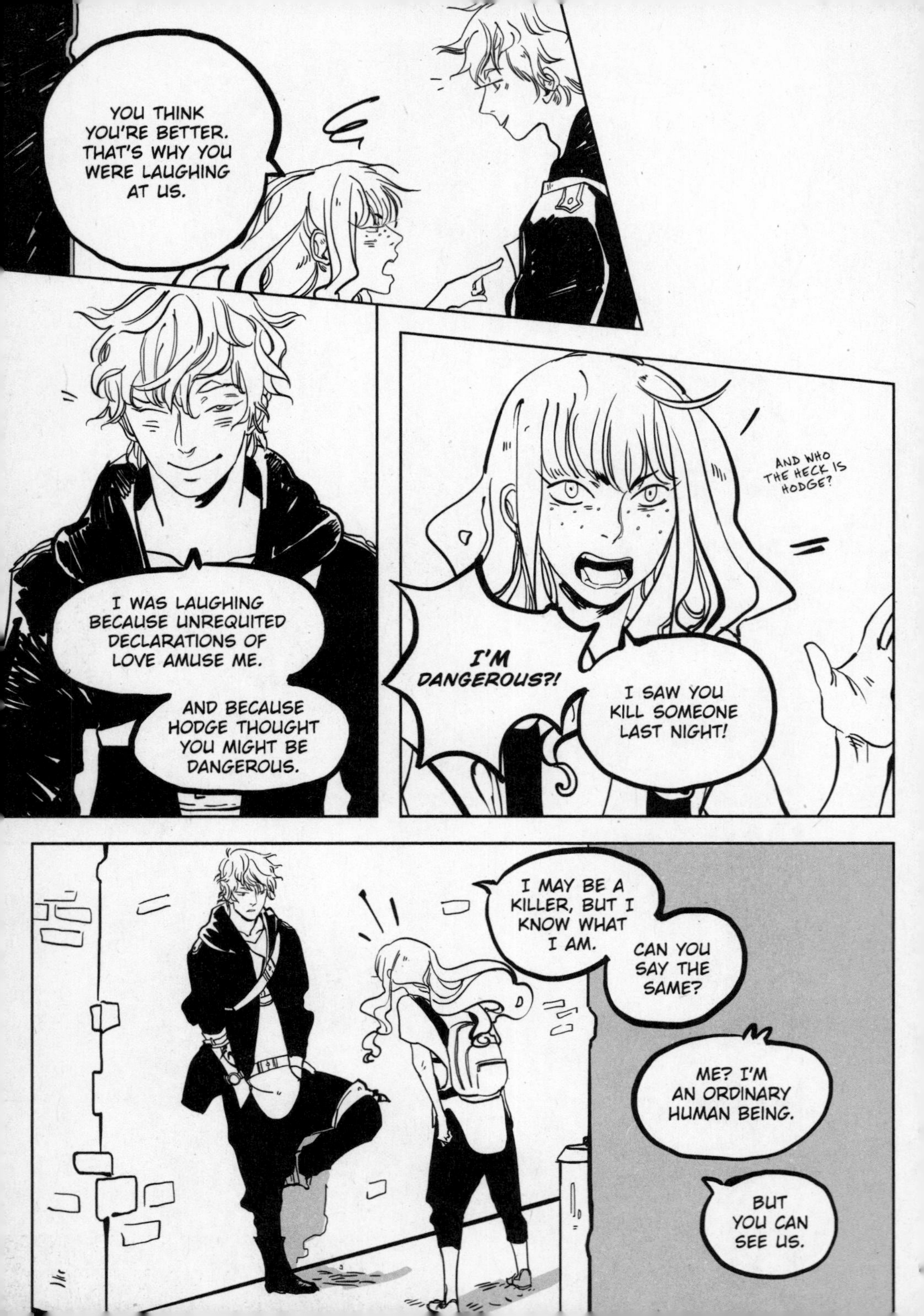
YOU THINK YOU'RE BETTER. THAT'S WHY YOU WERE LAUGHING AT US.
I WAS LAUGHING BECAUSE UNREQUITED DECLARATIONS OF LOVE AMUSE ME.
AND BECAUSE HODGE THOUGHT YOU MIGHT BE DANGEROUS.
I'M DANGEROUS?!
I SAW YOU KILL SOMEONE LAST NIGHT!
AND WHO THE HECK IS HODGE?
I MAY BE A KILLER, BUT I KNOW WHAT I AM.
CAN YOU SAY THE SAME?
ME? I'M AN ORDINARY HUMAN BEING.
BUT YOU CAN SEE US.

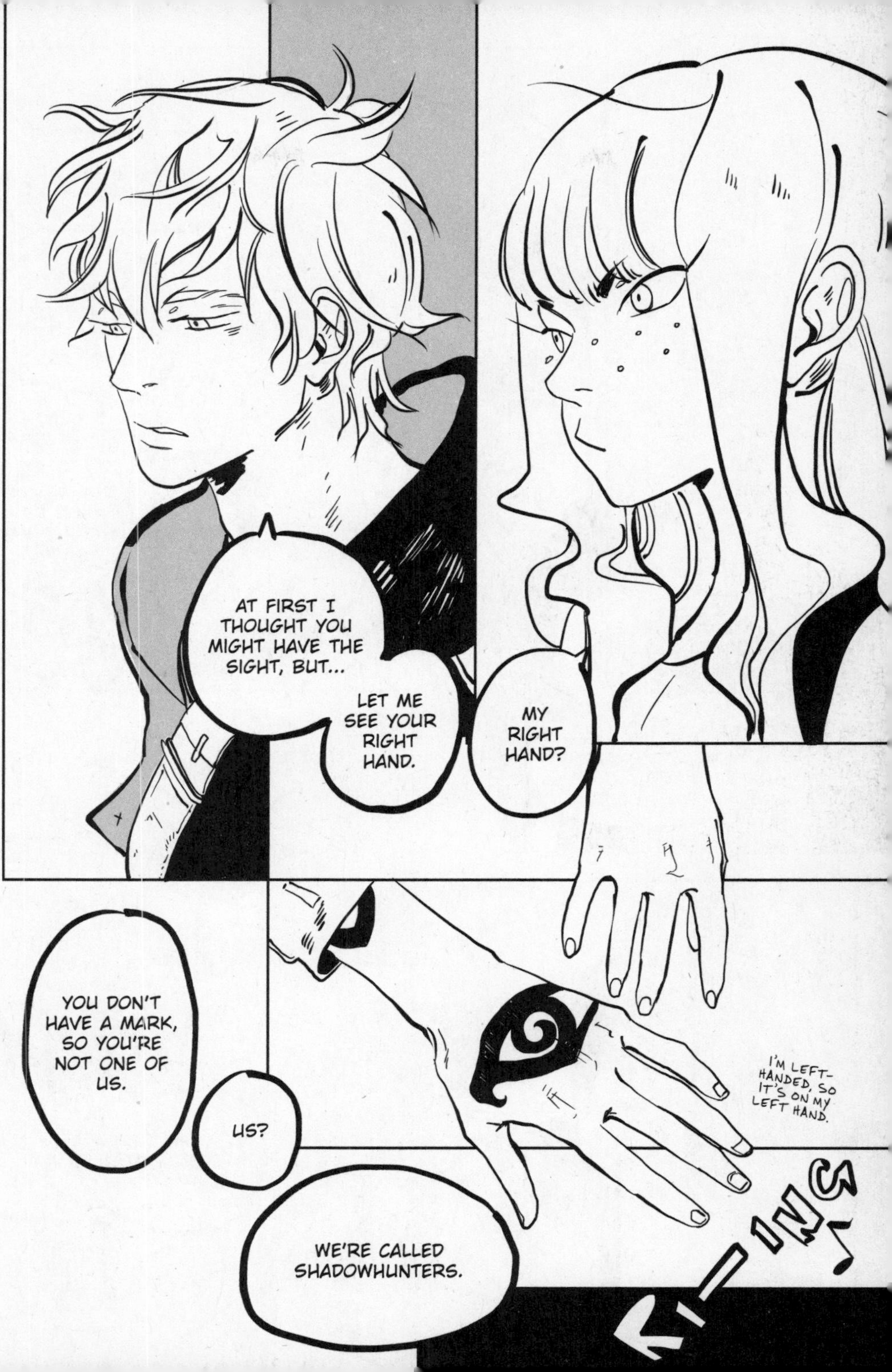
AT FIRST I THOUGHT YOU MIGHT HAVE THE SIGHT, BUT...
LET ME SEE YOUR RIGHT HAND.
MY RIGHT HAND?
YOU DON'T HAVE A MARK, SO YOU'RE NOT ONE OF US.
US?
I'M LEFT-HANDED, SO IT'S ON MY LEFT HAND.
WE'RE CALLED SHADOWHUNTERS.
RI—ING♪

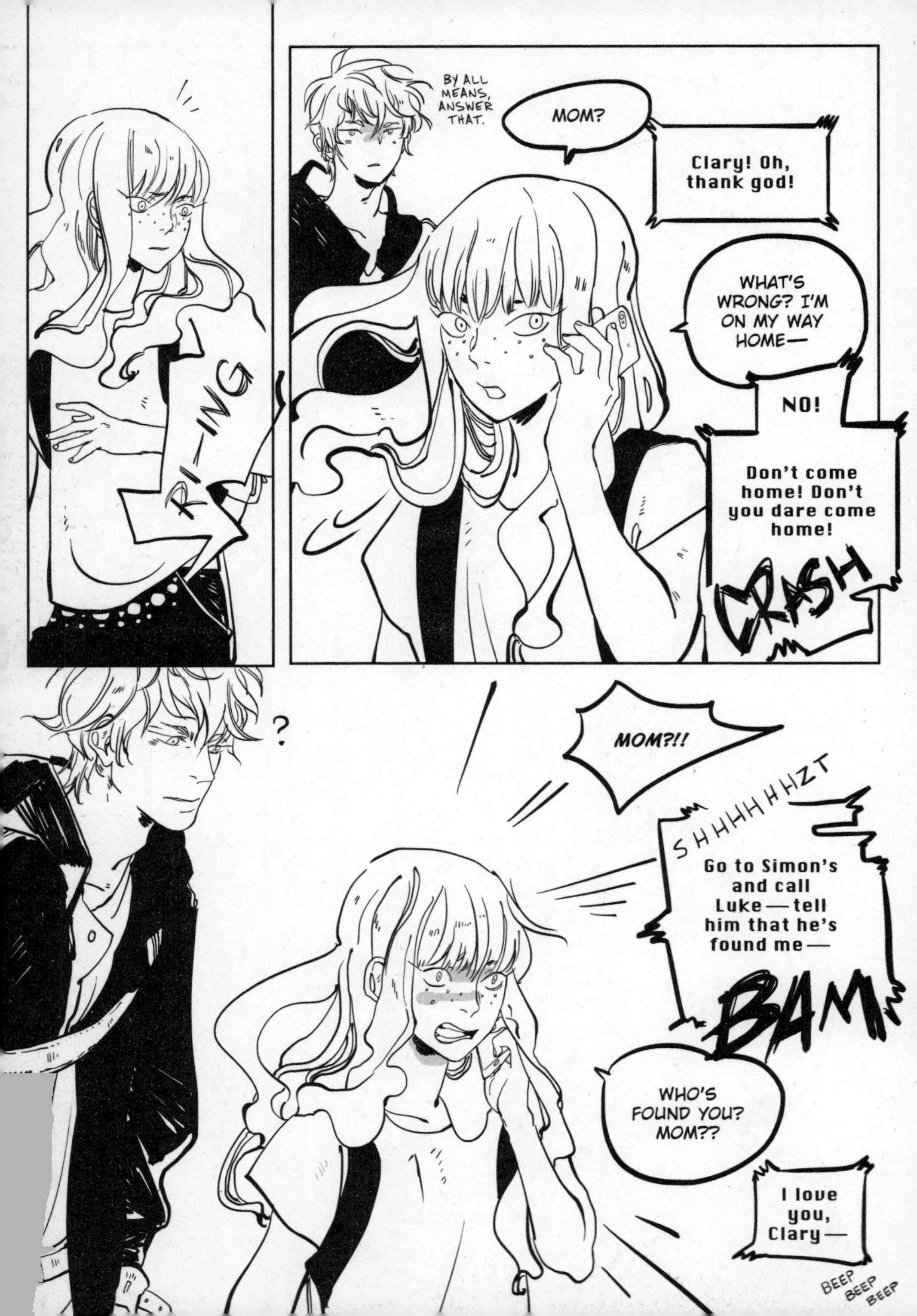
RI—ING
BY ALL MEANS, ANSWER THAT.
MOM?
Clary! Oh, thank god!
WHAT'S WRONG? I'M ON MY WAY HOME—
NO!
Don't come home! Don't you dare come home!
CRASH
?
MOM?!!
SHHHHHHZT
Go to Simon's and call Luke—tell him that he's found me—
BAM
WHO'S FOUND YOU? MOM??
I love you, Clary—
BEEP BEEP BEEP

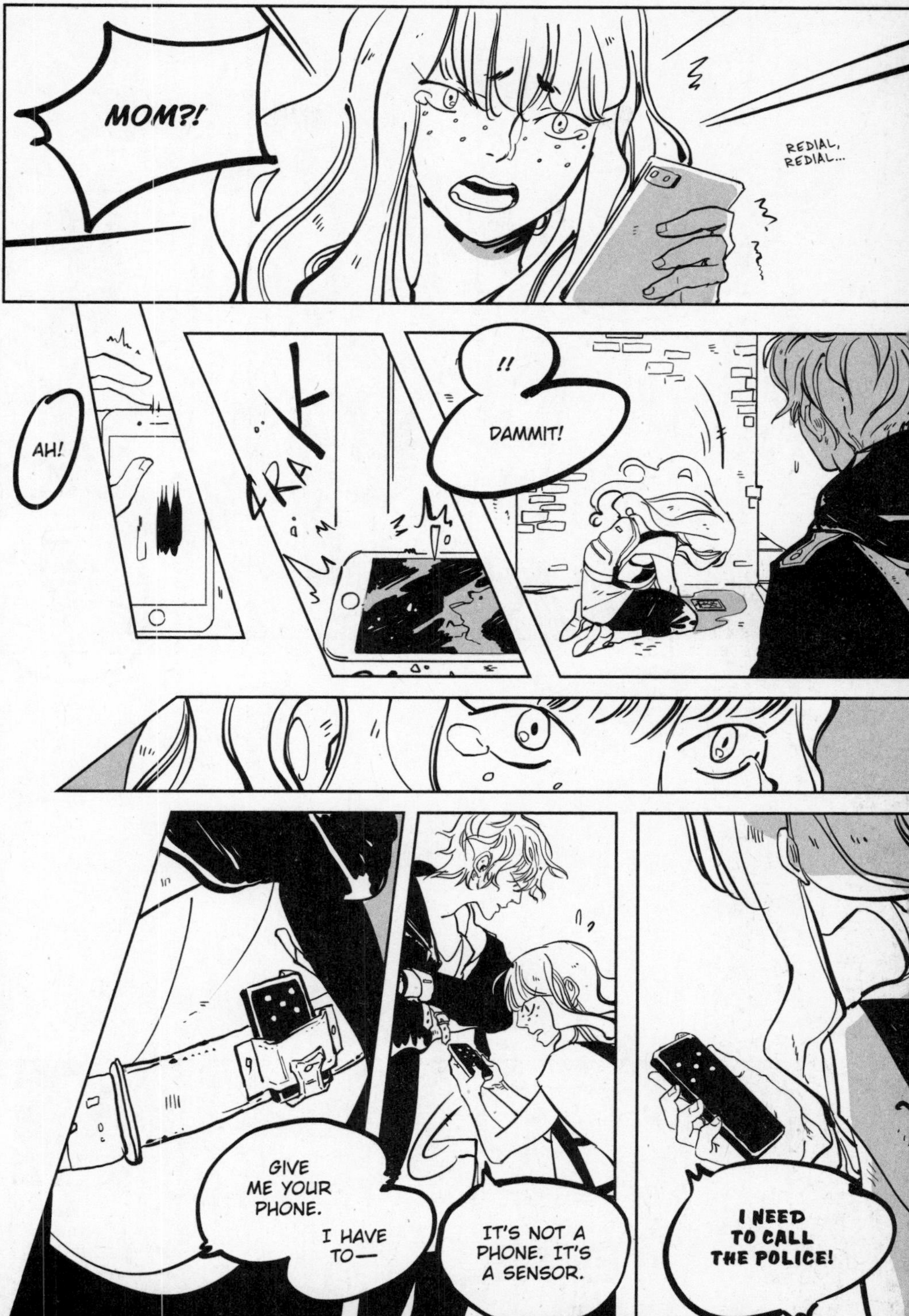
MOM?!
REDIAL, REDIAL...
AH!
CRAK
!!
DAMMIT!
GIVE ME YOUR PHONE.
I HAVE TO—
IT'S NOT A PHONE. IT'S A SENSOR.
I NEED TO CALL THE POLICE!

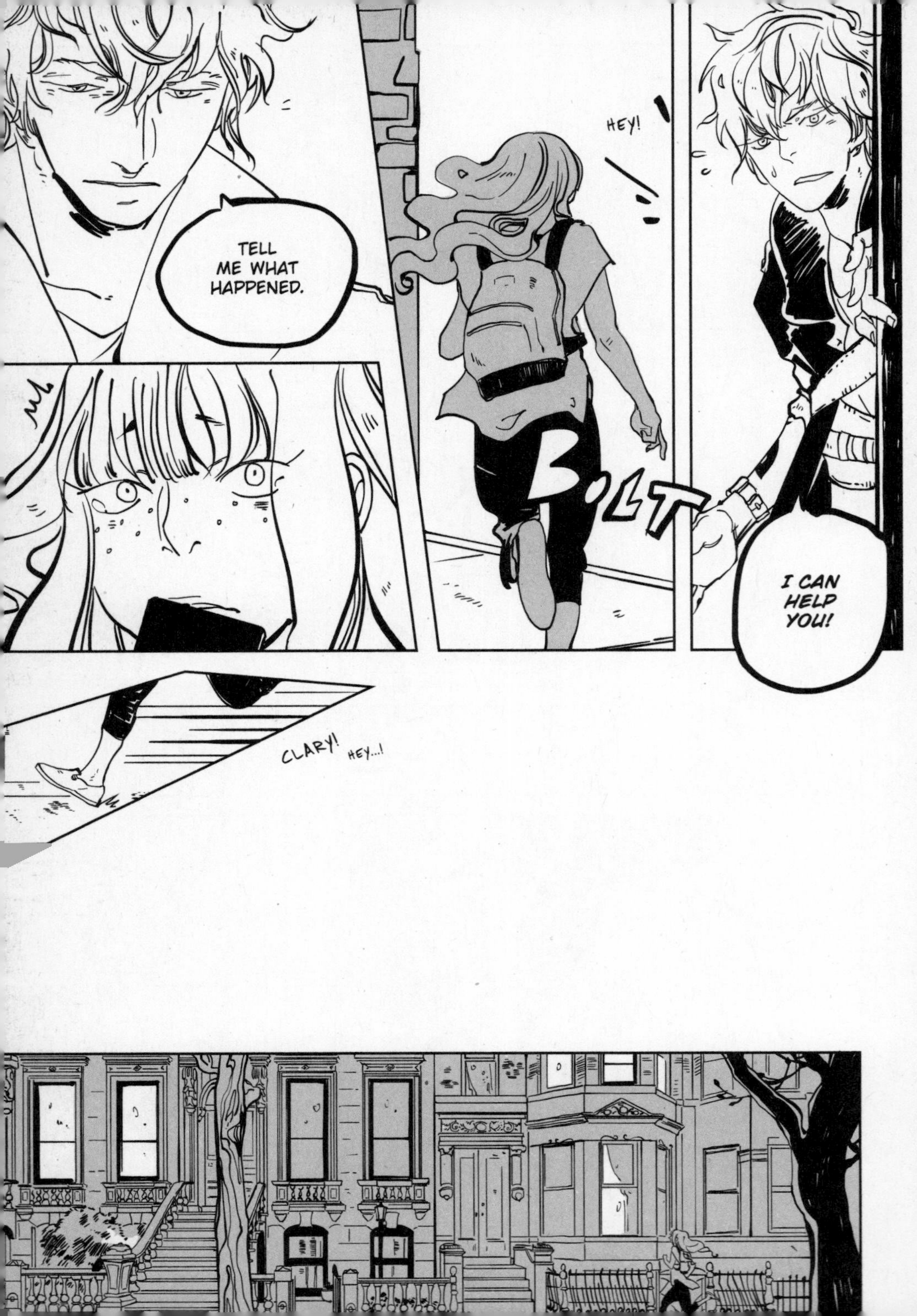
TELL ME WHAT HAPPENED.
HEY!
BOLT
I CAN HELP YOU!
CLARY!
HEY...!

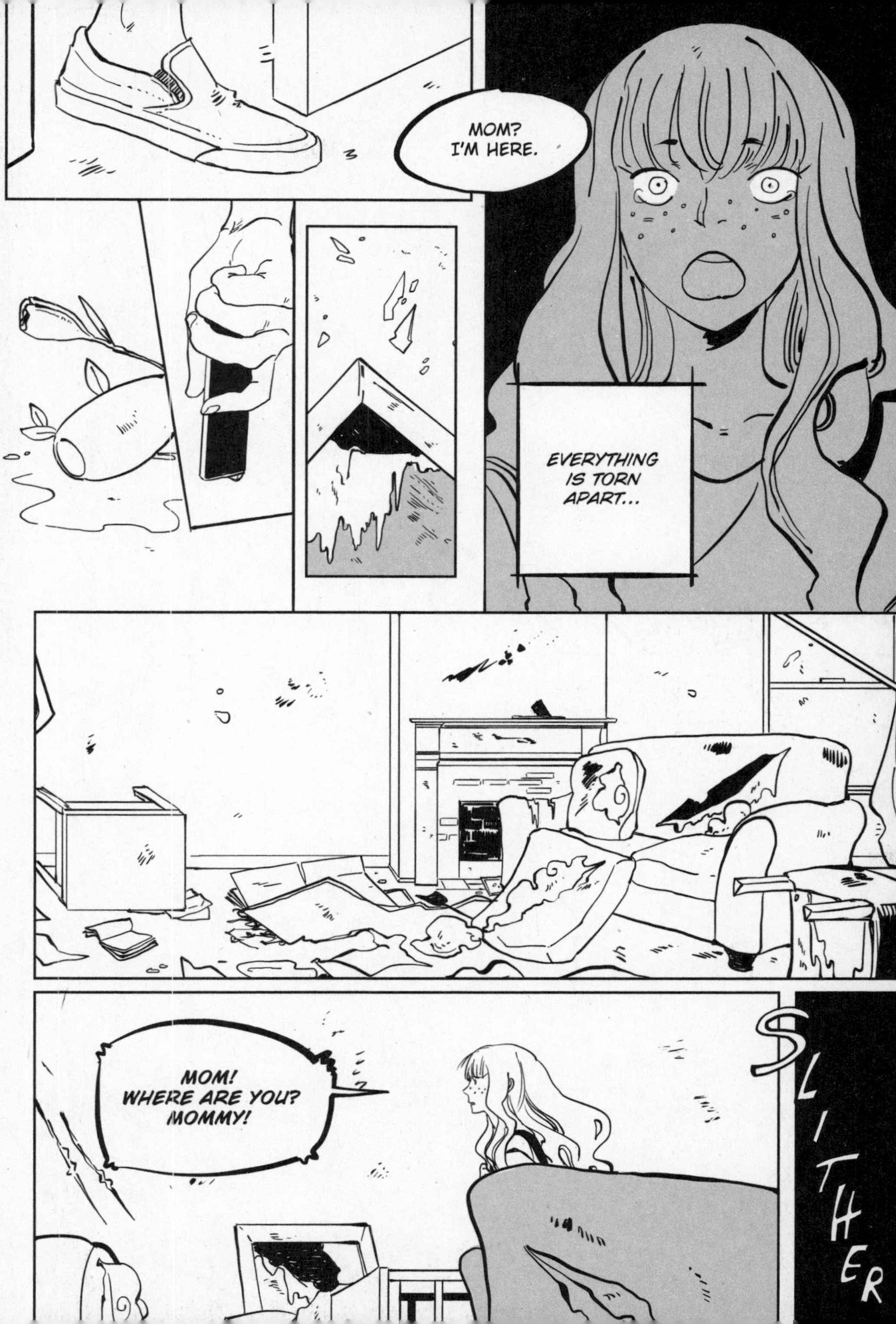
MOM? I'M HERE.
EVERYTHING IS TORN APART...
MOM! WHERE ARE YOU? MOMMY!
SLITHER

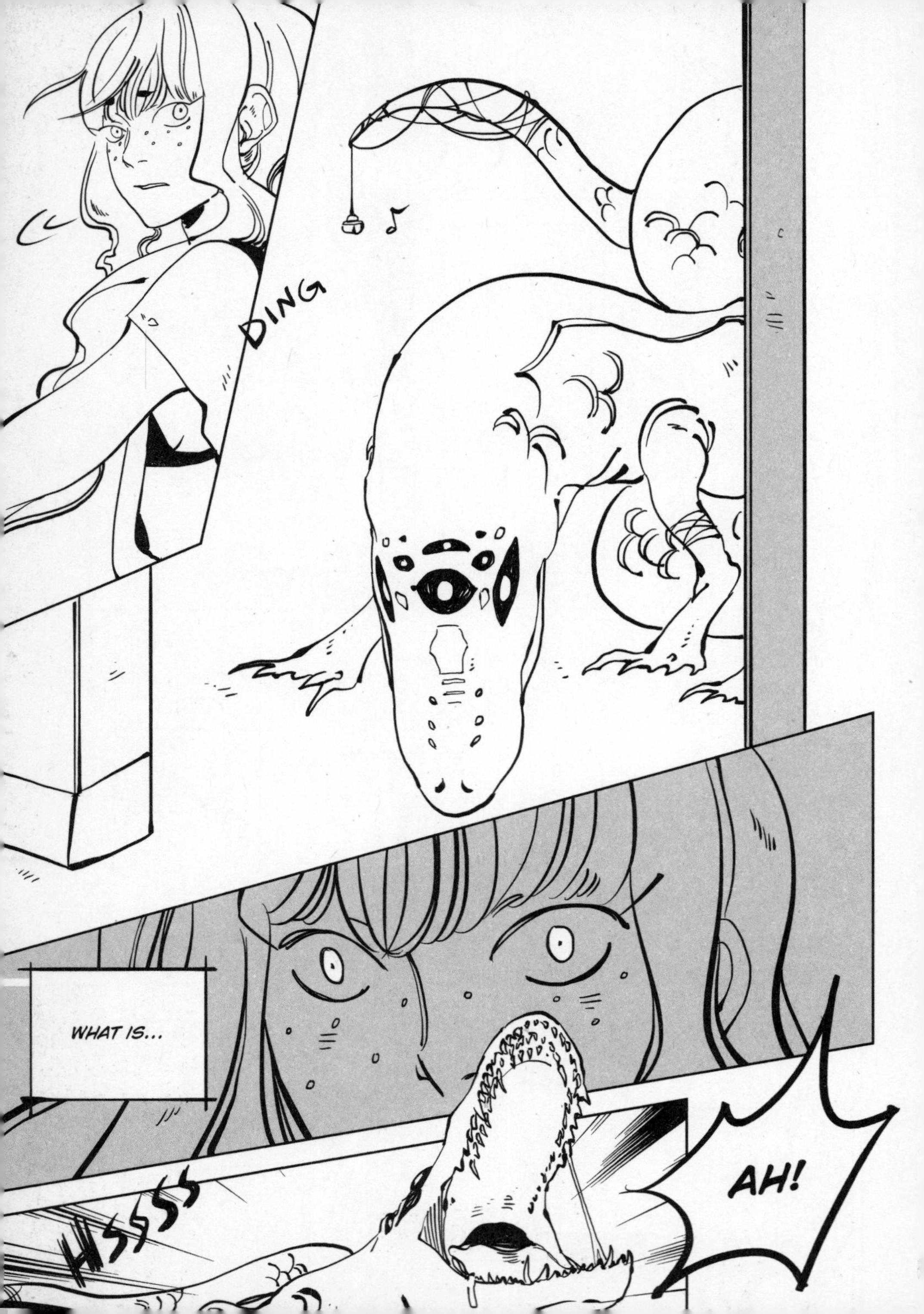
DING
WHAT IS...
HSSSS
AH!

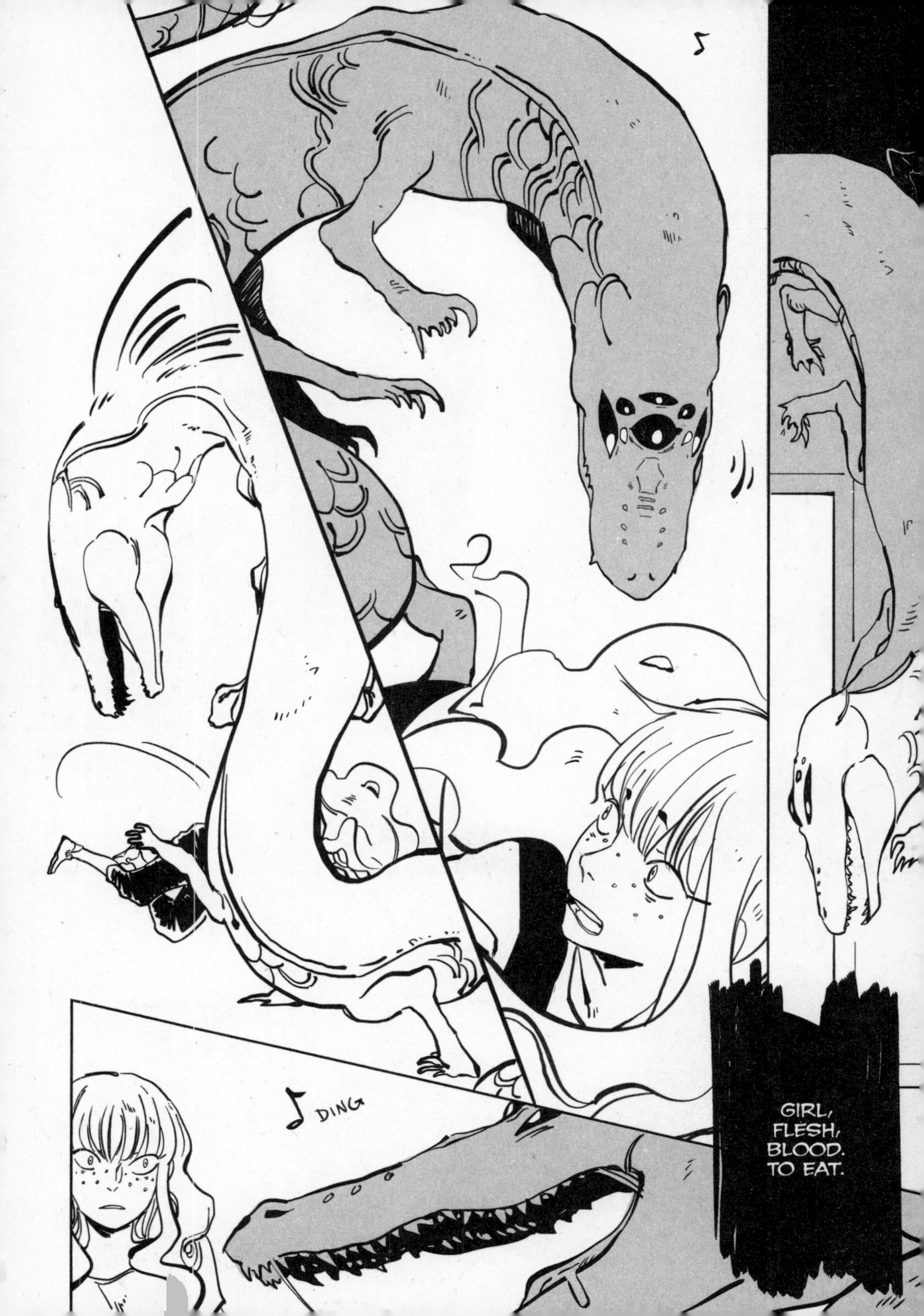
DING
GIRL,
FLESH,
BLOOD.
TO EAT.

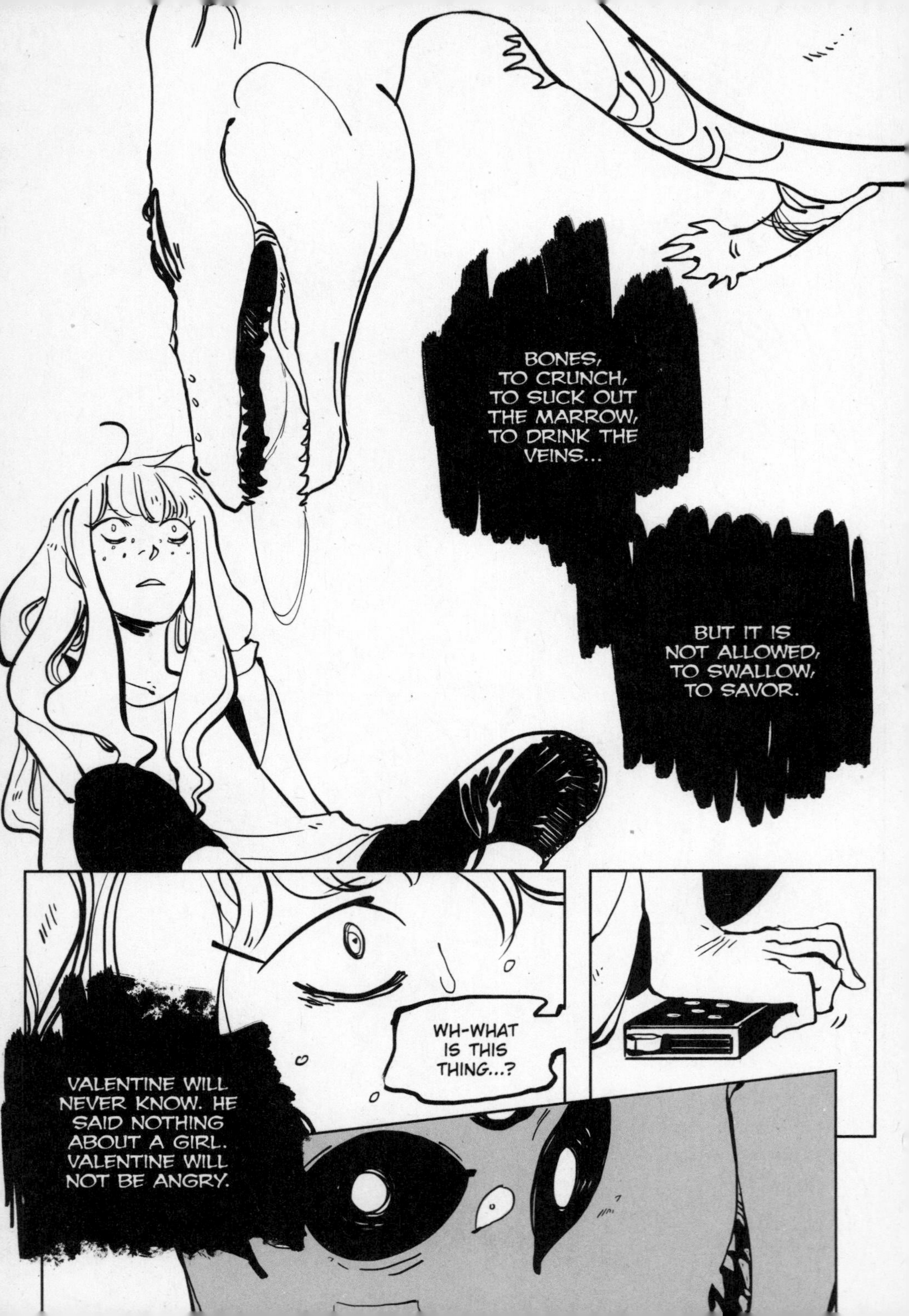
BONES, TO CRUNCH, TO SUCK OUT THE MARROW, TO DRINK THE VEINS...
BUT IT IS NOT ALLOWED, TO SWALLOW, TO SAVOR.
WH-WHAT IS THIS THING...?
VALENTINE WILL NEVER KNOW. HE SAID NOTHING ABOUT A GIRL. VALENTINE WILL NOT BE ANGRY.

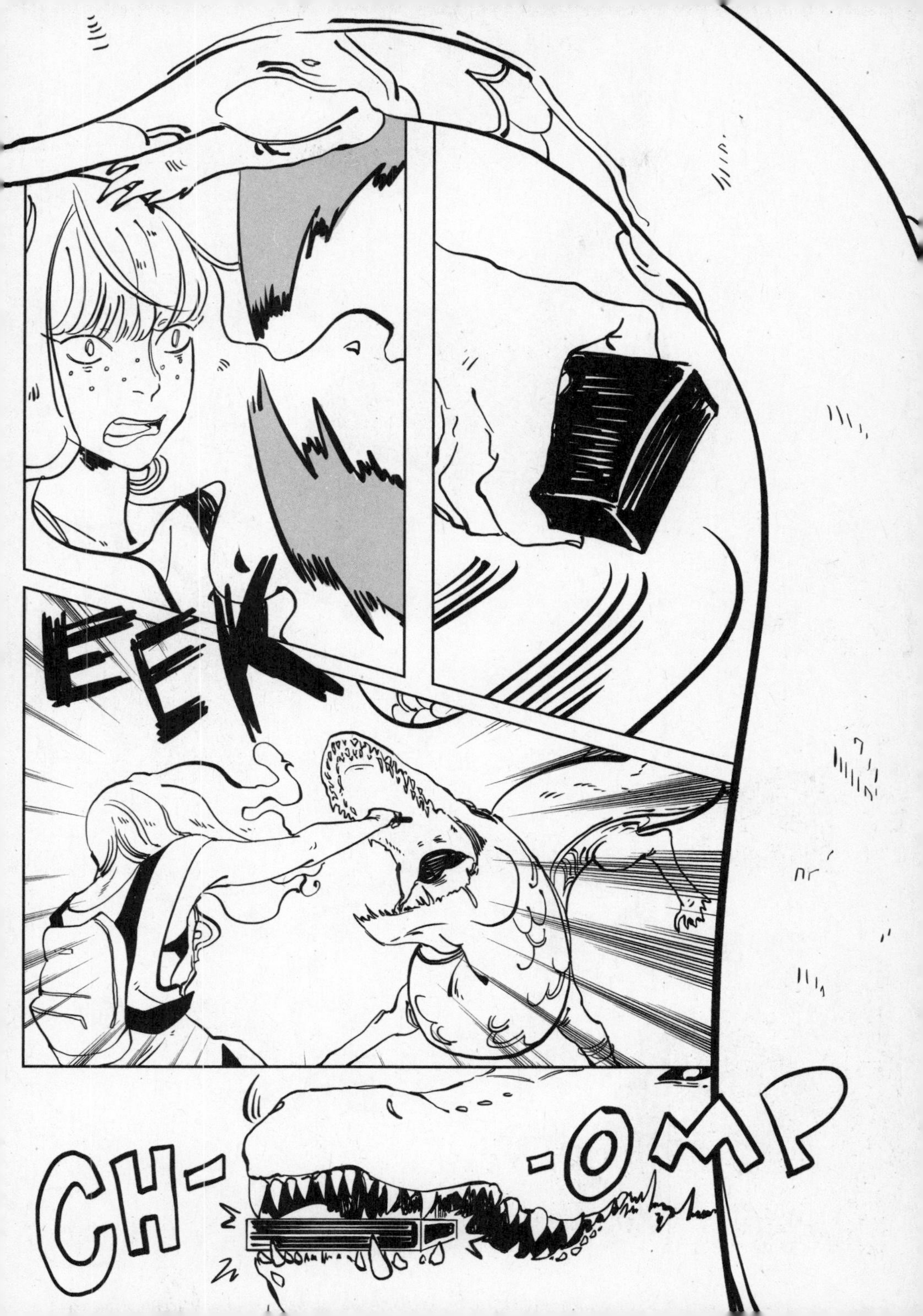
EEK
CH-
-OMP

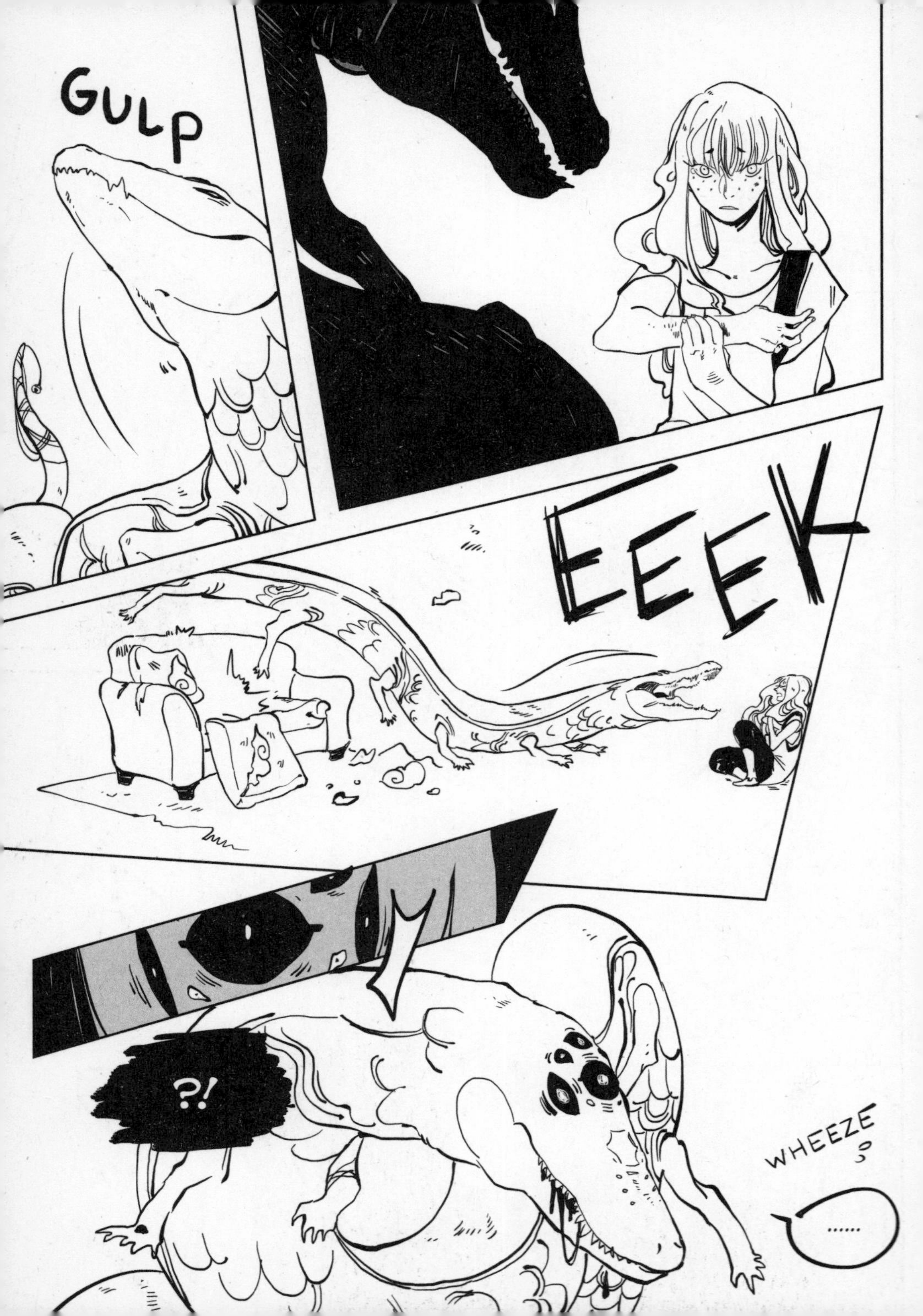
GULP
EEEK
?!
WHEEZE
......

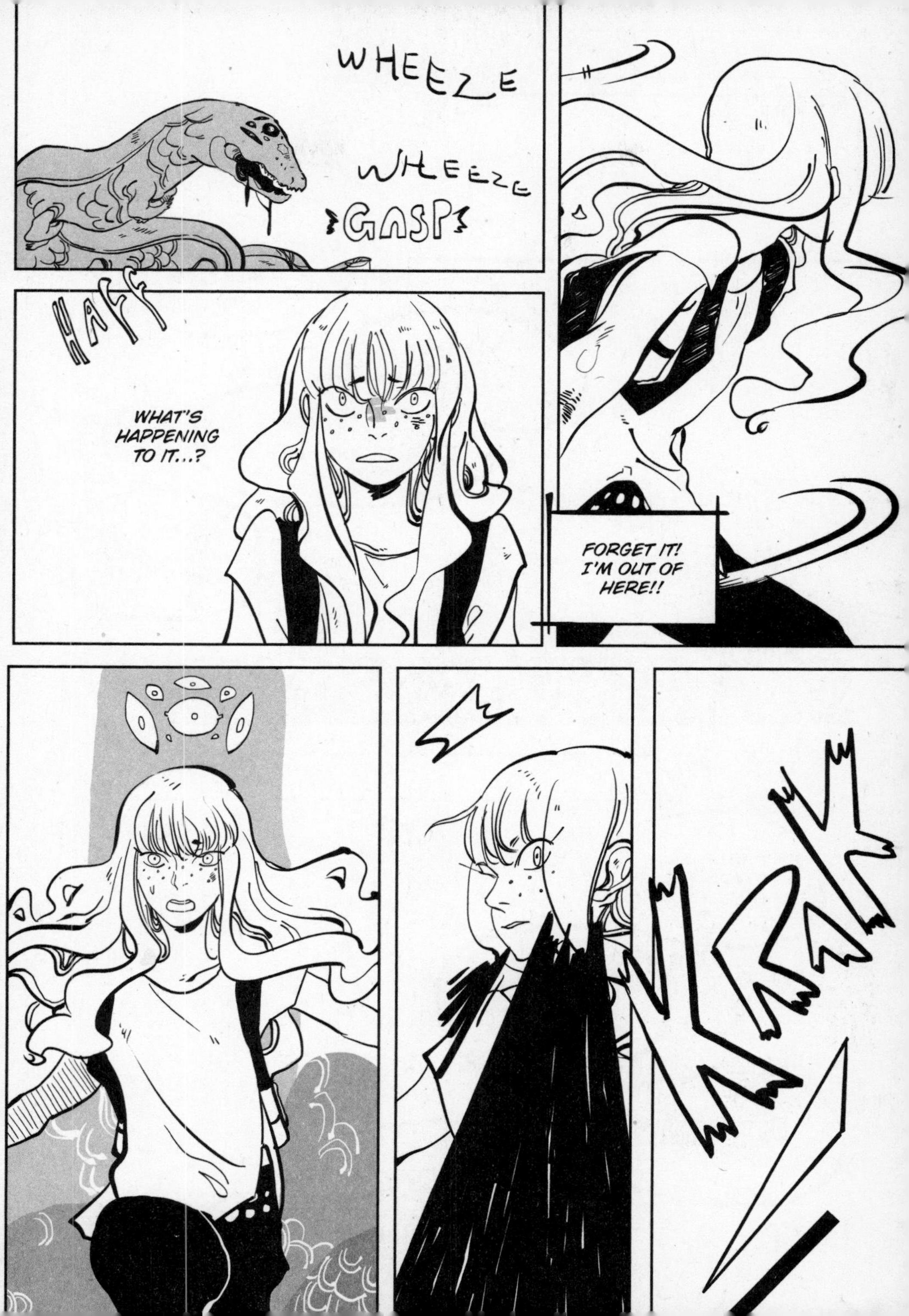
WHEEZE
WHEEZE
GASP
HAFF
WHAT'S HAPPENING TO IT...?
FORGET IT! I'M OUT OF HERE!!

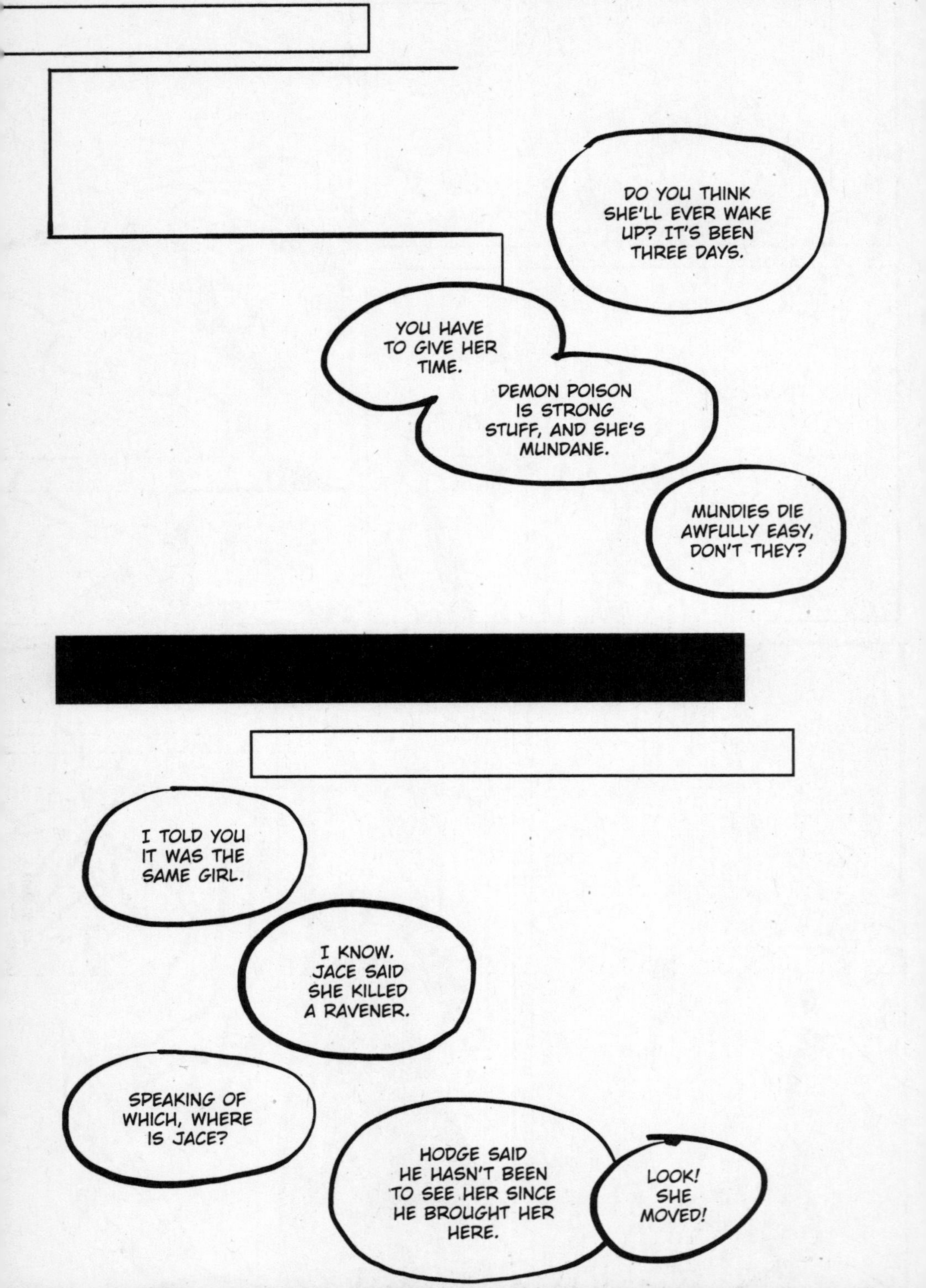
DO YOU THINK SHE'LL EVER WAKE UP? IT'S BEEN THREE DAYS.
YOU HAVE TO GIVE HER TIME.
DEMON POISON IS STRONG STUFF, AND SHE'S MUNDANE.
MUNDIES DIE AWFULLY EASY, DON'T THEY?
I TOLD YOU IT WAS THE SAME GIRL.
I KNOW. JACE SAID SHE KILLED A RAVENER.
SPEAKING OF WHICH, WHERE IS JACE?
HODGE SAID HE HASN'T BEEN TO SEE HER SINCE HE BROUGHT HER HERE.
LOOK! SHE MOVED!

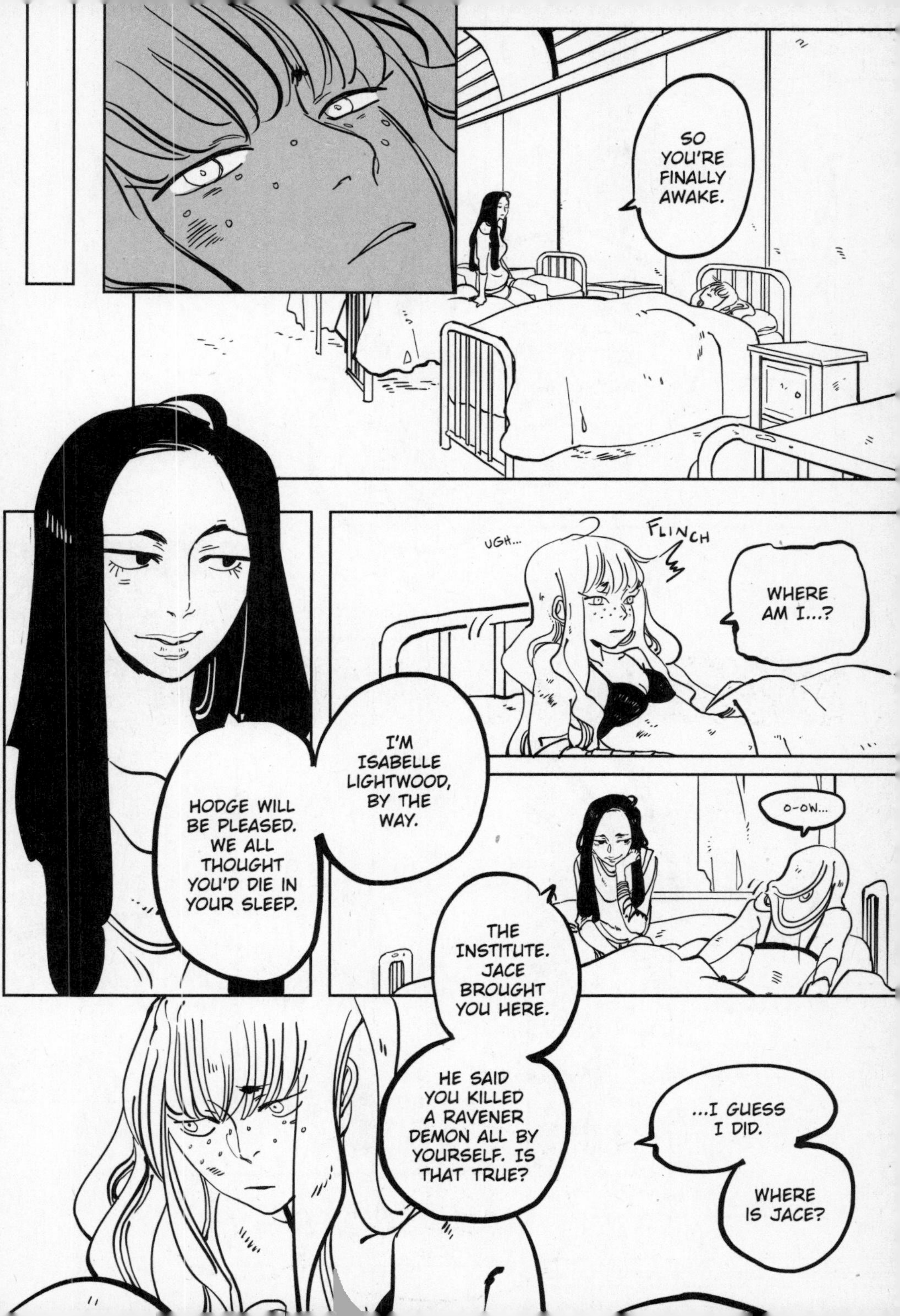
SO YOU'RE FINALLY AWAKE.
UGH...
FLINCH
WHERE AM I...?
O-OW...
THE INSTITUTE. JACE BROUGHT YOU HERE.
HODGE WILL BE PLEASED. WE ALL THOUGHT YOU'D DIE IN YOUR SLEEP.
I'M ISABELLE LIGHTWOOD, BY THE WAY.
HE SAID YOU KILLED A RAVENER DEMON ALL BY YOURSELF. IS THAT TRUE?
...I GUESS I DID.
WHERE IS JACE?

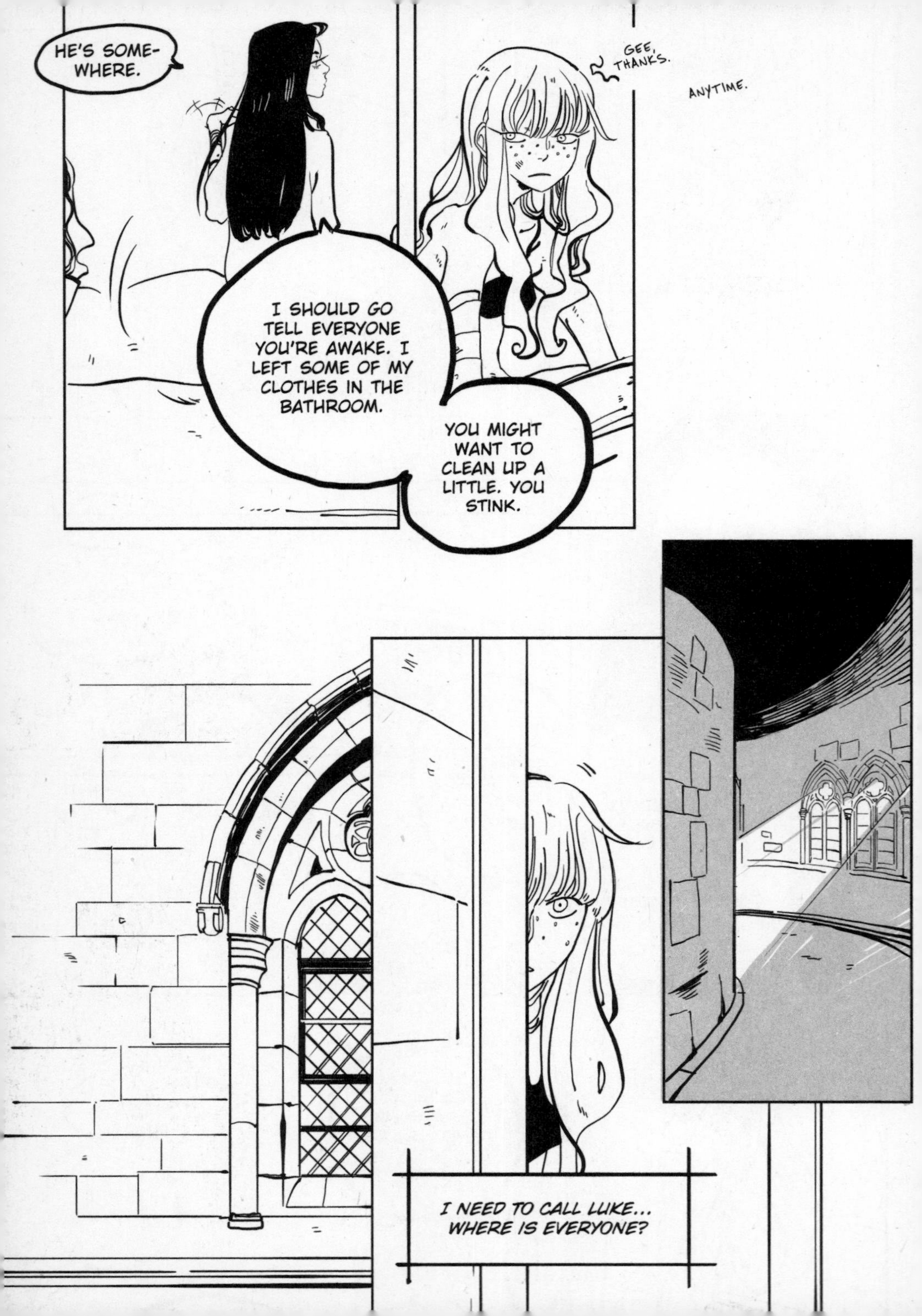
HE'S SOME-WHERE.
GEE, THANKS.
ANYTIME.
I SHOULD GO TELL EVERYONE YOU'RE AWAKE. I LEFT SOME OF MY CLOTHES IN THE BATHROOM.
YOU MIGHT WANT TO CLEAN UP A LITTLE. YOU STINK.
I NEED TO CALL LUKE... WHERE IS EVERYONE?

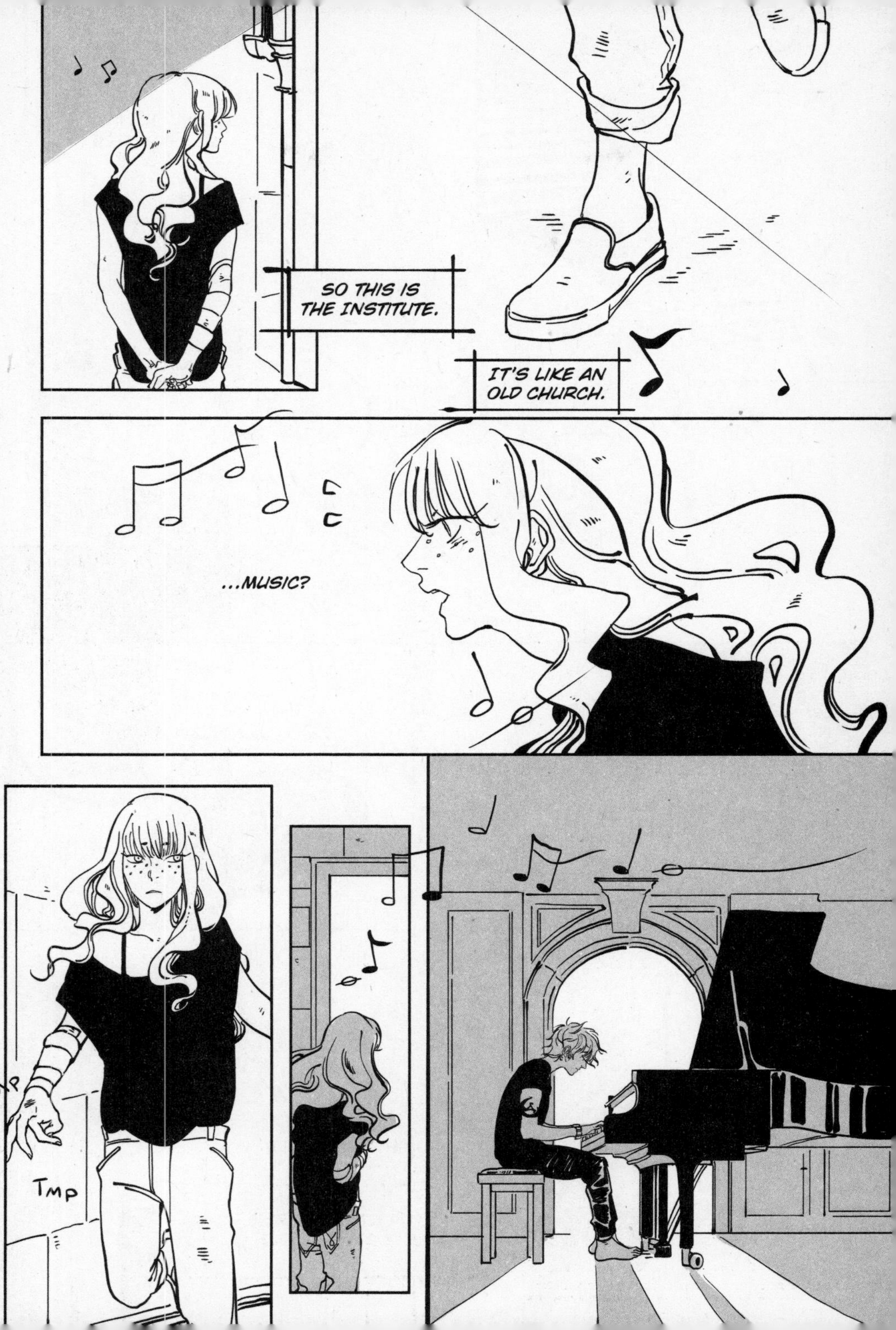
SO THIS IS THE INSTITUTE.
IT'S LIKE AN OLD CHURCH.
...MUSIC?
TMP
TMP

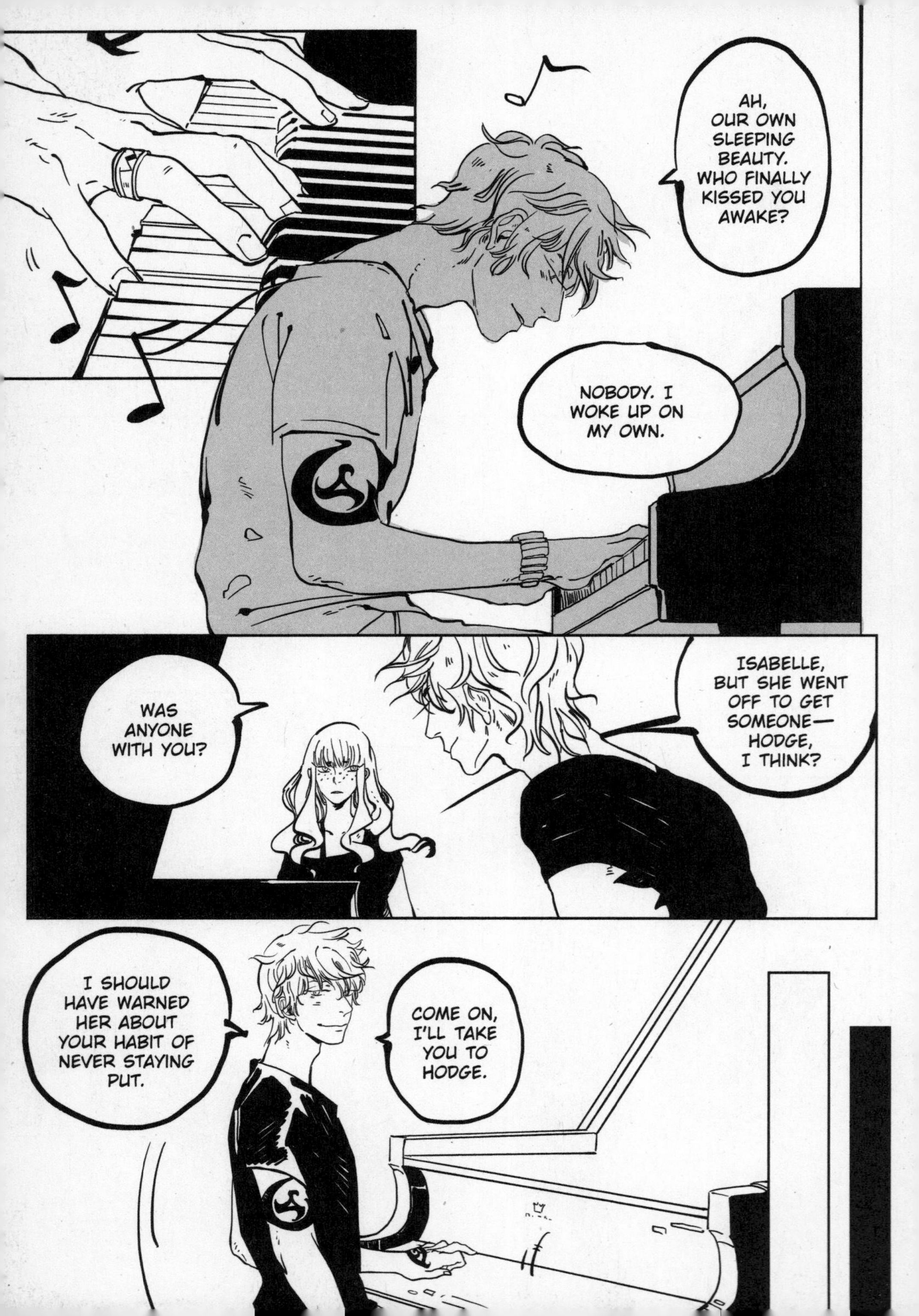
AH, OUR OWN SLEEPING BEAUTY. WHO FINALLY KISSED YOU AWAKE?
NOBODY. I WOKE UP ON MY OWN.
WAS ANYONE WITH YOU?
ISABELLE, BUT SHE WENT OFF TO GET SOMEONE—HODGE, I THINK?
I SHOULD HAVE WARNED HER ABOUT YOUR HABIT OF NEVER STAYING PUT.
COME ON, I'LL TAKE YOU TO HODGE.

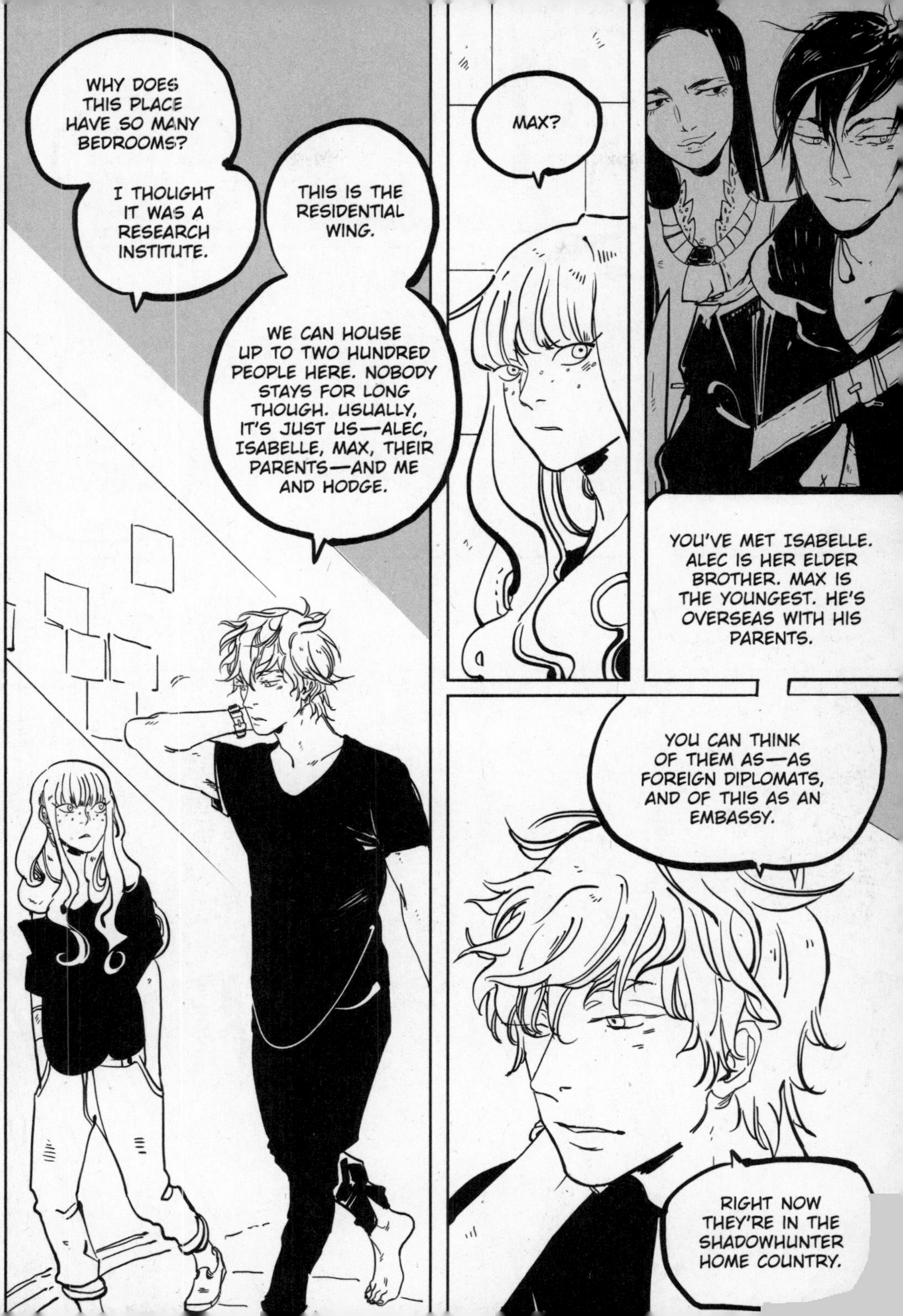
WHY DOES THIS PLACE HAVE SO MANY BEDROOMS?
I THOUGHT IT WAS A RESEARCH INSTITUTE.
THIS IS THE RESIDENTIAL WING.
WE CAN HOUSE UP TO TWO HUNDRED PEOPLE HERE. NOBODY STAYS FOR LONG THOUGH. USUALLY, IT'S JUST US—ALEC, ISABELLE, MAX, THEIR PARENTS—AND ME AND HODGE.
MAX?
YOU'VE MET ISABELLE. ALEC IS HER ELDER BROTHER. MAX IS THE YOUNGEST. HE'S OVERSEAS WITH HIS PARENTS.
YOU CAN THINK OF THEM AS—AS FOREIGN DIPLOMATS, AND OF THIS AS AN EMBASSY.
RIGHT NOW THEY'RE IN THE SHADOWHUNTER HOME COUNTRY.

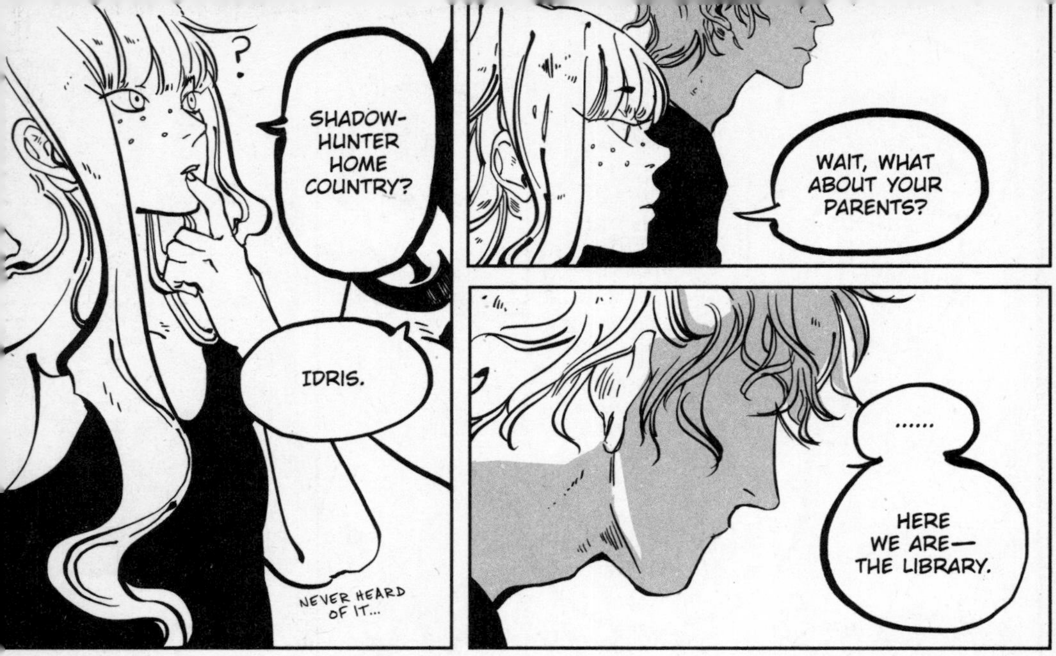
?
SHADOW-HUNTER HOME COUNTRY?
IDRIS.
NEVER HEARD OF IT...
WAIT, WHAT ABOUT YOUR PARENTS?
......
HERE WE ARE— THE LIBRARY.
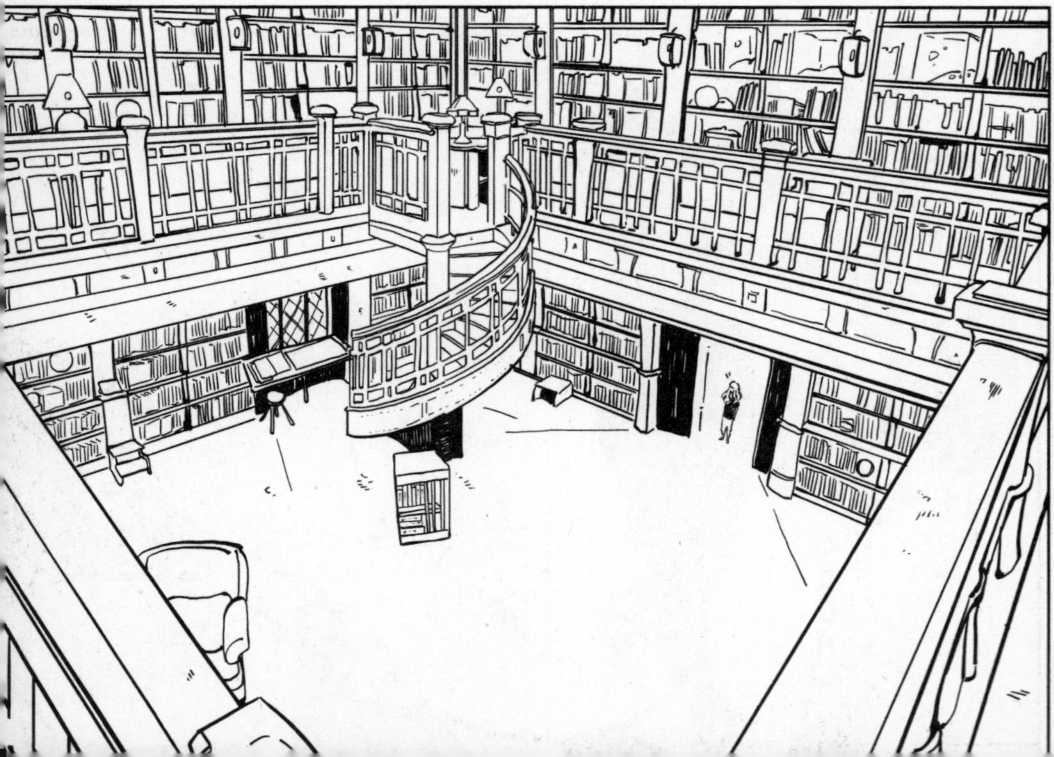

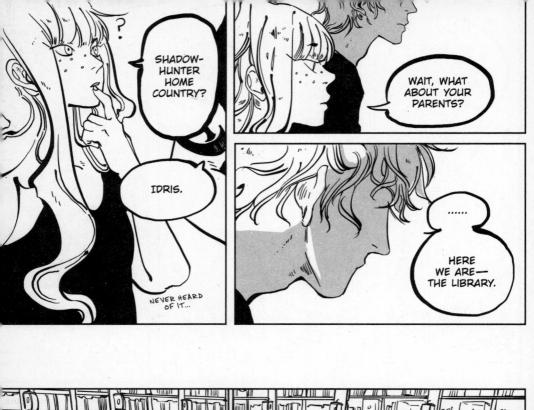

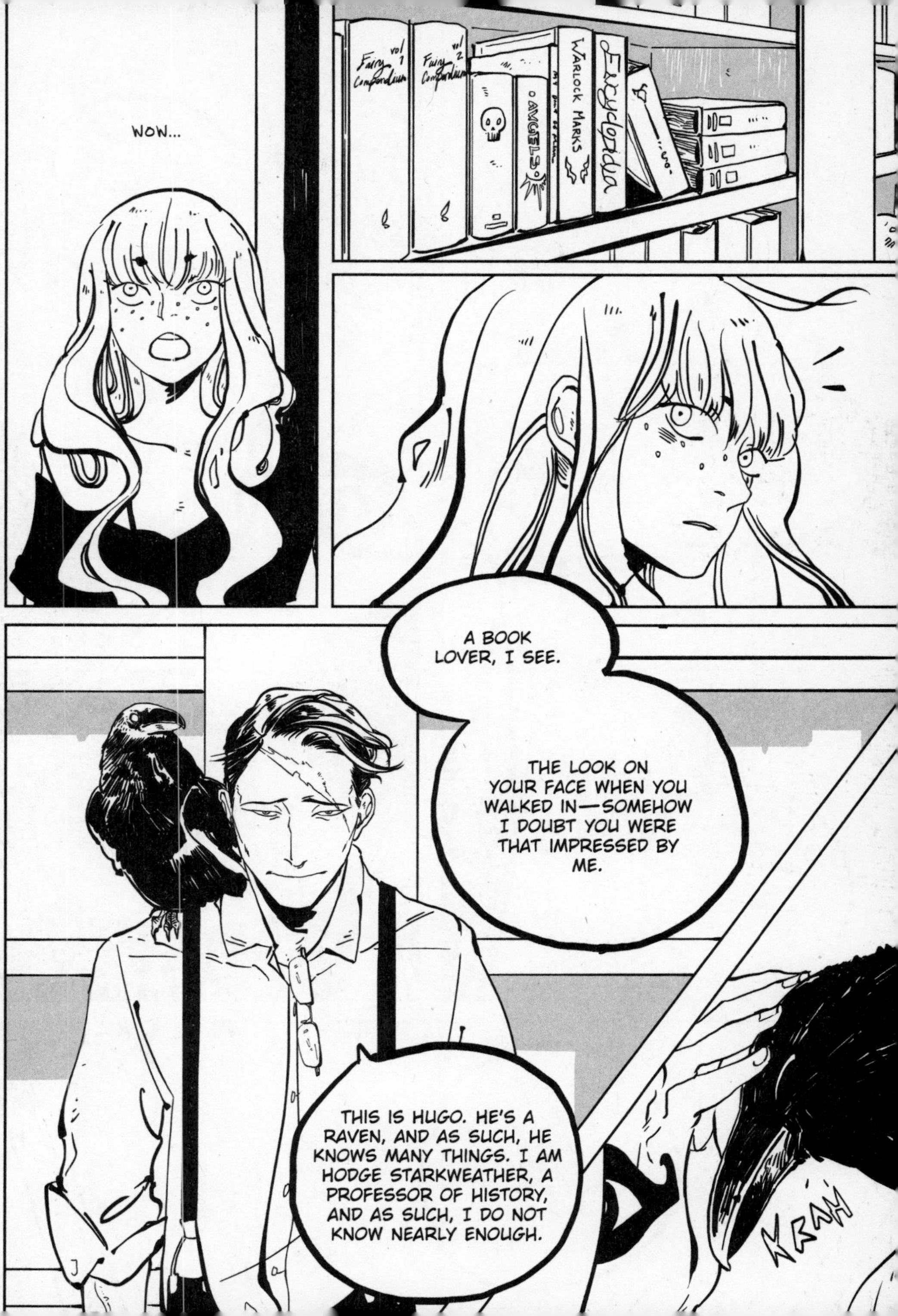
WOW...
Fairy Compendium vol 1
Fairy Compendium vol 2
ANGELS
WARLOCK MARKS
Encyclopedia
A BOOK LOVER, I SEE.
THE LOOK ON YOUR FACE WHEN YOU WALKED IN—SOMEHOW I DOUBT YOU WERE THAT IMPRESSED BY ME.
THIS IS HUGO. HE'S A RAVEN, AND AS SUCH, HE KNOWS MANY THINGS. I AM HODGE STARKWEATHER, A PROFESSOR OF HISTORY, AND AS SUCH, I DO NOT KNOW NEARLY ENOUGH.
KRAH

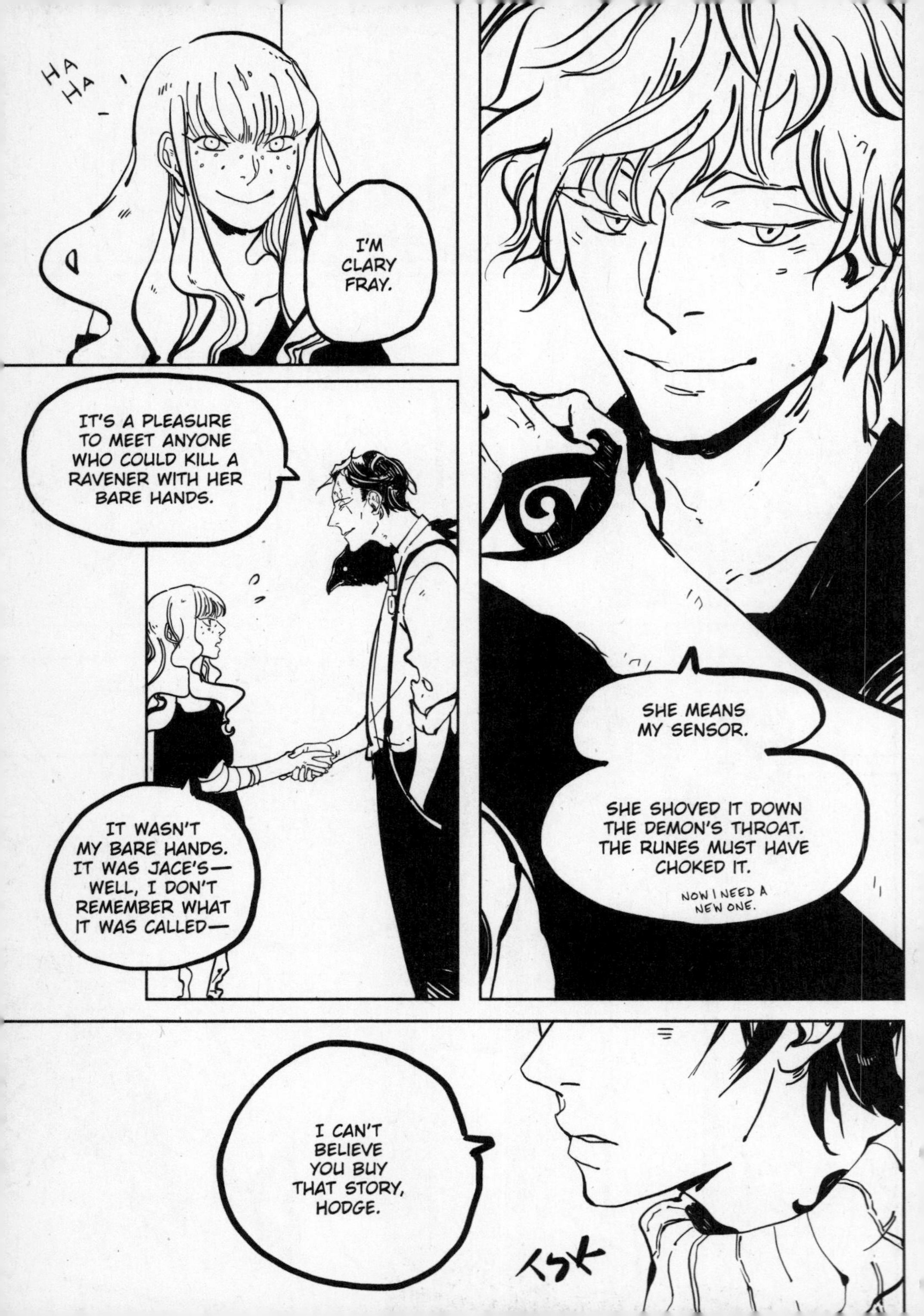
HA HA —
I'M CLARY FRAY.
IT'S A PLEASURE TO MEET ANYONE WHO COULD KILL A RAVENER WITH HER BARE HANDS.
IT WASN'T MY BARE HANDS. IT WAS JACE'S— WELL, I DON'T REMEMBER WHAT IT WAS CALLED—
SHE MEANS MY SENSOR.
SHE SHOVED IT DOWN THE DEMON'S THROAT. THE RUNES MUST HAVE CHOKED IT.
NOW I NEED A NEW ONE.
I CAN'T BELIEVE YOU BUY THAT STORY, HODGE.
TSK

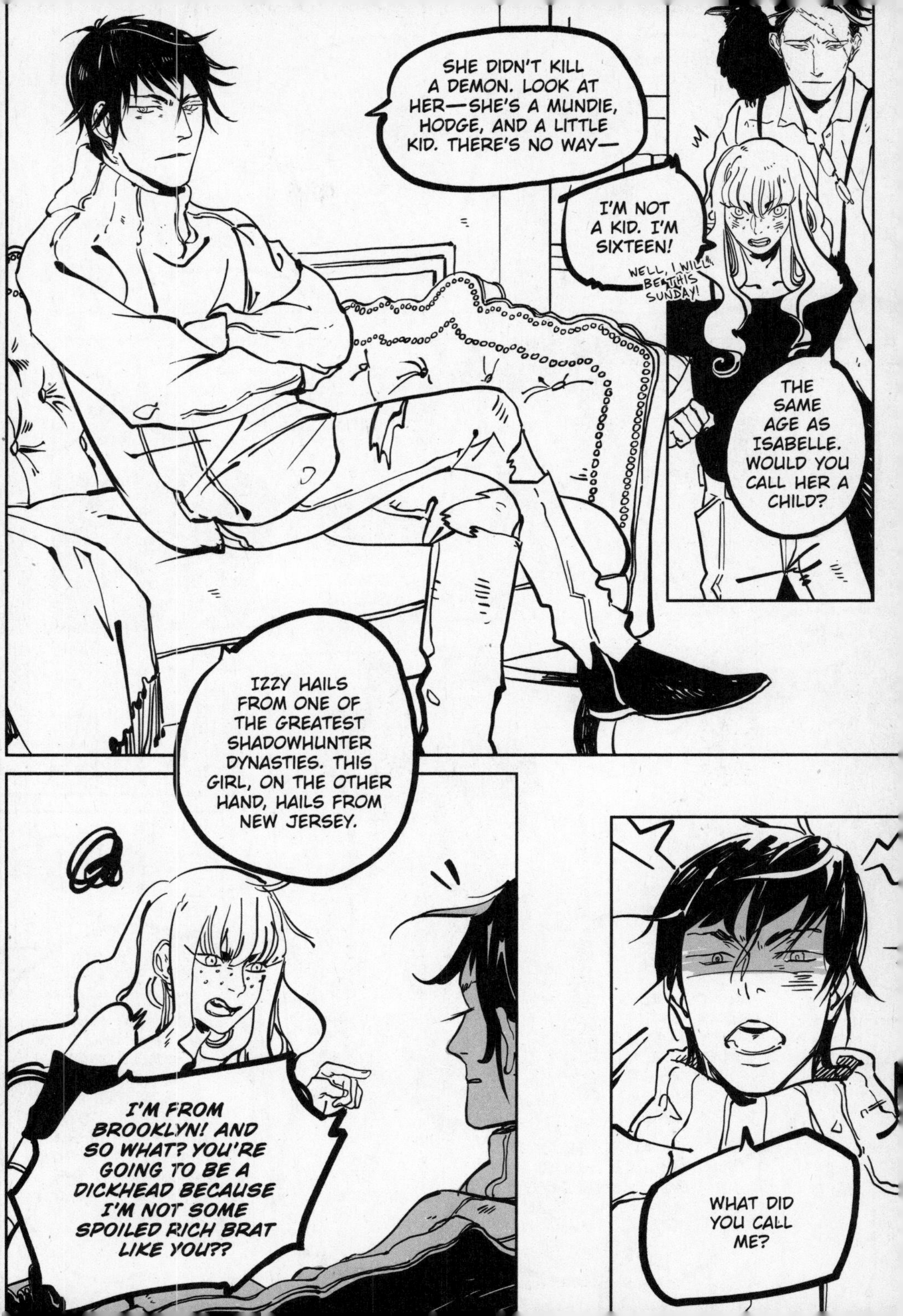
SHE DIDN'T KILL A DEMON. LOOK AT HER—SHE'S A MUNDIE, HODGE, AND A LITTLE KID. THERE'S NO WAY—
I'M NOT A KID. I'M SIXTEEN!
WELL, I WILL BE THIS SUNDAY!
THE SAME AGE AS ISABELLE. WOULD YOU CALL HER A CHILD?
IZZY HAILS FROM ONE OF THE GREATEST SHADOWHUNTER DYNASTIES. THIS GIRL, ON THE OTHER HAND, HAILS FROM NEW JERSEY.
I'M FROM BROOKLYN! AND SO WHAT? YOU'RE GOING TO BE A DICKHEAD BECAUSE I'M NOT SOME SPOILED RICH BRAT LIKE YOU??
WHAT DID YOU CALL ME?

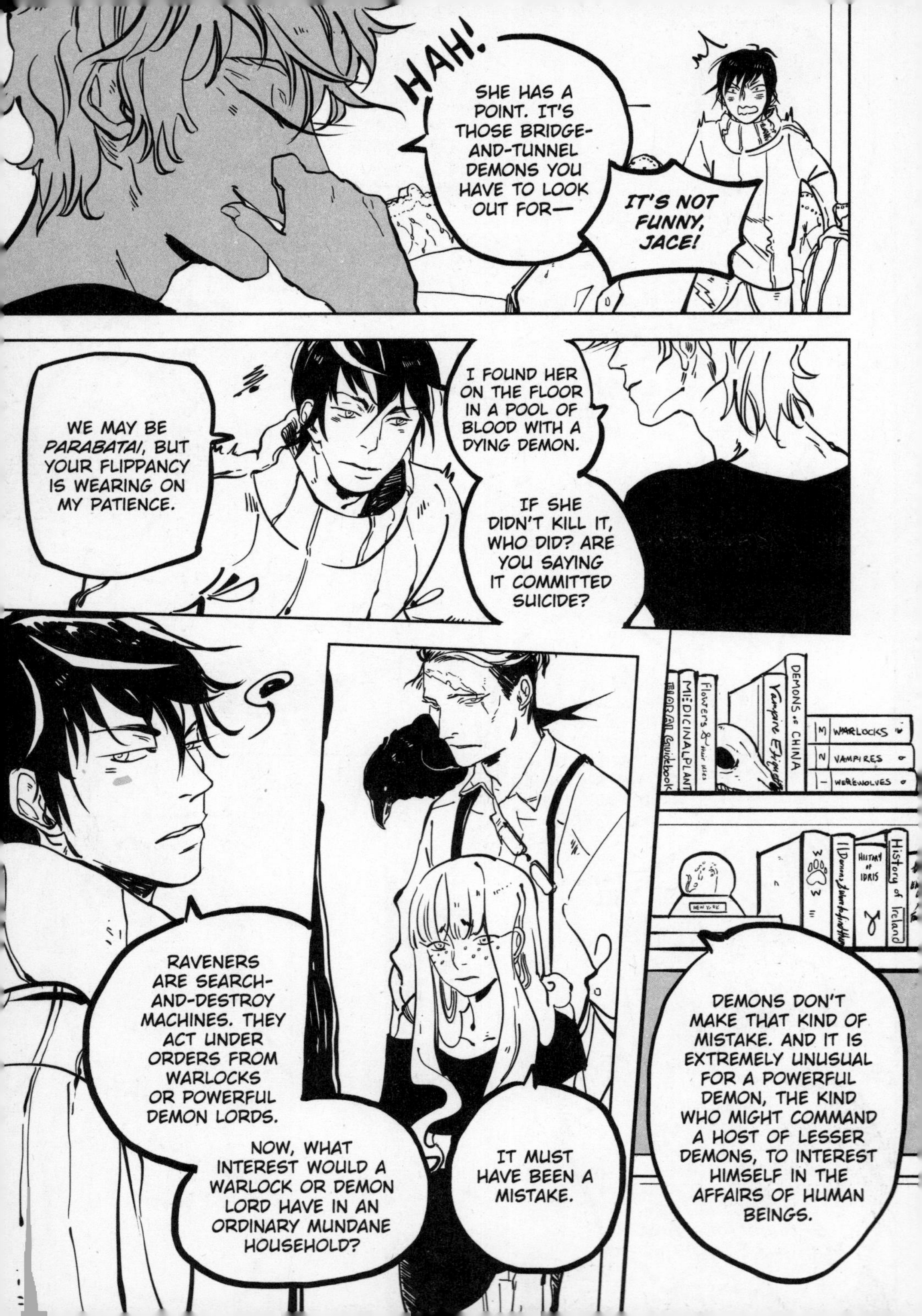
HAH!
SHE HAS A POINT. IT'S THOSE BRIDGE-AND-TUNNEL DEMONS YOU HAVE TO LOOK OUT FOR—
IT'S NOT FUNNY, JACE!
WE MAY BE *PARABATAI*, BUT YOUR FLIPPANCY IS WEARING ON MY PATIENCE.
I FOUND HER ON THE FLOOR IN A POOL OF BLOOD WITH A DYING DEMON.
IF SHE DIDN'T KILL IT, WHO DID? ARE YOU SAYING IT COMMITTED SUICIDE?
DEMONS of CHINA
WARLOCKS
VAMPIRES
WEREWOLVES
HISTORY of IDRIS
History of Ireland
NEW YORK
RAVENERS ARE SEARCH-AND-DESTROY MACHINES. THEY ACT UNDER ORDERS FROM WARLOCKS OR POWERFUL DEMON LORDS.
NOW, WHAT INTEREST WOULD A WARLOCK OR DEMON LORD HAVE IN AN ORDINARY MUNDANE HOUSEHOLD?
IT MUST HAVE BEEN A MISTAKE.
DEMONS DON'T MAKE THAT KIND OF MISTAKE. AND IT IS EXTREMELY UNUSUAL FOR A POWERFUL DEMON, THE KIND WHO MIGHT COMMAND A HOST OF LESSER DEMONS, TO INTEREST HIMSELF IN THE AFFAIRS OF HUMAN BEINGS.

MADAME DOROTHEA— SHE LIVES DOWN- STAIRS— SHE'S A WITCH. MAYBE THE DEMONS WERE AFTER HER AND GOT MY MOM BY MISTAKE?

SHE'S LIKE MOST WITCHES—A FAKE. I ALREADY LOOKED INTO IT. THERE'S NO REASON FOR ANY WARLOCK TO BE INTERESTED IN HER.

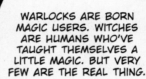

WARLOCKS ARE BORN MAGIC USERS. WITCHES ARE HUMANS WHO'VE TAUGHT THEMSELVES A LITTLE MAGIC. BUT VERY FEW ARE THE REAL THING.

BESIDES...

...CLARY IS NOT MUNDANE.

BUT I AM...

NO, YOU AREN'T.

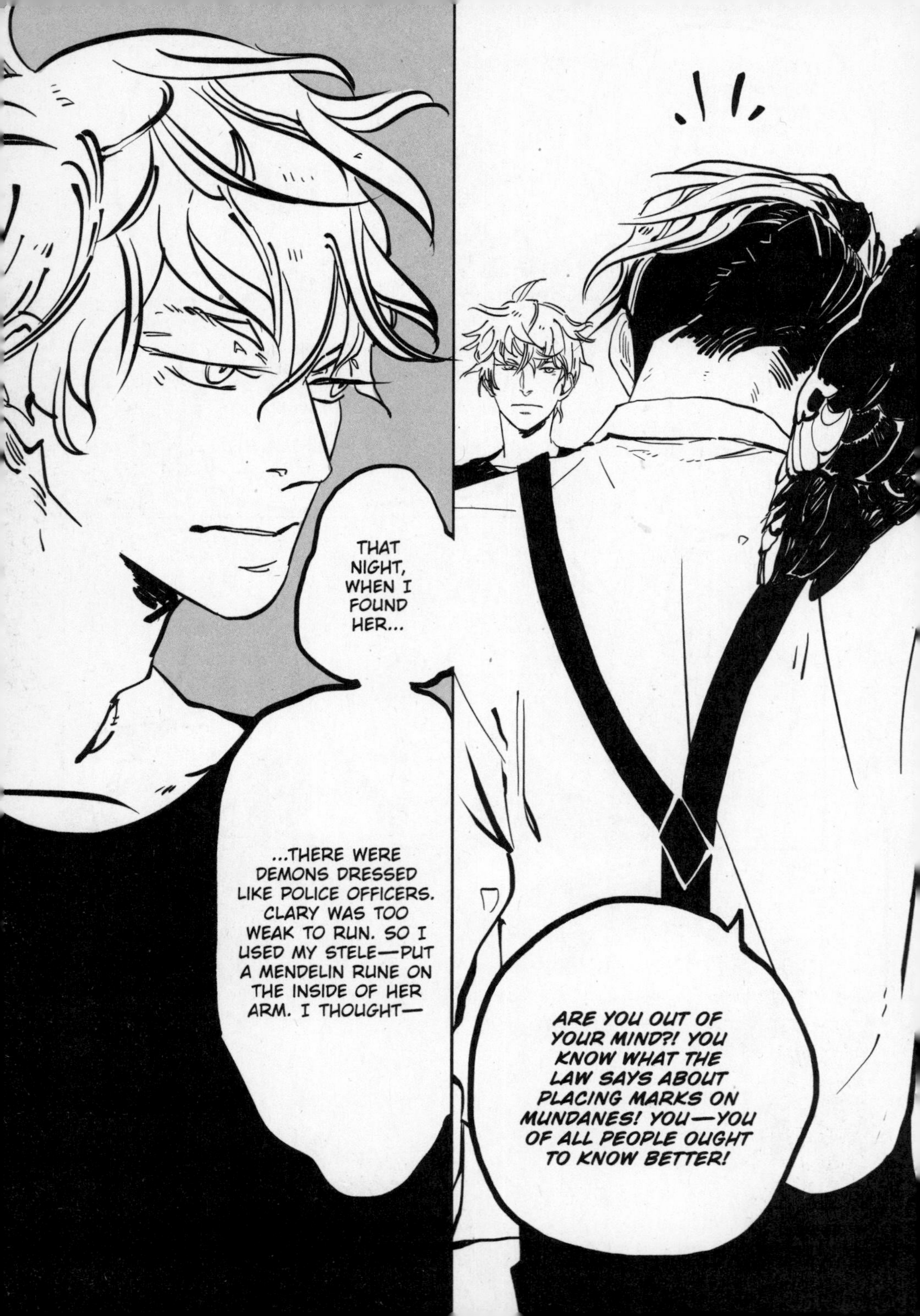
THAT NIGHT, WHEN I FOUND HER...
...THERE WERE DEMONS DRESSED LIKE POLICE OFFICERS. CLARY WAS TOO WEAK TO RUN. SO I USED MY STELE—PUT A MENDELIN RUNE ON THE INSIDE OF HER ARM. I THOUGHT—
ARE YOU OUT OF YOUR MIND?! YOU KNOW WHAT THE LAW SAYS ABOUT PLACING MARKS ON MUNDANES! YOU—YOU OF ALL PEOPLE OUGHT TO KNOW BETTER!

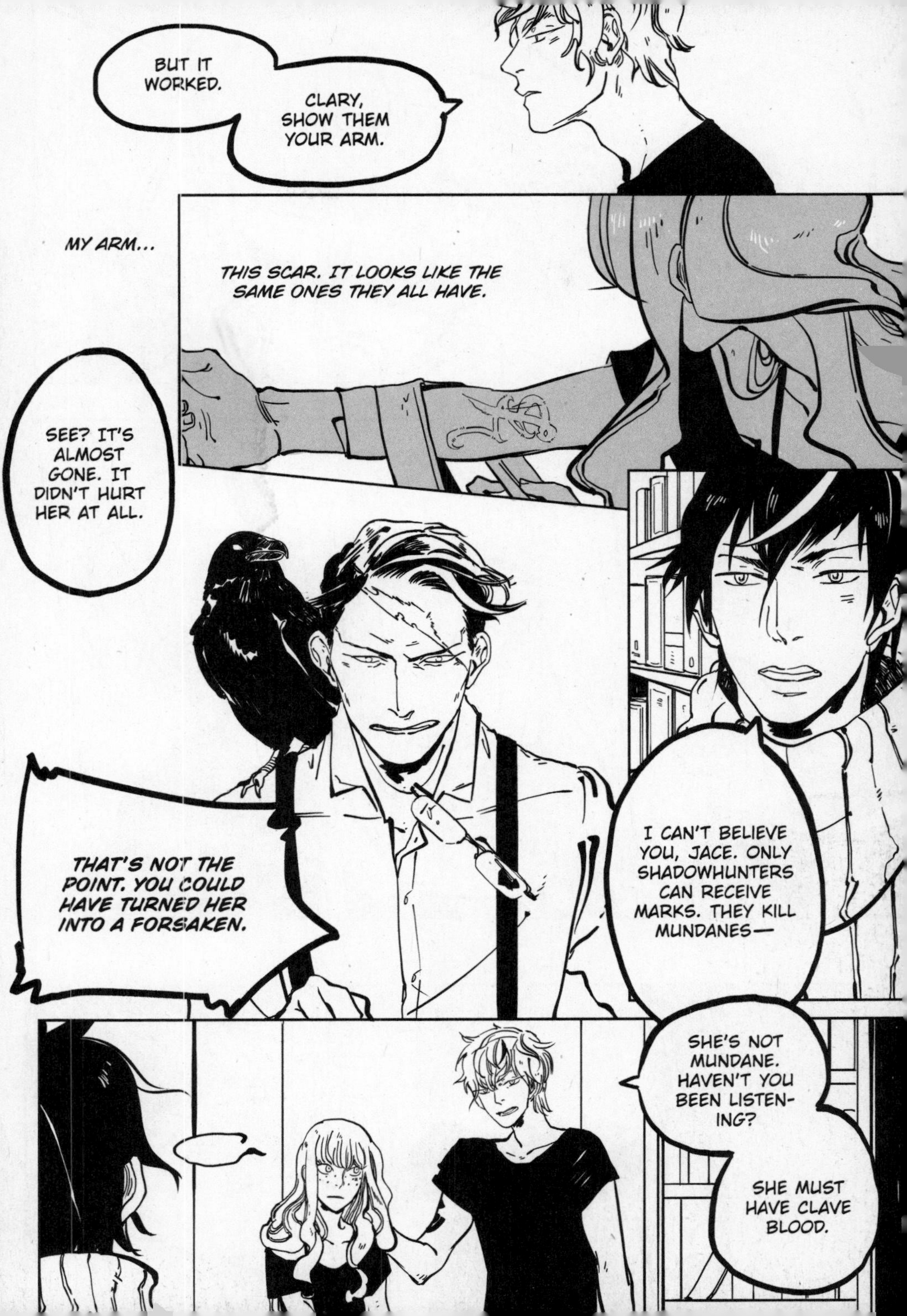

BUT IT WORKED.
CLARY, SHOW THEM YOUR ARM.
MY ARM...
THIS SCAR. IT LOOKS LIKE THE SAME ONES THEY ALL HAVE.
SEE? IT'S ALMOST GONE. IT DIDN'T HURT HER AT ALL.
THAT'S NOT THE POINT. YOU COULD HAVE TURNED HER INTO A FORSAKEN.
I CAN'T BELIEVE YOU, JACE. ONLY SHADOWHUNTERS CAN RECEIVE MARKS. THEY KILL MUNDANES—
SHE'S NOT MUNDANE. HAVEN'T YOU BEEN LISTEN-ING?
SHE MUST HAVE CLAVE BLOOD.

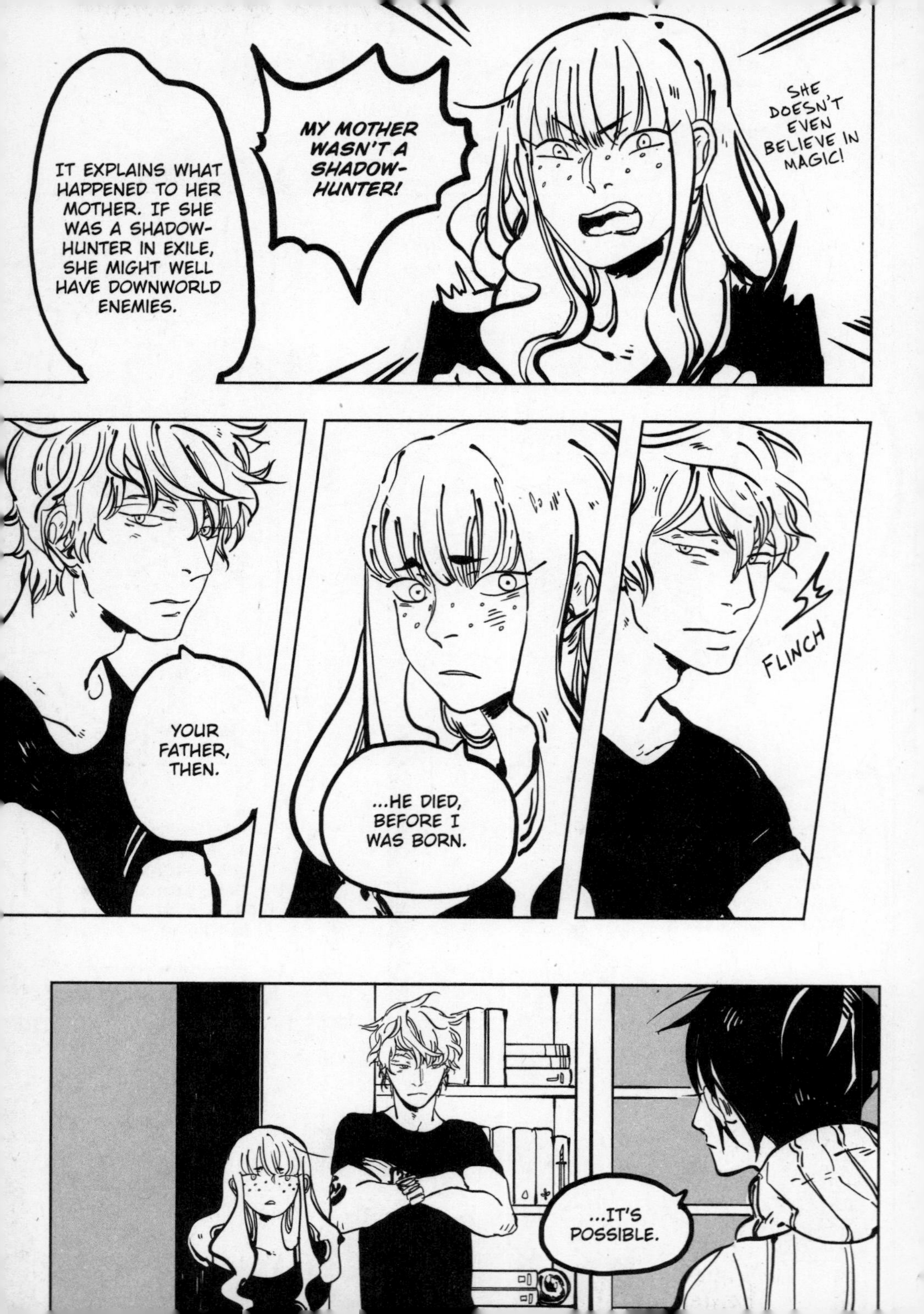
IT EXPLAINS WHAT HAPPENED TO HER MOTHER. IF SHE WAS A SHADOW-HUNTER IN EXILE, SHE MIGHT WELL HAVE DOWNWORLD ENEMIES.
MY MOTHER WASN'T A SHADOW-HUNTER!
SHE DOESN'T EVEN BELIEVE IN MAGIC!
YOUR FATHER, THEN.
...HE DIED, BEFORE I WAS BORN.
FLINCH
...IT'S POSSIBLE.

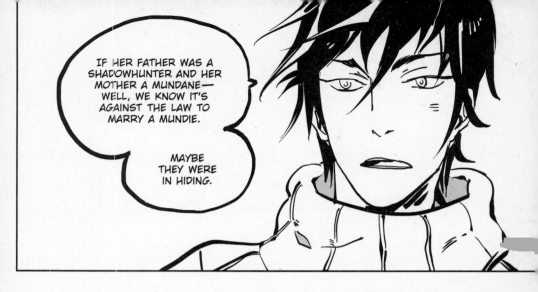

IF HER FATHER WAS A SHADOWHUNTER AND HER MOTHER A MUNDANE— WELL, WE KNOW IT'S AGAINST THE LAW TO MARRY A MUNDIE.

MAYBE THEY WERE IN HIDING.

MOM NEVER TALKS ABOUT DAD. SHE DOESN'T EVEN KEEP PICTURES...

WHAT IF MY DAD WAS...

OH! LUKE!

MY MOM'S FRIEND. HE WOULD KNOW. CAN I CALL HIM?

...YES, ON THE DESK.

LUKE IS PROBABLY SO WORRIED HE'S FRANTIC. I'VE BEEN MISSING FOR DAYS.

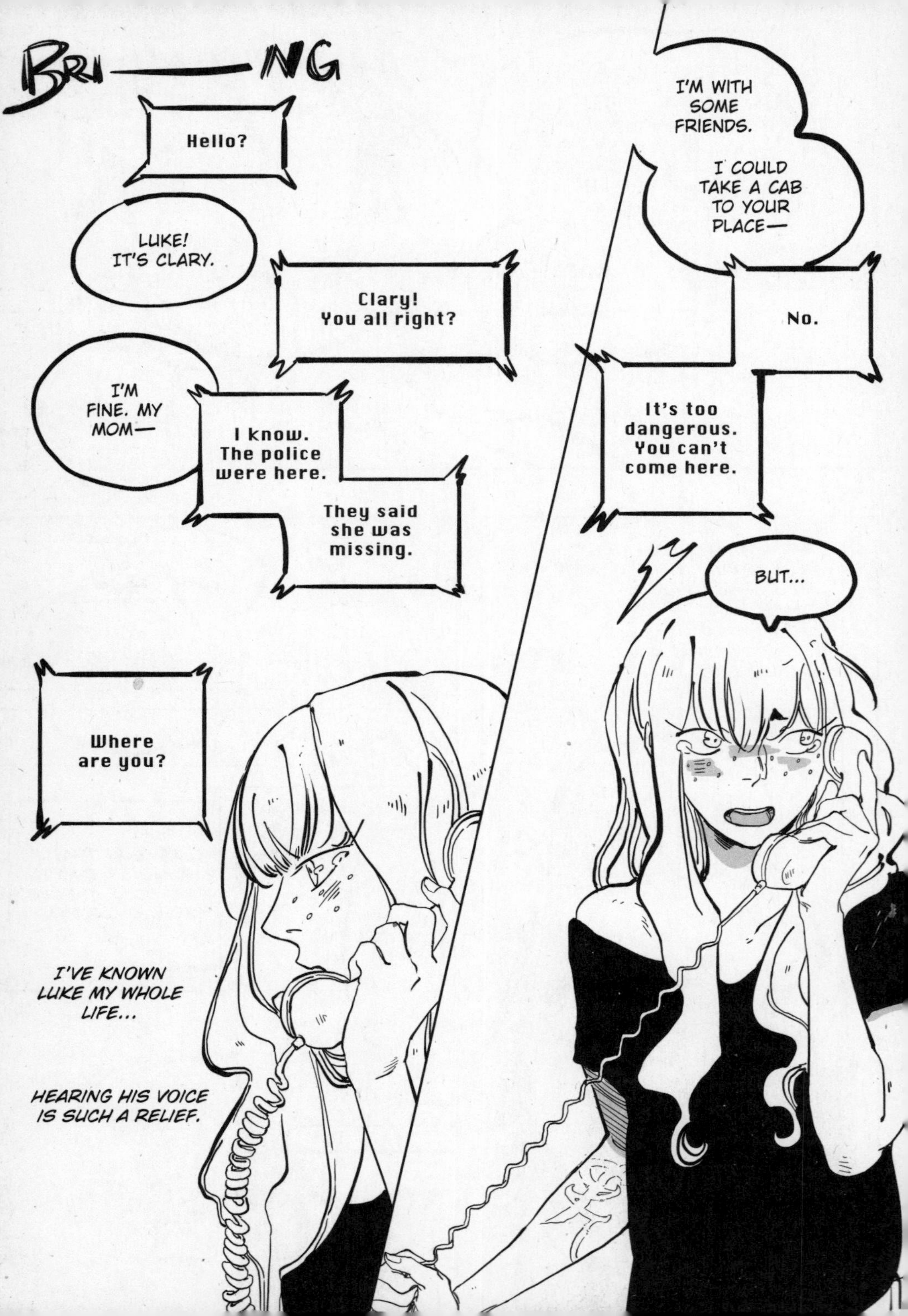
BRI——NG
Hello?
LUKE! IT'S CLARY.
Clary! You all right?
I'M FINE. MY MOM—
I know. The police were here.
They said she was missing.
Where are you?
I'VE KNOWN LUKE MY WHOLE LIFE...
HEARING HIS VOICE IS SUCH A RELIEF.
I'M WITH SOME FRIENDS.
I COULD TAKE A CAB TO YOUR PLACE—
No.
It's too dangerous. You can't come here.
BUT...

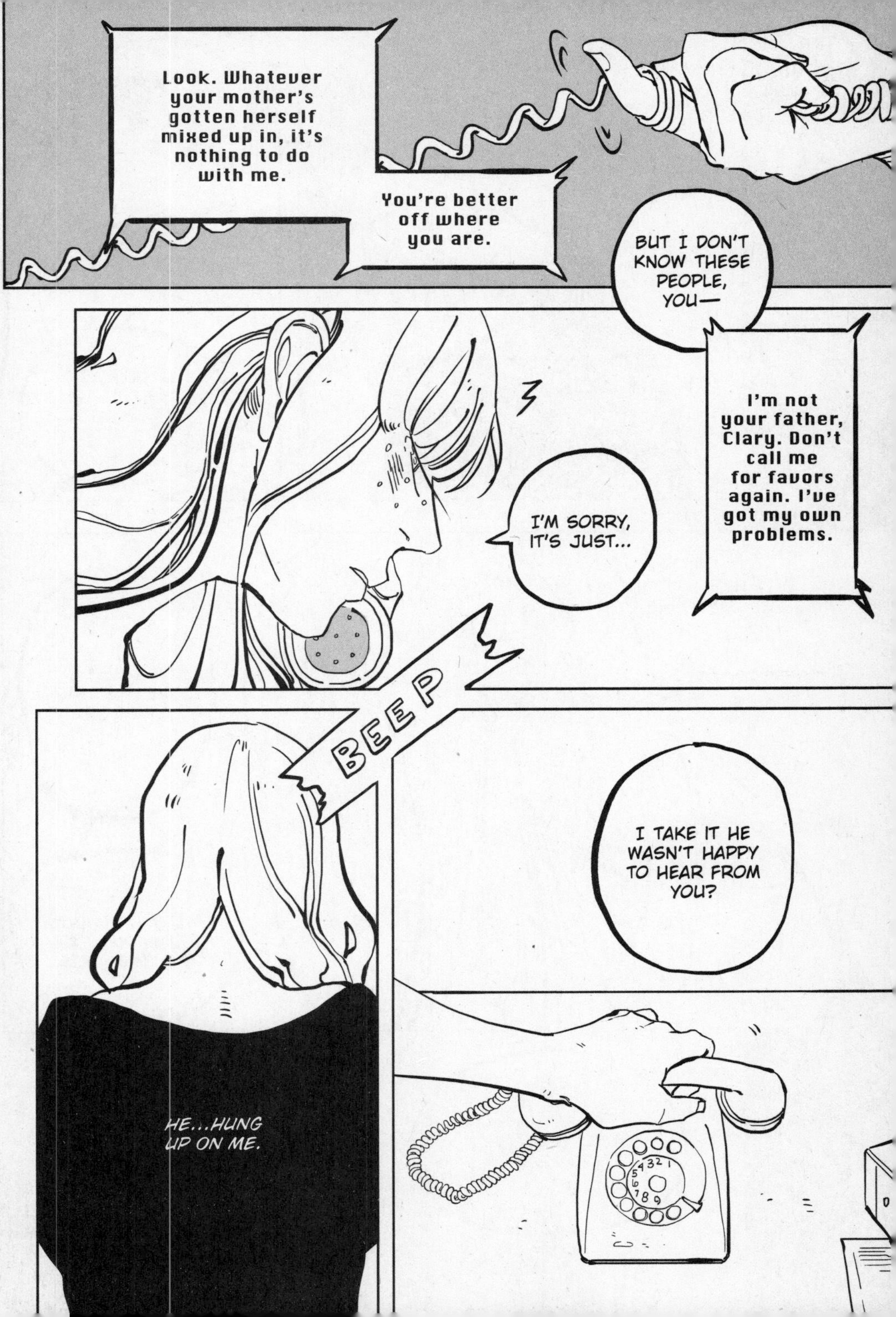
Look. Whatever your mother's gotten herself mixed up in, it's nothing to do with me.
You're better off where you are.
BUT I DON'T KNOW THESE PEOPLE, YOU—
I'm not your father, Clary. Don't call me for favors again. I've got my own problems.
I'M SORRY, IT'S JUST...
BEEP
HE...HUNG UP ON ME.
I TAKE IT HE WASN'T HAPPY TO HEAR FROM YOU?

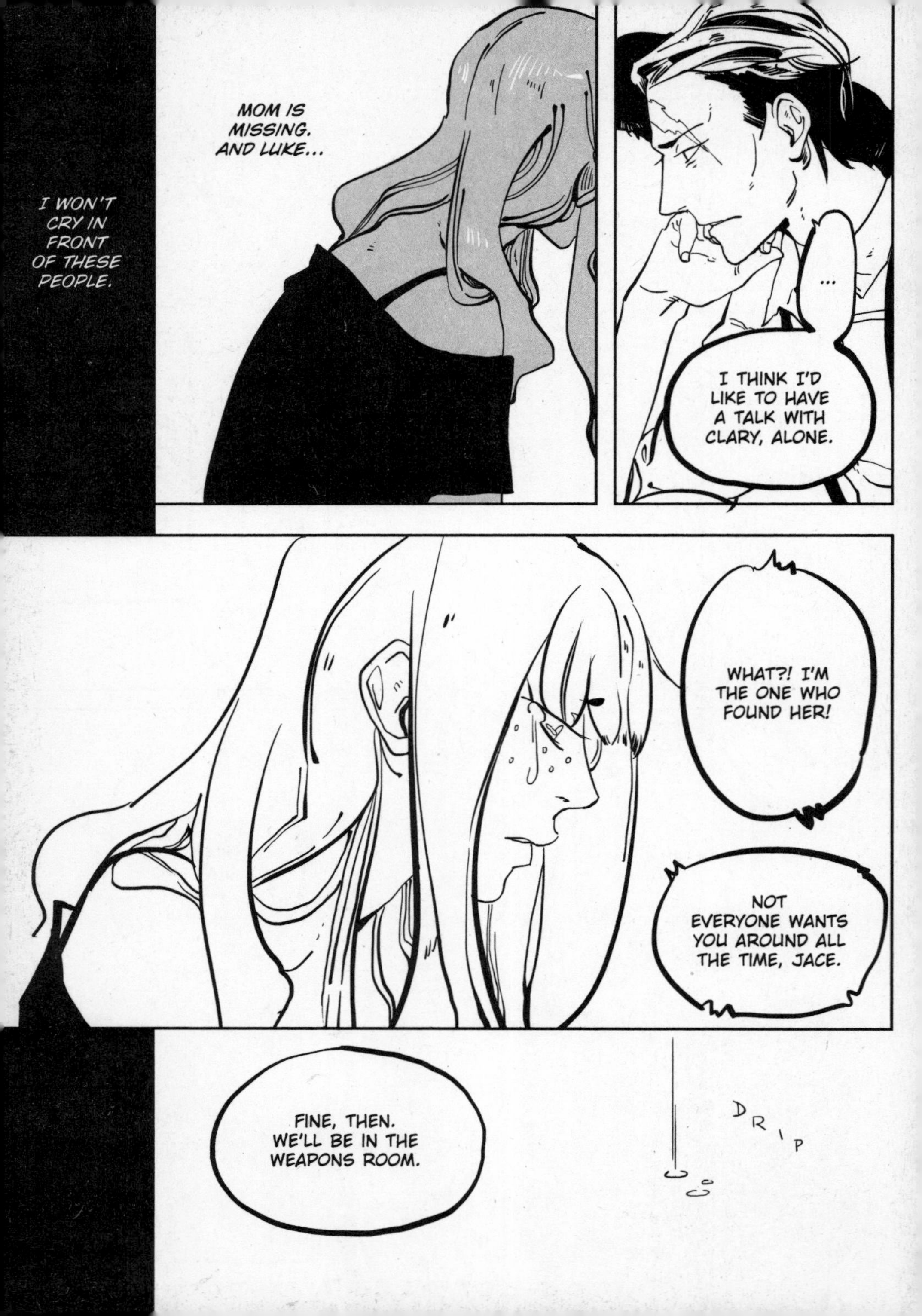
I WON'T CRY IN FRONT OF THESE PEOPLE.
MOM IS MISSING. AND LUKE...
...
I THINK I'D LIKE TO HAVE A TALK WITH CLARY, ALONE.
WHAT?! I'M THE ONE WHO FOUND HER!
NOT EVERYONE WANTS YOU AROUND ALL THE TIME, JACE.
FINE, THEN. WE'LL BE IN THE WEAPONS ROOM.
DRIP

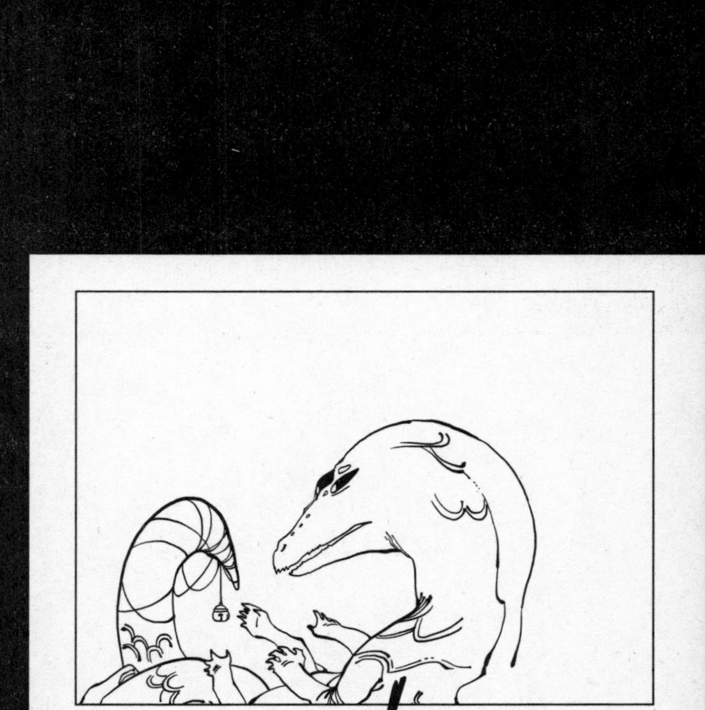

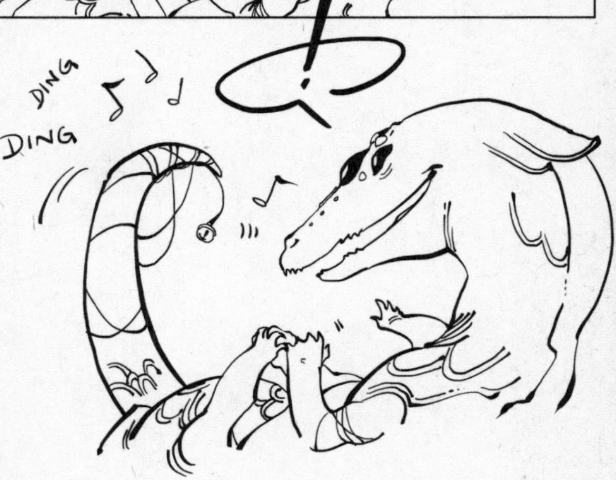
DING
DING
!

THE MORTAL INSTRUMENTS

THE GRAPHIC NOVEL

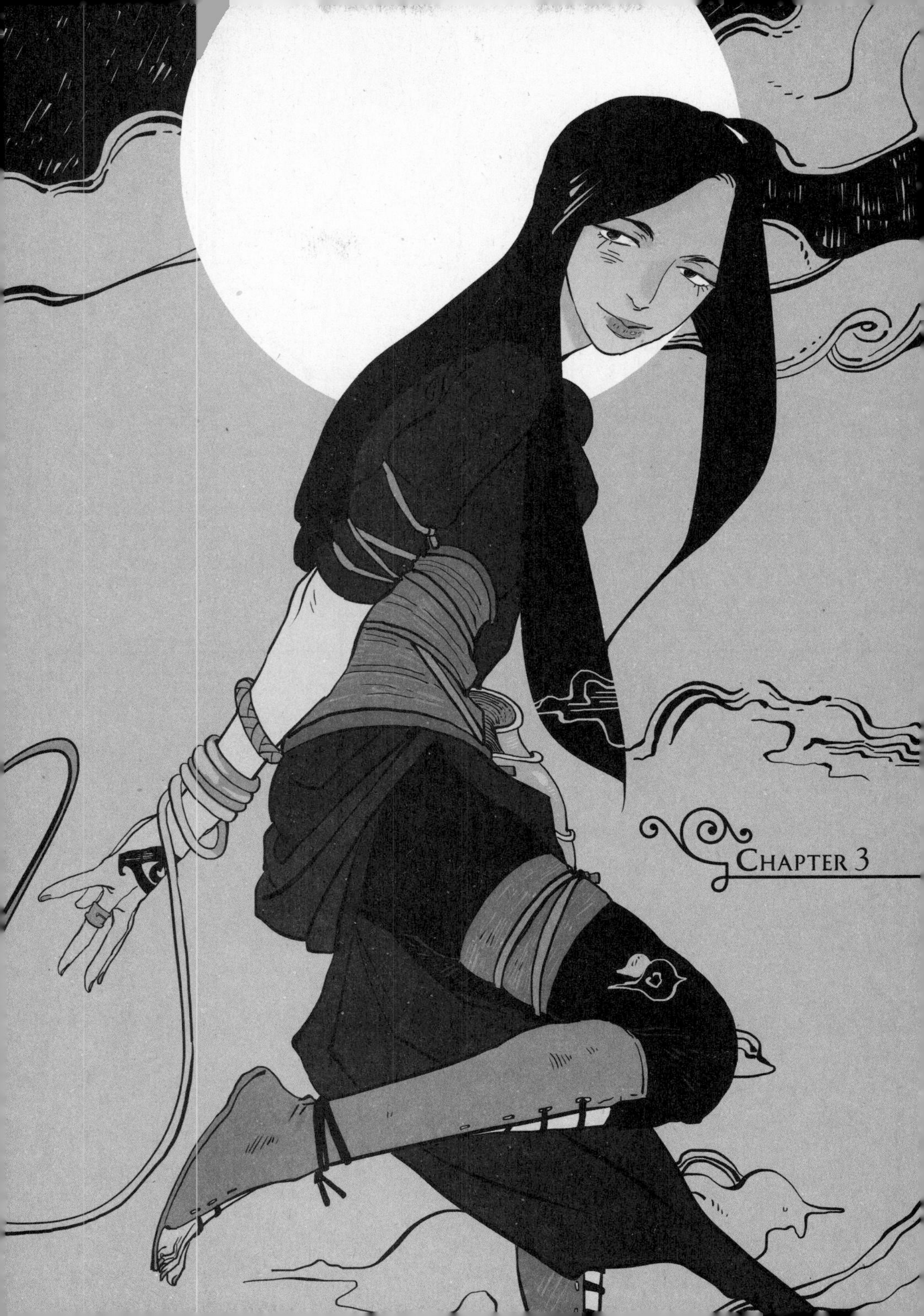
CHAPTER 3

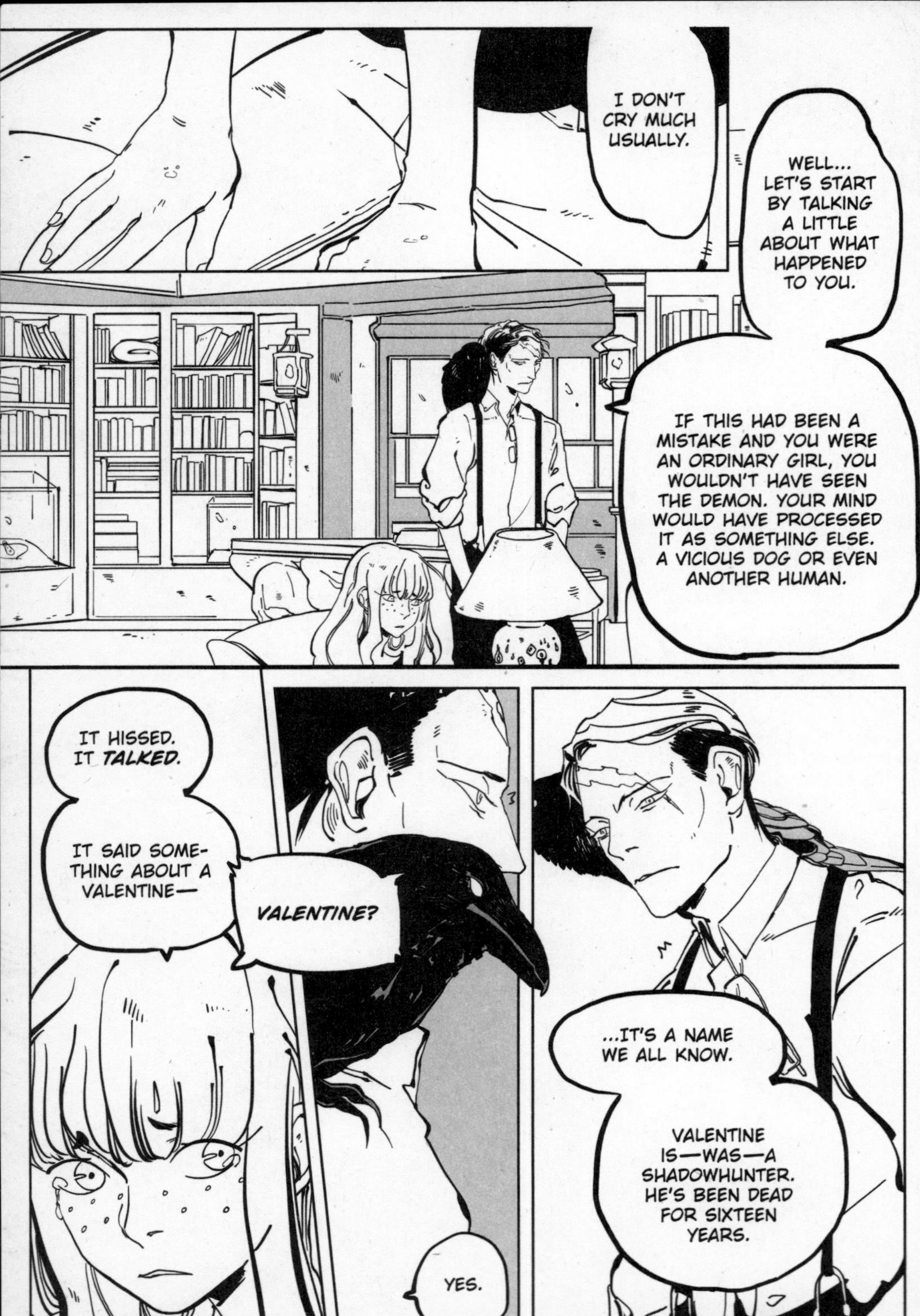
I DON'T CRY MUCH USUALLY.
WELL... LET'S START BY TALKING A LITTLE ABOUT WHAT HAPPENED TO YOU.
IF THIS HAD BEEN A MISTAKE AND YOU WERE AN ORDINARY GIRL, YOU WOULDN'T HAVE SEEN THE DEMON. YOUR MIND WOULD HAVE PROCESSED IT AS SOMETHING ELSE. A VICIOUS DOG OR EVEN ANOTHER HUMAN.
IT HISSED. IT *TALKED*.
IT SAID SOMETHING ABOUT A VALENTINE—
VALENTINE?
...IT'S A NAME WE ALL KNOW.
VALENTINE IS—WAS—A SHADOWHUNTER. HE'S BEEN DEAD FOR SIXTEEN YEARS.
YES.

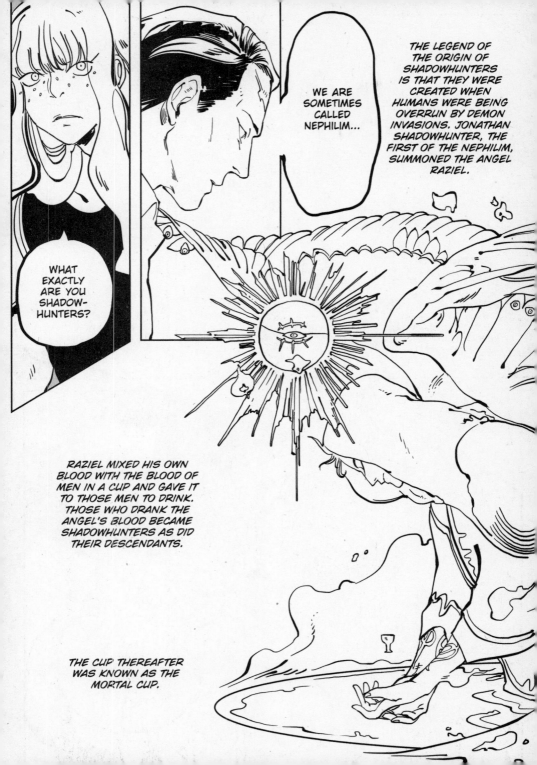

WHAT EXACTLY ARE YOU SHADOW-HUNTERS?

WE ARE SOMETIMES CALLED NEPHILIM...

THE LEGEND OF THE ORIGIN OF SHADOWHUNTERS IS THAT THEY WERE CREATED WHEN HUMANS WERE BEING OVERRUN BY DEMON INVASIONS. JONATHAN SHADOWHUNTER, THE FIRST OF THE NEPHILIM, SUMMONED THE ANGEL RAZIEL.

RAZIEL MIXED HIS OWN BLOOD WITH THE BLOOD OF MEN IN A CUP AND GAVE IT TO THOSE MEN TO DRINK. THOSE WHO DRANK THE ANGEL'S BLOOD BECAME SHADOWHUNTERS AS DID THEIR DESCENDANTS.

THE CUP THEREAFTER WAS KNOWN AS THE MORTAL CUP.

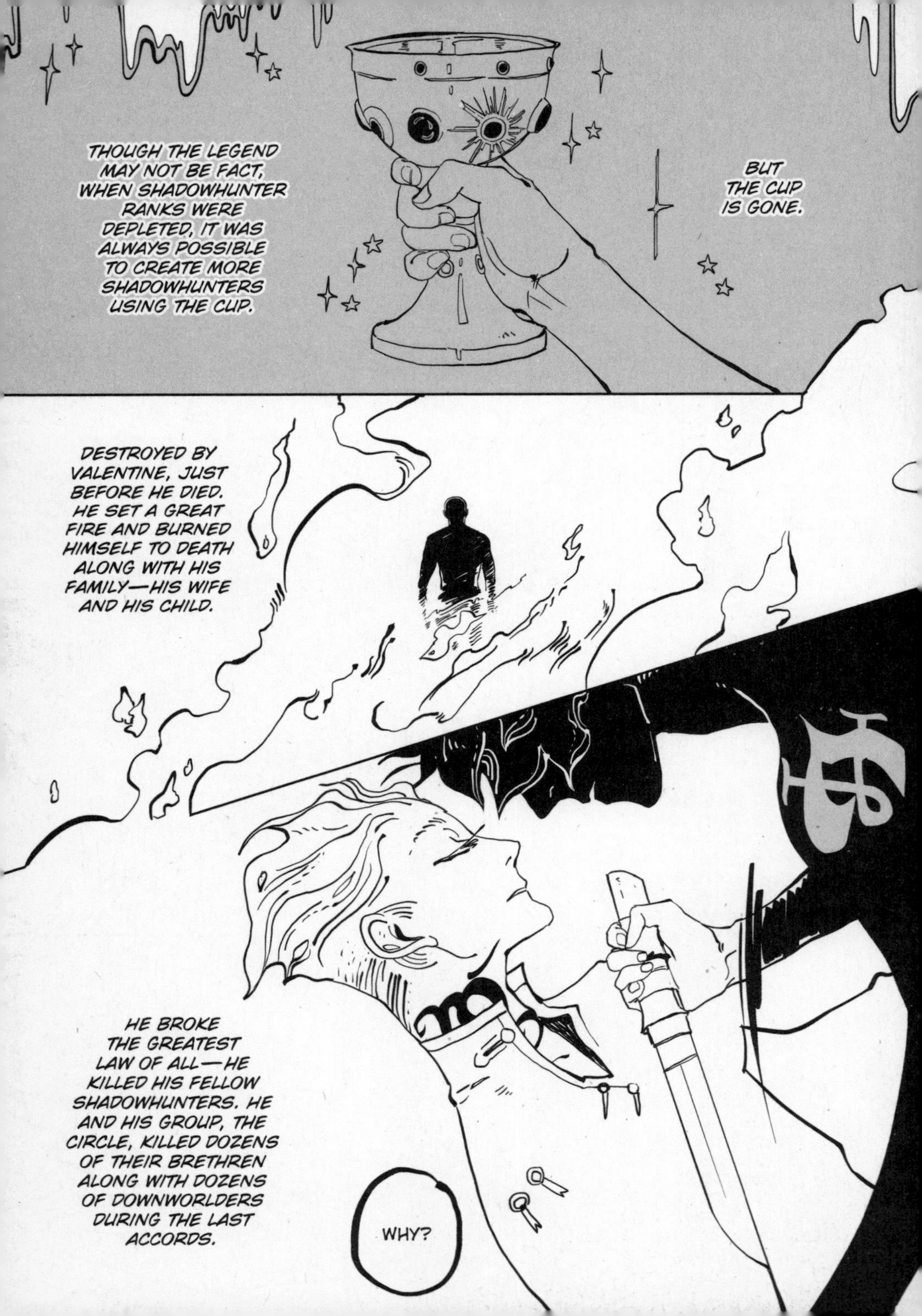
THOUGH THE LEGEND MAY NOT BE FACT, WHEN SHADOWHUNTER RANKS WERE DEPLETED, IT WAS ALWAYS POSSIBLE TO CREATE MORE SHADOWHUNTERS USING THE CUP.
BUT THE CUP IS GONE.
DESTROYED BY VALENTINE, JUST BEFORE HE DIED. HE SET A GREAT FIRE AND BURNED HIMSELF TO DEATH ALONG WITH HIS FAMILY—HIS WIFE AND HIS CHILD.
HE BROKE THE GREATEST LAW OF ALL—HE KILLED HIS FELLOW SHADOWHUNTERS. HE AND HIS GROUP, THE CIRCLE, KILLED DOZENS OF THEIR BRETHREN ALONG WITH DOZENS OF DOWNWORLDERS DURING THE LAST ACCORDS.
WHY?

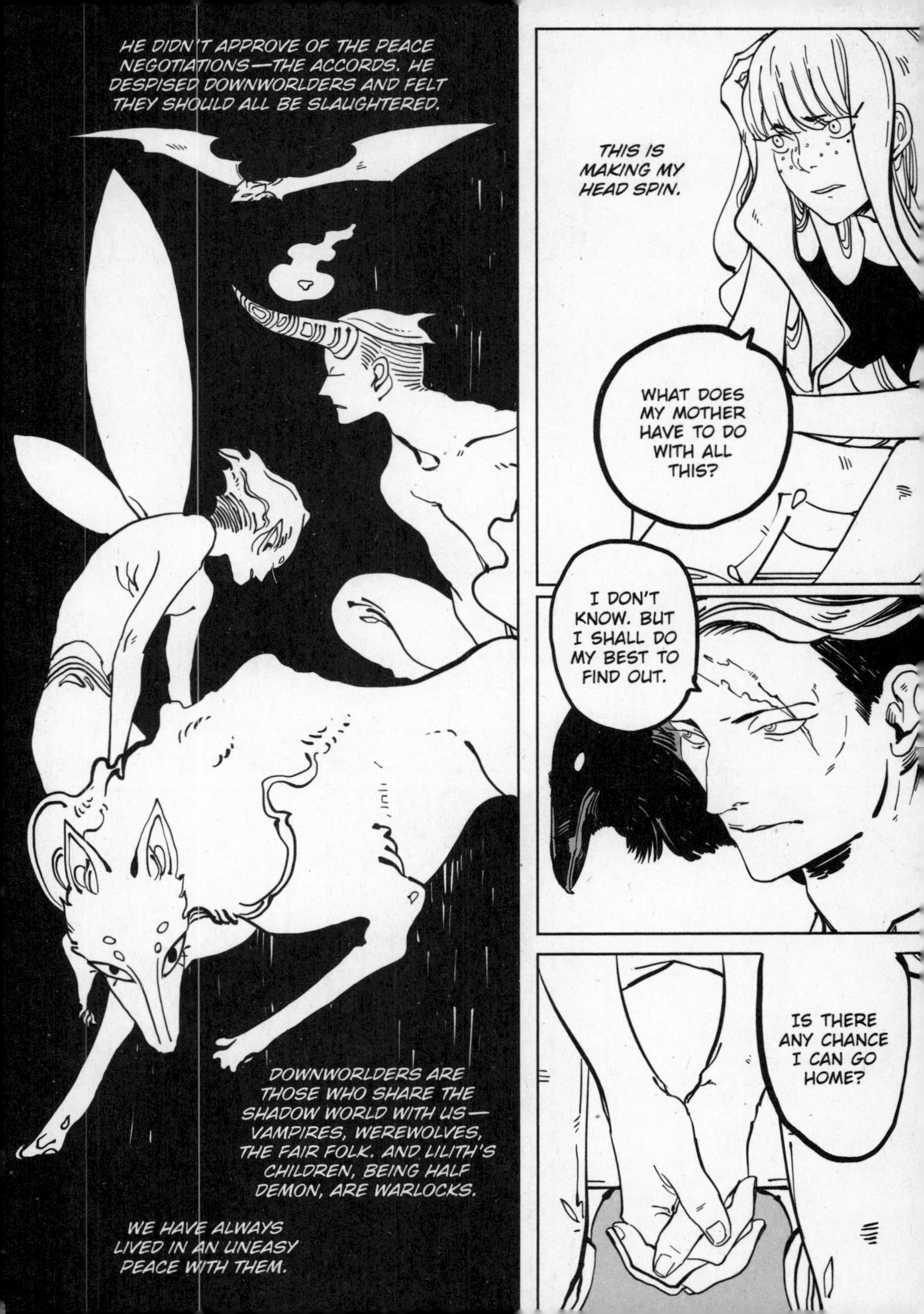
HE DIDN'T APPROVE OF THE PEACE NEGOTIATIONS—THE ACCORDS. HE DESPISED DOWNWORLDERS AND FELT THEY SHOULD ALL BE SLAUGHTERED.
DOWNWORLDERS ARE THOSE WHO SHARE THE SHADOW WORLD WITH US—VAMPIRES, WEREWOLVES, THE FAIR FOLK. AND LILITH'S CHILDREN, BEING HALF DEMON, ARE WARLOCKS.
WE HAVE ALWAYS LIVED IN AN UNEASY PEACE WITH THEM.
THIS IS MAKING MY HEAD SPIN.
WHAT DOES MY MOTHER HAVE TO DO WITH ALL THIS?
I DON'T KNOW. BUT I SHALL DO MY BEST TO FIND OUT.
IS THERE ANY CHANCE I CAN GO HOME?

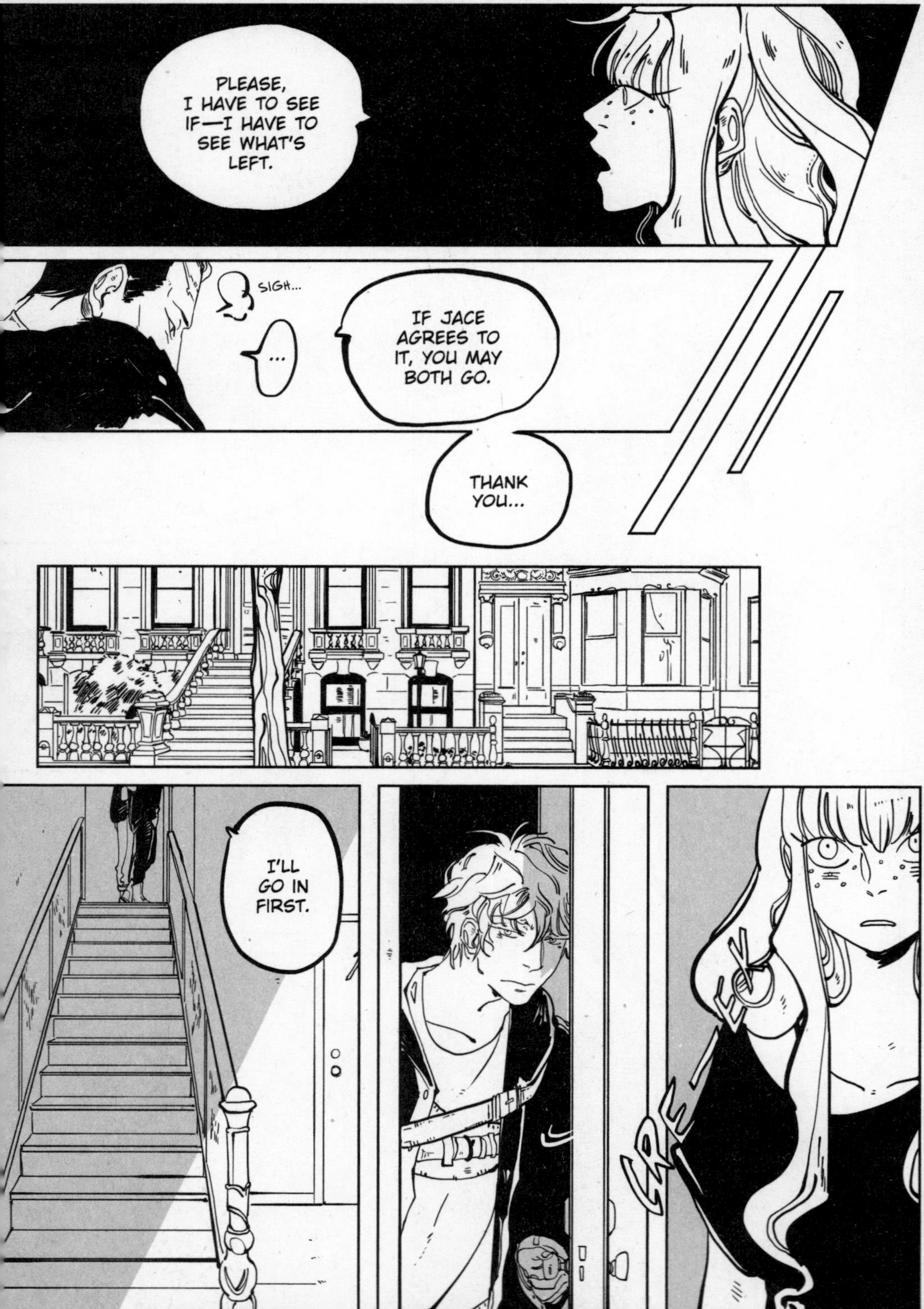
PLEASE, I HAVE TO SEE IF—I HAVE TO SEE WHAT'S LEFT.
SIGH...
...
IF JACE AGREES TO IT, YOU MAY BOTH GO.
THANK YOU...
I'LL GO IN FIRST.
CREEK

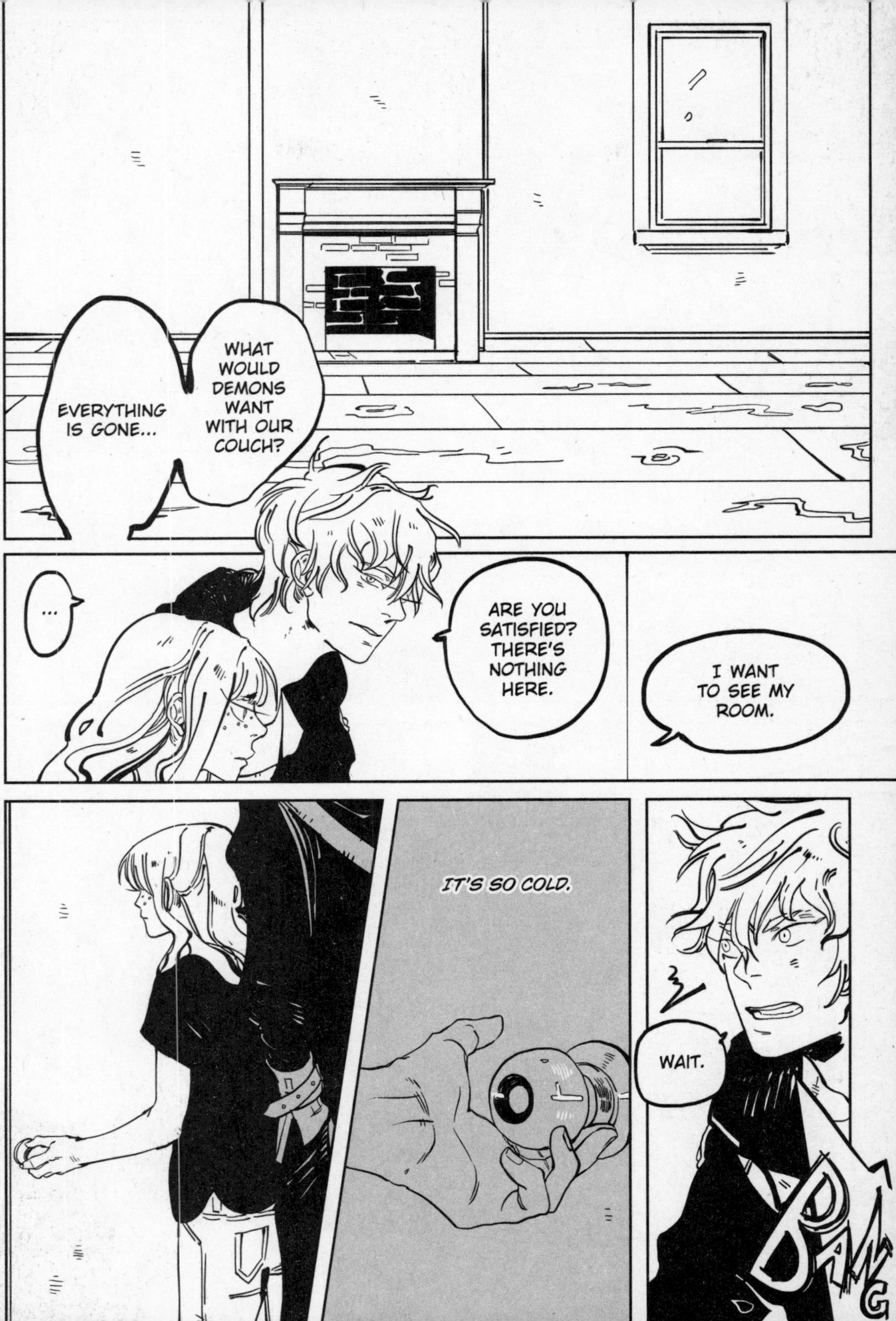
EVERYTHING IS GONE...
WHAT WOULD DEMONS WANT WITH OUR COUCH?
...
ARE YOU SATISFIED? THERE'S NOTHING HERE.
I WANT TO SEE MY ROOM.
IT'S SO COLD.
WAIT.
BANG

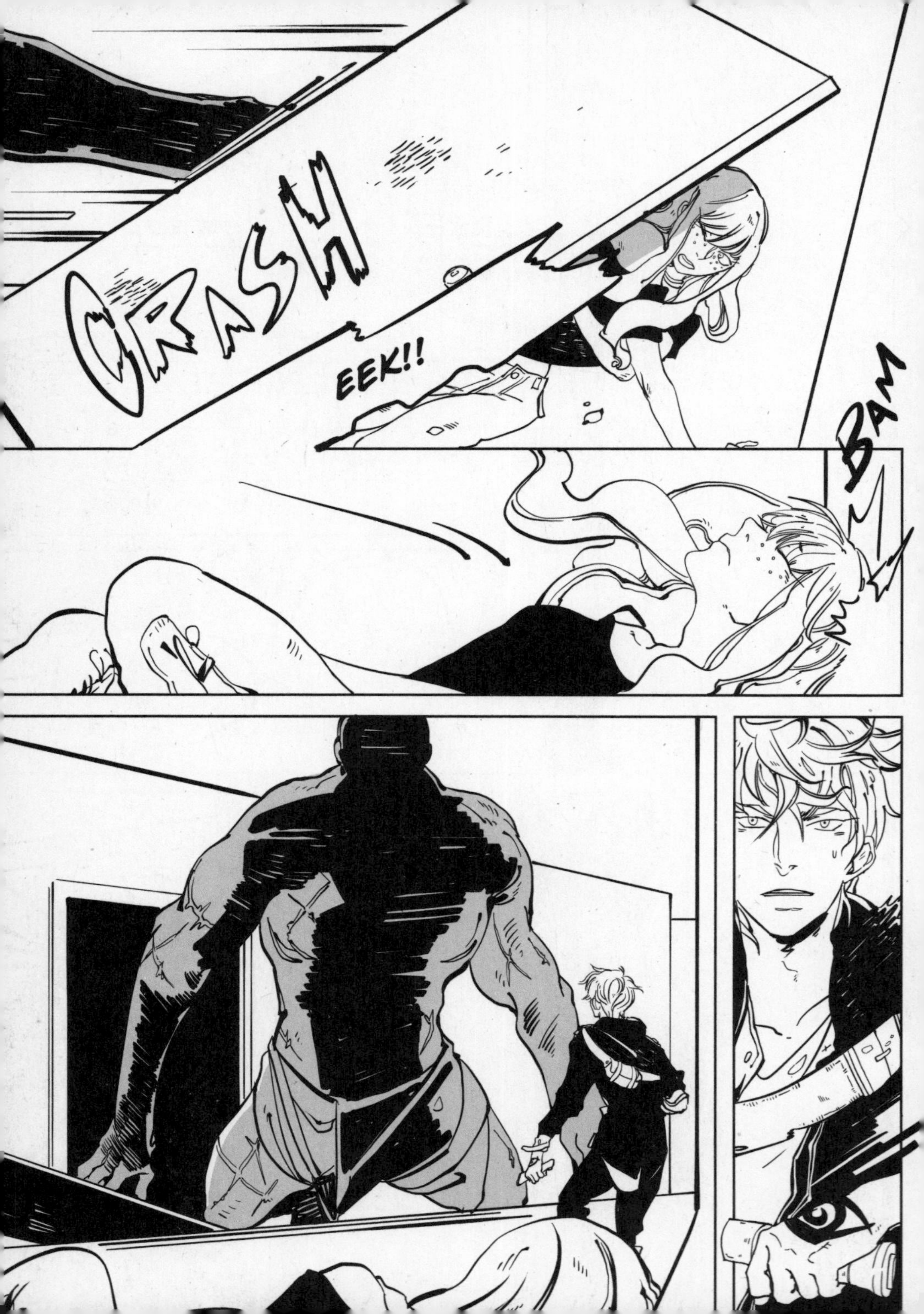

CRASH
EEK!!
BAM

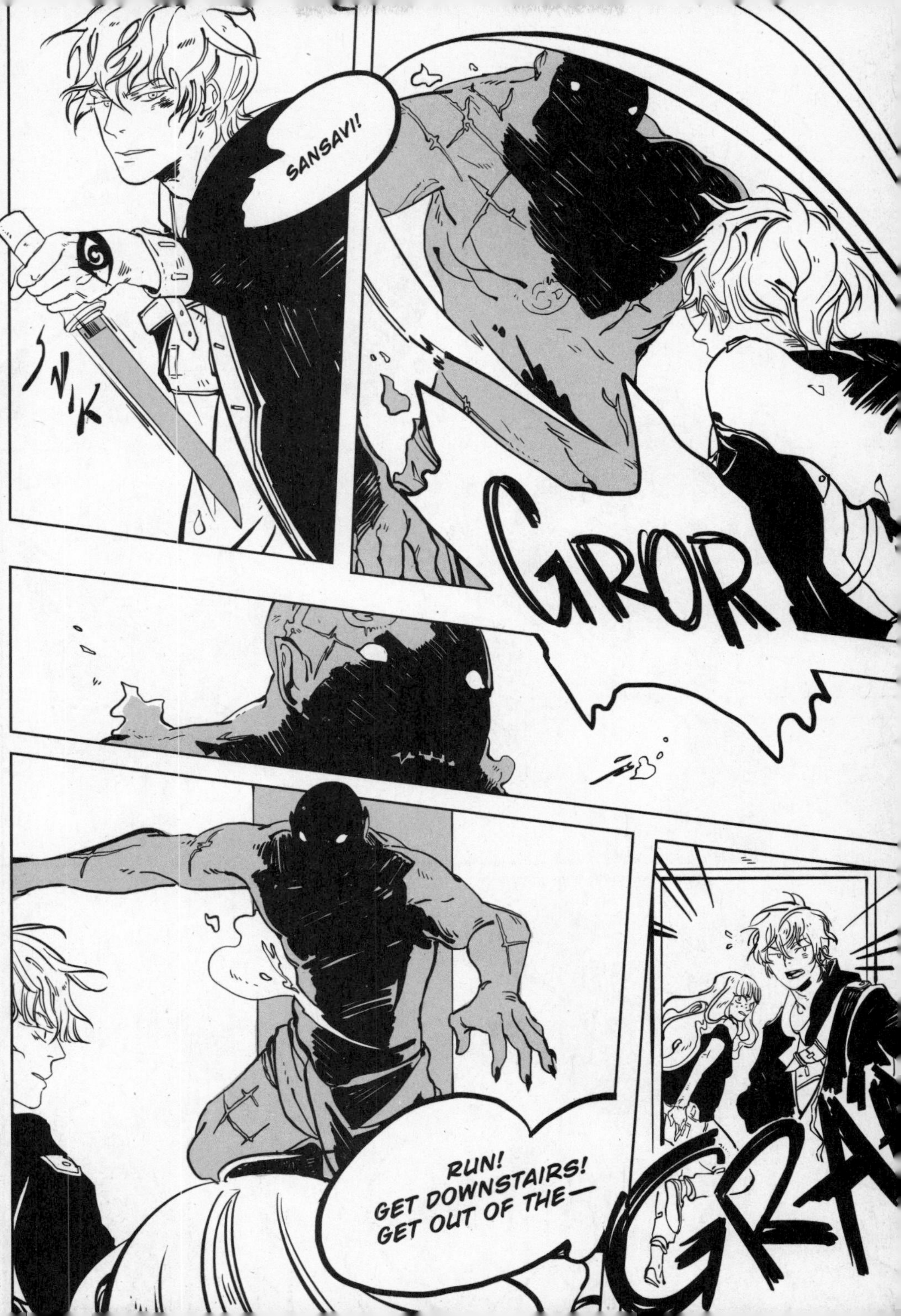
SANSAVI!
SNIK
GROR
RUN! GET DOWNSTAIRS! GET OUT OF THE—

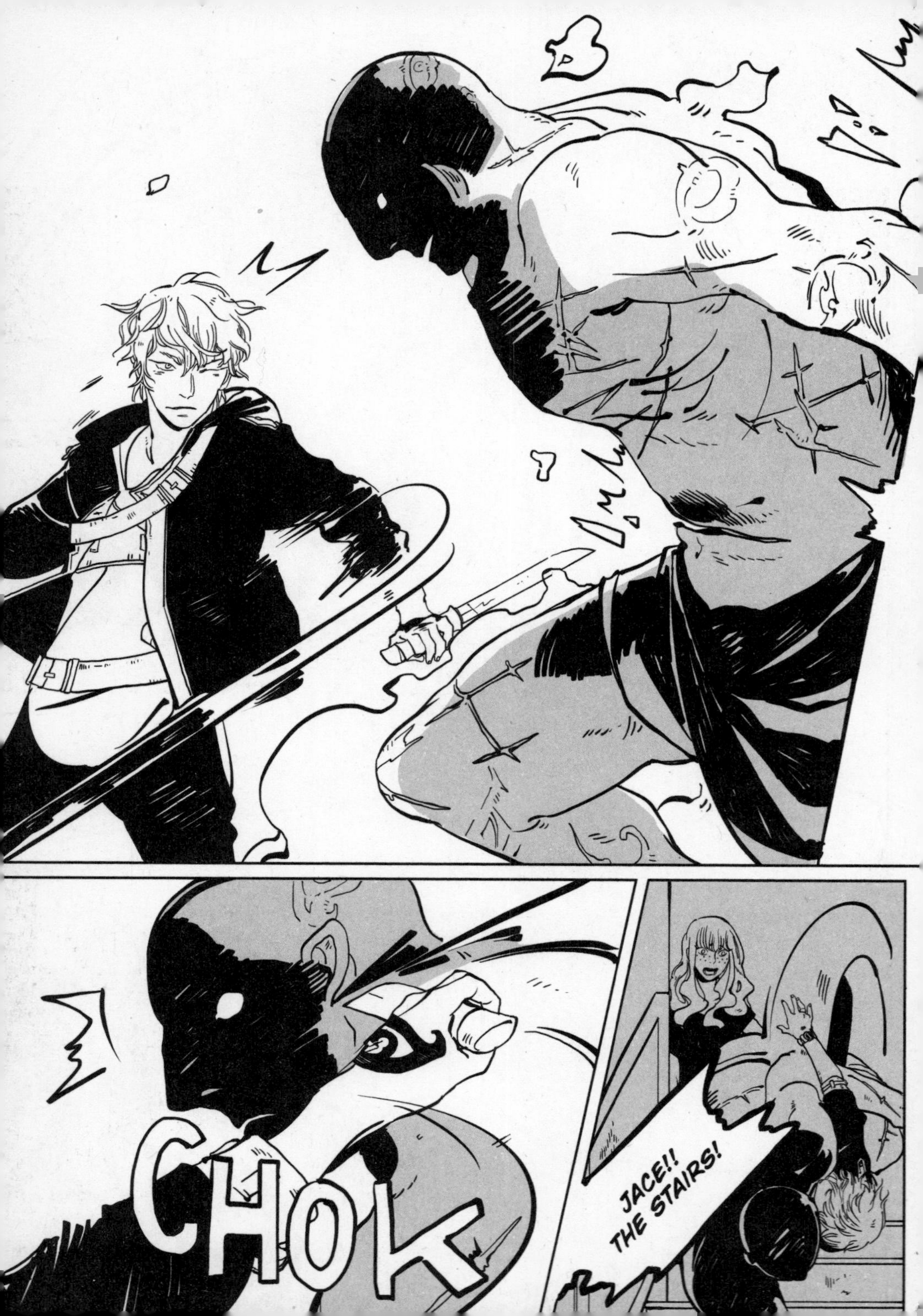
CHOK
JACE!! THE STAIRS!

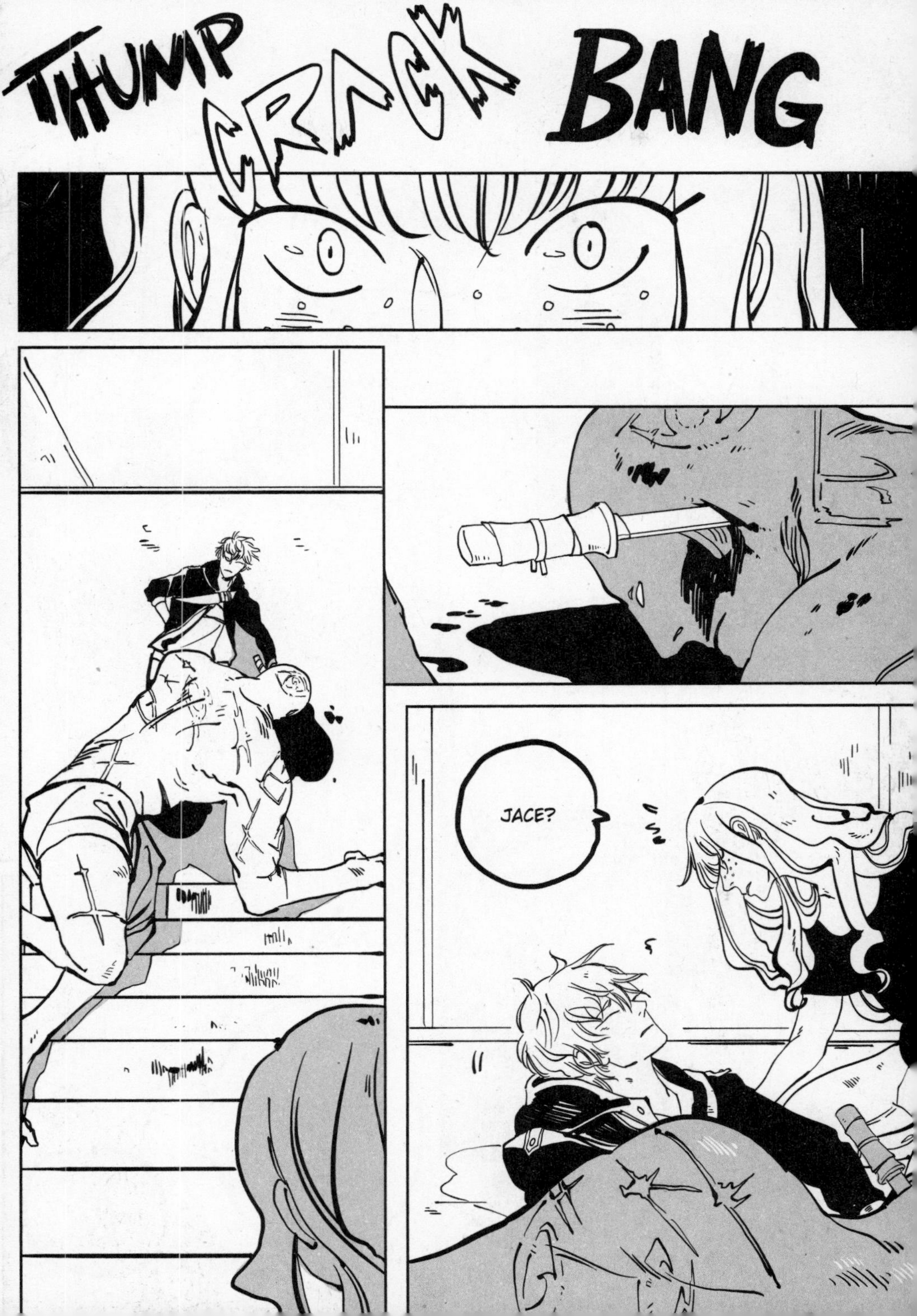
THUMP
CRACK
BANG
JACE?

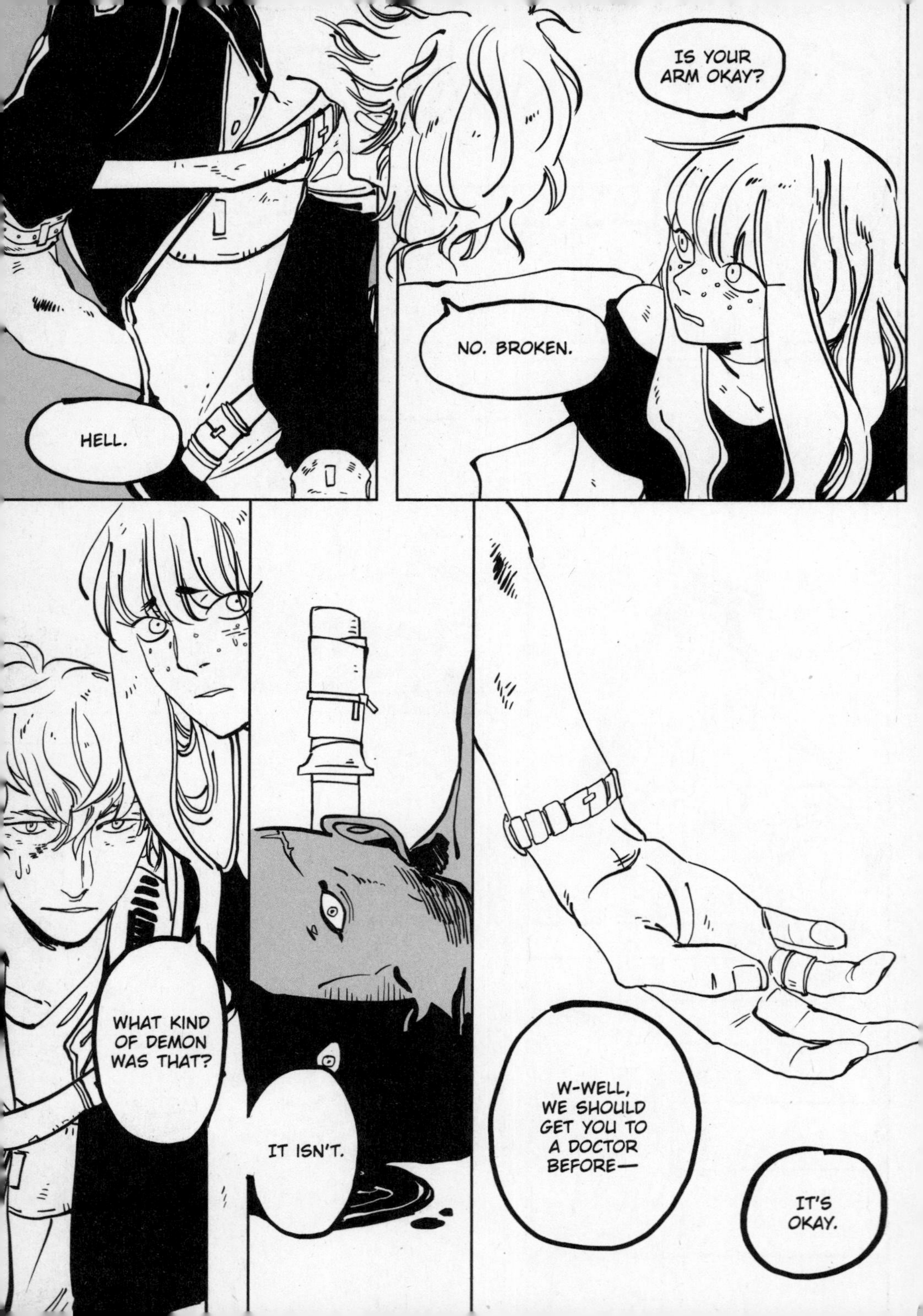
HELL.
IS YOUR ARM OKAY?
NO. BROKEN.
WHAT KIND OF DEMON WAS THAT?
IT ISN'T.
W-WELL, WE SHOULD GET YOU TO A DOCTOR BEFORE—
IT'S OKAY.

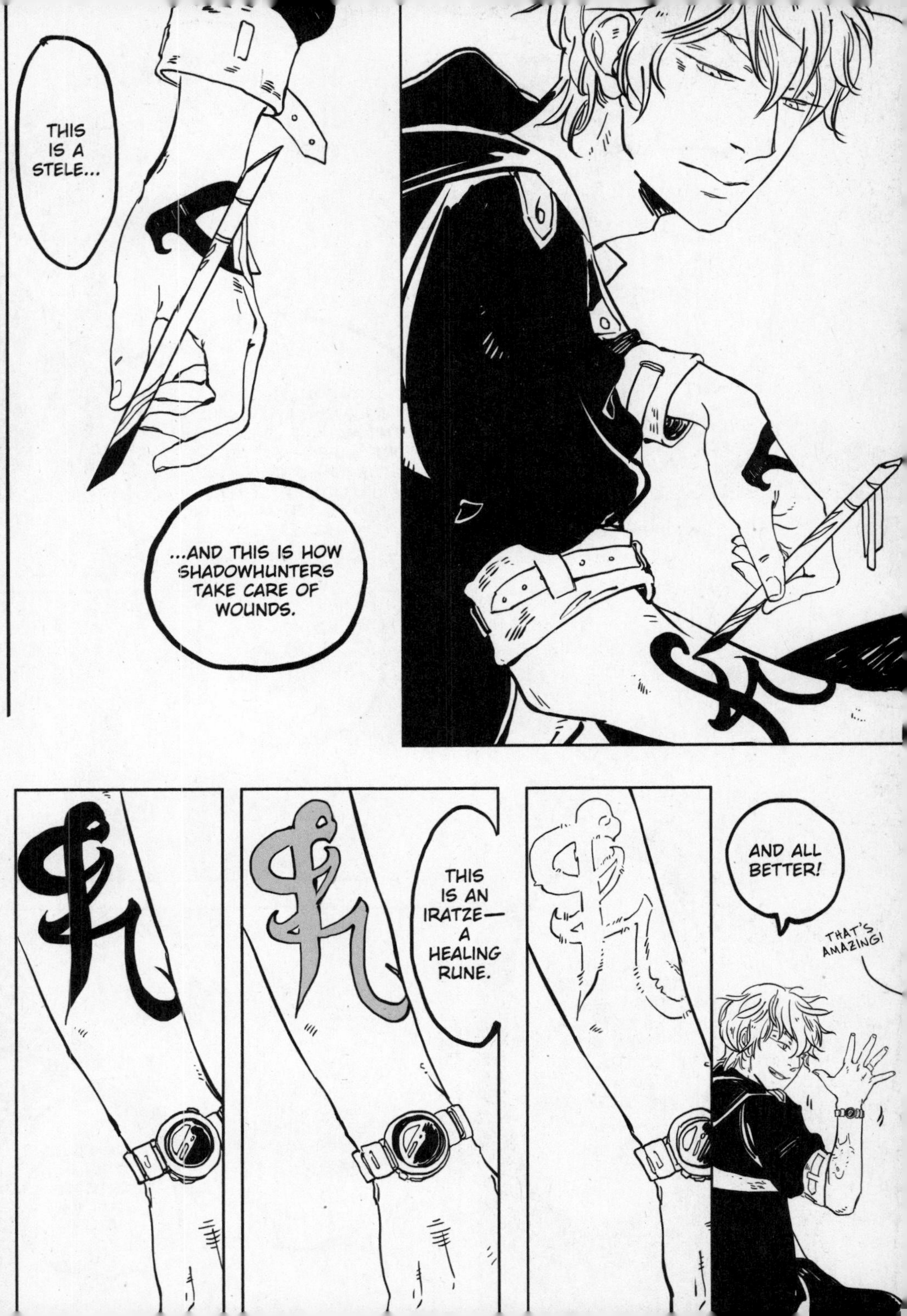
THIS IS A STELE...
...AND THIS IS HOW SHADOWHUNTERS TAKE CARE OF WOUNDS.
THIS IS AN IRATZE—A HEALING RUNE.
AND ALL BETTER!
THAT'S AMAZING!

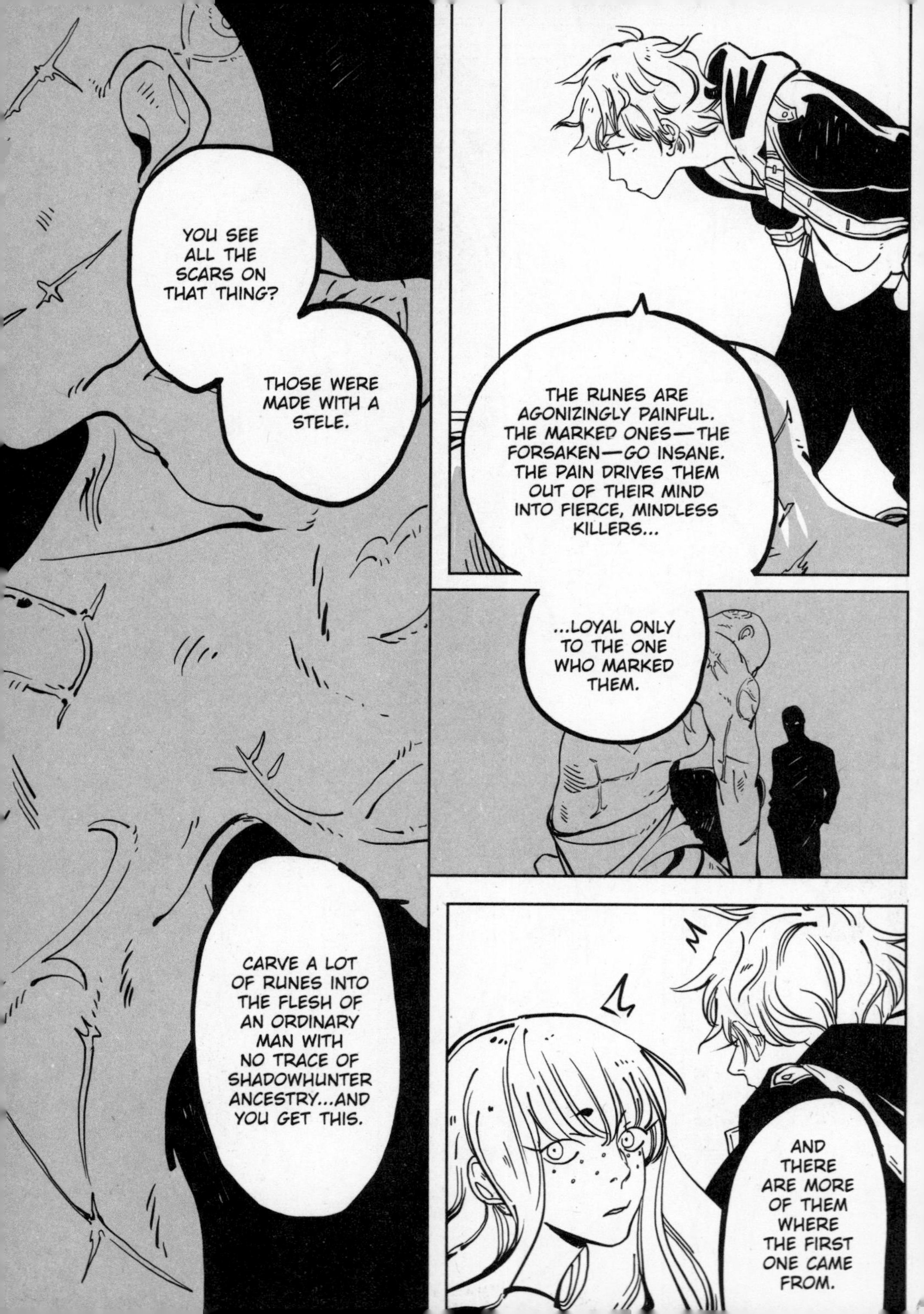
YOU SEE ALL THE SCARS ON THAT THING?
THOSE WERE MADE WITH A STELE.
CARVE A LOT OF RUNES INTO THE FLESH OF AN ORDINARY MAN WITH NO TRACE OF SHADOWHUNTER ANCESTRY...AND YOU GET THIS.
THE RUNES ARE AGONIZINGLY PAINFUL. THE MARKED ONES—THE FORSAKEN—GO INSANE. THE PAIN DRIVES THEM OUT OF THEIR MIND INTO FIERCE, MINDLESS KILLERS...
...LOYAL ONLY TO THE ONE WHO MARKED THEM.
AND THERE ARE MORE OF THEM WHERE THE FIRST ONE CAME FROM.

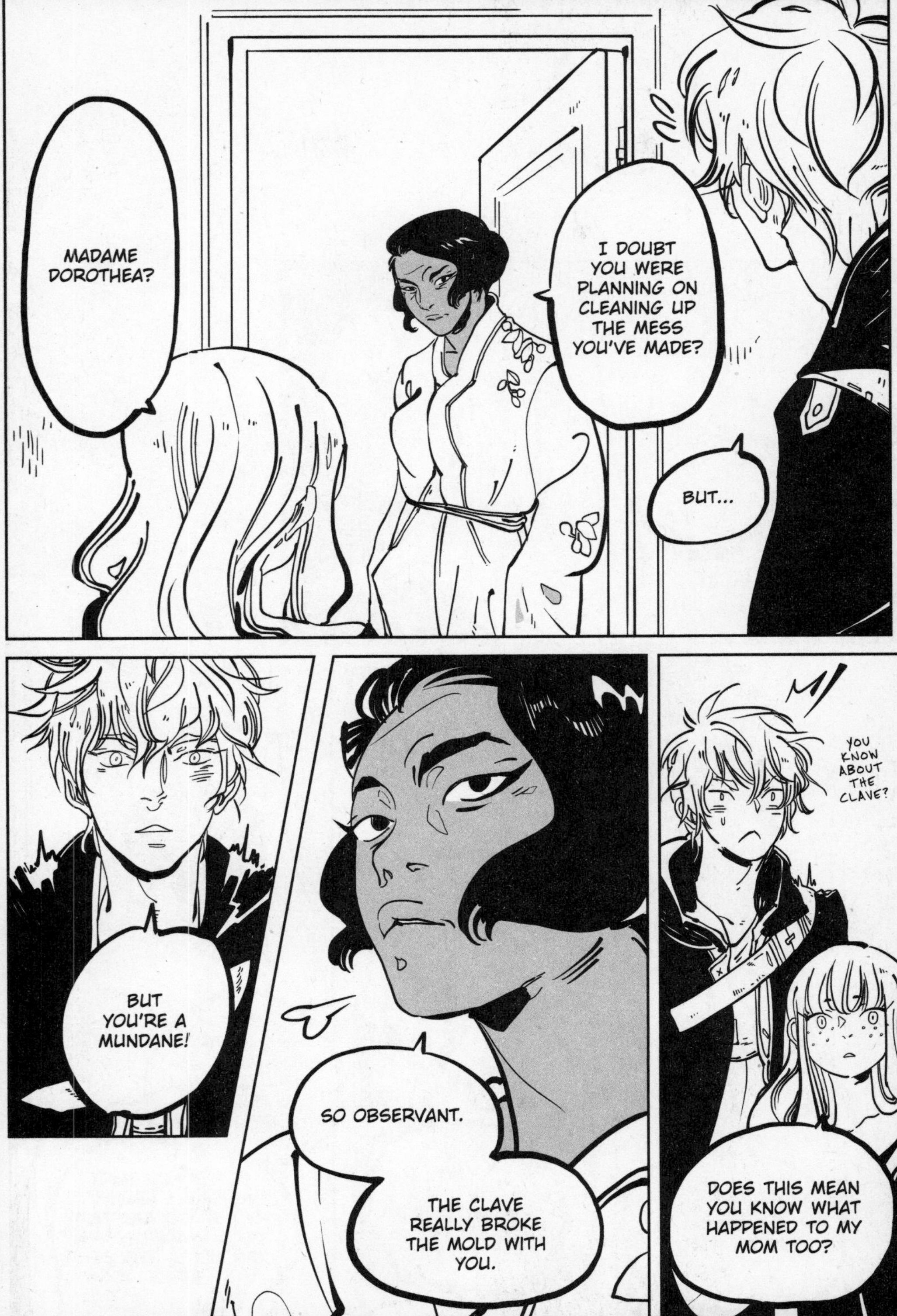
MADAME DOROTHEA?
I DOUBT YOU WERE PLANNING ON CLEANING UP THE MESS YOU'VE MADE?
BUT...
BUT YOU'RE A MUNDANE!
SO OBSERVANT.
THE CLAVE REALLY BROKE THE MOLD WITH YOU.
YOU KNOW ABOUT THE CLAVE?
DOES THIS MEAN YOU KNOW WHAT HAPPENED TO MY MOM TOO?

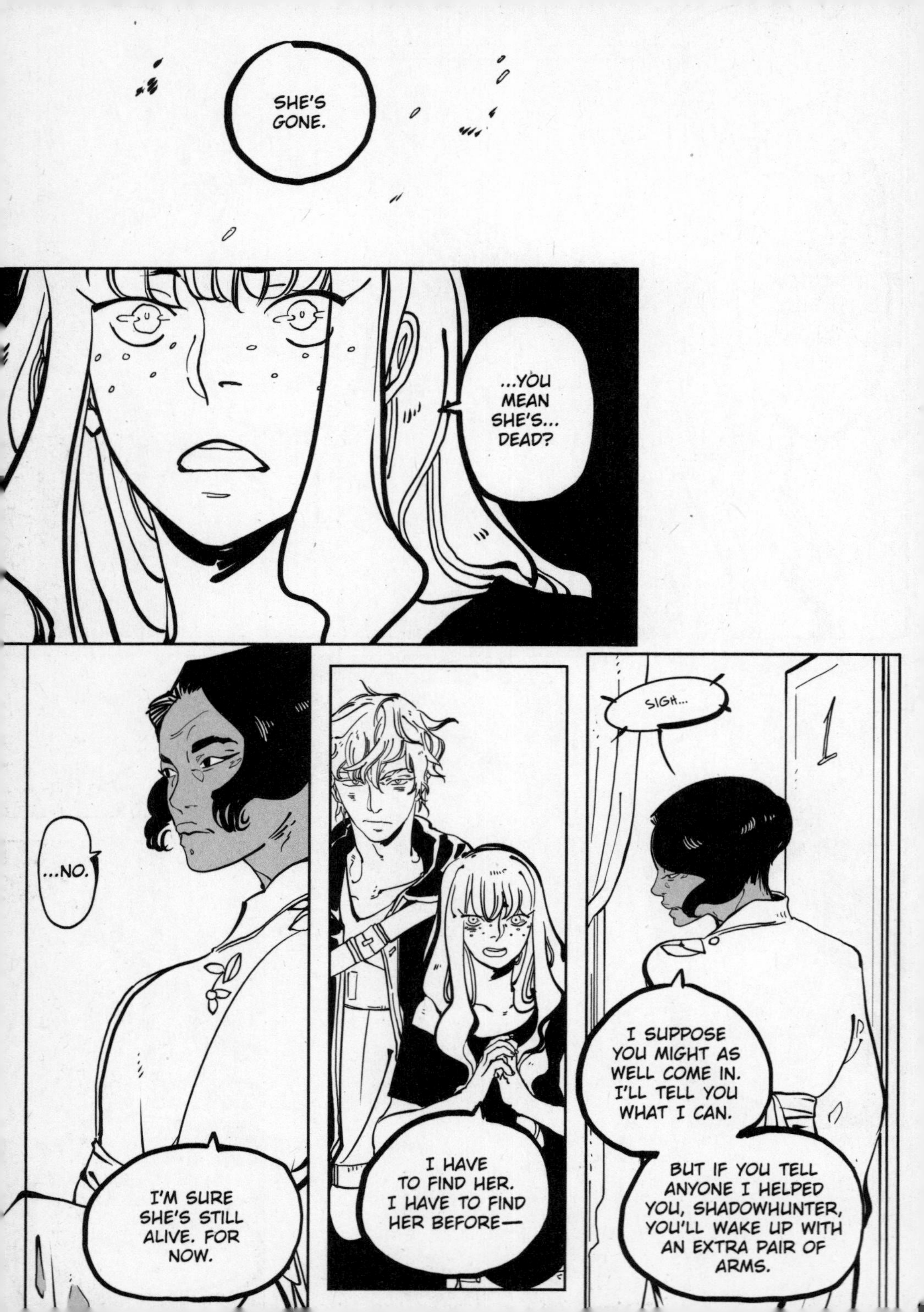
SHE'S GONE.
...YOU MEAN SHE'S... DEAD?
...NO.
I'M SURE SHE'S STILL ALIVE. FOR NOW.
I HAVE TO FIND HER. I HAVE TO FIND HER BEFORE—
SIGH...
I SUPPOSE YOU MIGHT AS WELL COME IN. I'LL TELL YOU WHAT I CAN.
BUT IF YOU TELL ANYONE I HELPED YOU, SHADOWHUNTER, YOU'LL WAKE UP WITH AN EXTRA PAIR OF ARMS.

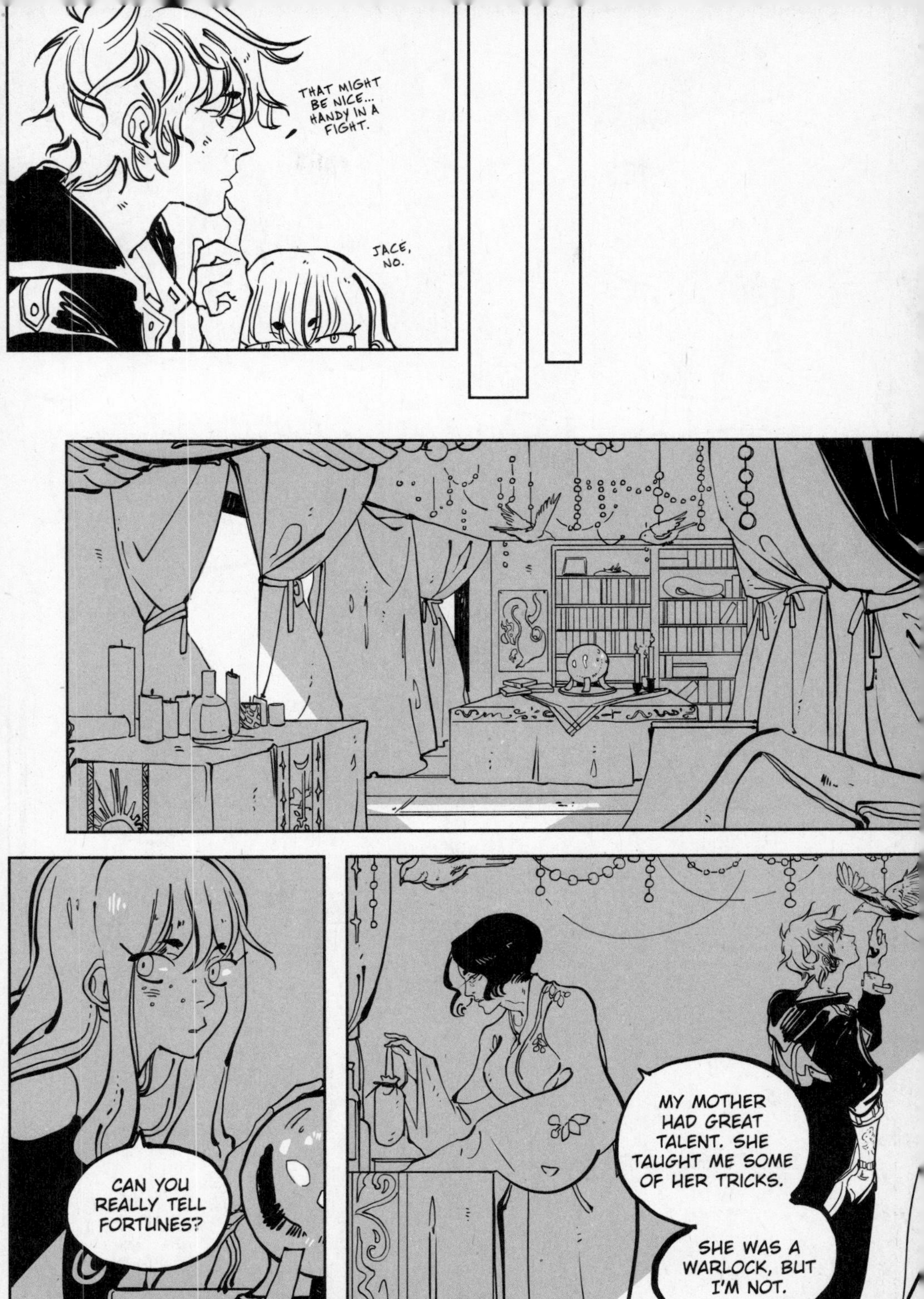
THAT MIGHT BE NICE... HANDY IN A FIGHT.
JACE, NO.
CAN YOU REALLY TELL FORTUNES?
MY MOTHER HAD GREAT TALENT. SHE TAUGHT ME SOME OF HER TRICKS.
SHE WAS A WARLOCK, BUT I'M NOT.

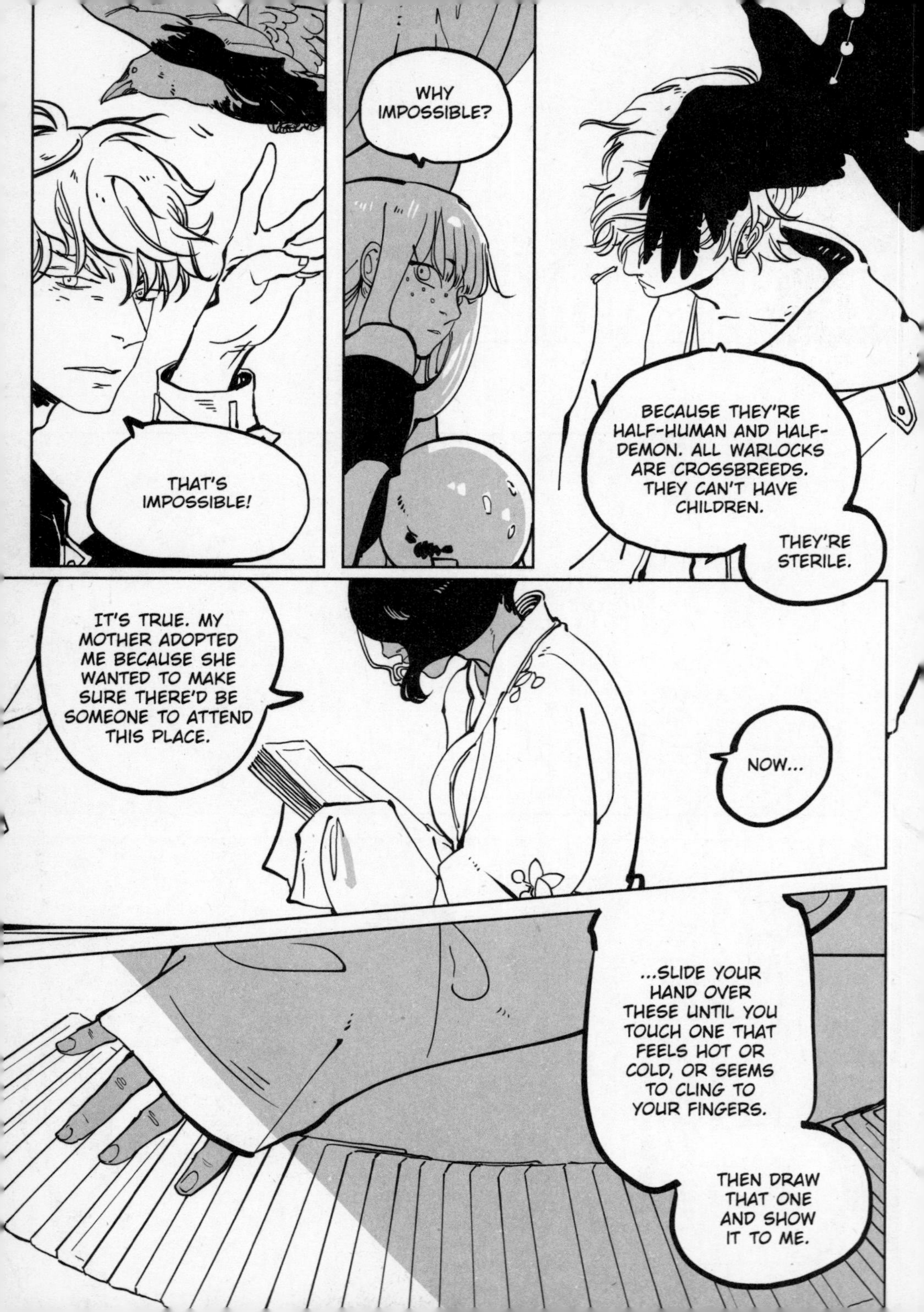
THAT'S IMPOSSIBLE!
WHY IMPOSSIBLE?
BECAUSE THEY'RE HALF-HUMAN AND HALF-DEMON. ALL WARLOCKS ARE CROSSBREEDS. THEY CAN'T HAVE CHILDREN.
THEY'RE STERILE.
IT'S TRUE. MY MOTHER ADOPTED ME BECAUSE SHE WANTED TO MAKE SURE THERE'D BE SOMEONE TO ATTEND THIS PLACE.
NOW...
...SLIDE YOUR HAND OVER THESE UNTIL YOU TOUCH ONE THAT FEELS HOT OR COLD, OR SEEMS TO CLING TO YOUR FINGERS.
THEN DRAW THAT ONE AND SHOW IT TO ME.

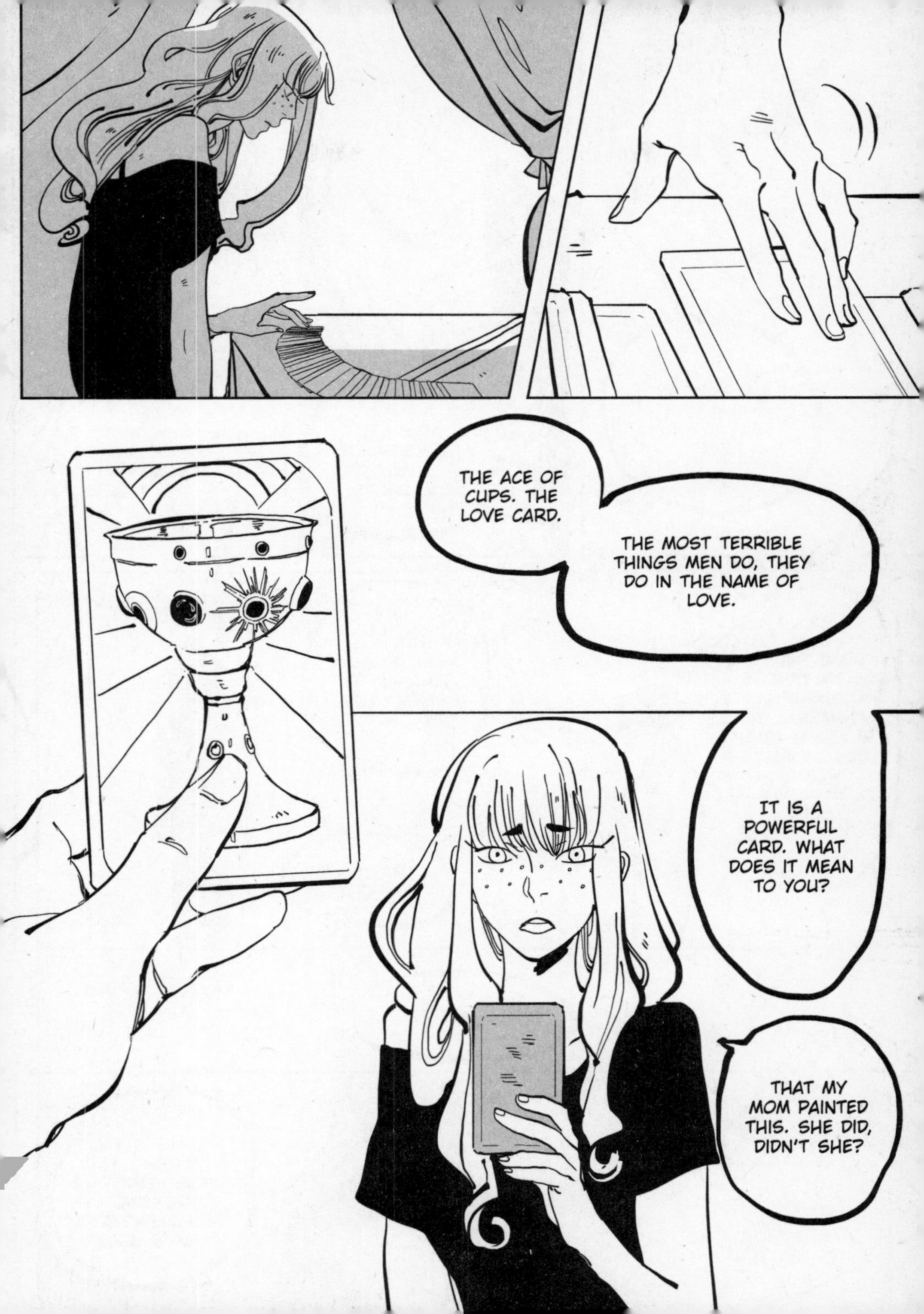
THE ACE OF CUPS. THE LOVE CARD.
THE MOST TERRIBLE THINGS MEN DO, THEY DO IN THE NAME OF LOVE.
IT IS A POWERFUL CARD. WHAT DOES IT MEAN TO YOU?
THAT MY MOM PAINTED THIS. SHE DID, DIDN'T SHE?

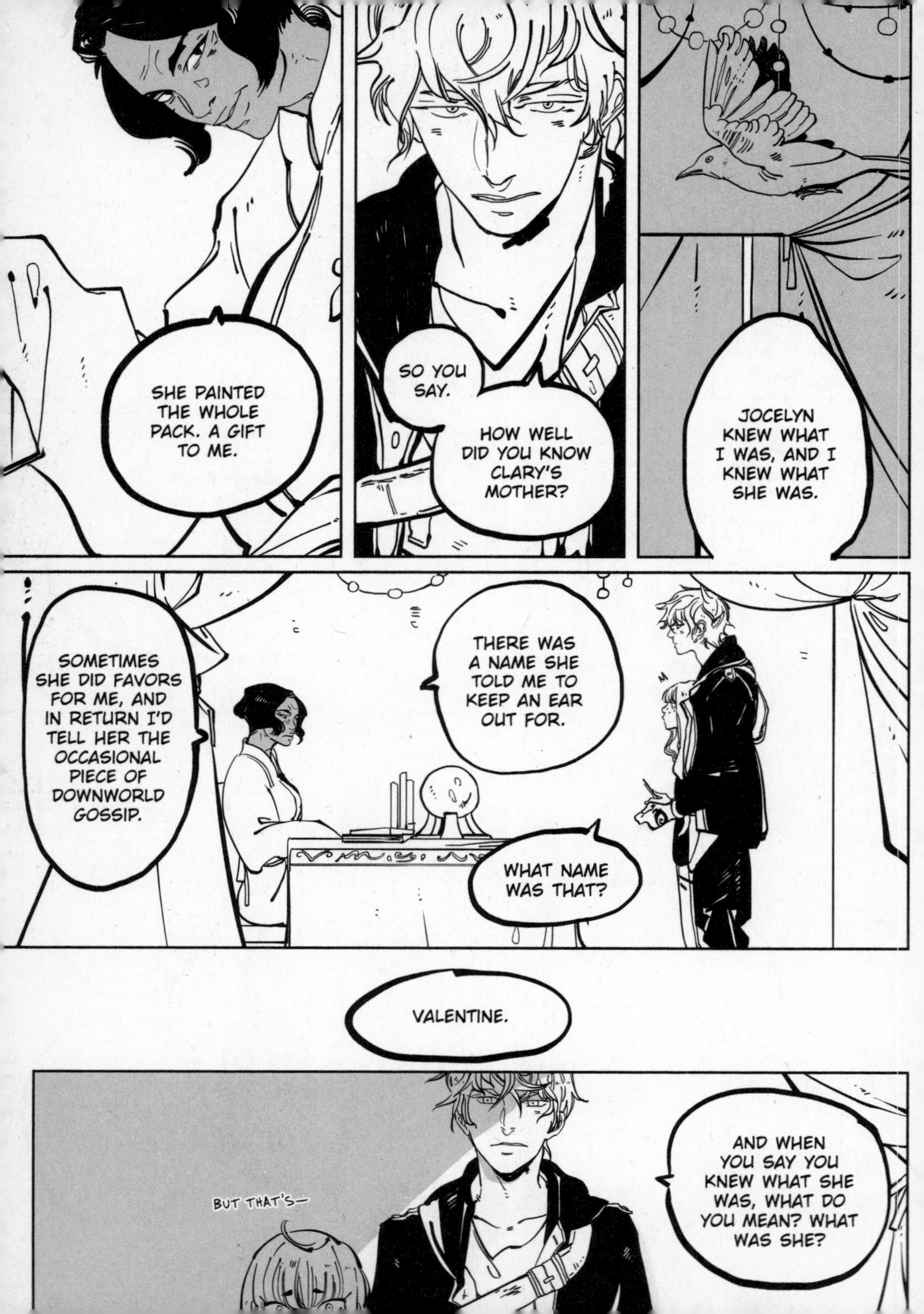
SHE PAINTED THE WHOLE PACK. A GIFT TO ME.
SO YOU SAY.
HOW WELL DID YOU KNOW CLARY'S MOTHER?
JOCELYN KNEW WHAT I WAS, AND I KNEW WHAT SHE WAS.
SOMETIMES SHE DID FAVORS FOR ME, AND IN RETURN I'D TELL HER THE OCCASIONAL PIECE OF DOWNWORLD GOSSIP.
THERE WAS A NAME SHE TOLD ME TO KEEP AN EAR OUT FOR.
WHAT NAME WAS THAT?
VALENTINE.
BUT THAT'S—
AND WHEN YOU SAY YOU KNEW WHAT SHE WAS, WHAT DO YOU MEAN? WHAT WAS SHE?

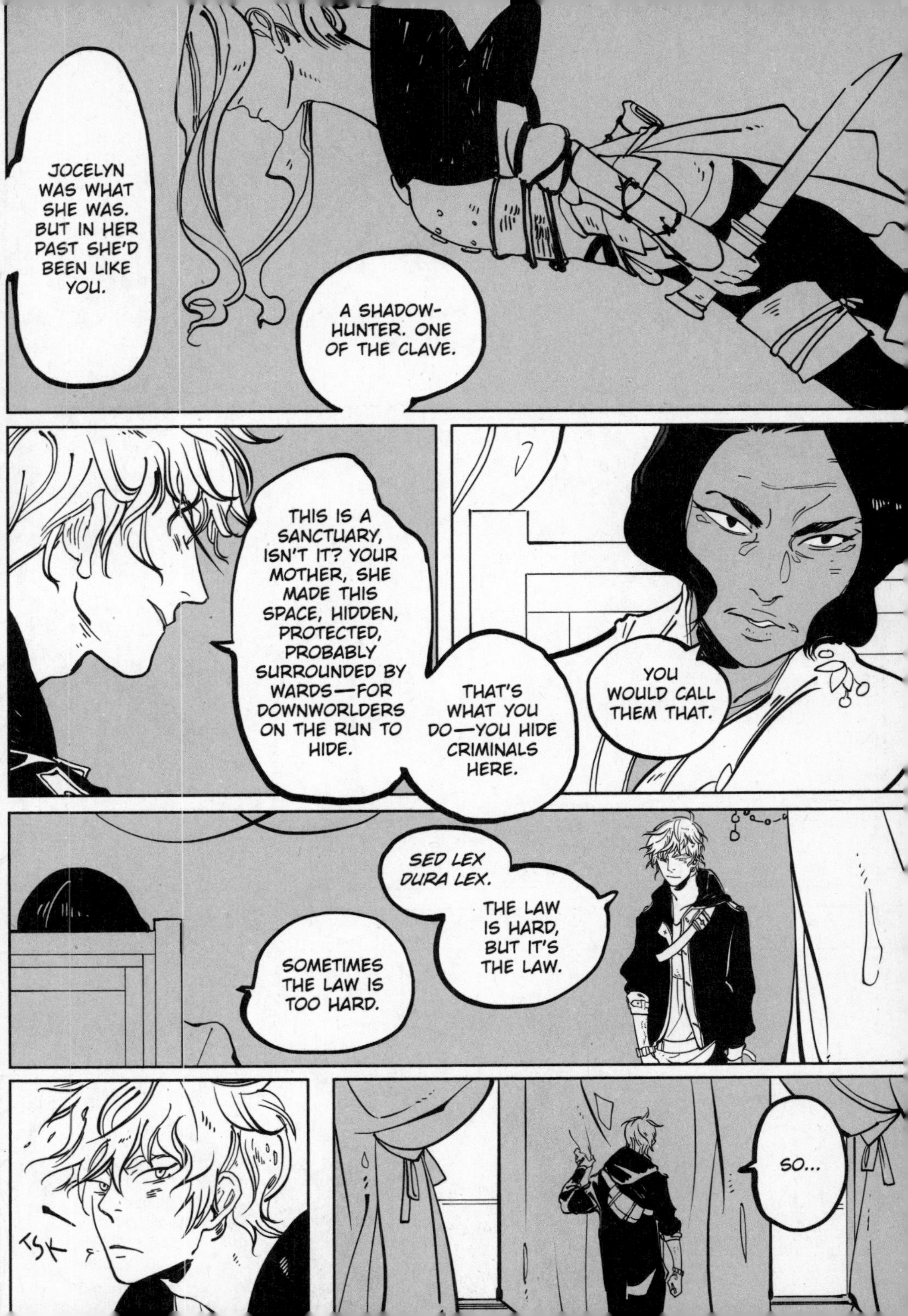
JOCELYN WAS WHAT SHE WAS. BUT IN HER PAST SHE'D BEEN LIKE YOU.
A SHADOW-HUNTER. ONE OF THE CLAVE.
THIS IS A SANCTUARY, ISN'T IT? YOUR MOTHER, SHE MADE THIS SPACE, HIDDEN, PROTECTED, PROBABLY SURROUNDED BY WARDS—FOR DOWNWORLDERS ON THE RUN TO HIDE.
THAT'S WHAT YOU DO—YOU HIDE CRIMINALS HERE.
YOU WOULD CALL THEM THAT.
SED LEX DURA LEX.
THE LAW IS HARD, BUT IT'S THE LAW.
SOMETIMES THE LAW IS TOO HARD.
TSK
SO...

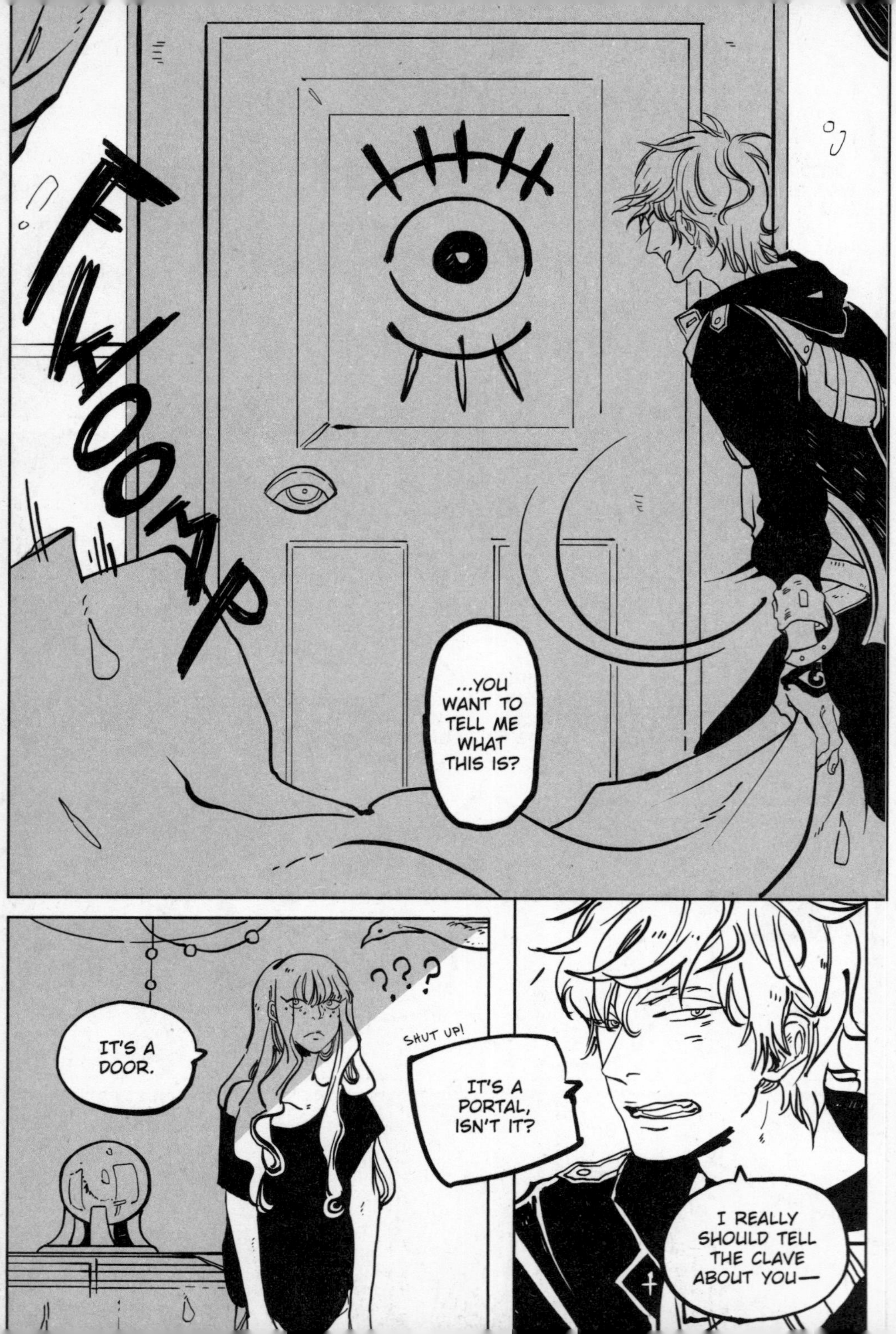
FWOOMP
...YOU WANT TO TELL ME WHAT THIS IS?
???
IT'S A DOOR.
SHUT UP!
IT'S A PORTAL, ISN'T IT?
I REALLY SHOULD TELL THE CLAVE ABOUT YOU—

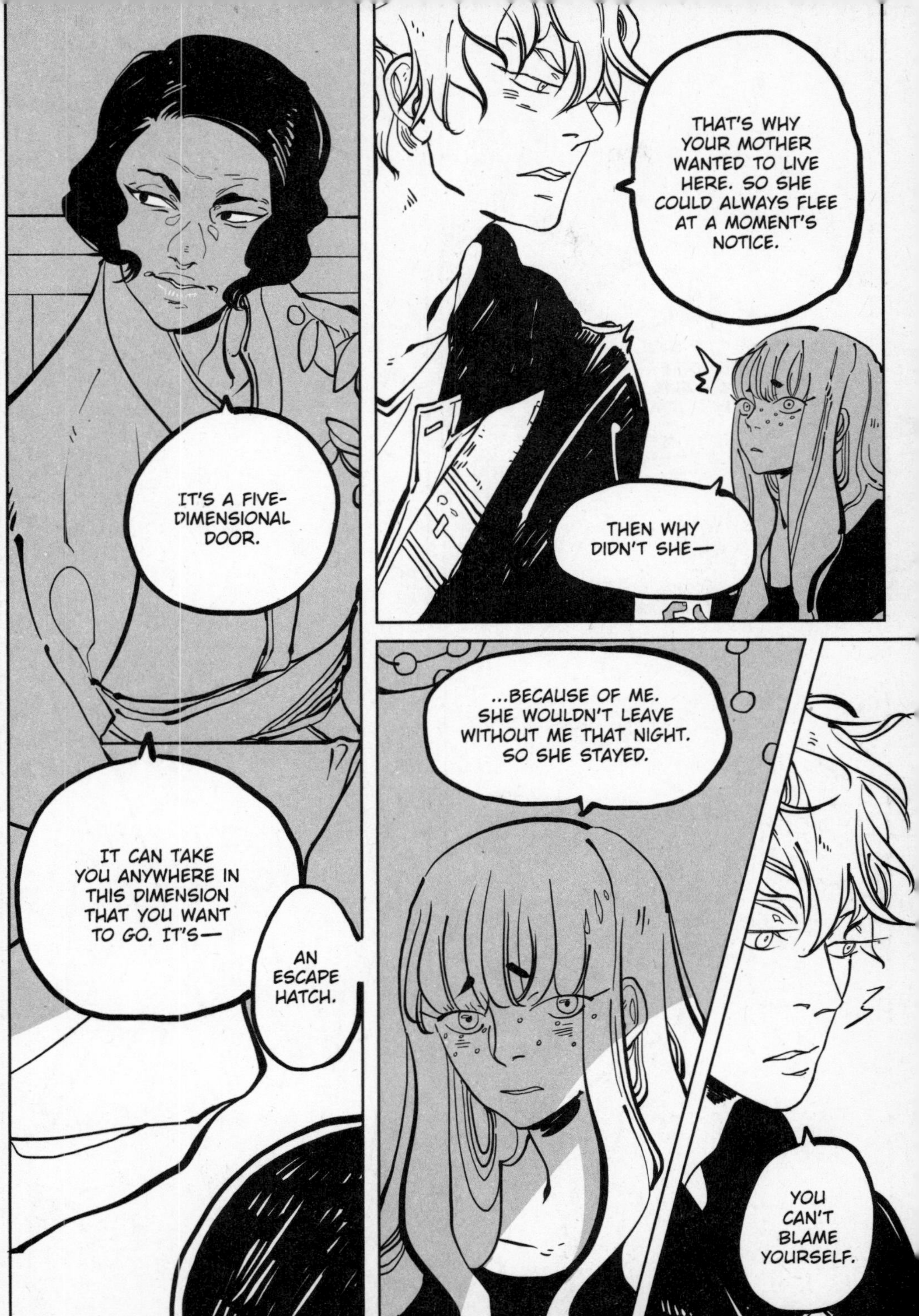
IT'S A FIVE-DIMENSIONAL DOOR.
IT CAN TAKE YOU ANYWHERE IN THIS DIMENSION THAT YOU WANT TO GO. IT'S—
AN ESCAPE HATCH.
THAT'S WHY YOUR MOTHER WANTED TO LIVE HERE. SO SHE COULD ALWAYS FLEE AT A MOMENT'S NOTICE.
THEN WHY DIDN'T SHE—
...BECAUSE OF ME. SHE WOULDN'T LEAVE WITHOUT ME THAT NIGHT. SO SHE STAYED.
YOU CAN'T BLAME YOURSELF.

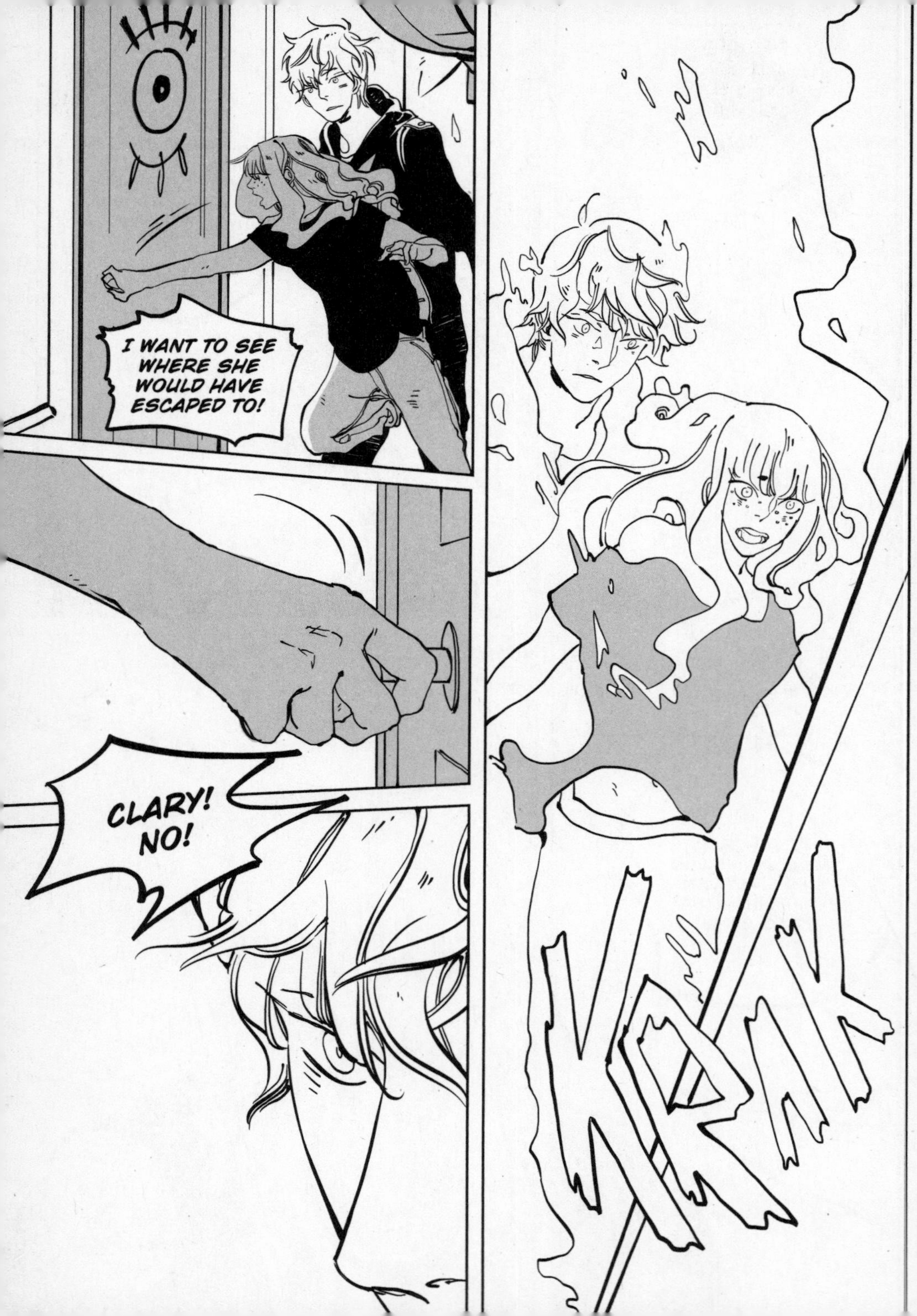
I WANT TO SEE WHERE SHE WOULD HAVE ESCAPED TO!
CLARY! NO!
KRAK

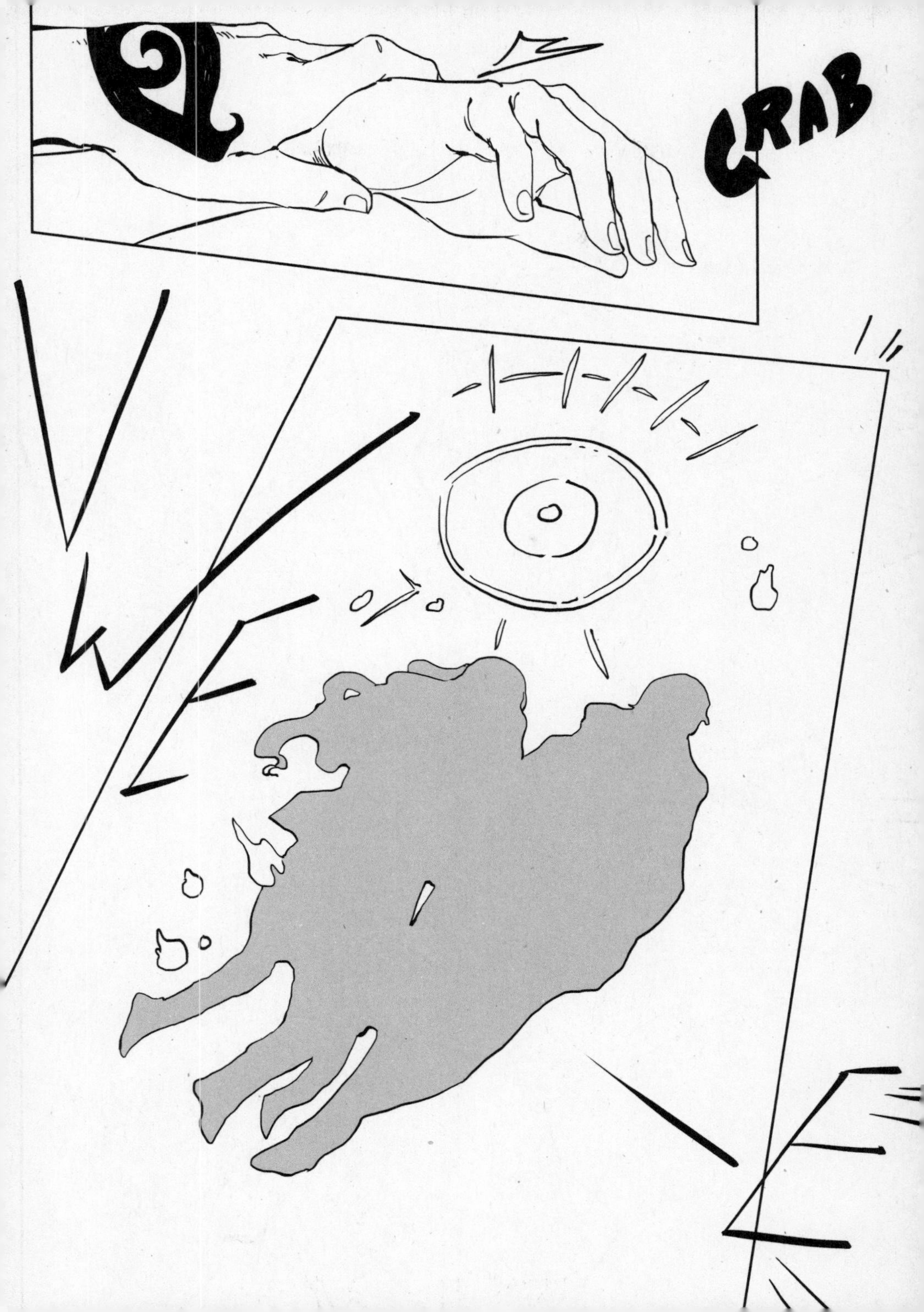
GRAB

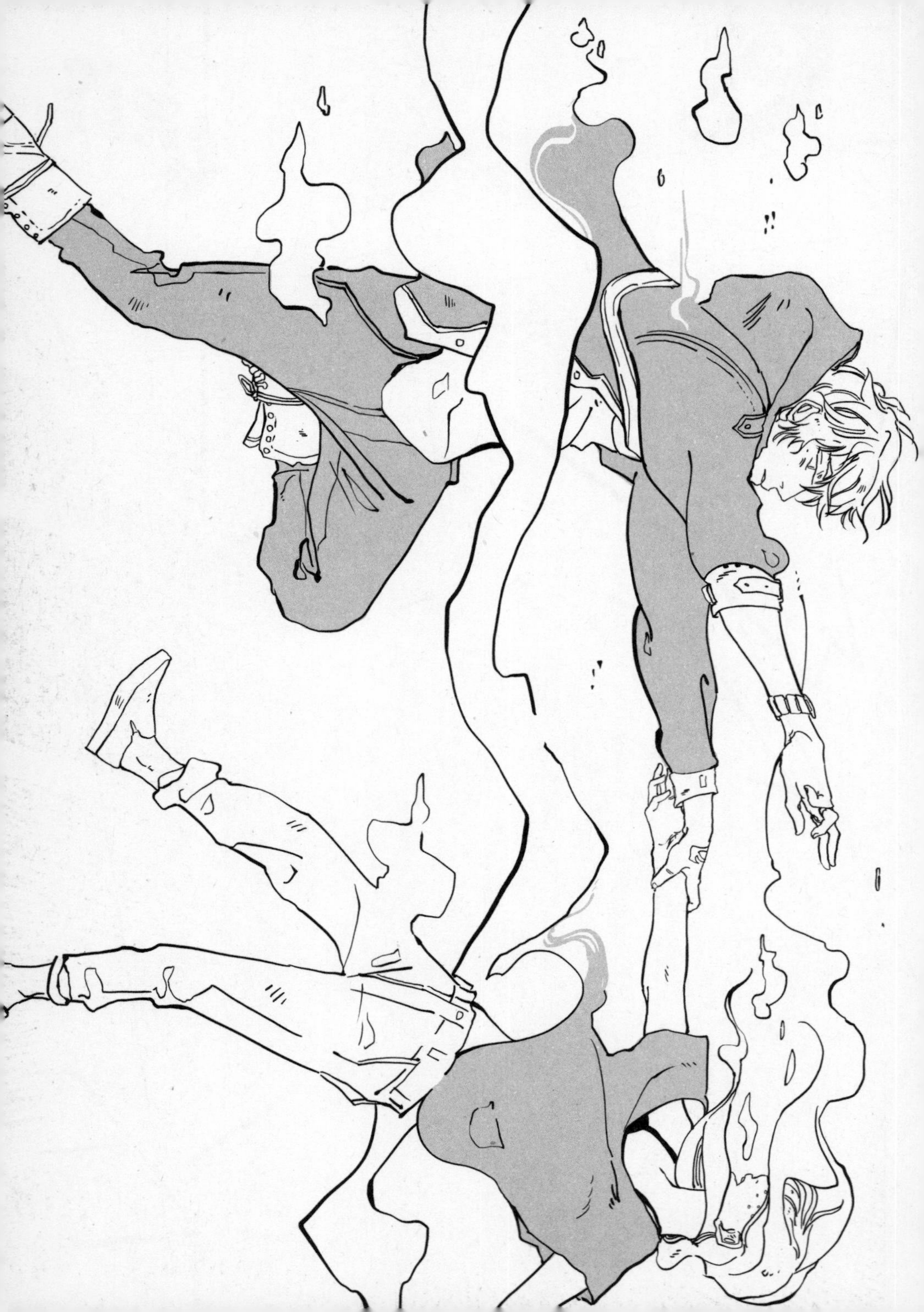

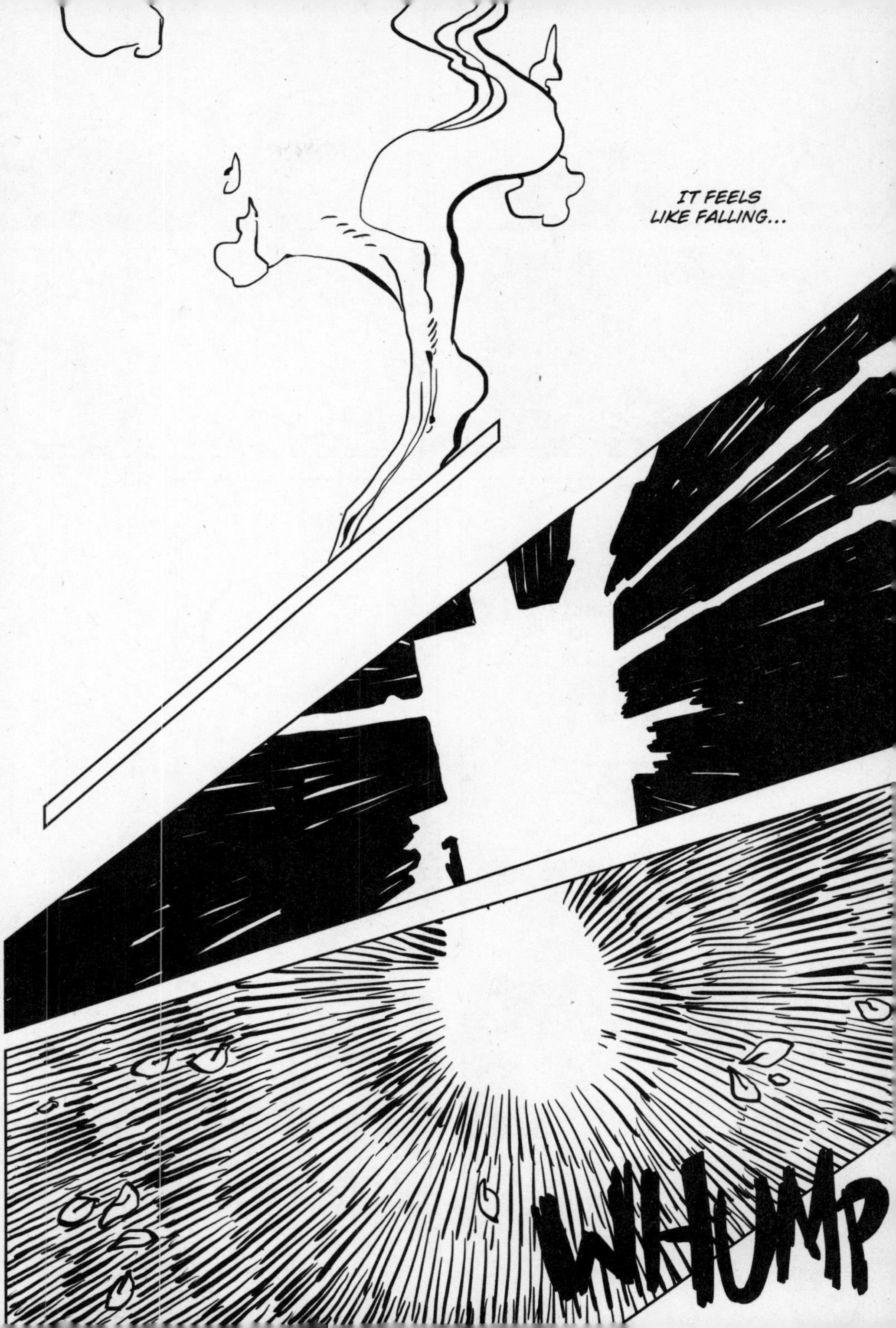
IT FEELS
LIKE FALLING...
WHUMP

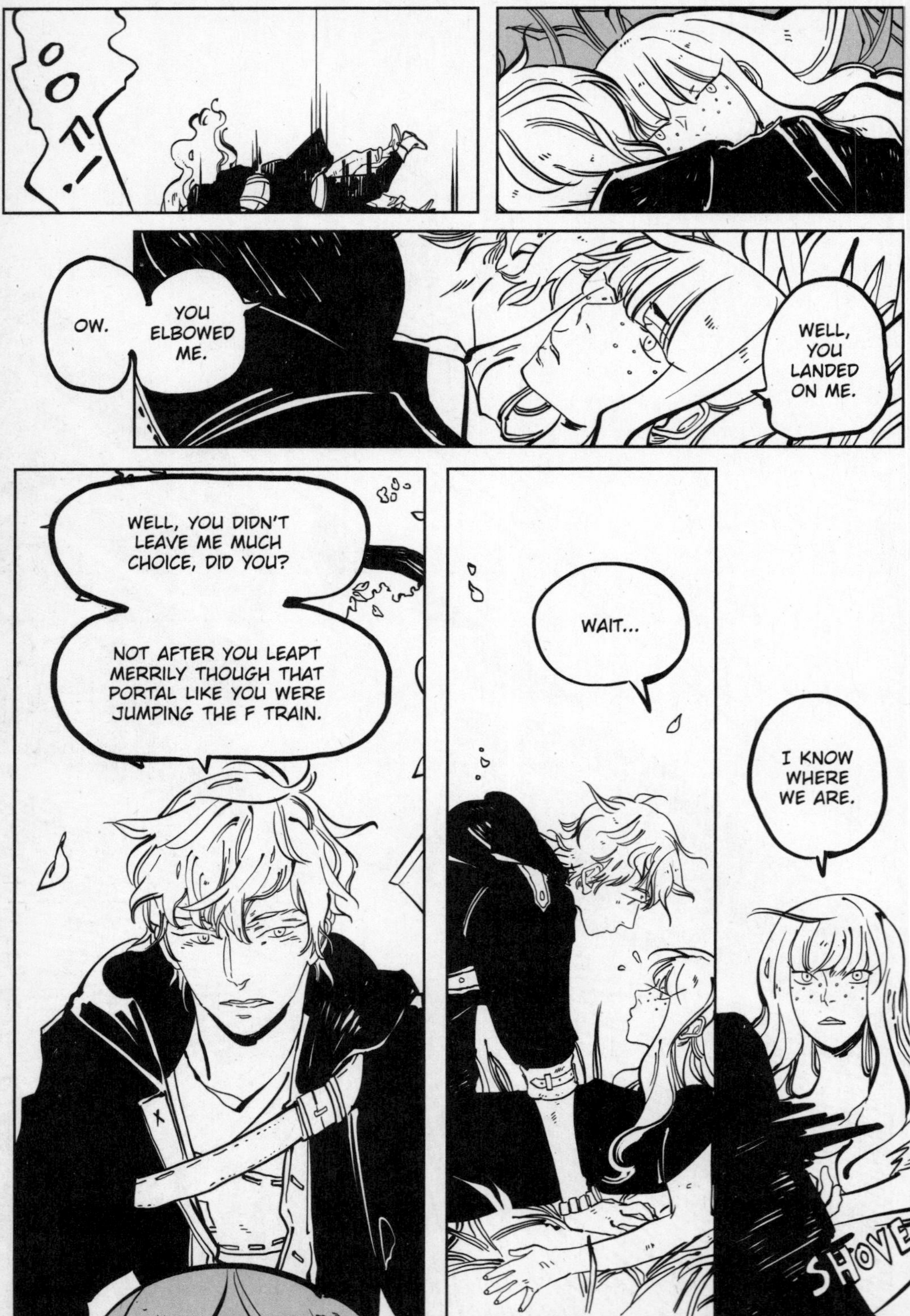
OOF!
OW.
YOU ELBOWED ME.
WELL, YOU LANDED ON ME.
WELL, YOU DIDN'T LEAVE ME MUCH CHOICE, DID YOU?
NOT AFTER YOU LEAPT MERRILY THOUGH THAT PORTAL LIKE YOU WERE JUMPING THE F TRAIN.
WAIT...
I KNOW WHERE WE ARE.
SHOVE

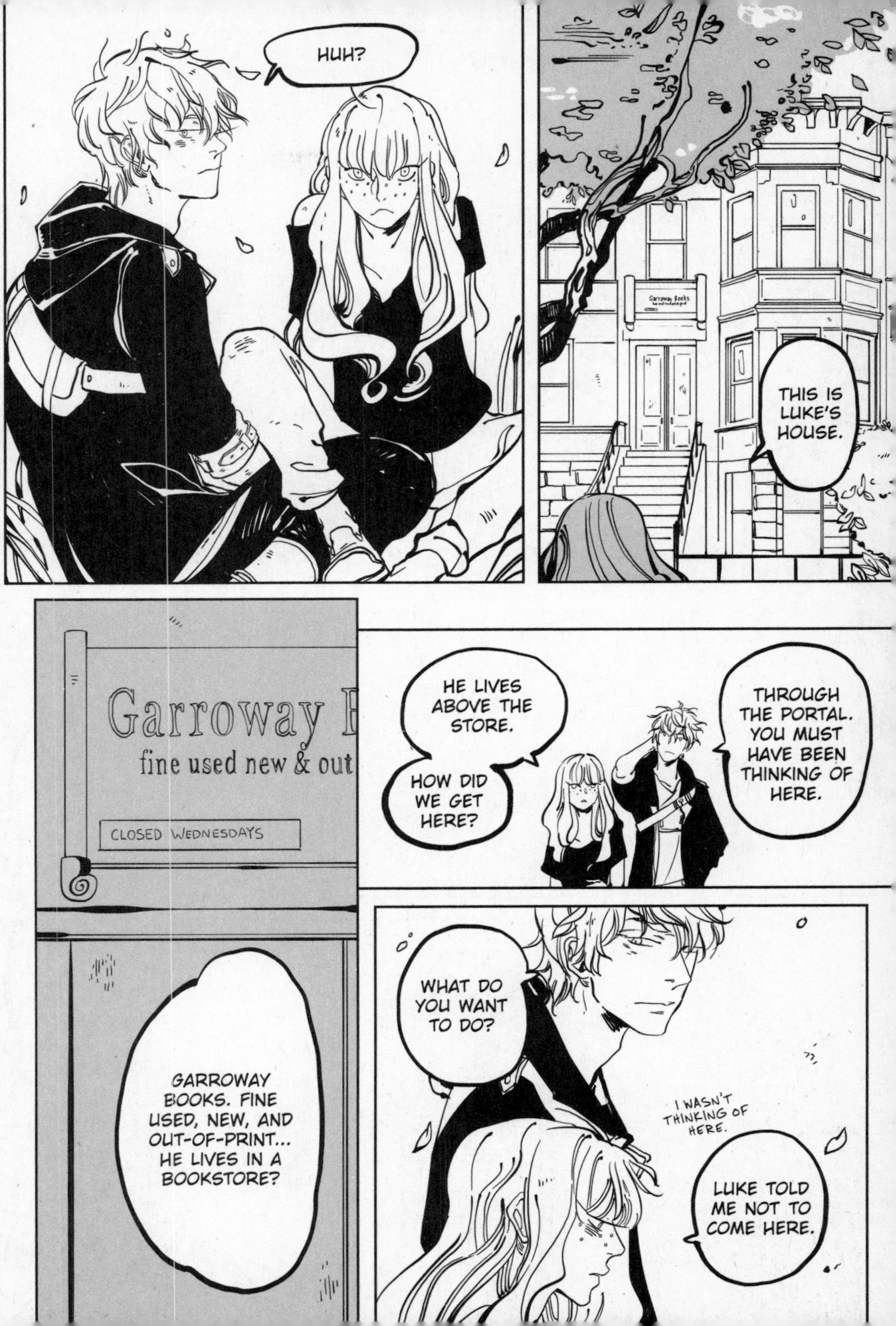
HUH?
Garroway Books
THIS IS LUKE'S HOUSE.
Garroway B
fine used new & out
CLOSED WEDNESDAYS
GARROWAY BOOKS. FINE USED, NEW, AND OUT-OF-PRINT... HE LIVES IN A BOOKSTORE?
HE LIVES ABOVE THE STORE.
HOW DID WE GET HERE?
THROUGH THE PORTAL. YOU MUST HAVE BEEN THINKING OF HERE.
WHAT DO YOU WANT TO DO?
I WASN'T THINKING OF HERE.
LUKE TOLD ME NOT TO COME HERE.

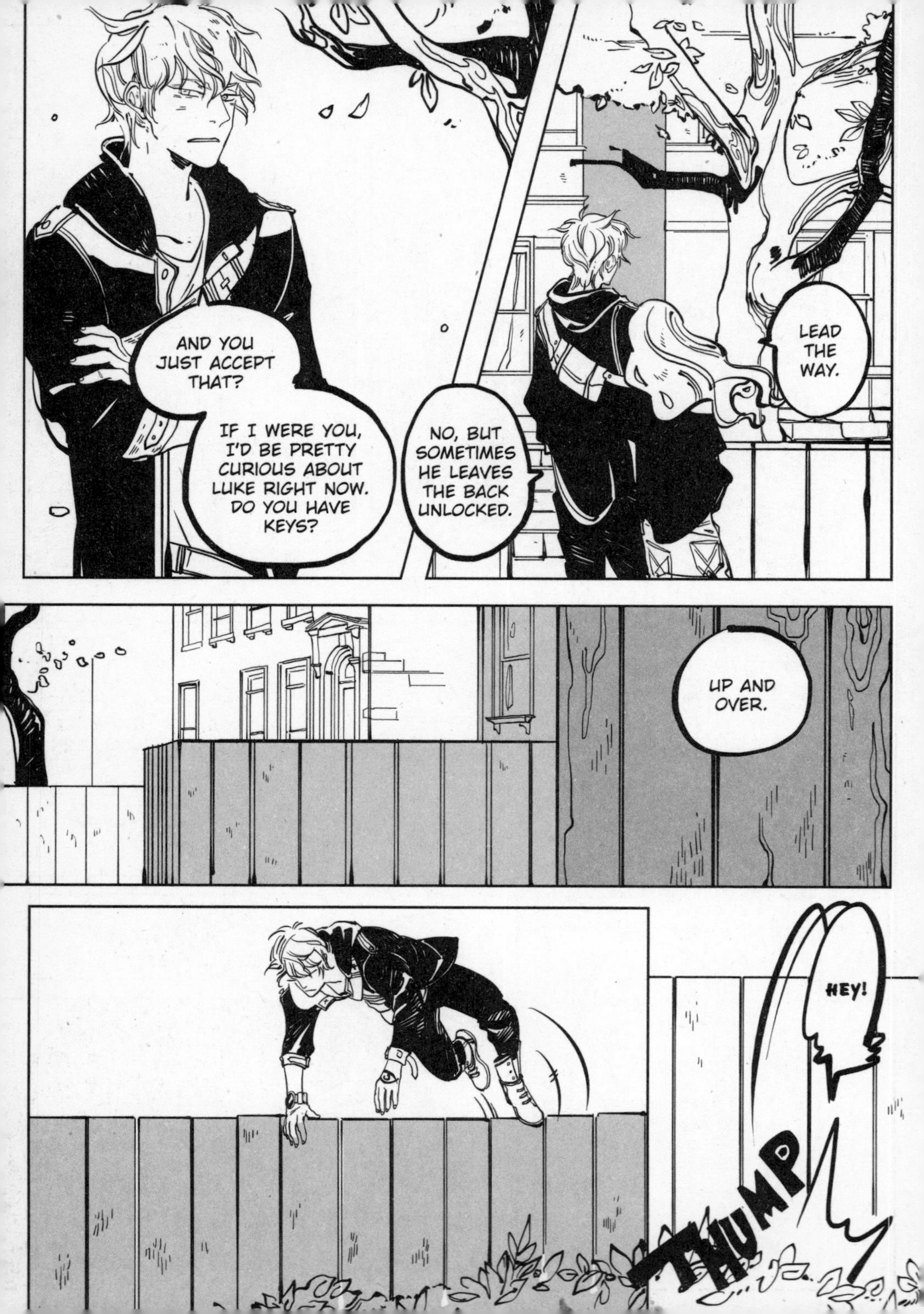
AND YOU JUST ACCEPT THAT?
IF I WERE YOU, I'D BE PRETTY CURIOUS ABOUT LUKE RIGHT NOW. DO YOU HAVE KEYS?
NO, BUT SOMETIMES HE LEAVES THE BACK UNLOCKED.
LEAD THE WAY.
UP AND OVER.
HEY!
THUMP

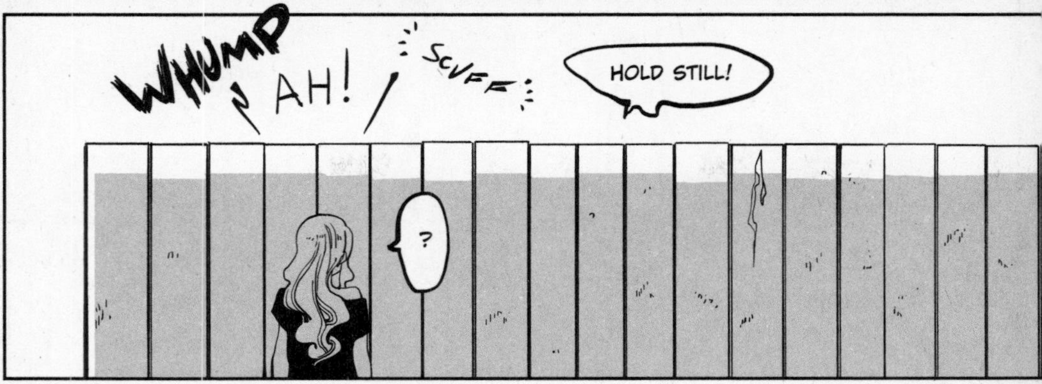
WHUMP
AH!
SCUFF
HOLD STILL!
?

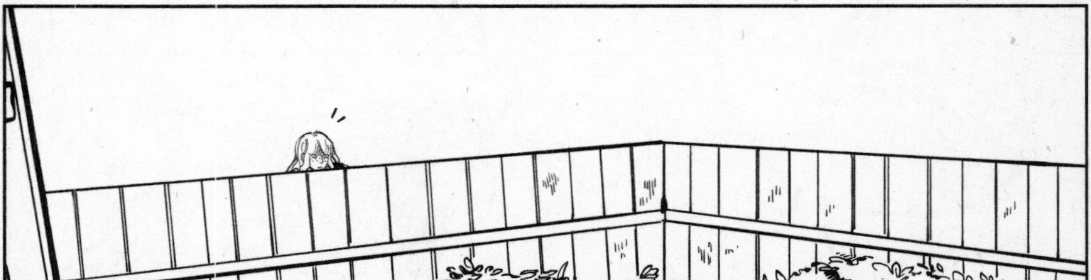

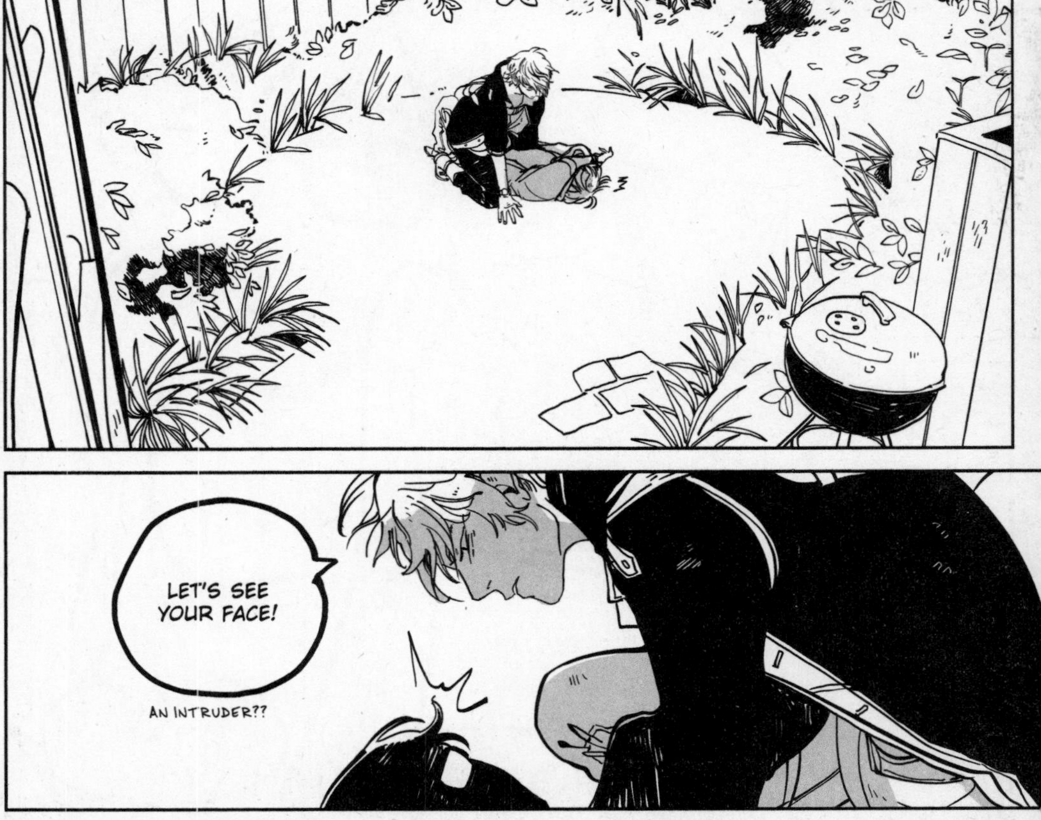
LET'S SEE YOUR FACE!
AN INTRUDER??

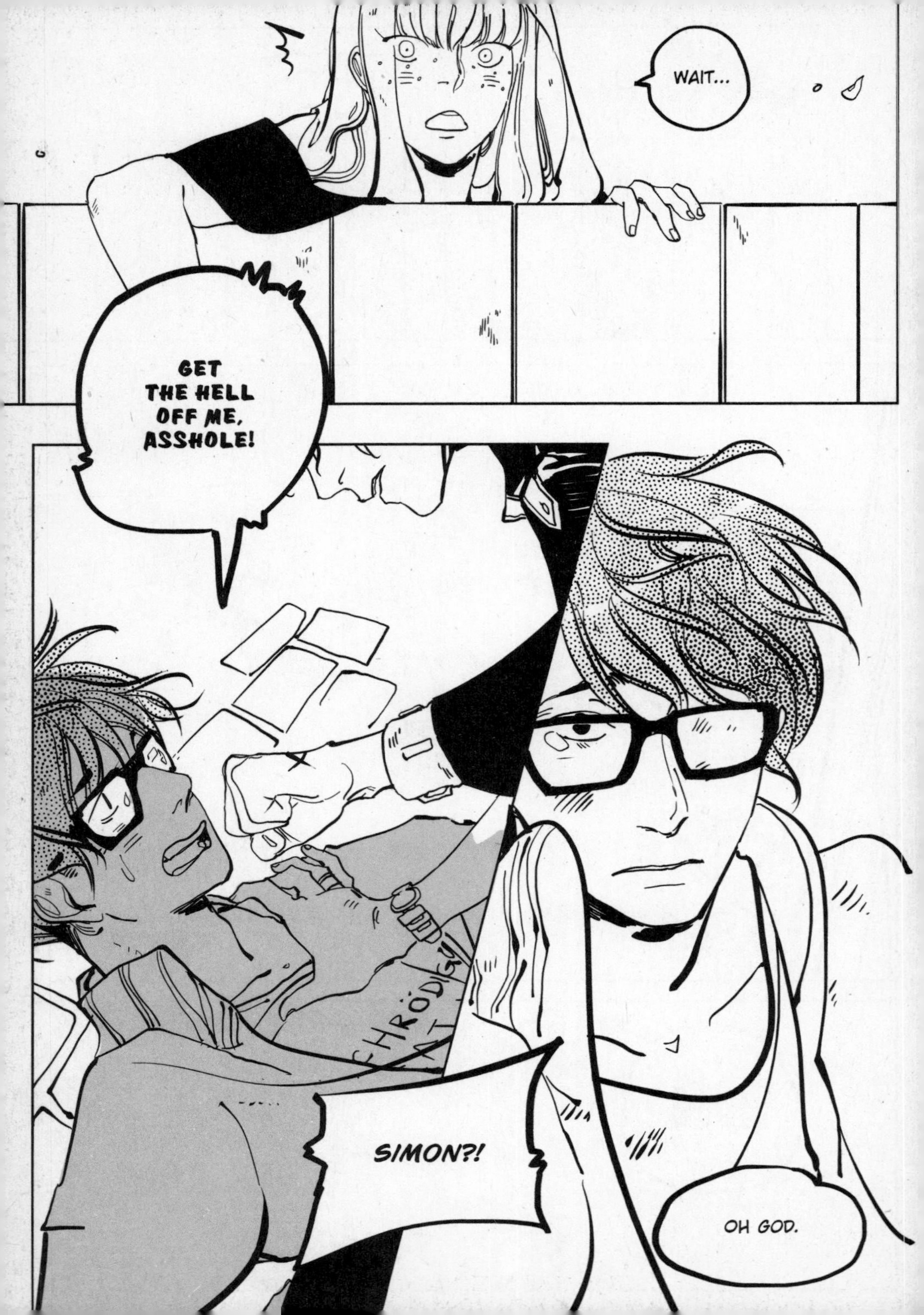
WAIT...
GET THE HELL OFF ME, ASSHOLE!
SIMON?!
OH GOD.

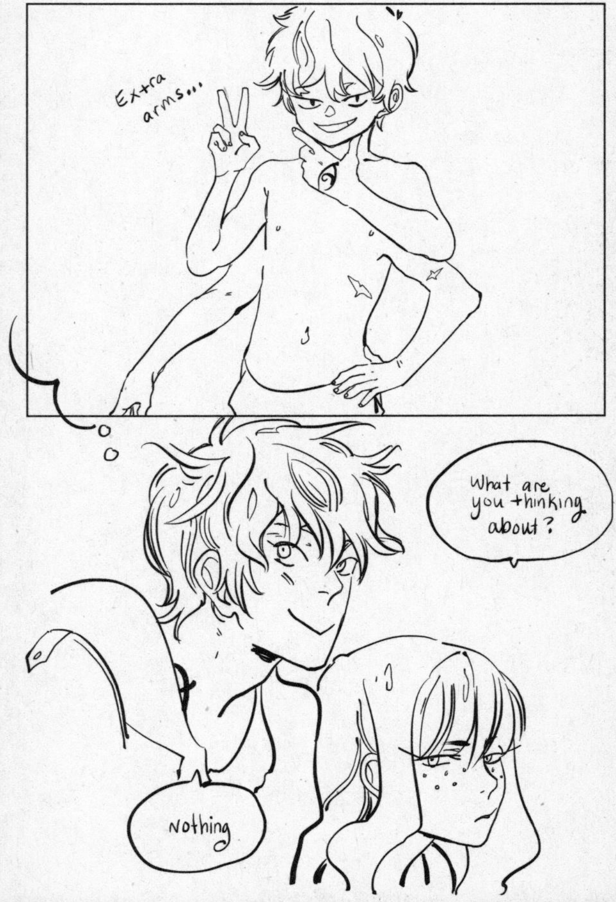
Extra arms...
What are you thinking about?
Nothing

THE MORTAL INSTRUMENTS

THE GRAPHIC NOVEL

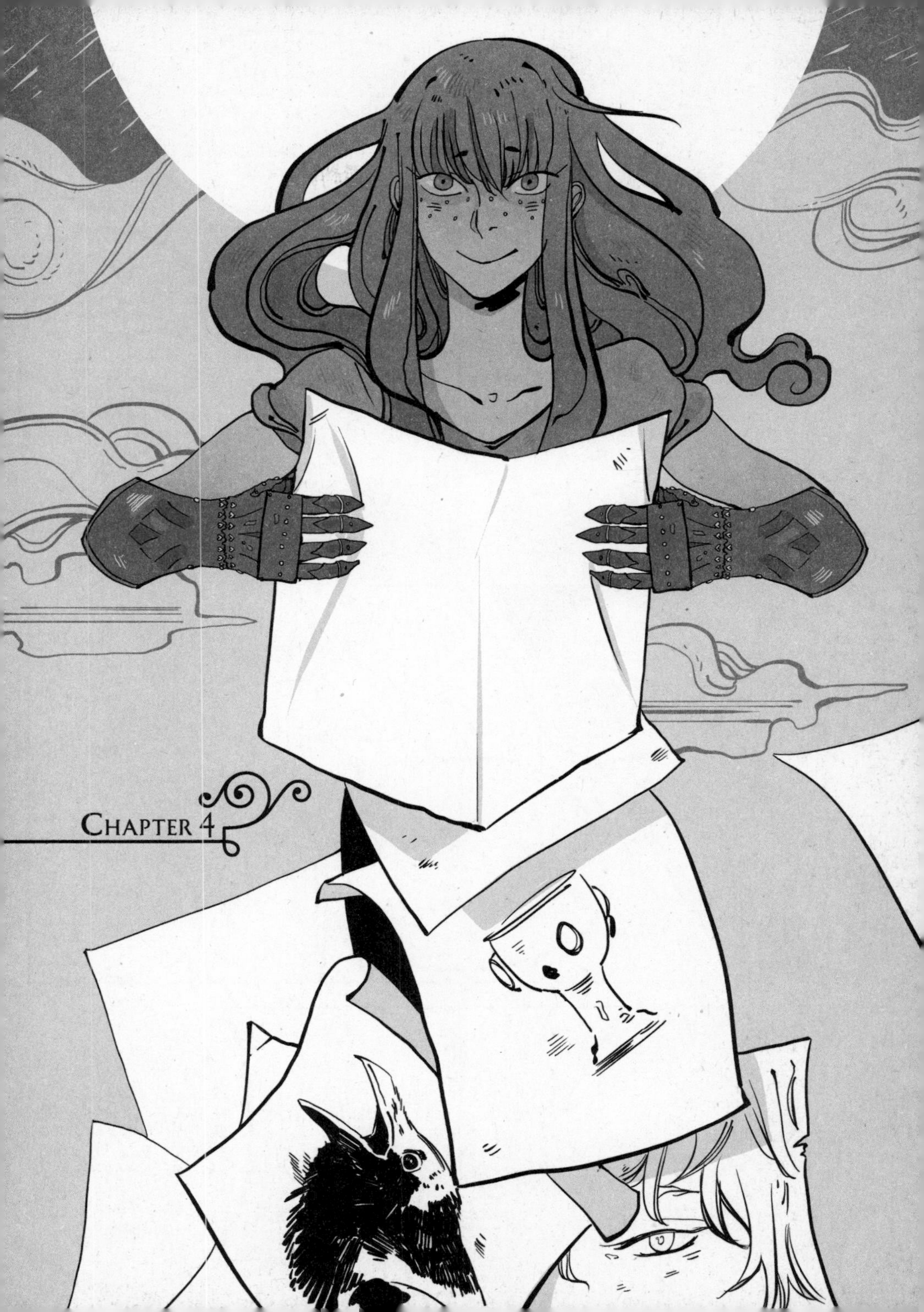

Chapter 4

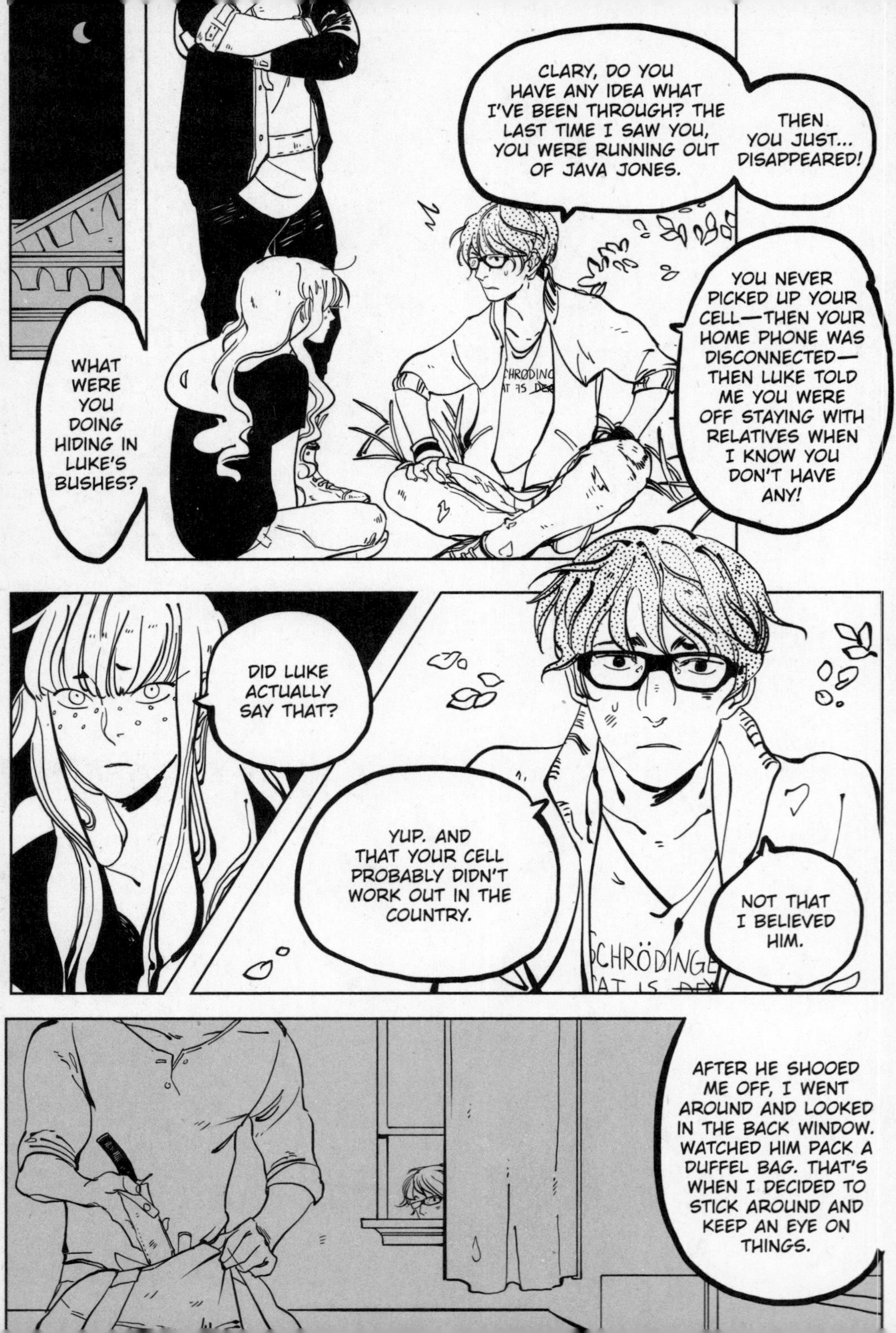
CLARY, DO YOU HAVE ANY IDEA WHAT I'VE BEEN THROUGH? THE LAST TIME I SAW YOU, YOU WERE RUNNING OUT OF JAVA JONES.
THEN YOU JUST... DISAPPEARED!
WHAT WERE YOU DOING HIDING IN LUKE'S BUSHES?
YOU NEVER PICKED UP YOUR CELL—THEN YOUR HOME PHONE WAS DISCONNECTED—THEN LUKE TOLD ME YOU WERE OFF STAYING WITH RELATIVES WHEN I KNOW YOU DON'T HAVE ANY!
DID LUKE ACTUALLY SAY THAT?
YUP. AND THAT YOUR CELL PROBABLY DIDN'T WORK OUT IN THE COUNTRY.
NOT THAT I BELIEVED HIM.
AFTER HE SHOOED ME OFF, I WENT AROUND AND LOOKED IN THE BACK WINDOW. WATCHED HIM PACK A DUFFEL BAG. THAT'S WHEN I DECIDED TO STICK AROUND AND KEEP AN EYE ON THINGS.

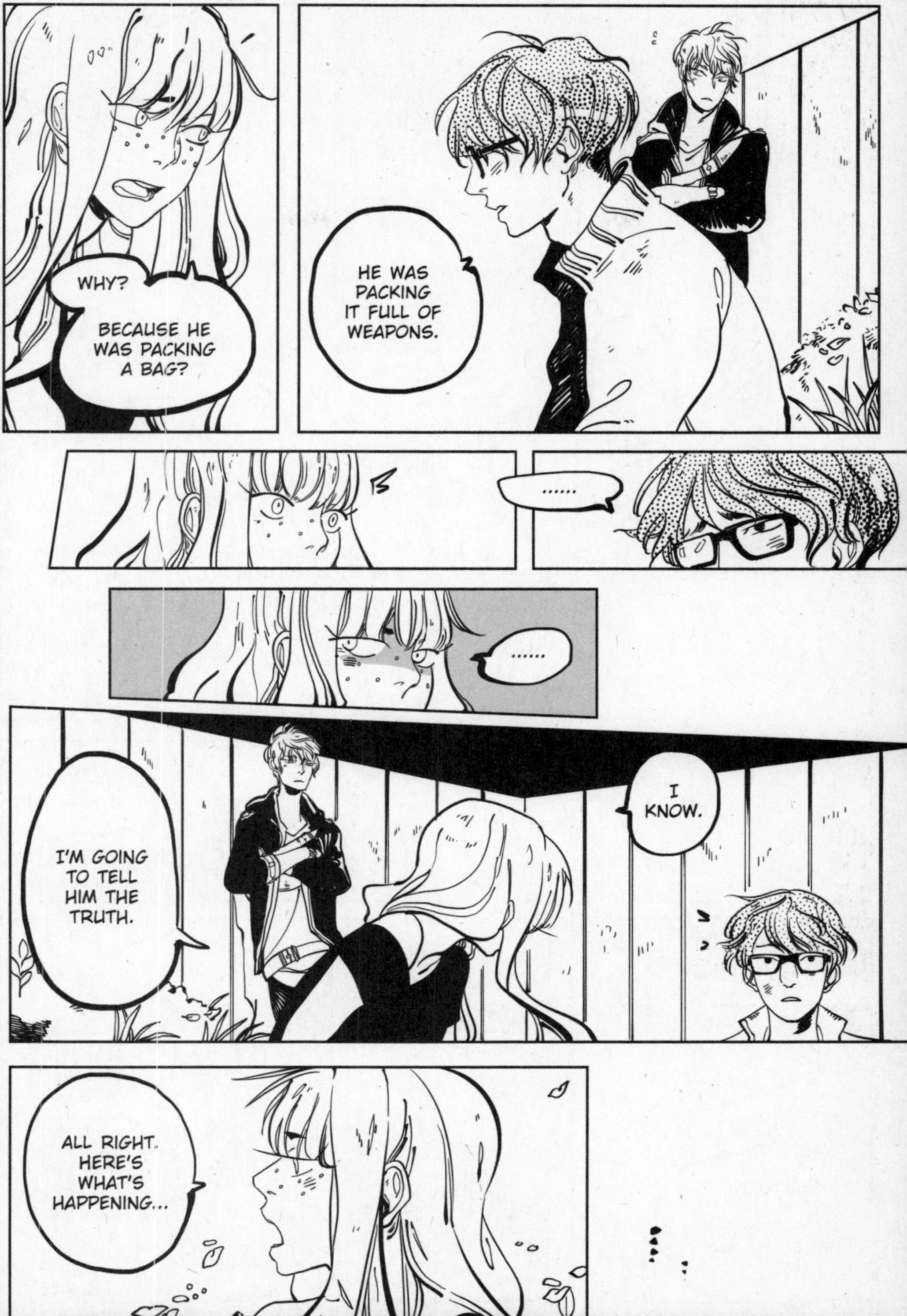
WHY?
BECAUSE HE WAS PACKING A BAG?
HE WAS PACKING IT FULL OF WEAPONS.
......
......
I'M GOING TO TELL HIM THE TRUTH.
I KNOW.
ALL RIGHT. HERE'S WHAT'S HAPPENING...

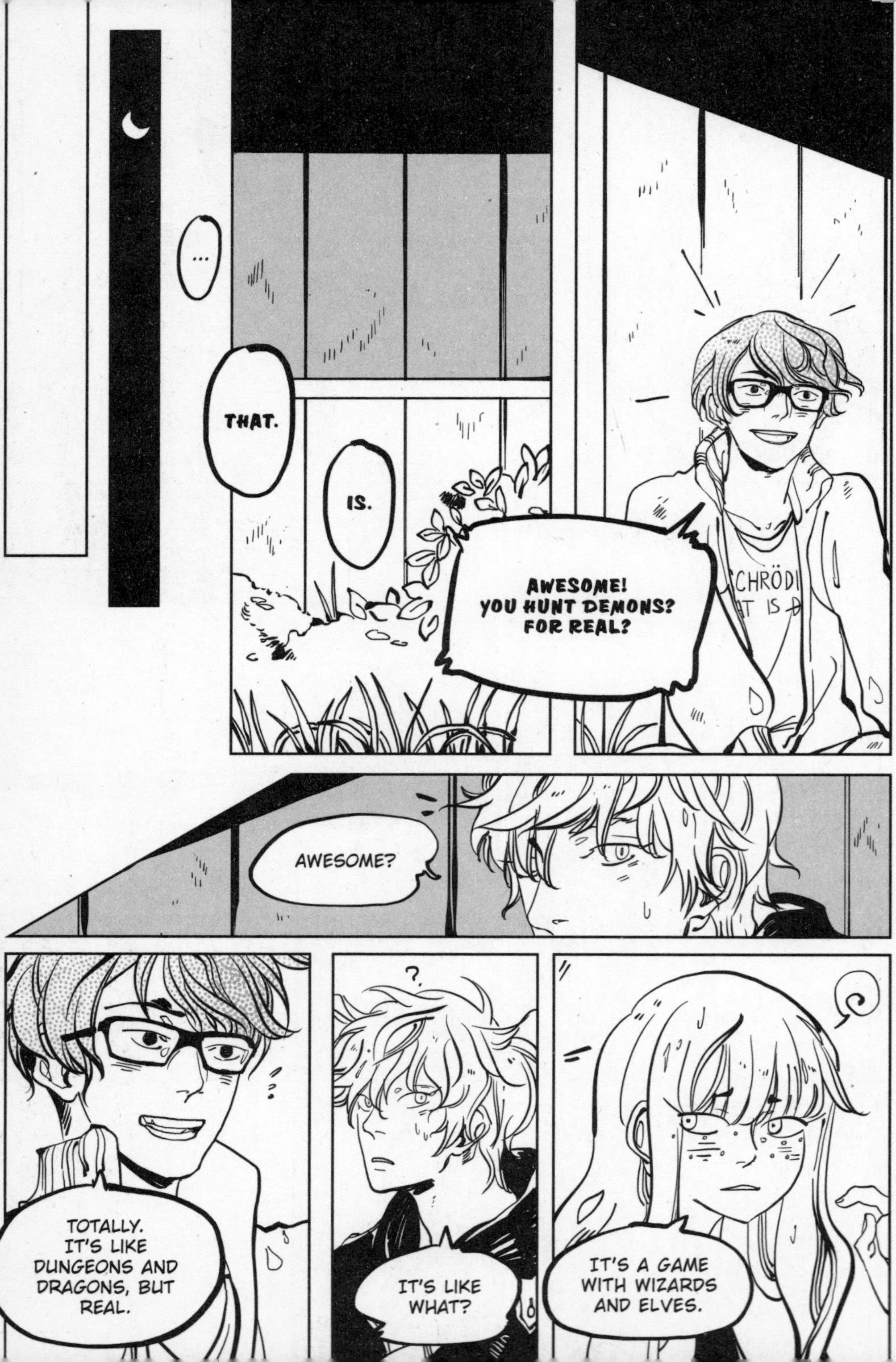
...
THAT.
IS.
AWESOME! YOU HUNT DEMONS? FOR REAL?
SCHRÖDI
AT IS D
AWESOME?
TOTALLY. IT'S LIKE DUNGEONS AND DRAGONS, BUT REAL.
?
IT'S LIKE WHAT?
IT'S A GAME WITH WIZARDS AND ELVES.

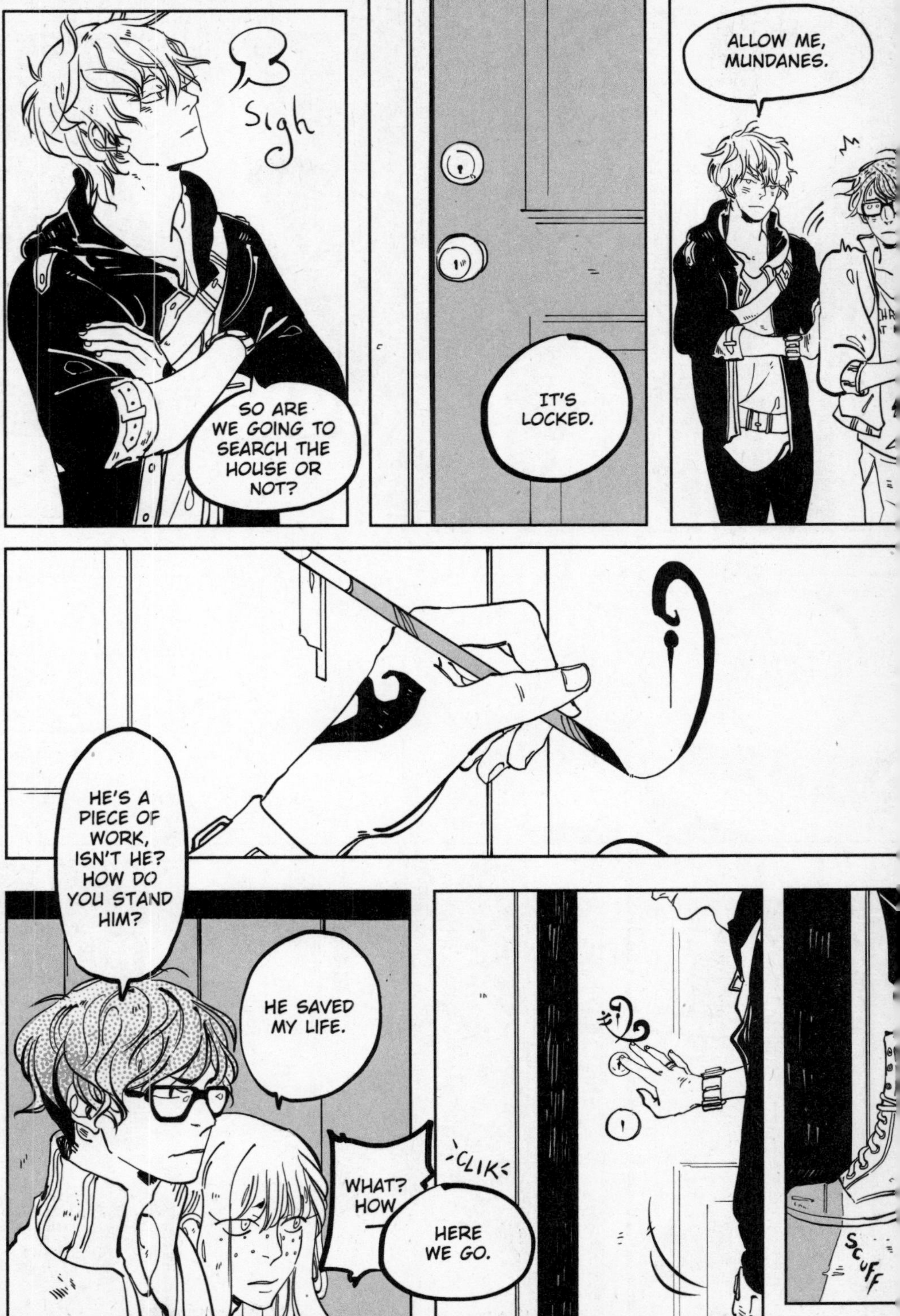
Sigh
SO ARE WE GOING TO SEARCH THE HOUSE OR NOT?
IT'S LOCKED.
ALLOW ME, MUNDANES.
HE'S A PIECE OF WORK, ISN'T HE? HOW DO YOU STAND HIM?
HE SAVED MY LIFE.
WHAT? HOW
-CLIK-
HERE WE GO.
SCUFF

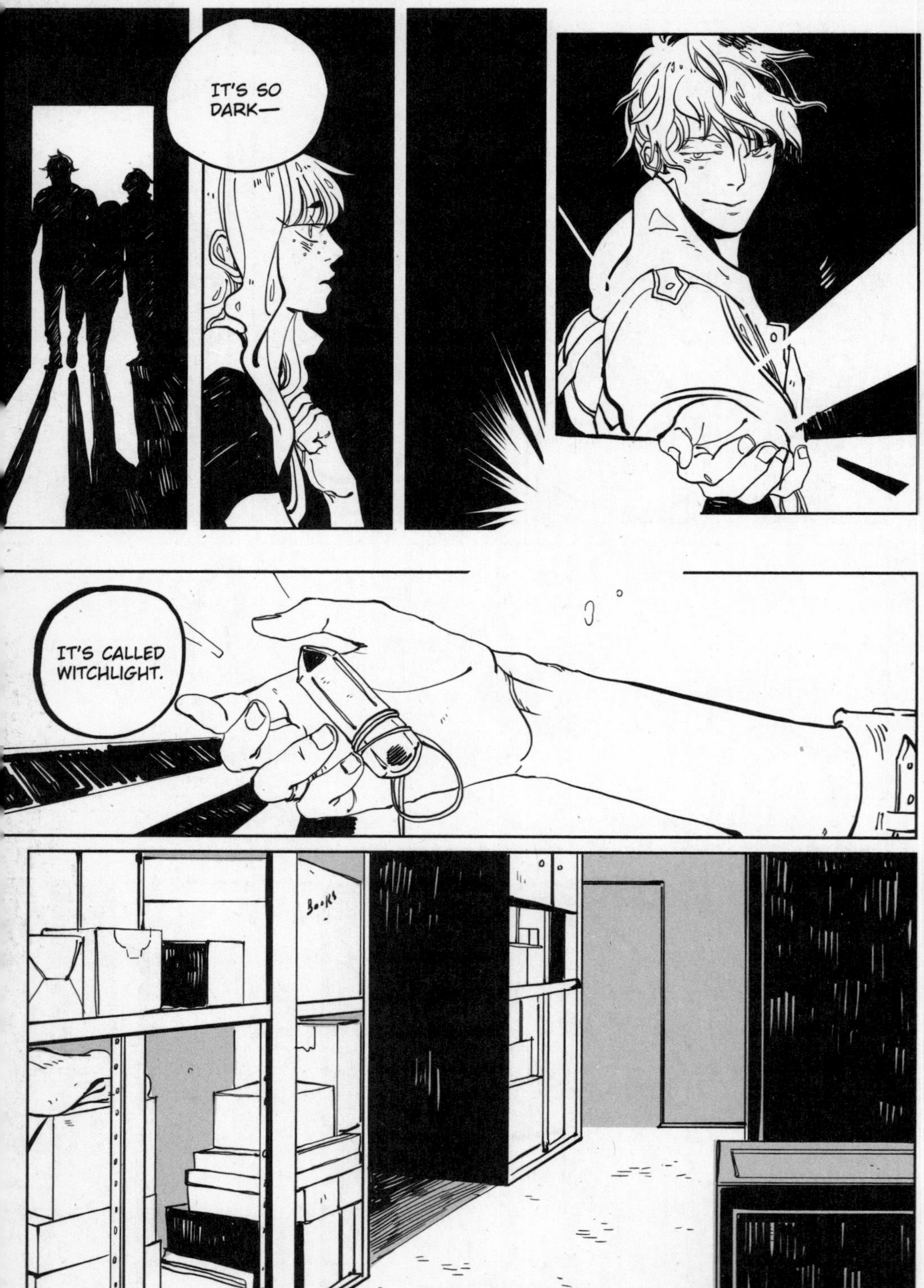

IT'S SO DARK—
IT'S CALLED WITCHLIGHT.

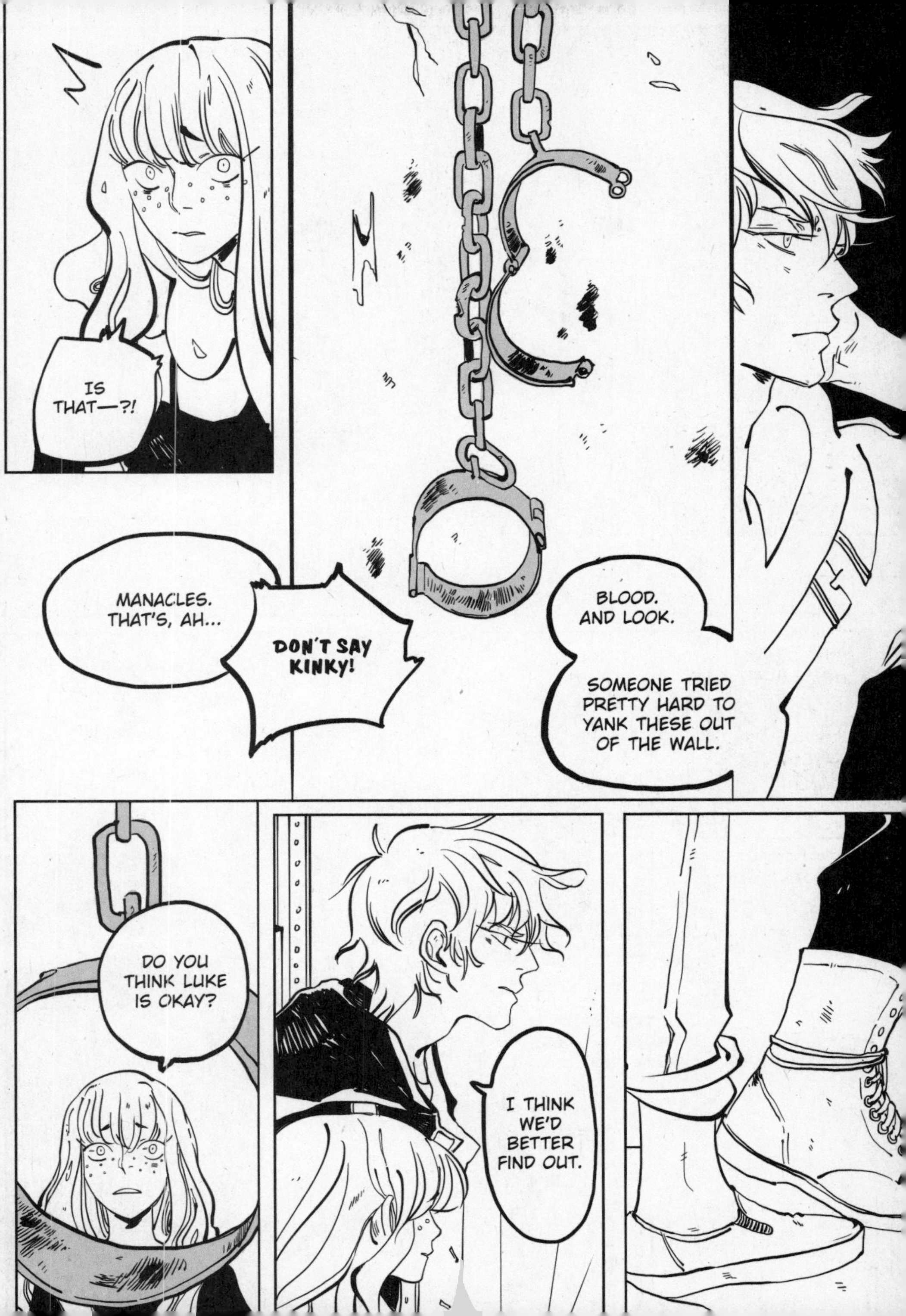
IS THAT—?!
MANACLES. THAT'S, AH...
DON'T SAY KINKY!
BLOOD. AND LOOK.
SOMEONE TRIED PRETTY HARD TO YANK THESE OUT OF THE WALL.
DO YOU THINK LUKE IS OKAY?
I THINK WE'D BETTER FIND OUT.

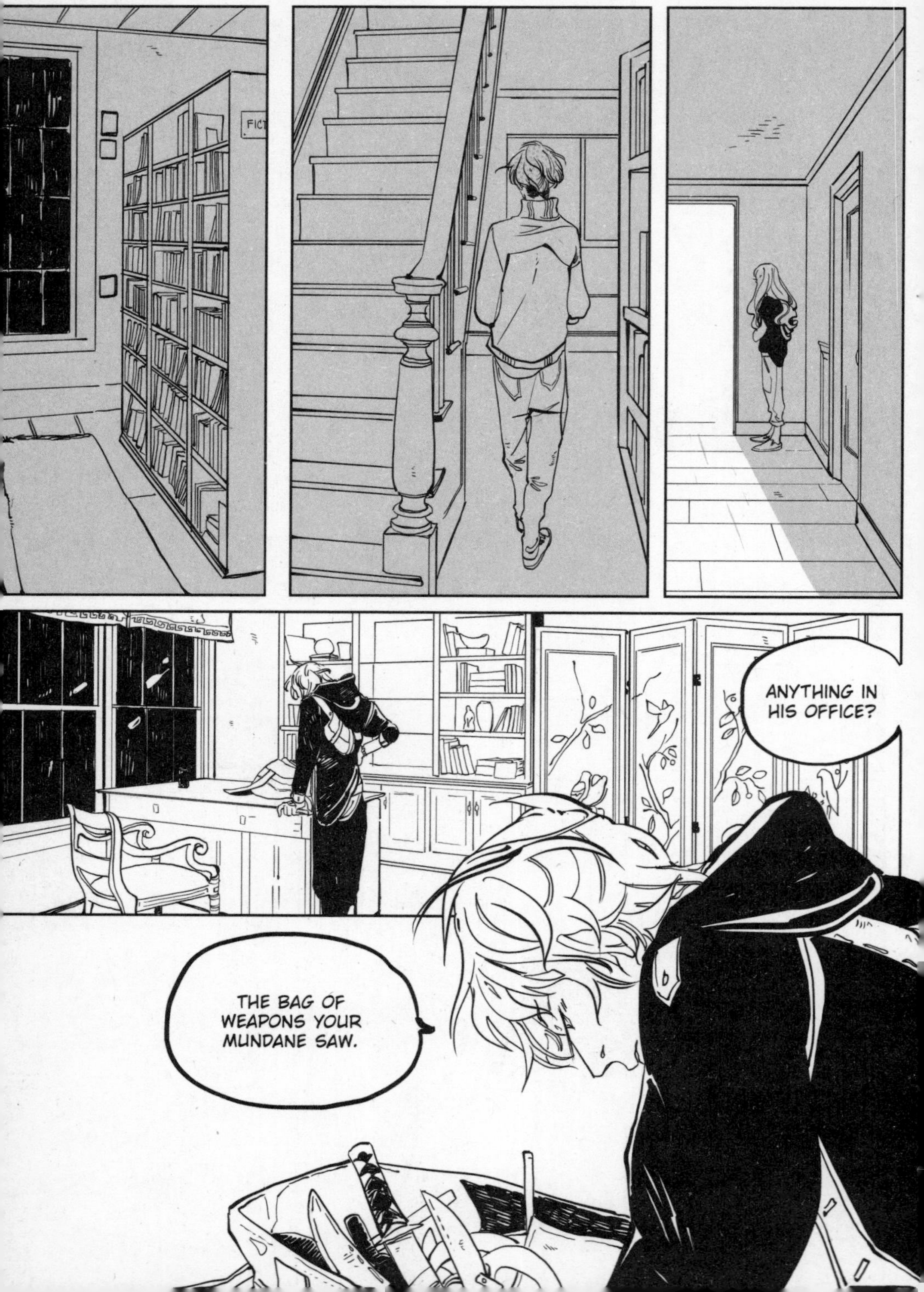
ANYTHING IN HIS OFFICE?
THE BAG OF WEAPONS YOUR MUNDANE SAW.

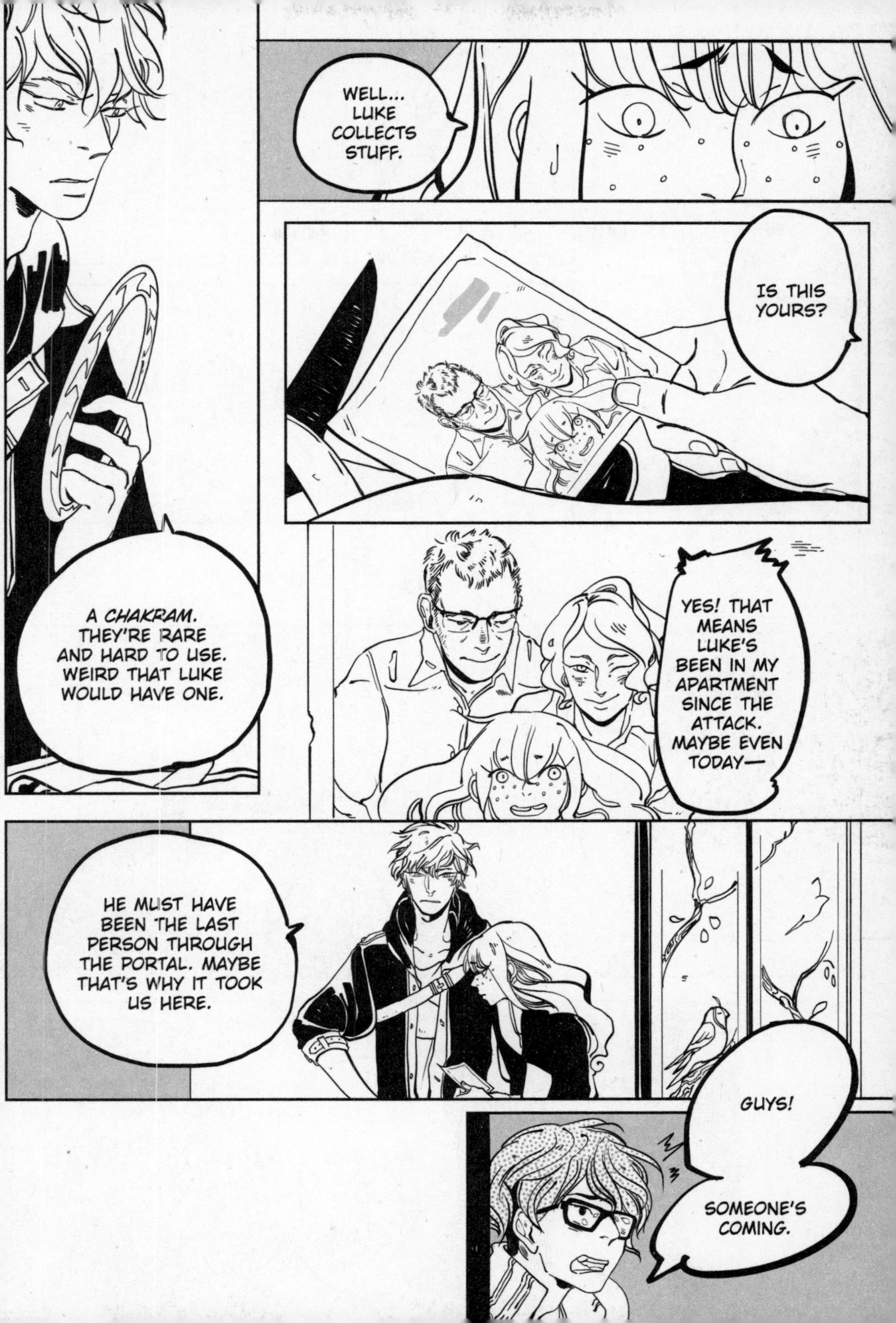
A *CHAKRAM*. THEY'RE RARE AND HARD TO USE. WEIRD THAT LUKE WOULD HAVE ONE.
WELL... LUKE COLLECTS STUFF.
IS THIS YOURS?
YES! THAT MEANS LUKE'S BEEN IN MY APARTMENT SINCE THE ATTACK. MAYBE EVEN TODAY—
HE MUST HAVE BEEN THE LAST PERSON THROUGH THE PORTAL. MAYBE THAT'S WHY IT TOOK US HERE.
GUYS!
SOMEONE'S COMING.

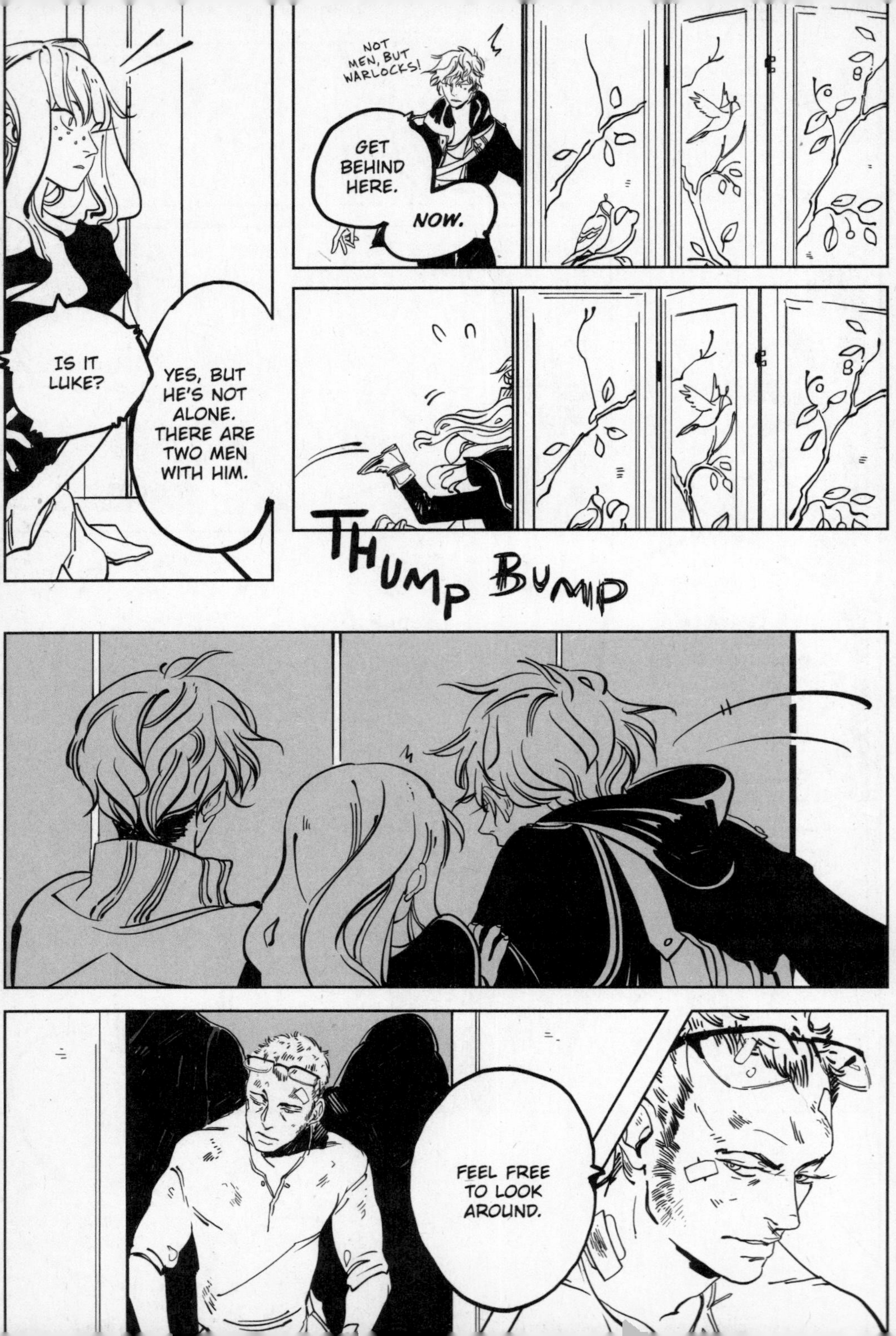
IS IT LUKE?
YES, BUT HE'S NOT ALONE. THERE ARE TWO MEN WITH HIM.
NOT MEN, BUT WARLOCKS!
GET BEHIND HERE.
NOW.
THUMP BUMP
FEEL FREE TO LOOK AROUND.

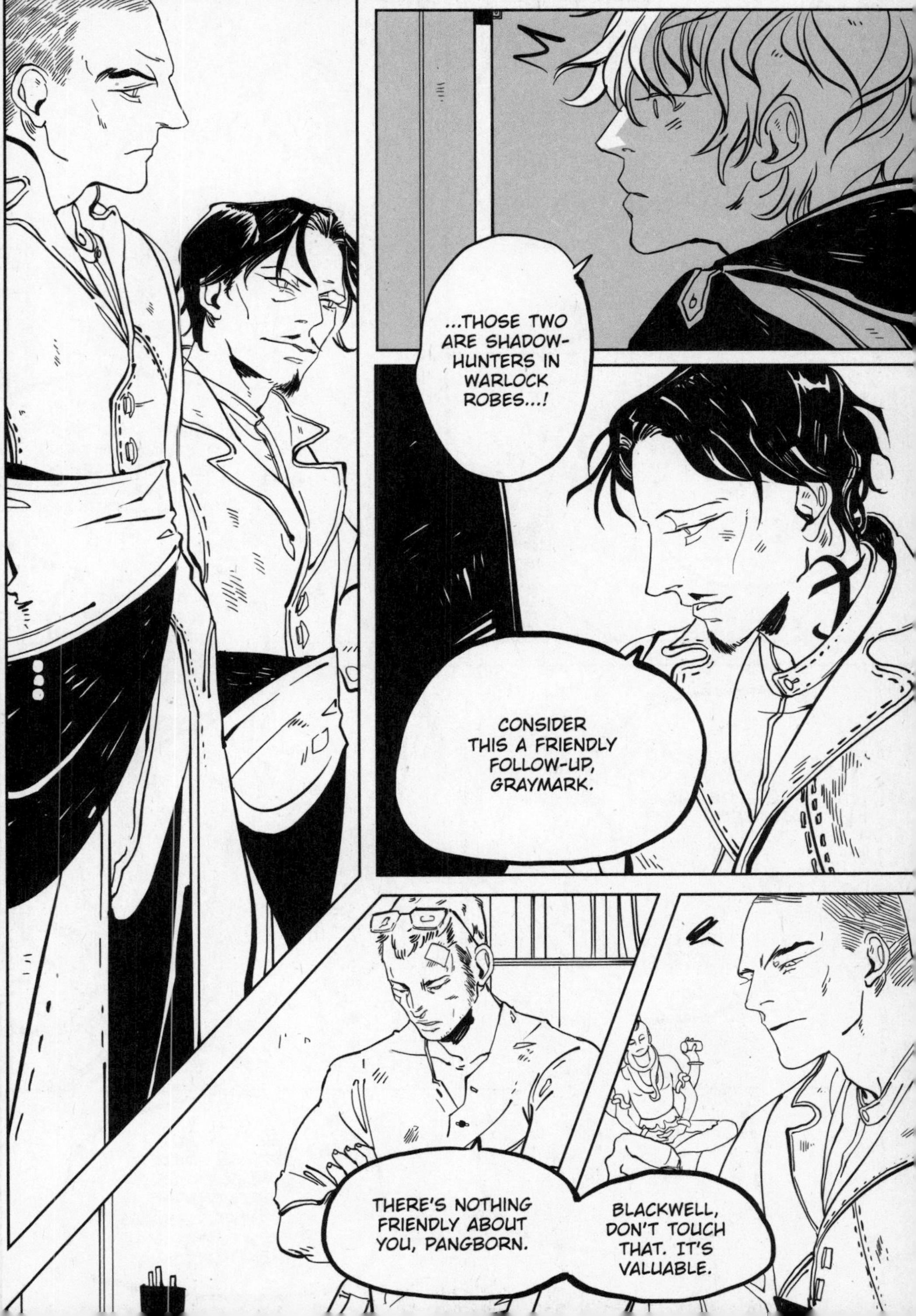
...THOSE TWO ARE SHADOW-HUNTERS IN WARLOCK ROBES...!
CONSIDER THIS A FRIENDLY FOLLOW-UP, GRAYMARK.
THERE'S NOTHING FRIENDLY ABOUT YOU, PANGBORN.
BLACKWELL, DON'T TOUCH THAT. IT'S VALUABLE.

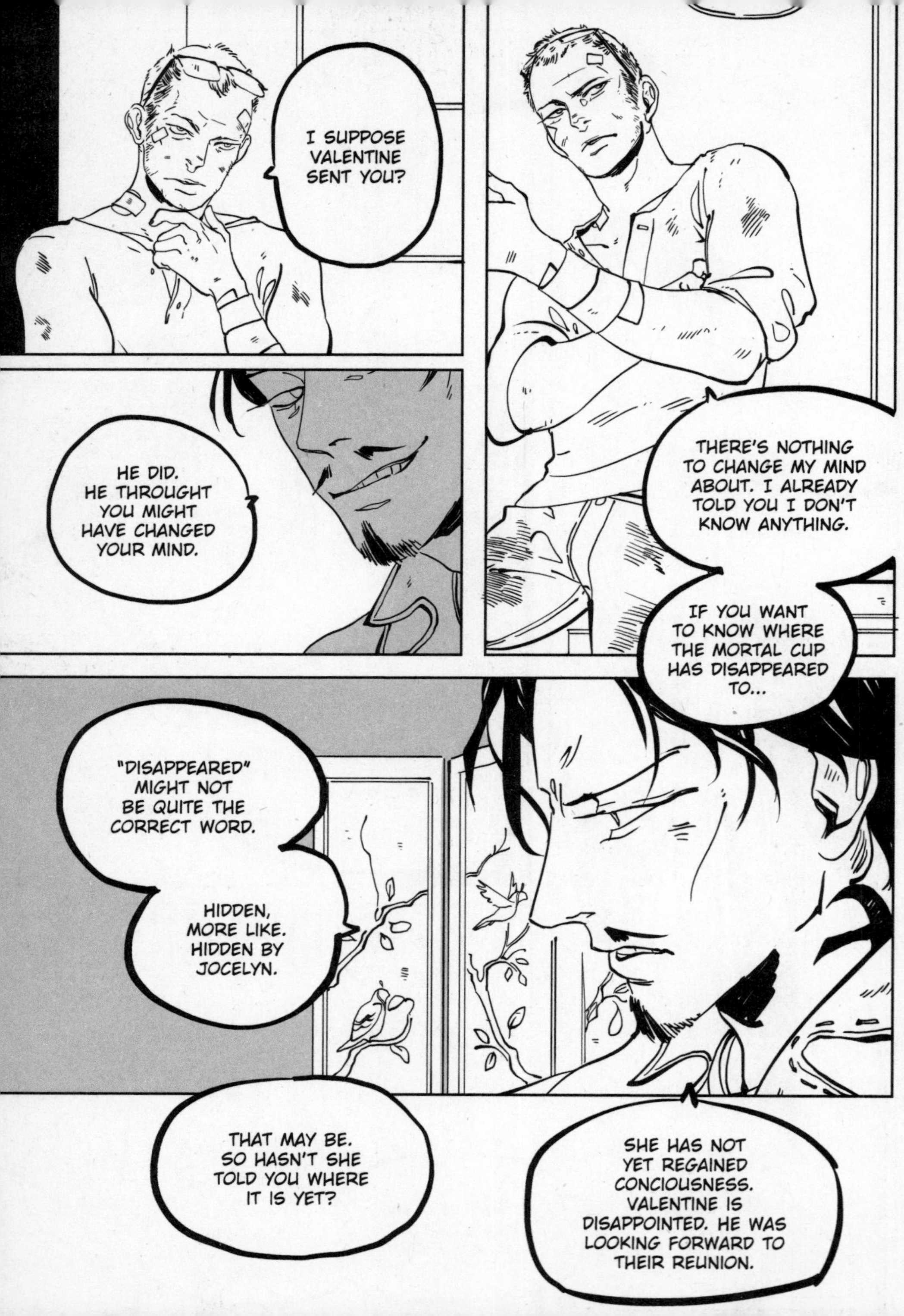
I SUPPOSE VALENTINE SENT YOU?
HE DID. HE THROUGHT YOU MIGHT HAVE CHANGED YOUR MIND.
THERE'S NOTHING TO CHANGE MY MIND ABOUT. I ALREADY TOLD YOU I DON'T KNOW ANYTHING.
IF YOU WANT TO KNOW WHERE THE MORTAL CUP HAS DISAPPEARED TO...
"DISAPPEARED" MIGHT NOT BE QUITE THE CORRECT WORD.
HIDDEN, MORE LIKE. HIDDEN BY JOCELYN.
THAT MAY BE. SO HASN'T SHE TOLD YOU WHERE IT IS YET?
SHE HAS NOT YET REGAINED CONCIOUSNESS. VALENTINE IS DISAPPOINTED. HE WAS LOOKING FORWARD TO THEIR REUNION.

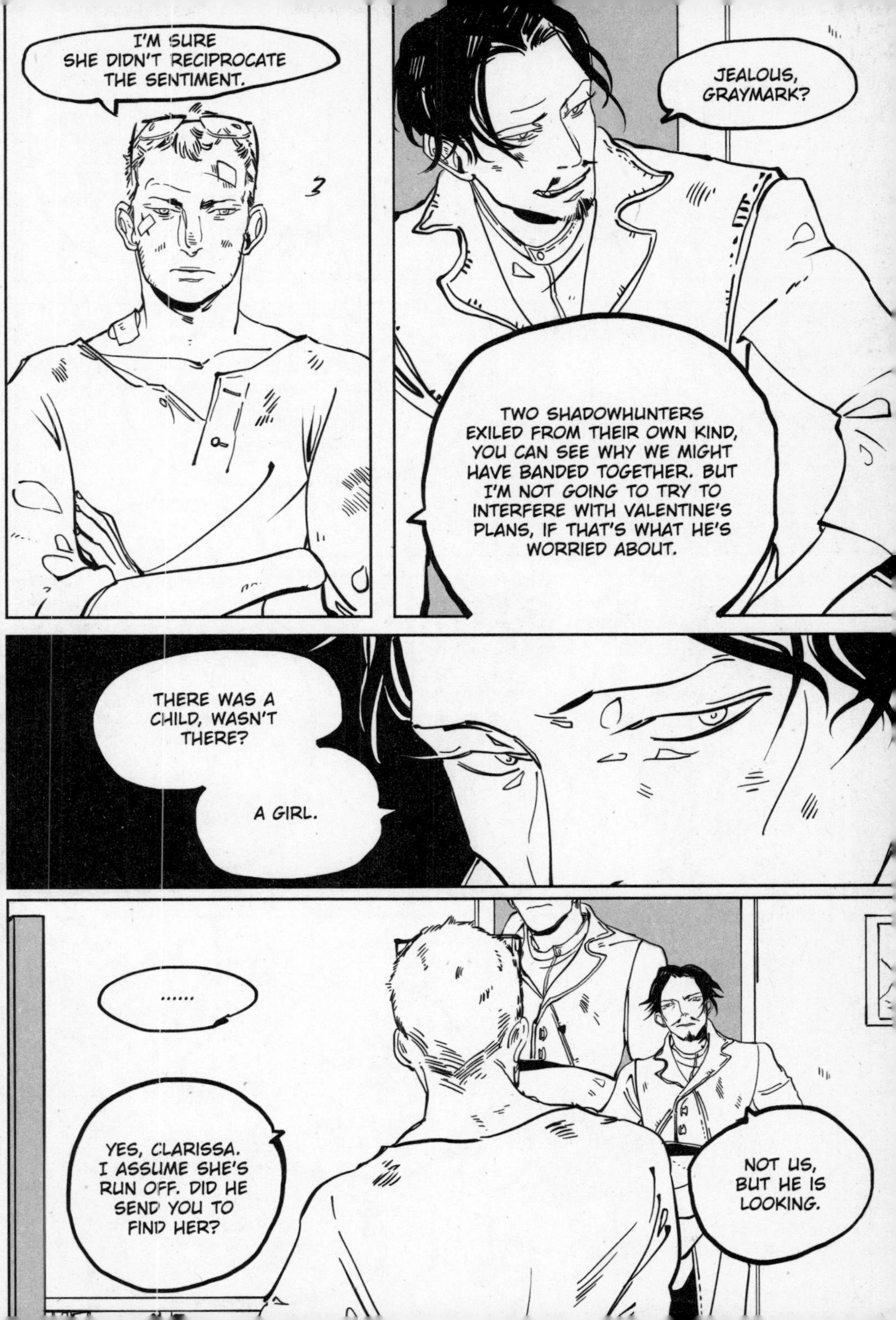
I'M SURE SHE DIDN'T RECIPROCATE THE SENTIMENT.
JEALOUS, GRAYMARK?
TWO SHADOWHUNTERS EXILED FROM THEIR OWN KIND, YOU CAN SEE WHY WE MIGHT HAVE BANDED TOGETHER. BUT I'M NOT GOING TO TRY TO INTERFERE WITH VALENTINE'S PLANS, IF THAT'S WHAT HE'S WORRIED ABOUT.
THERE WAS A CHILD, WASN'T THERE?
A GIRL.
......
YES, CLARISSA. I ASSUME SHE'S RUN OFF. DID HE SEND YOU TO FIND HER?
NOT US, BUT HE IS LOOKING.

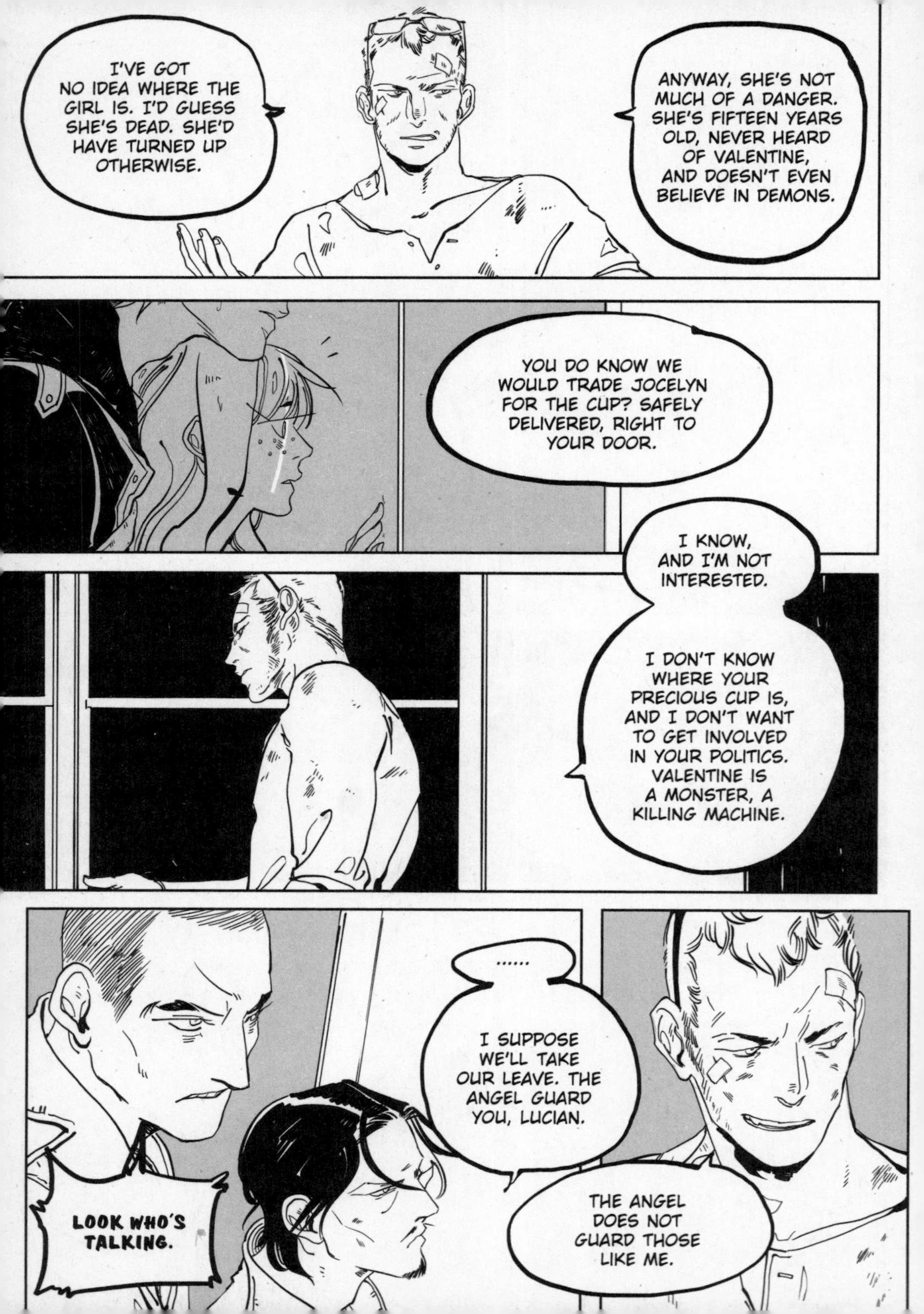
I'VE GOT NO IDEA WHERE THE GIRL IS. I'D GUESS SHE'S DEAD. SHE'D HAVE TURNED UP OTHERWISE.
ANYWAY, SHE'S NOT MUCH OF A DANGER. SHE'S FIFTEEN YEARS OLD, NEVER HEARD OF VALENTINE, AND DOESN'T EVEN BELIEVE IN DEMONS.
YOU DO KNOW WE WOULD TRADE JOCELYN FOR THE CUP? SAFELY DELIVERED, RIGHT TO YOUR DOOR.
I KNOW, AND I'M NOT INTERESTED.
I DON'T KNOW WHERE YOUR PRECIOUS CUP IS, AND I DON'T WANT TO GET INVOLVED IN YOUR POLITICS. VALENTINE IS A MONSTER, A KILLING MACHINE.
......
I SUPPOSE WE'LL TAKE OUR LEAVE. THE ANGEL GUARD YOU, LUCIAN.
LOOK WHO'S TALKING.
THE ANGEL DOES NOT GUARD THOSE LIKE ME.

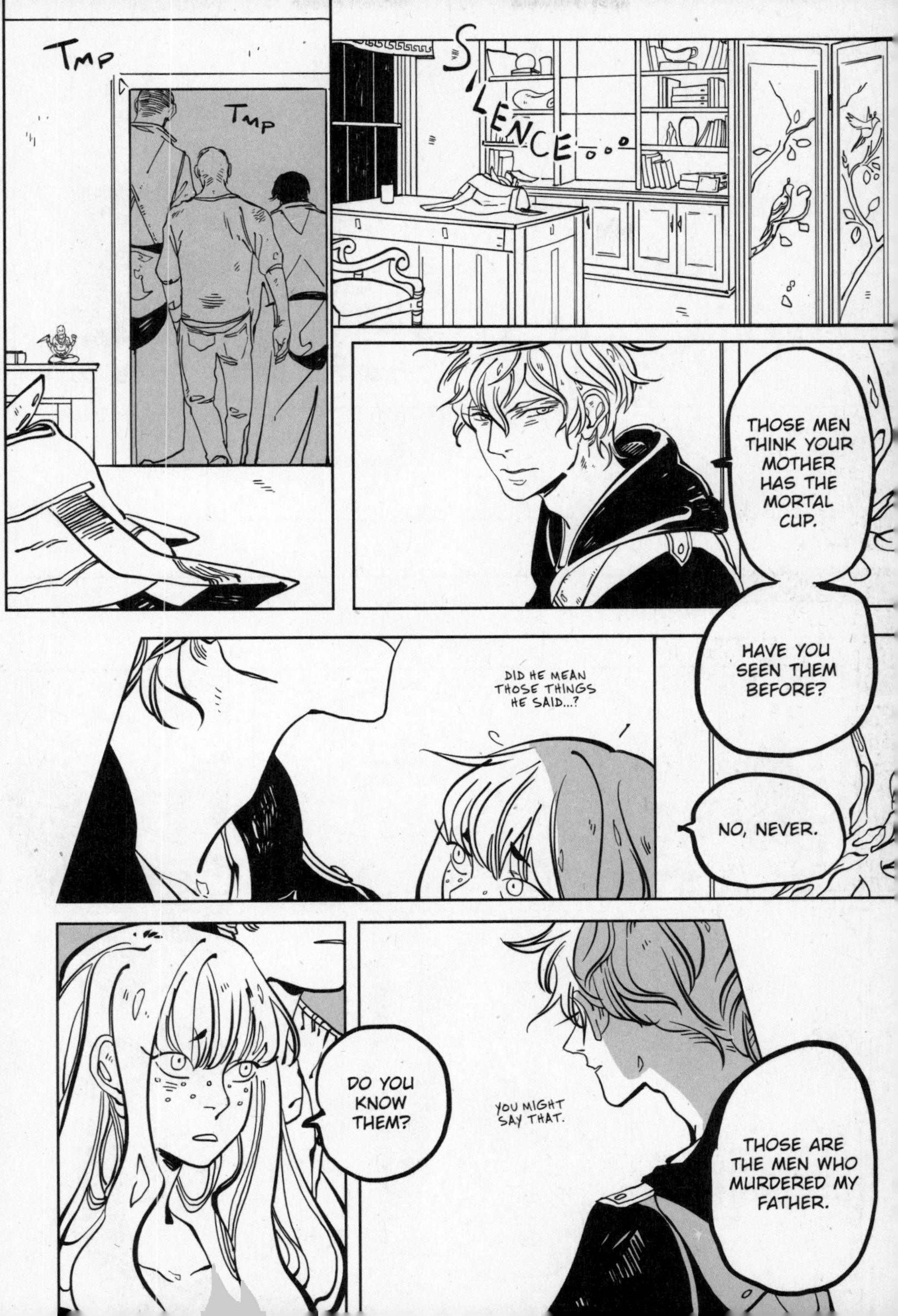
TMP
TMP
SILENCE...
THOSE MEN THINK YOUR MOTHER HAS THE MORTAL CUP.
HAVE YOU SEEN THEM BEFORE?
DID HE MEAN THOSE THINGS HE SAID...?
NO, NEVER.
DO YOU KNOW THEM?
YOU MIGHT SAY THAT.
THOSE ARE THE MEN WHO MURDERED MY FATHER.

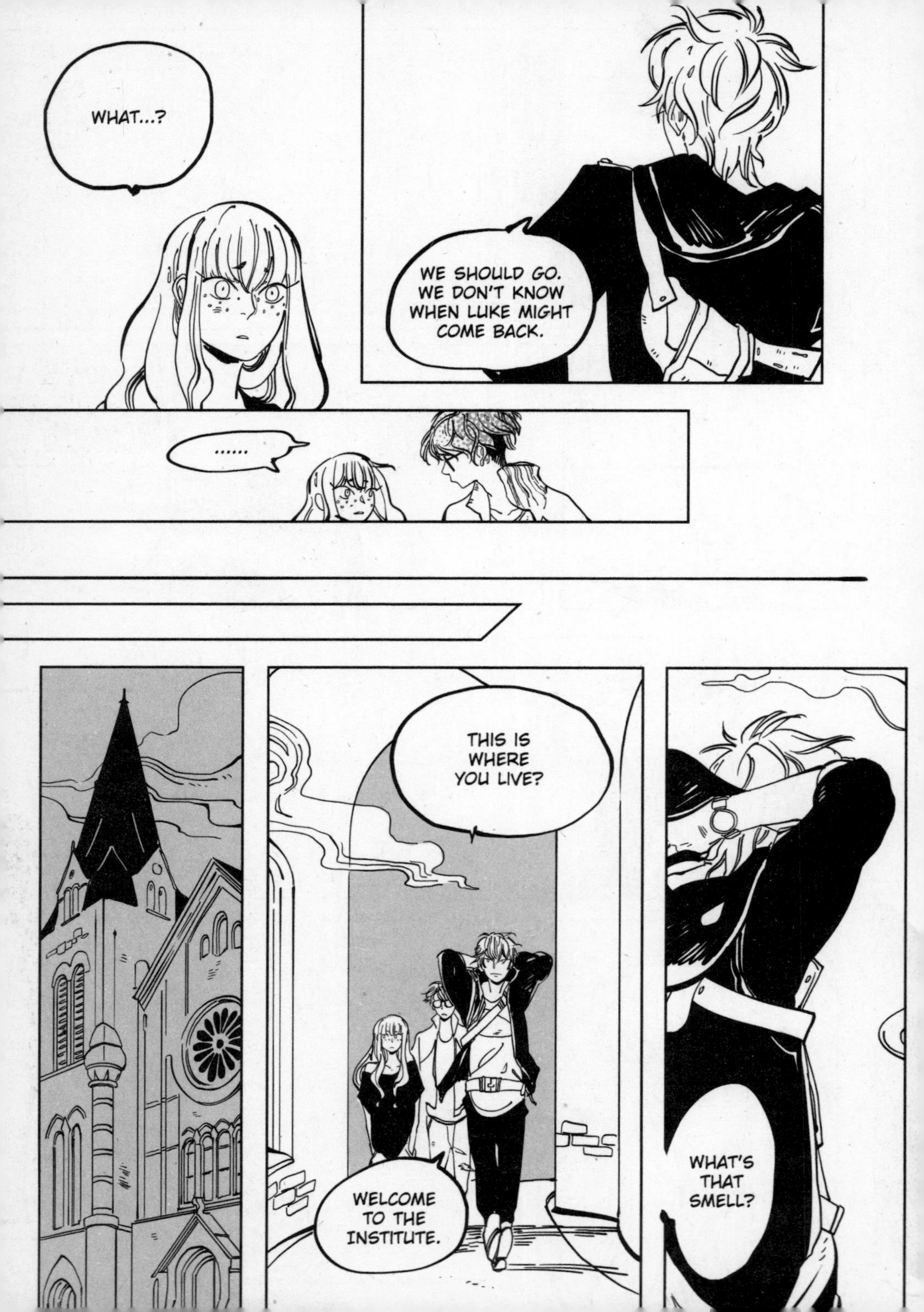
WHAT...?
WE SHOULD GO. WE DON'T KNOW WHEN LUKE MIGHT COME BACK.
......
THIS IS WHERE YOU LIVE?
WELCOME TO THE INSTITUTE.
WHAT'S THAT SMELL?

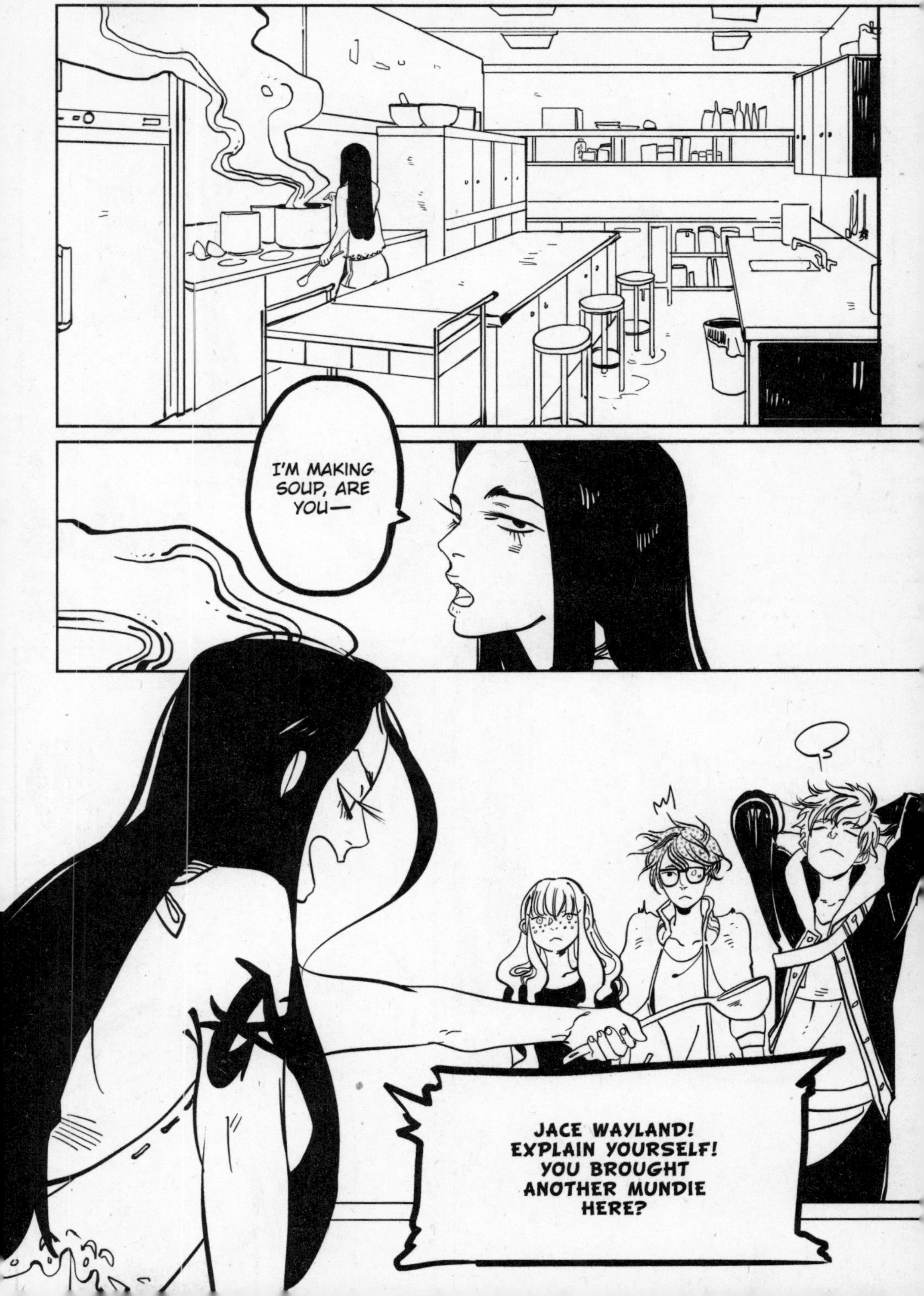
I'M MAKING SOUP, ARE YOU—
JACE WAYLAND! EXPLAIN YOURSELF! YOU BROUGHT ANOTHER MUNDIE HERE?

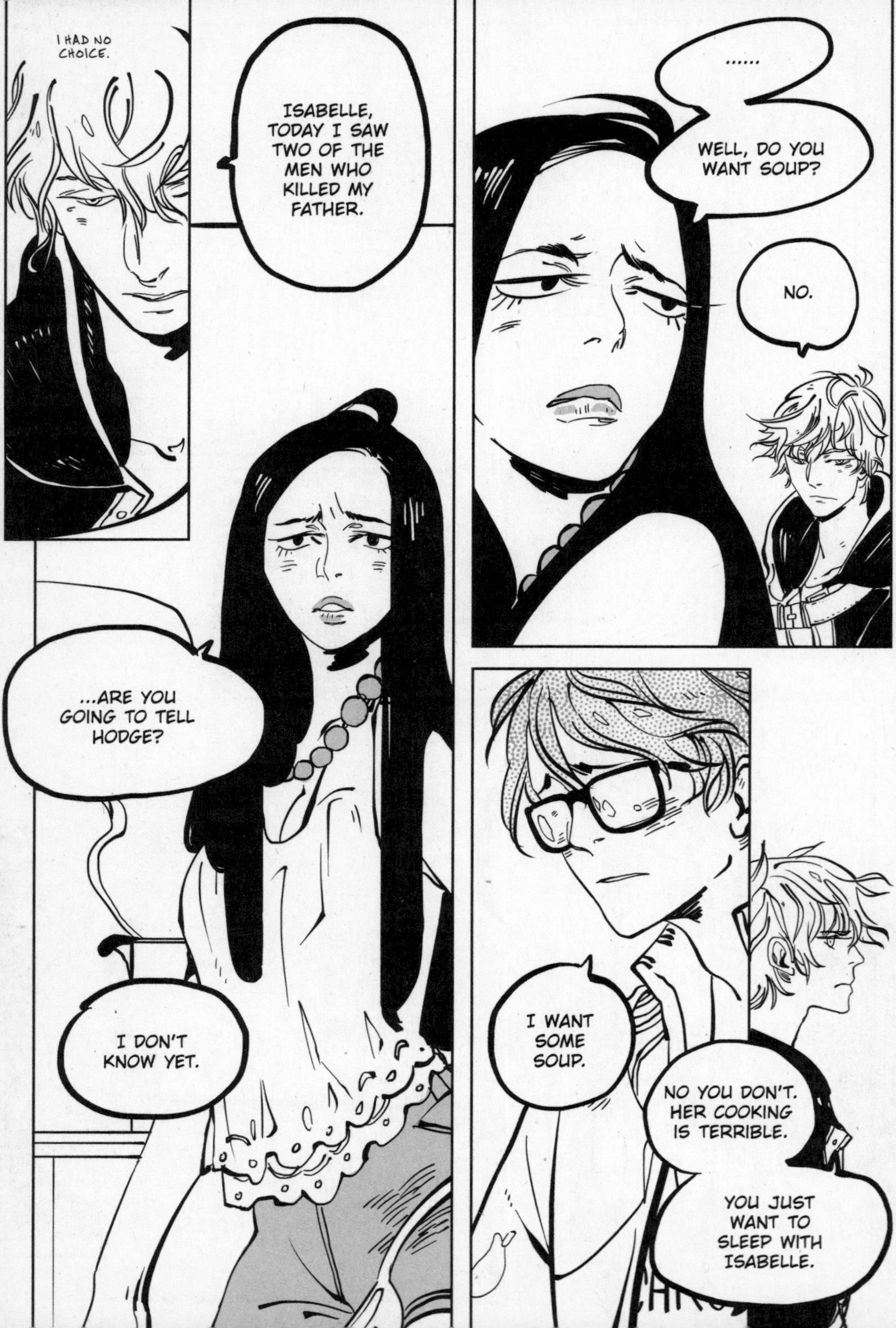

I HAD NO CHOICE.
ISABELLE, TODAY I SAW TWO OF THE MEN WHO KILLED MY FATHER.
...ARE YOU GOING TO TELL HODGE?
I DON'T KNOW YET.
......
WELL, DO YOU WANT SOUP?
NO.
I WANT SOME SOUP.
NO YOU DON'T. HER COOKING IS TERRIBLE.
YOU JUST WANT TO SLEEP WITH ISABELLE.

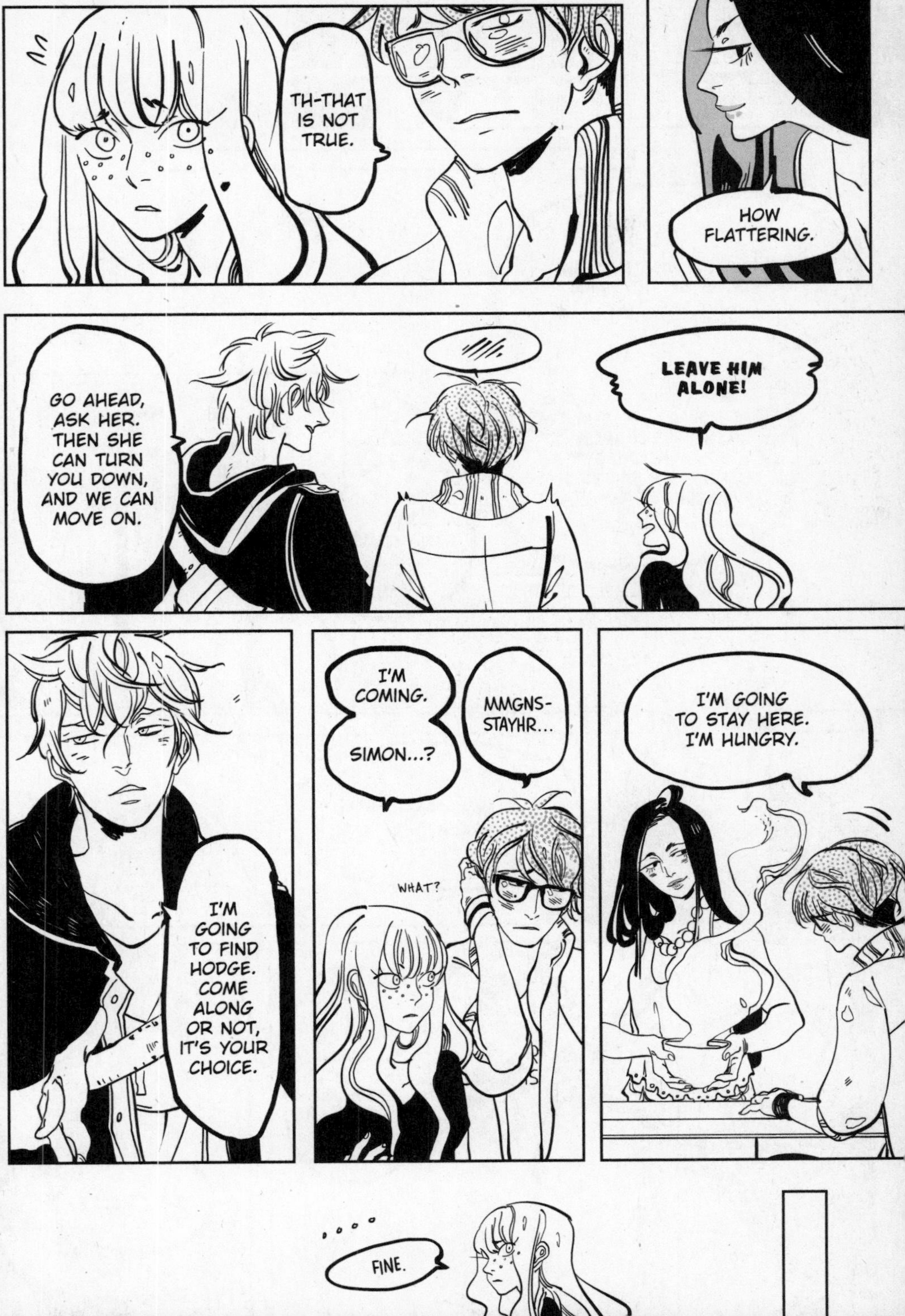
TH-THAT IS NOT TRUE.
HOW FLATTERING.
GO AHEAD, ASK HER. THEN SHE CAN TURN YOU DOWN, AND WE CAN MOVE ON.
LEAVE HIM ALONE!
I'M GOING TO FIND HODGE. COME ALONG OR NOT, IT'S YOUR CHOICE.
I'M COMING.
SIMON...?
MMGNS-STAYHR...
WHAT?
I'M GOING TO STAY HERE. I'M HUNGRY.
FINE.

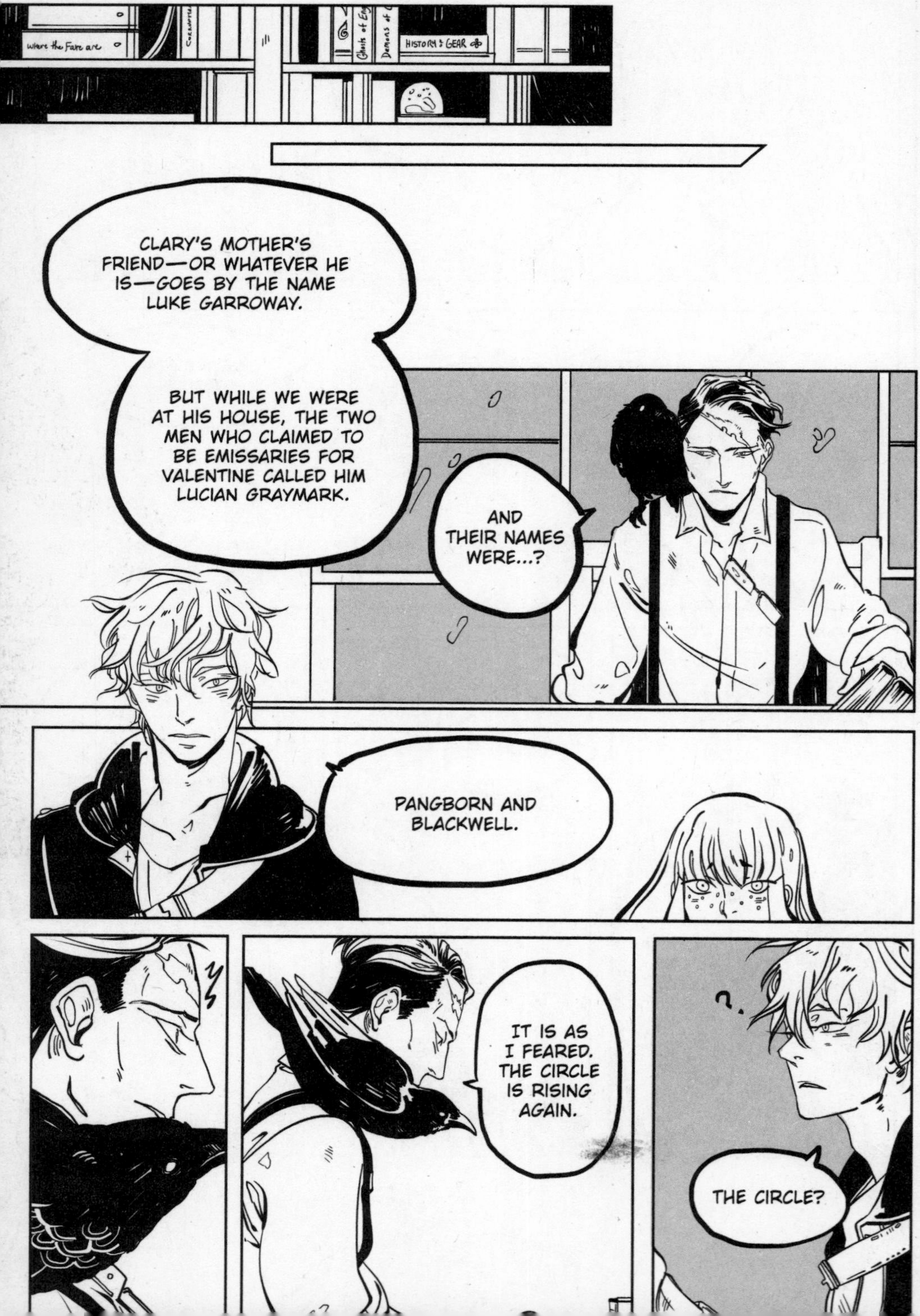
HISTORY & GEAR
CLARY'S MOTHER'S FRIEND—OR WHATEVER HE IS—GOES BY THE NAME LUKE GARROWAY.
BUT WHILE WE WERE AT HIS HOUSE, THE TWO MEN WHO CLAIMED TO BE EMISSARIES FOR VALENTINE CALLED HIM LUCIAN GRAYMARK.
AND THEIR NAMES WERE...?
PANGBORN AND BLACKWELL.
IT IS AS I FEARED. THE CIRCLE IS RISING AGAIN.
THE CIRCLE?

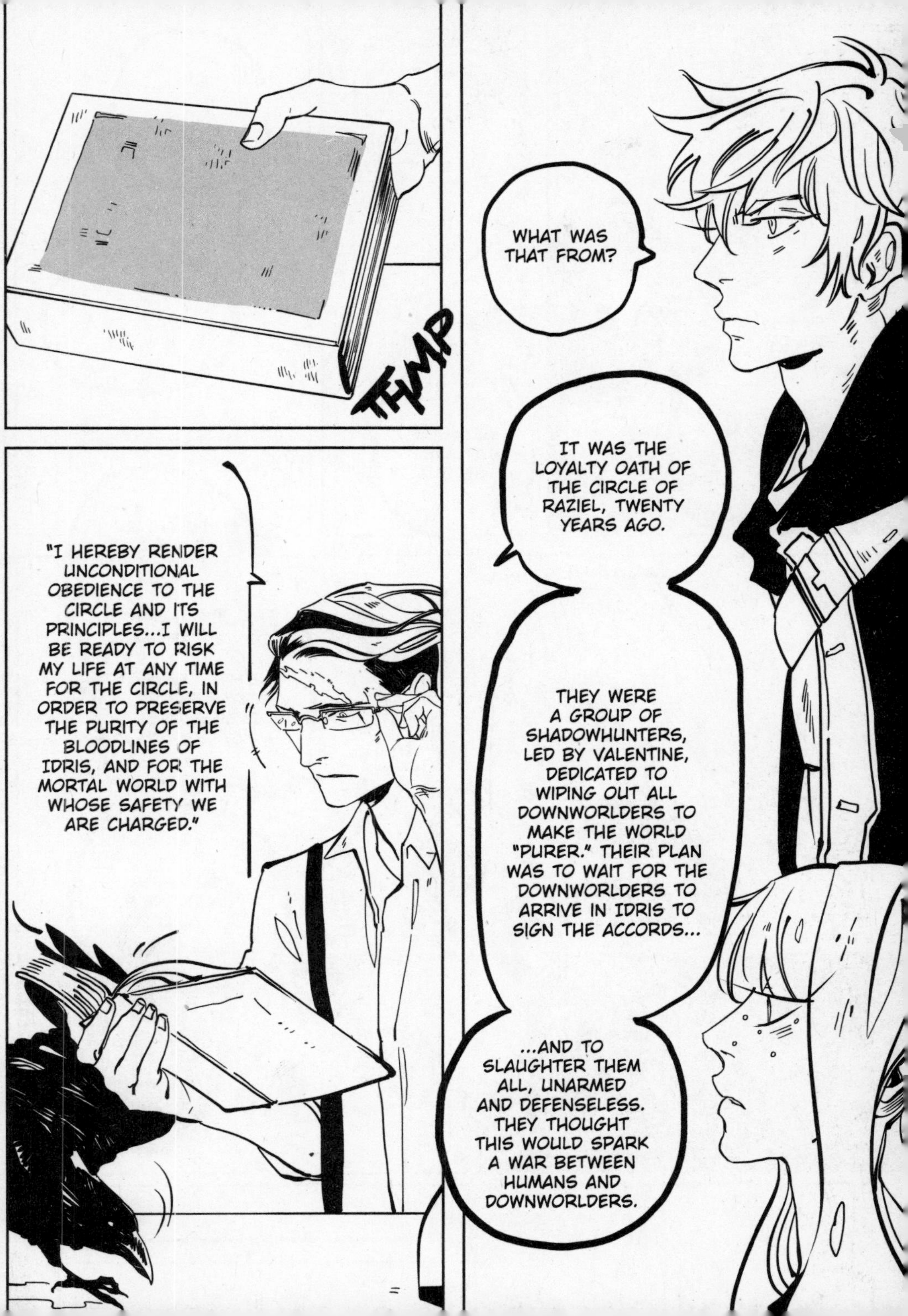
THMP
"I HEREBY RENDER UNCONDITIONAL OBEDIENCE TO THE CIRCLE AND ITS PRINCIPLES...I WILL BE READY TO RISK MY LIFE AT ANY TIME FOR THE CIRCLE, IN ORDER TO PRESERVE THE PURITY OF THE BLOODLINES OF IDRIS, AND FOR THE MORTAL WORLD WITH WHOSE SAFETY WE ARE CHARGED."
WHAT WAS THAT FROM?
IT WAS THE LOYALTY OATH OF THE CIRCLE OF RAZIEL, TWENTY YEARS AGO.
THEY WERE A GROUP OF SHADOWHUNTERS, LED BY VALENTINE, DEDICATED TO WIPING OUT ALL DOWNWORLDERS TO MAKE THE WORLD "PURER." THEIR PLAN WAS TO WAIT FOR THE DOWNWORLDERS TO ARRIVE IN IDRIS TO SIGN THE ACCORDS...
...AND TO SLAUGHTER THEM ALL, UNARMED AND DEFENSELESS. THEY THOUGHT THIS WOULD SPARK A WAR BETWEEN HUMANS AND DOWNWORLDERS.

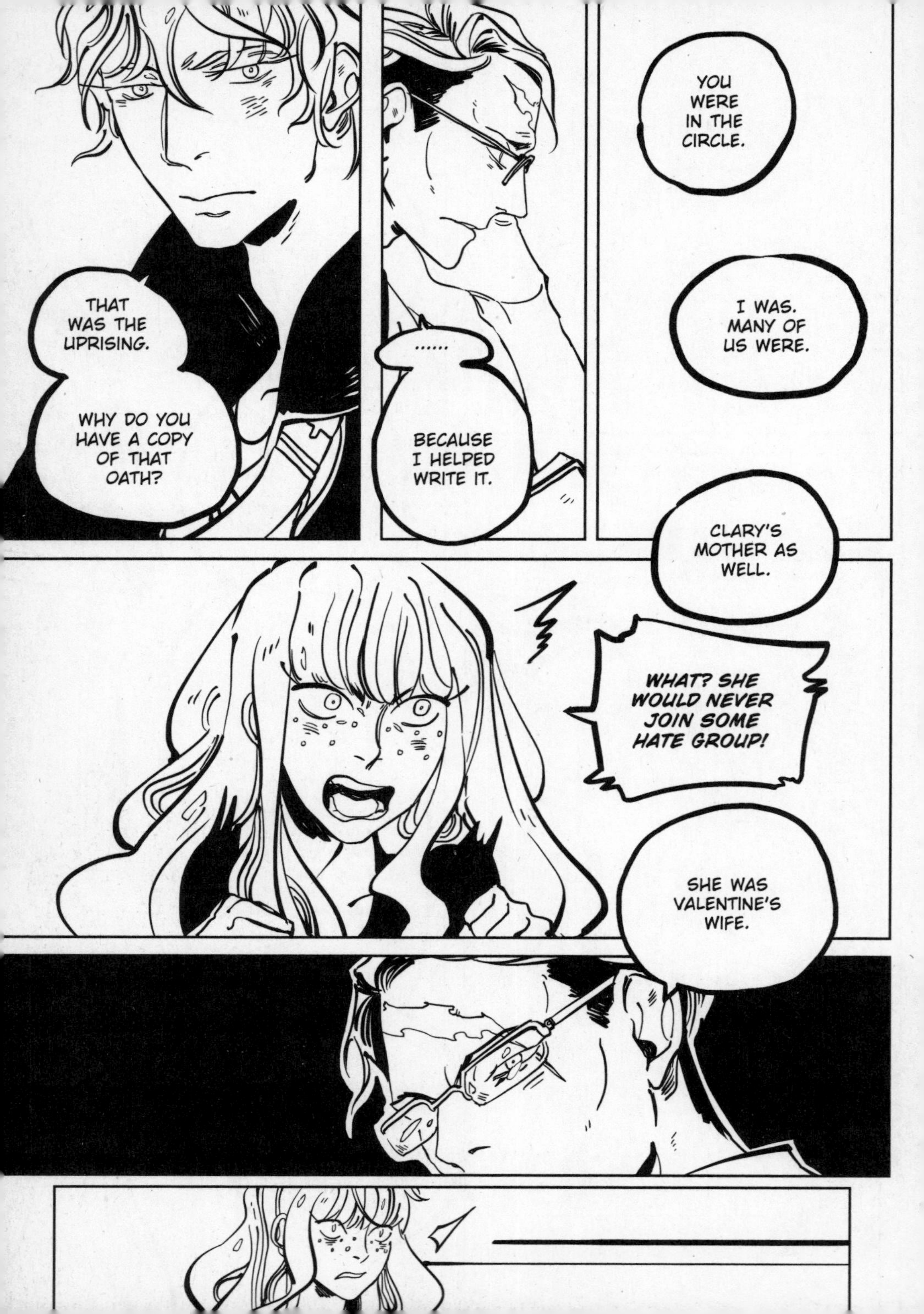
THAT WAS THE UPRISING.
WHY DO YOU HAVE A COPY OF THAT OATH?
......
BECAUSE I HELPED WRITE IT.
YOU WERE IN THE CIRCLE.
I WAS. MANY OF US WERE.
CLARY'S MOTHER AS WELL.
WHAT? SHE WOULD NEVER JOIN SOME HATE GROUP!
SHE WAS VALENTINE'S WIFE.

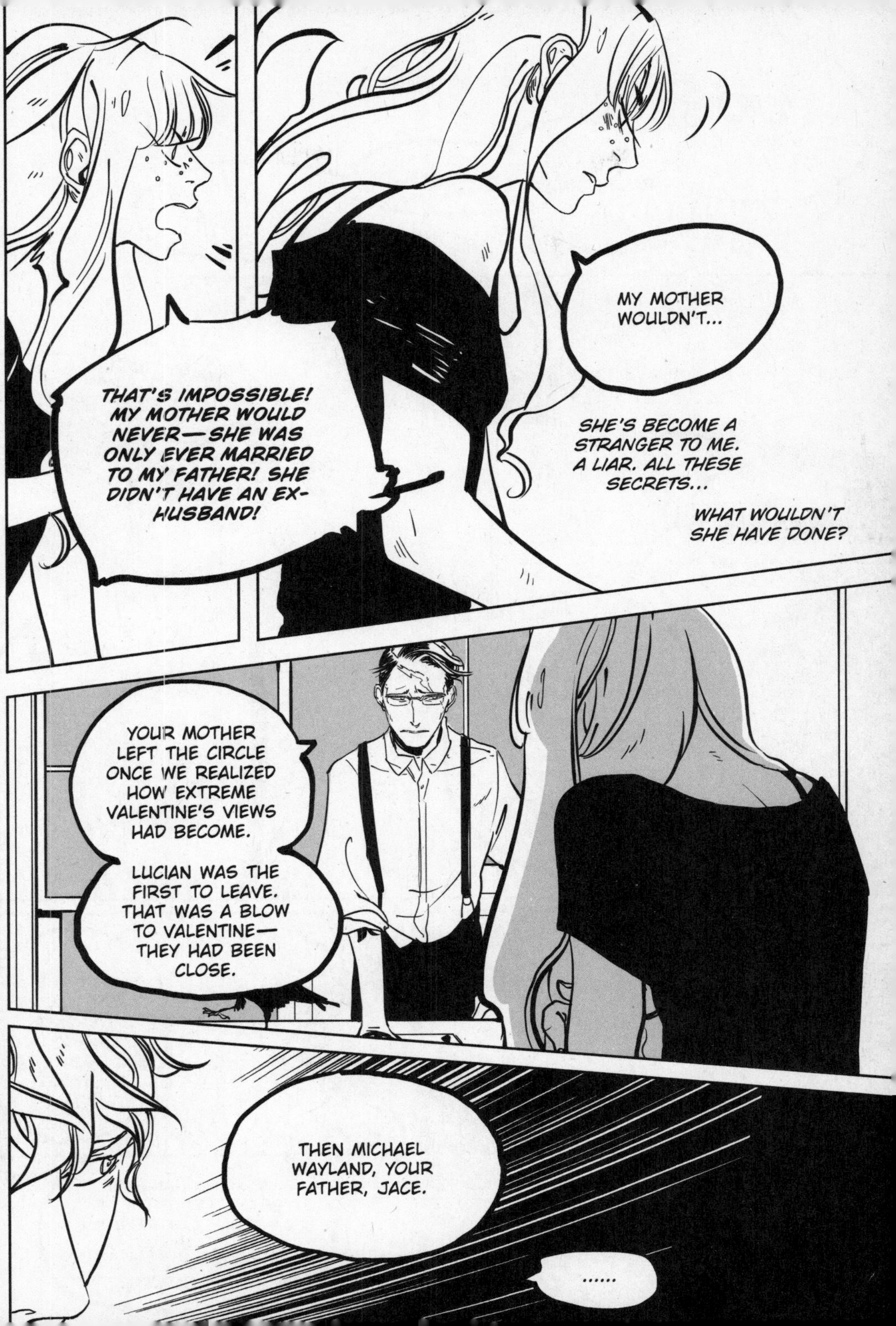
THAT'S IMPOSSIBLE! MY MOTHER WOULD NEVER—SHE WAS ONLY EVER MARRIED TO MY FATHER! SHE DIDN'T HAVE AN EX-HUSBAND!
MY MOTHER WOULDN'T...
SHE'S BECOME A STRANGER TO ME. A LIAR. ALL THESE SECRETS...
WHAT WOULDN'T SHE HAVE DONE?
YOUR MOTHER LEFT THE CIRCLE ONCE WE REALIZED HOW EXTREME VALENTINE'S VIEWS HAD BECOME.
LUCIAN WAS THE FIRST TO LEAVE. THAT WAS A BLOW TO VALENTINE— THEY HAD BEEN CLOSE.
THEN MICHAEL WAYLAND, YOUR FATHER, JACE.
......

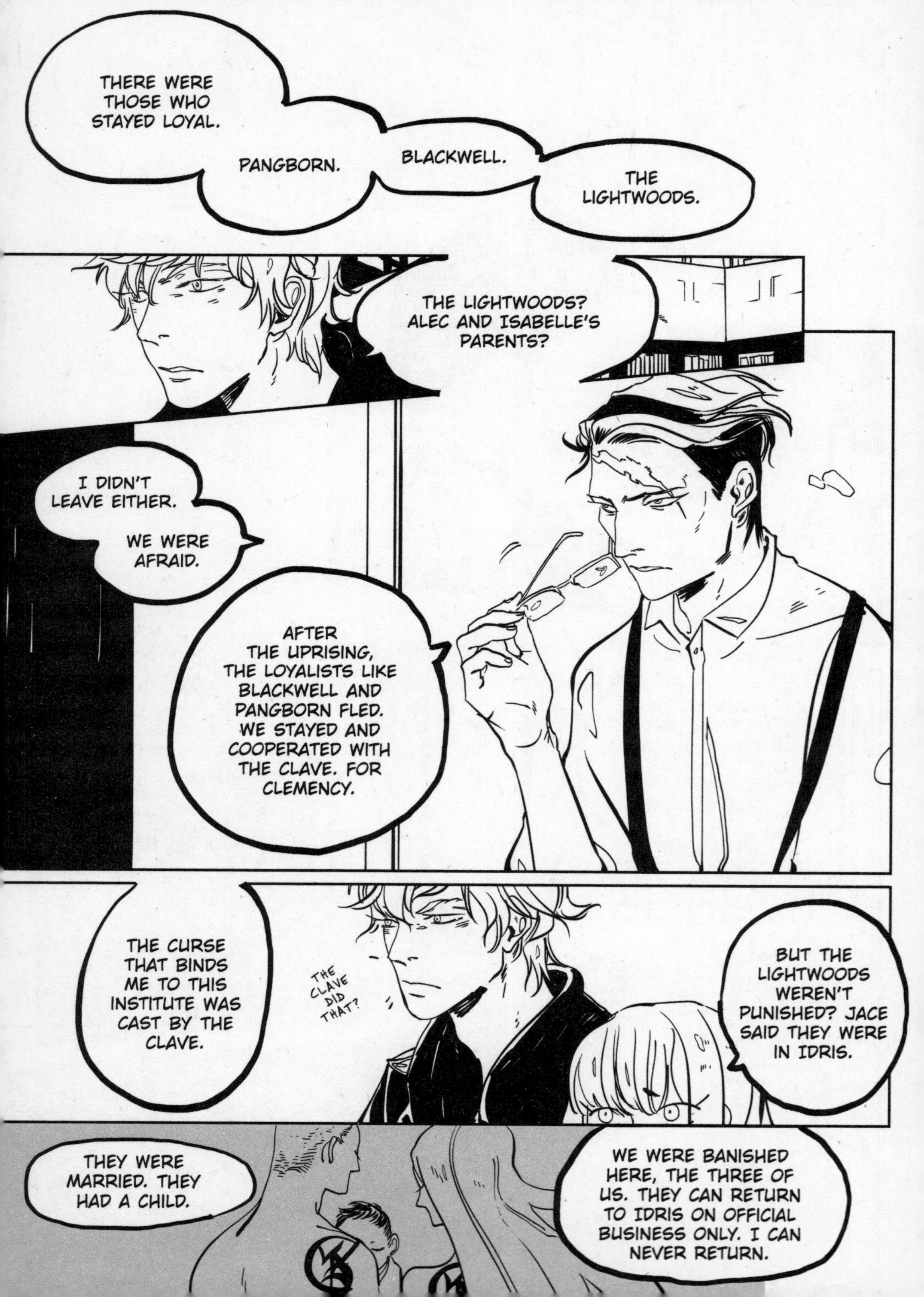
THERE WERE THOSE WHO STAYED LOYAL.
PANGBORN.
BLACKWELL.
THE LIGHTWOODS.
THE LIGHTWOODS? ALEC AND ISABELLE'S PARENTS?
I DIDN'T LEAVE EITHER.
WE WERE AFRAID.
AFTER THE UPRISING, THE LOYALISTS LIKE BLACKWELL AND PANGBORN FLED. WE STAYED AND COOPERATED WITH THE CLAVE. FOR CLEMENCY.
THE CURSE THAT BINDS ME TO THIS INSTITUTE WAS CAST BY THE CLAVE.
THE CLAVE DID THAT?
BUT THE LIGHTWOODS WEREN'T PUNISHED? JACE SAID THEY WERE IN IDRIS.
THEY WERE MARRIED. THEY HAD A CHILD.
WE WERE BANISHED HERE, THE THREE OF US. THEY CAN RETURN TO IDRIS ON OFFICIAL BUSINESS ONLY. I CAN NEVER RETURN.

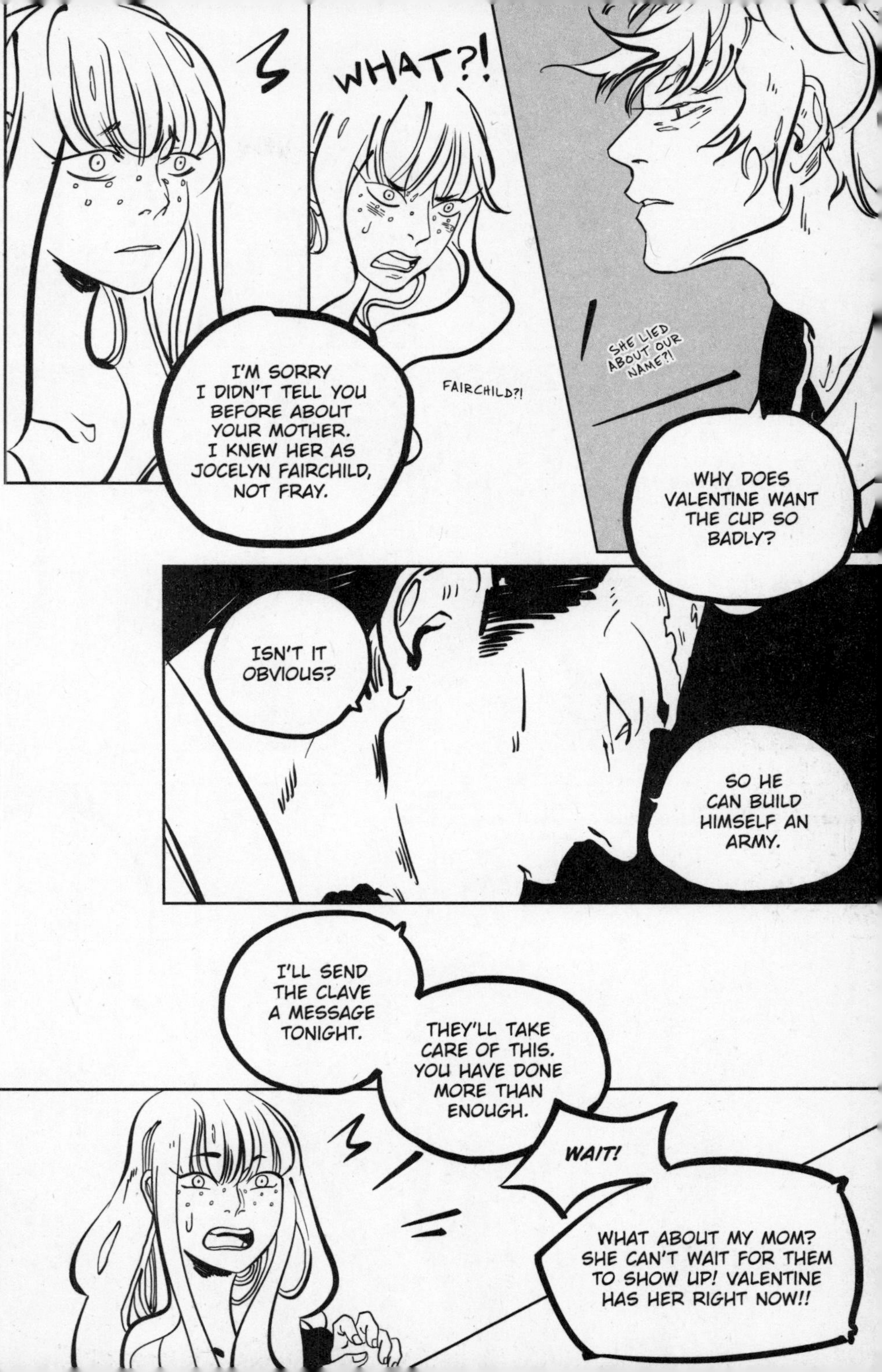
WHAT?!
I'M SORRY I DIDN'T TELL YOU BEFORE ABOUT YOUR MOTHER. I KNEW HER AS JOCELYN FAIRCHILD, NOT FRAY.
FAIRCHILD?!
SHE LIED ABOUT OUR NAME?!
WHY DOES VALENTINE WANT THE CUP SO BADLY?
ISN'T IT OBVIOUS?
SO HE CAN BUILD HIMSELF AN ARMY.
I'LL SEND THE CLAVE A MESSAGE TONIGHT.
THEY'LL TAKE CARE OF THIS. YOU HAVE DONE MORE THAN ENOUGH.
WAIT!
WHAT ABOUT MY MOM? SHE CAN'T WAIT FOR THEM TO SHOW UP! VALENTINE HAS HER RIGHT NOW!!

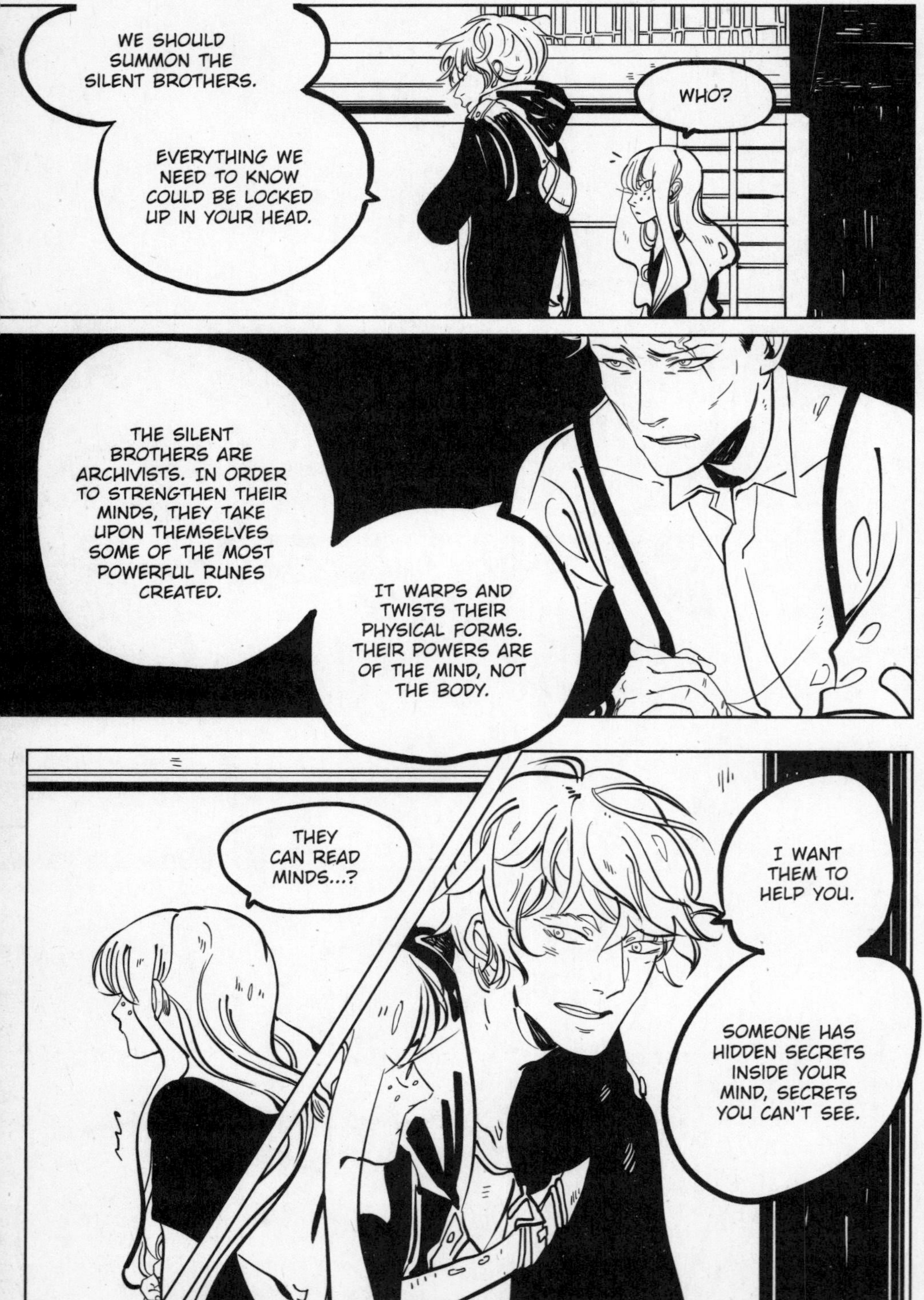
WE SHOULD SUMMON THE SILENT BROTHERS.
EVERYTHING WE NEED TO KNOW COULD BE LOCKED UP IN YOUR HEAD.
WHO?
THE SILENT BROTHERS ARE ARCHIVISTS. IN ORDER TO STRENGTHEN THEIR MINDS, THEY TAKE UPON THEMSELVES SOME OF THE MOST POWERFUL RUNES CREATED.
IT WARPS AND TWISTS THEIR PHYSICAL FORMS. THEIR POWERS ARE OF THE MIND, NOT THE BODY.
THEY CAN READ MINDS...?
I WANT THEM TO HELP YOU.
SOMEONE HAS HIDDEN SECRETS INSIDE YOUR MIND, SECRETS YOU CAN'T SEE.

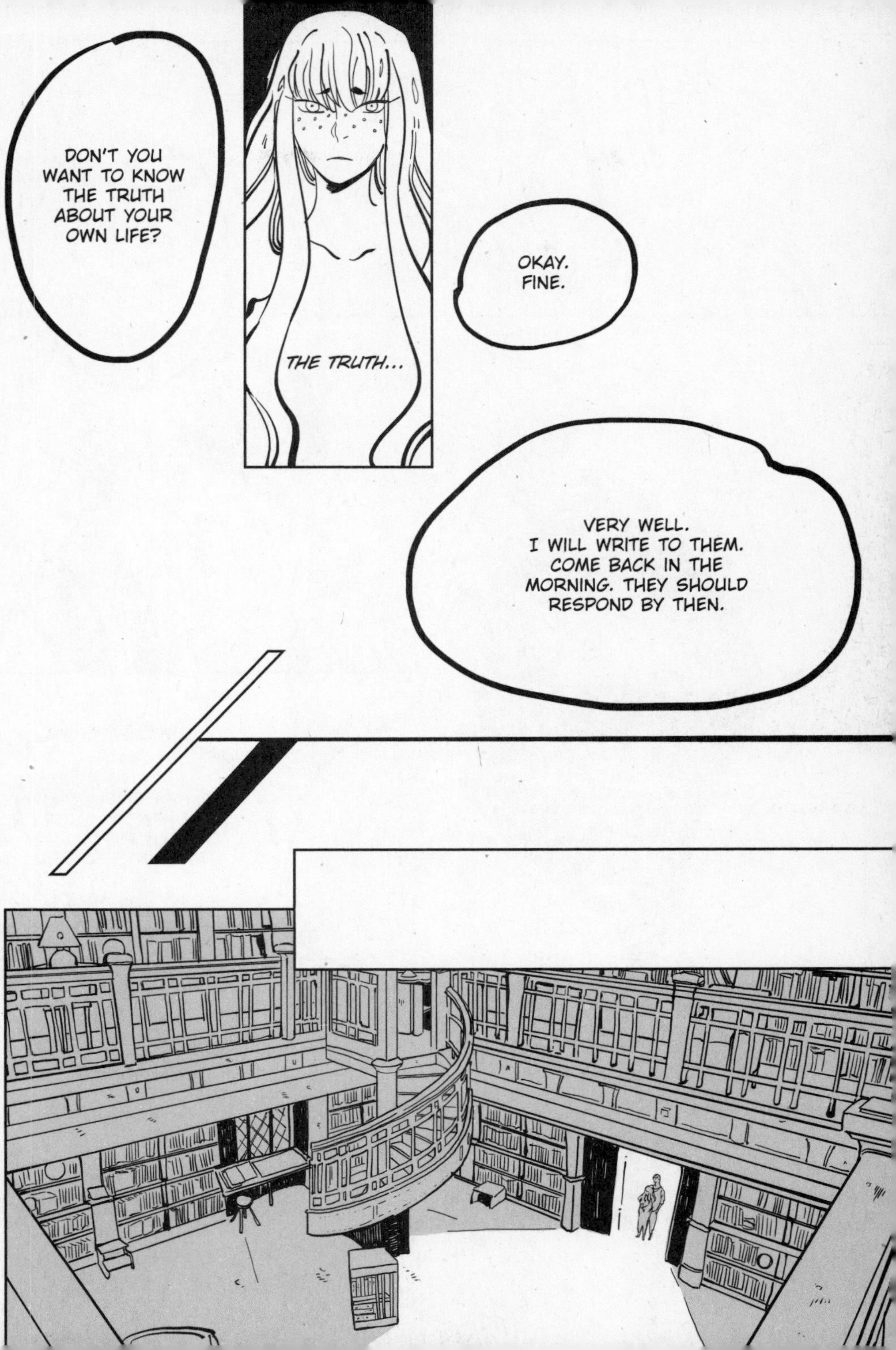
DON'T YOU WANT TO KNOW THE TRUTH ABOUT YOUR OWN LIFE?
THE TRUTH...
OKAY. FINE.
VERY WELL. I WILL WRITE TO THEM. COME BACK IN THE MORNING. THEY SHOULD RESPOND BY THEN.

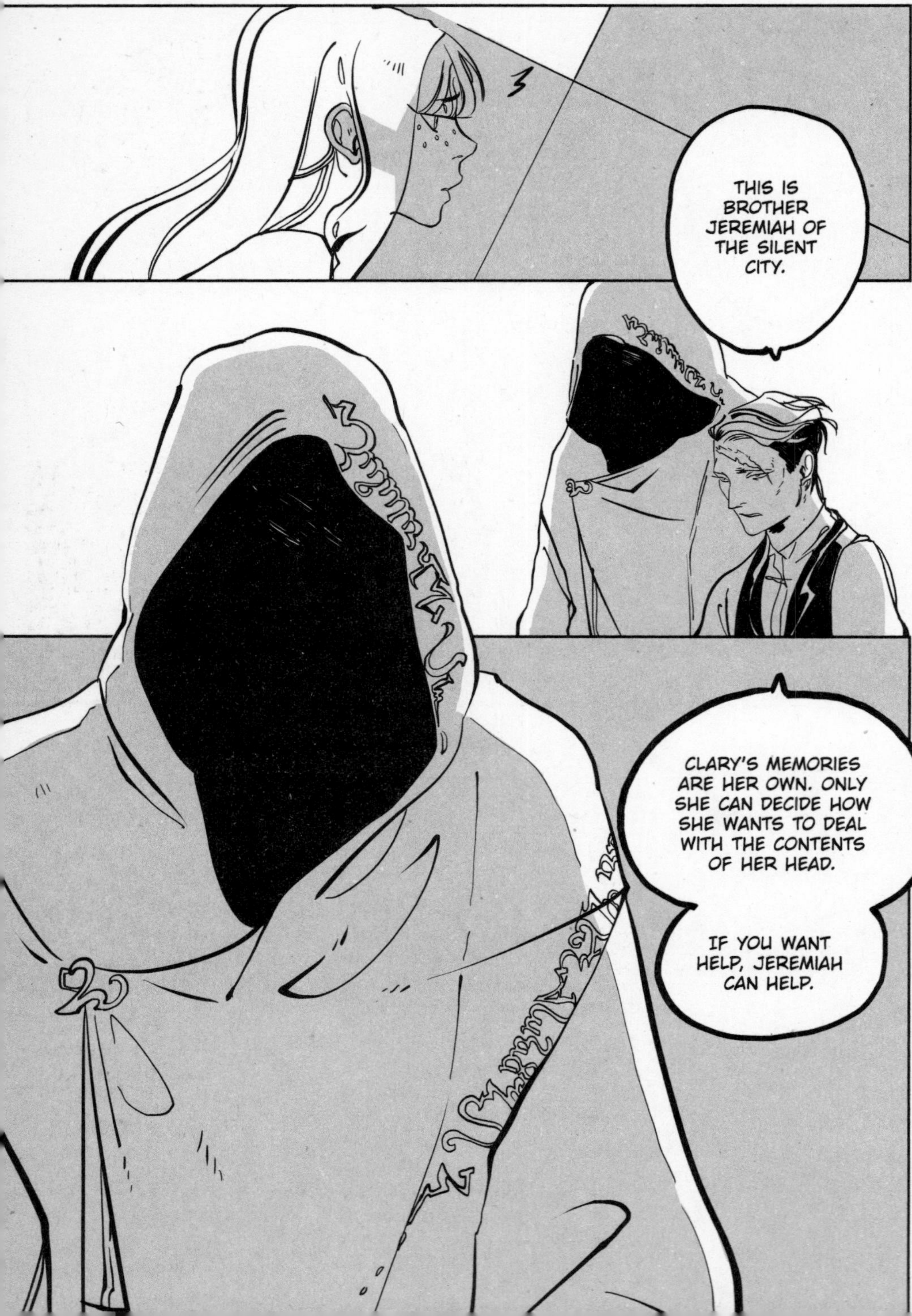
THIS IS BROTHER JEREMIAH OF THE SILENT CITY.
CLARY'S MEMORIES ARE HER OWN. ONLY SHE CAN DECIDE HOW SHE WANTS TO DEAL WITH THE CONTENTS OF HER HEAD.
IF YOU WANT HELP, JEREMIAH CAN HELP.

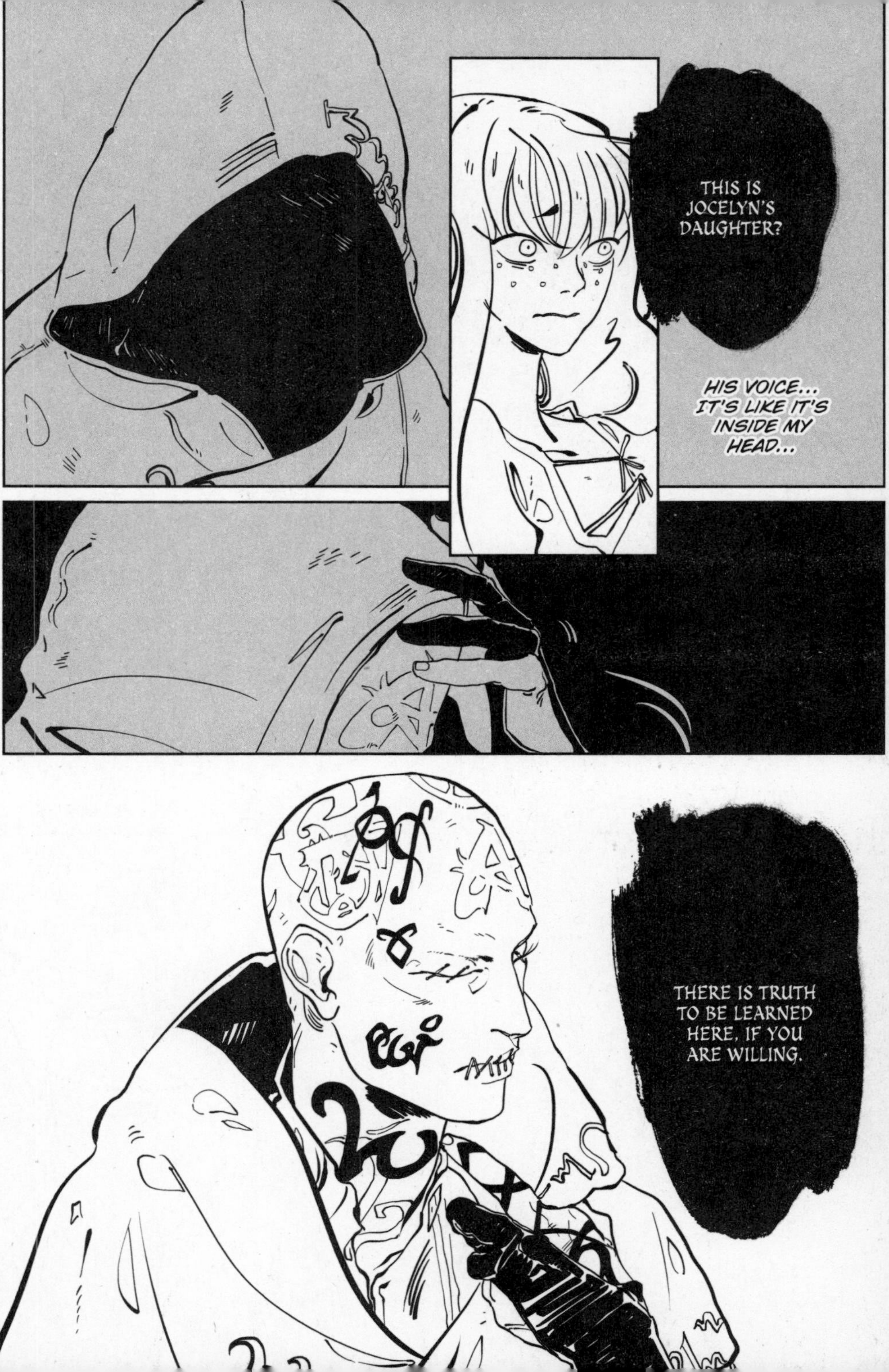
THIS IS JOCELYN'S DAUGHTER?
HIS VOICE... IT'S LIKE IT'S INSIDE MY HEAD...
THERE IS TRUTH TO BE LEARNED HERE, IF YOU ARE WILLING.

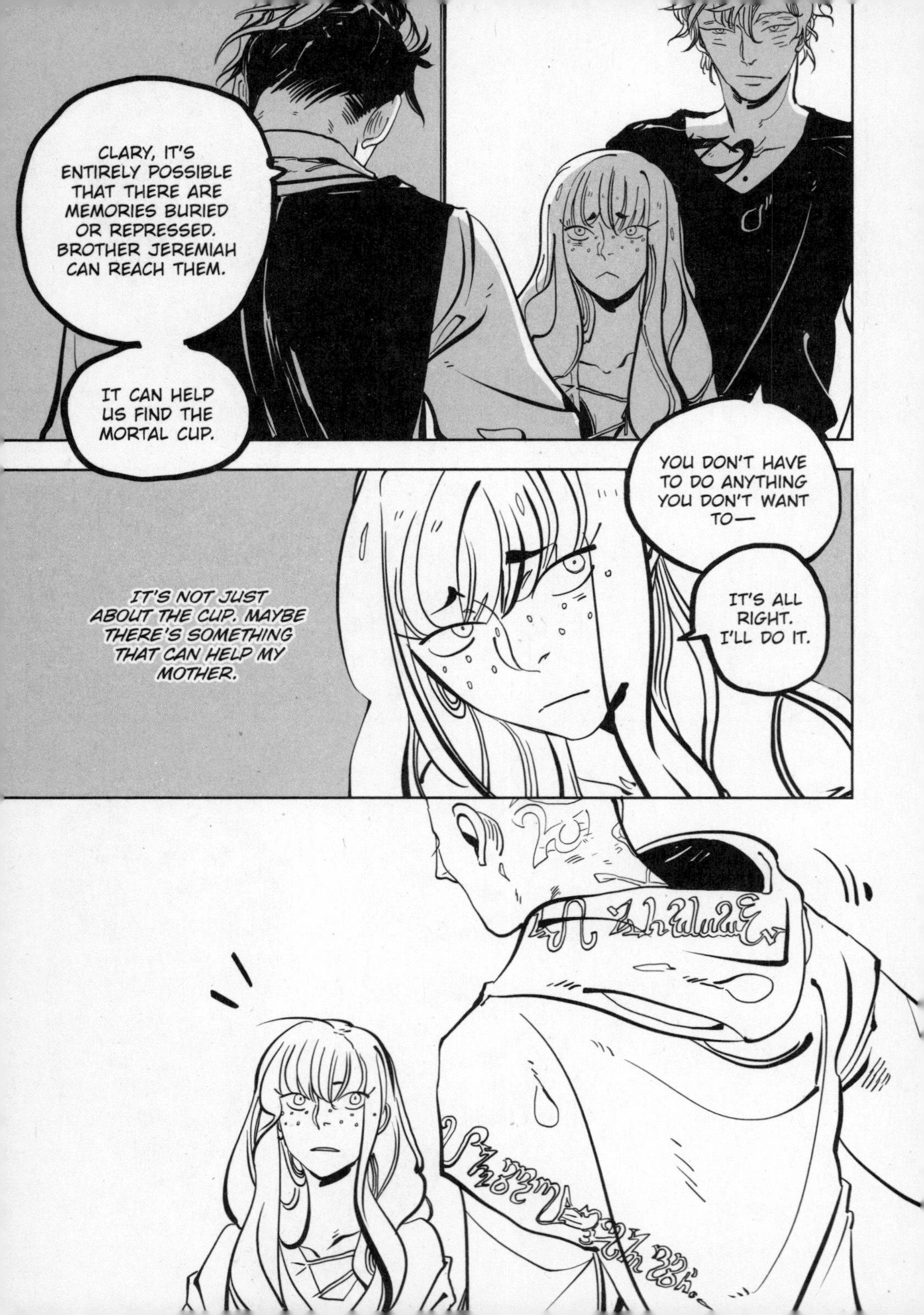
CLARY, IT'S ENTIRELY POSSIBLE THAT THERE ARE MEMORIES BURIED OR REPRESSED. BROTHER JEREMIAH CAN REACH THEM.
IT CAN HELP US FIND THE MORTAL CUP.
YOU DON'T HAVE TO DO ANYTHING YOU DON'T WANT TO—
IT'S NOT JUST ABOUT THE CUP. MAYBE THERE'S SOMETHING THAT CAN HELP MY MOTHER.
IT'S ALL RIGHT. I'LL DO IT.

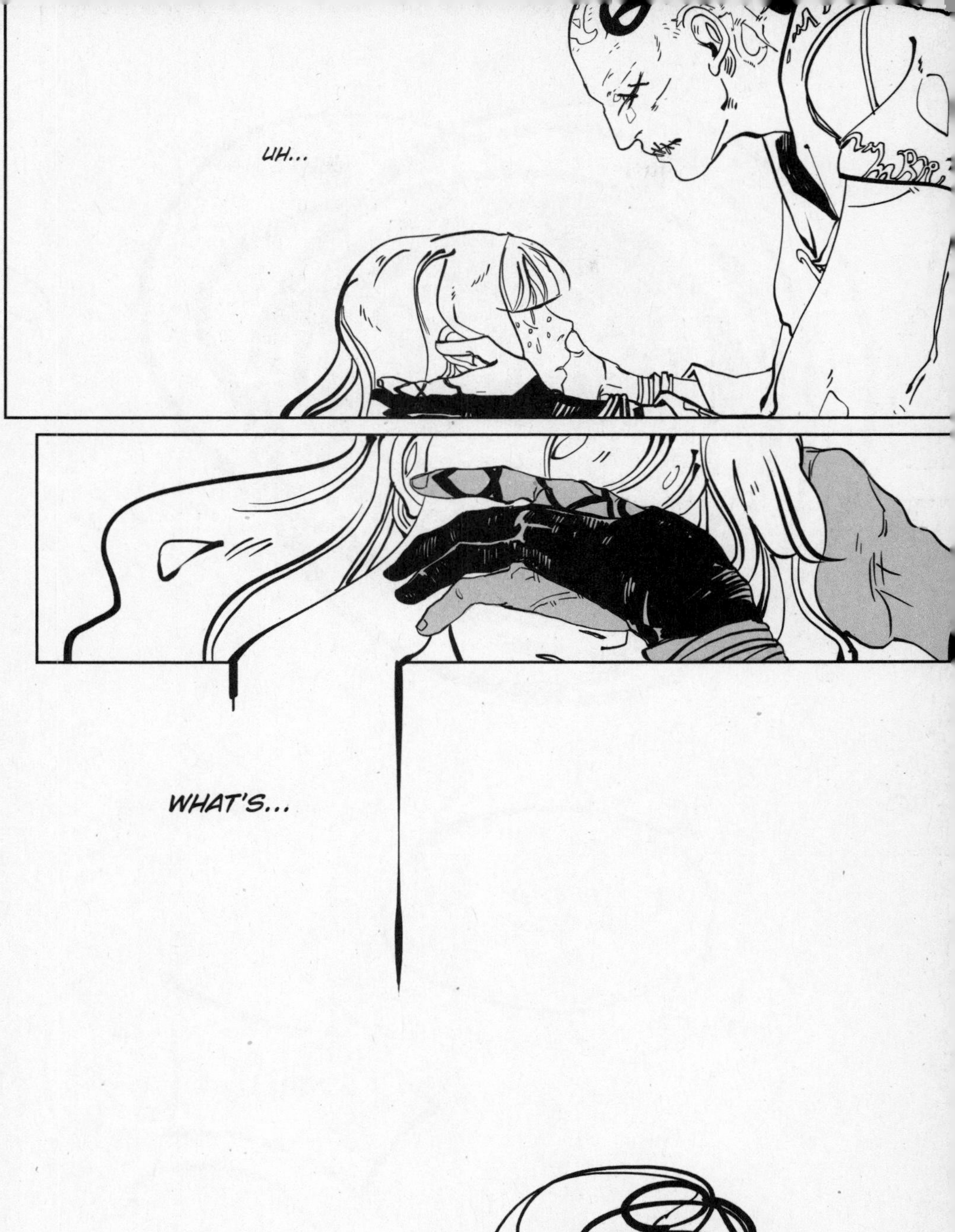
UH...
WHAT'S...

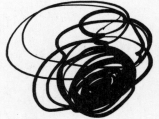

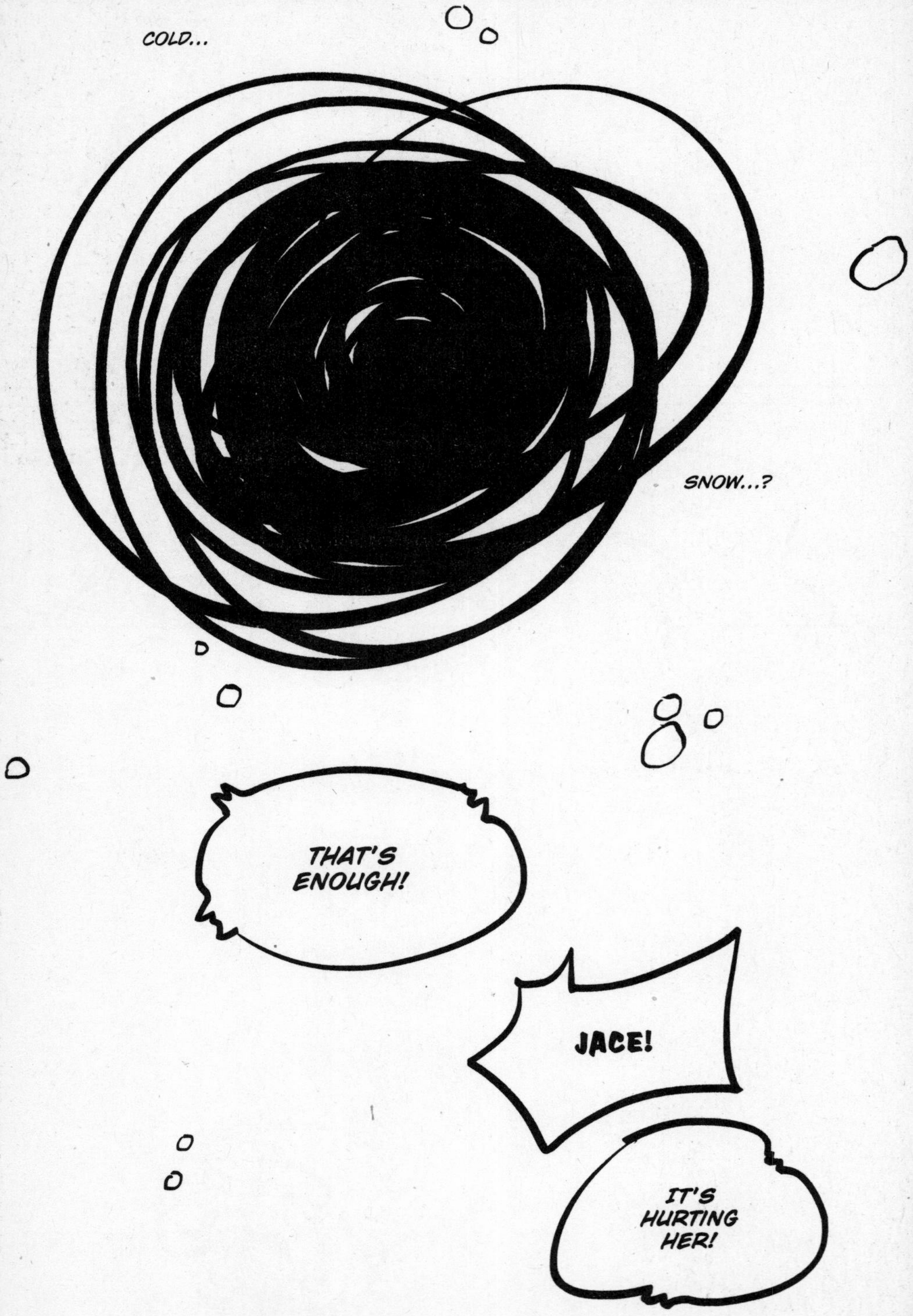
COLD...
SNOW...?
THAT'S ENOUGH!
JACE!
IT'S HURTING HER!

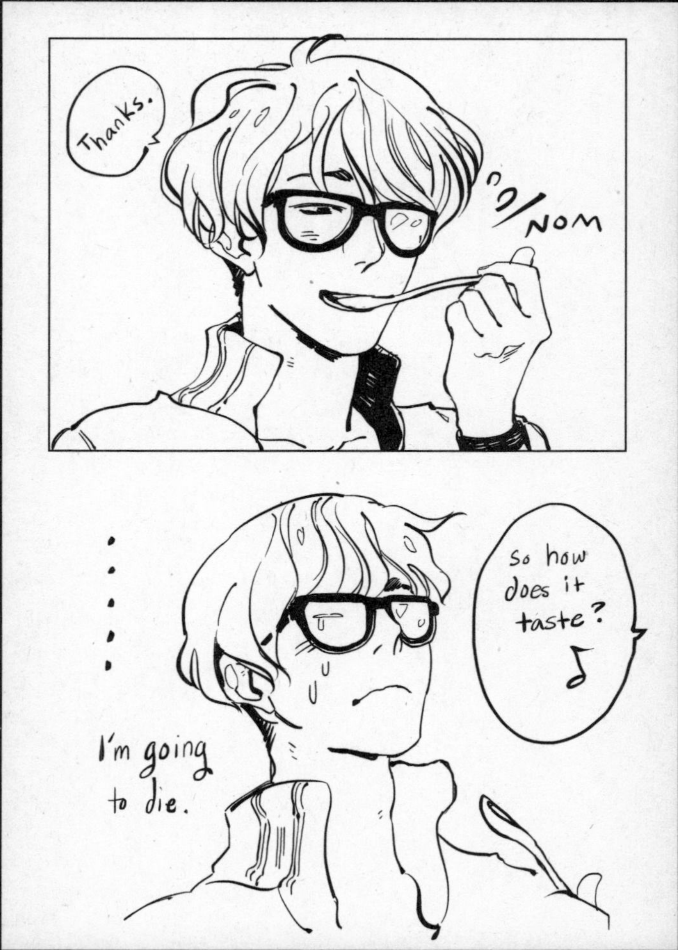
Thanks.
NOM
So how does it taste?
I'm going to die.

THE MORTAL INSTRUMENTS

THE GRAPHIC NOVEL

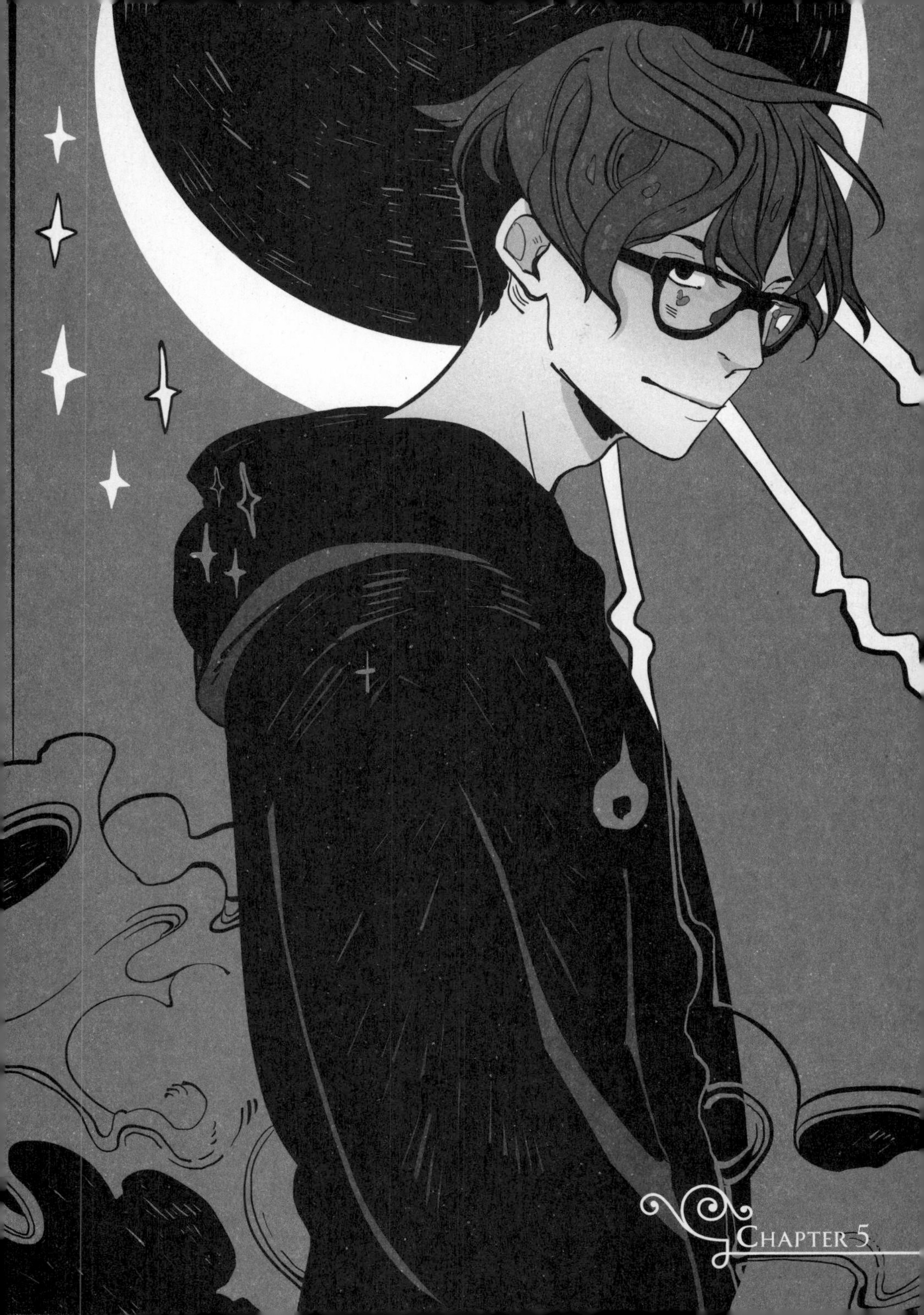
Chapter 5

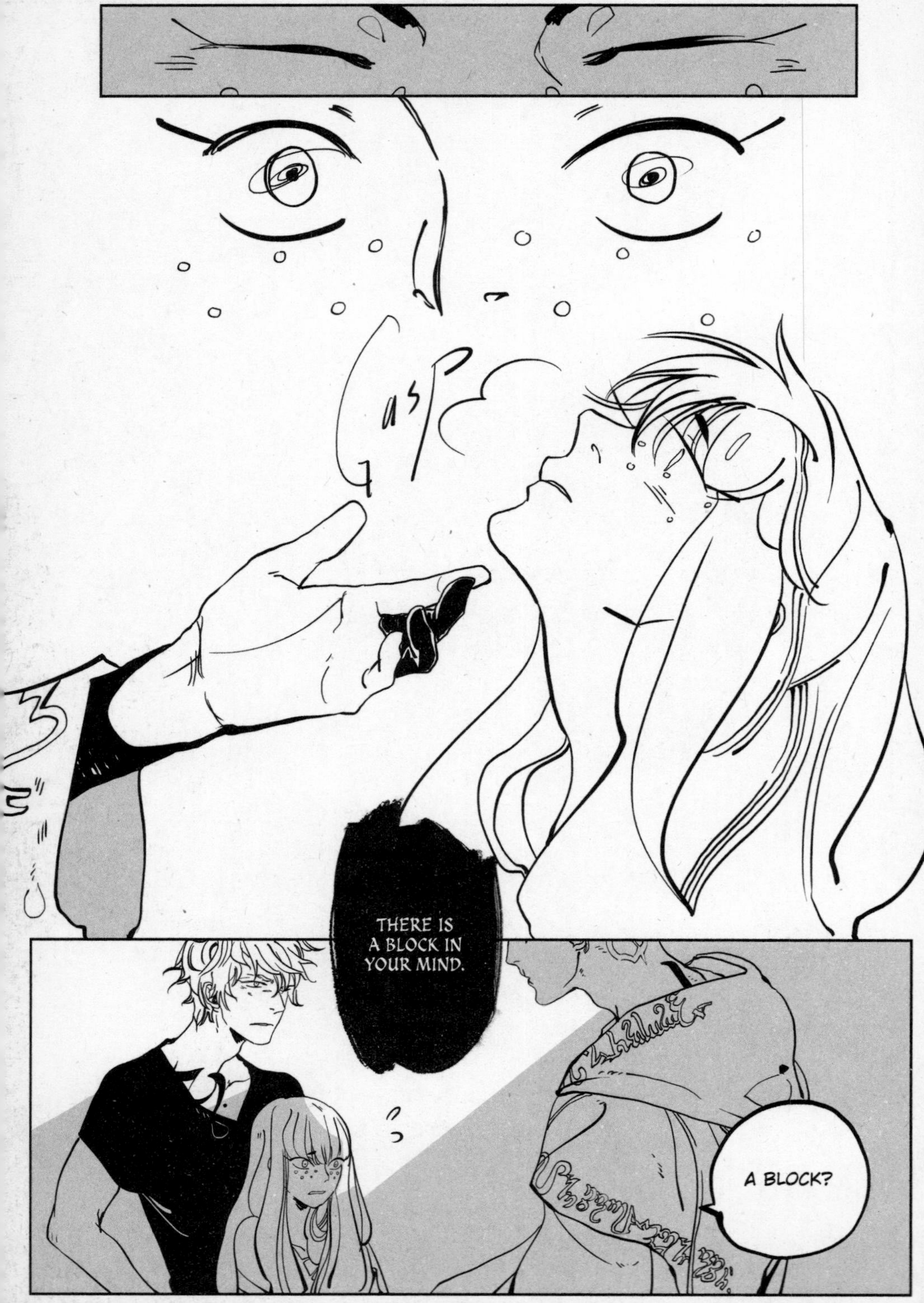
THERE IS A BLOCK IN YOUR MIND.
A BLOCK?

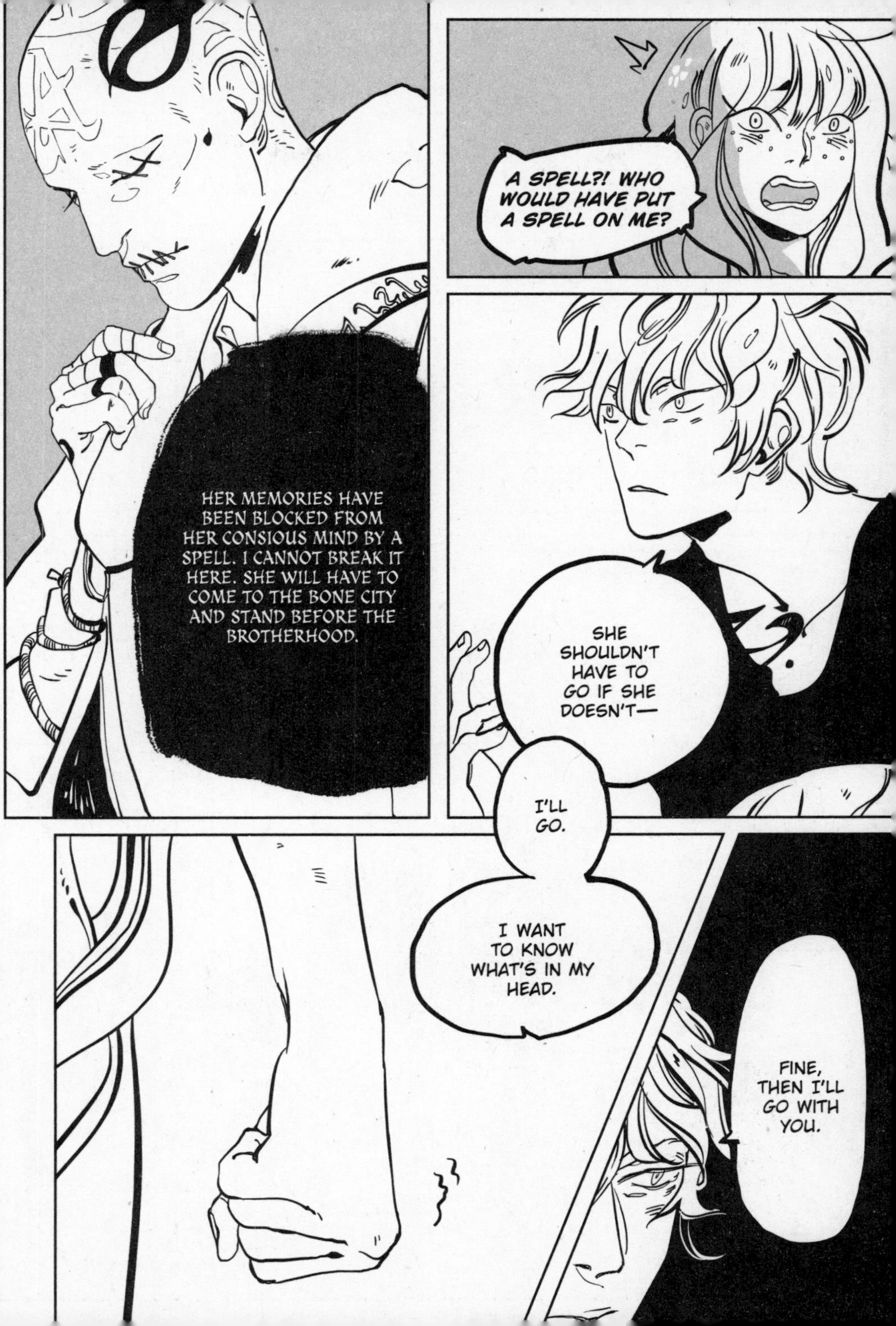
HER MEMORIES HAVE BEEN BLOCKED FROM HER CONSIOUS MIND BY A SPELL. I CANNOT BREAK IT HERE. SHE WILL HAVE TO COME TO THE BONE CITY AND STAND BEFORE THE BROTHERHOOD.
A SPELL?! WHO WOULD HAVE PUT A SPELL ON ME?
SHE SHOULDN'T HAVE TO GO IF SHE DOESN'T—
I'LL GO.
I WANT TO KNOW WHAT'S IN MY HEAD.
FINE, THEN I'LL GO WITH YOU.

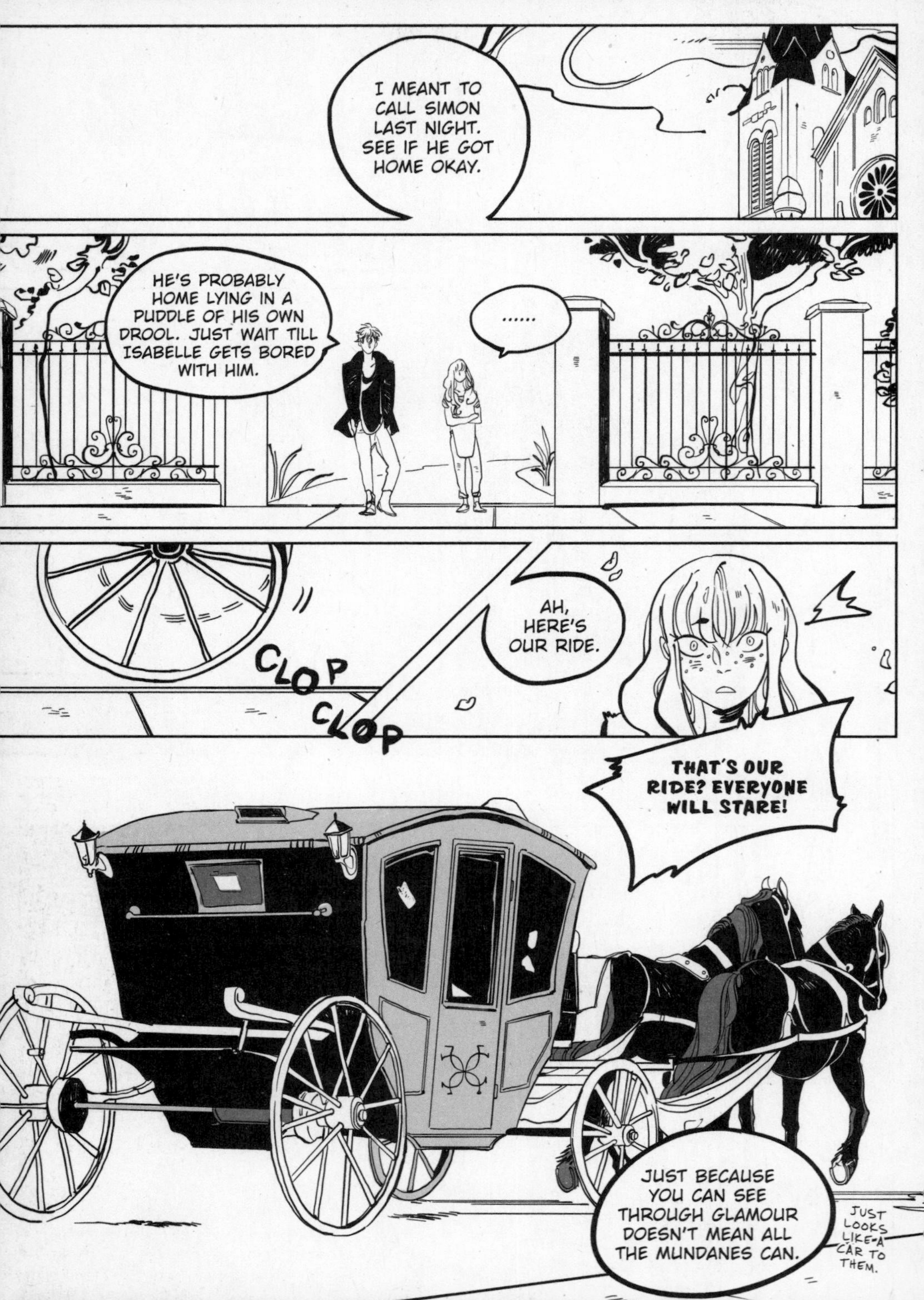
I MEANT TO CALL SIMON LAST NIGHT. SEE IF HE GOT HOME OKAY.
HE'S PROBABLY HOME LYING IN A PUDDLE OF HIS OWN DROOL. JUST WAIT TILL ISABELLE GETS BORED WITH HIM.
......
CLOP CLOP
AH, HERE'S OUR RIDE.
THAT'S OUR RIDE? EVERYONE WILL STARE!
JUST BECAUSE YOU CAN SEE THROUGH GLAMOUR DOESN'T MEAN ALL THE MUNDANES CAN.
JUST LOOKS LIKE A CAR TO THEM.

Huff

A PERSONAL ESCORT TO THE BONE CITY IS NOTHING TO TURN YOUR NOSE UP AT.

RELAX.

ENJOY THE NEW CARRIAGE SMELL!

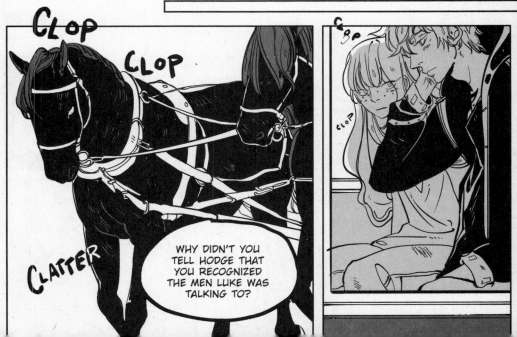

CLOP

CLOP

CLOP

CLATTER

WHY DIDN'T YOU TELL HODGE THAT YOU RECOGNIZED THE MEN LUKE WAS TALKING TO?

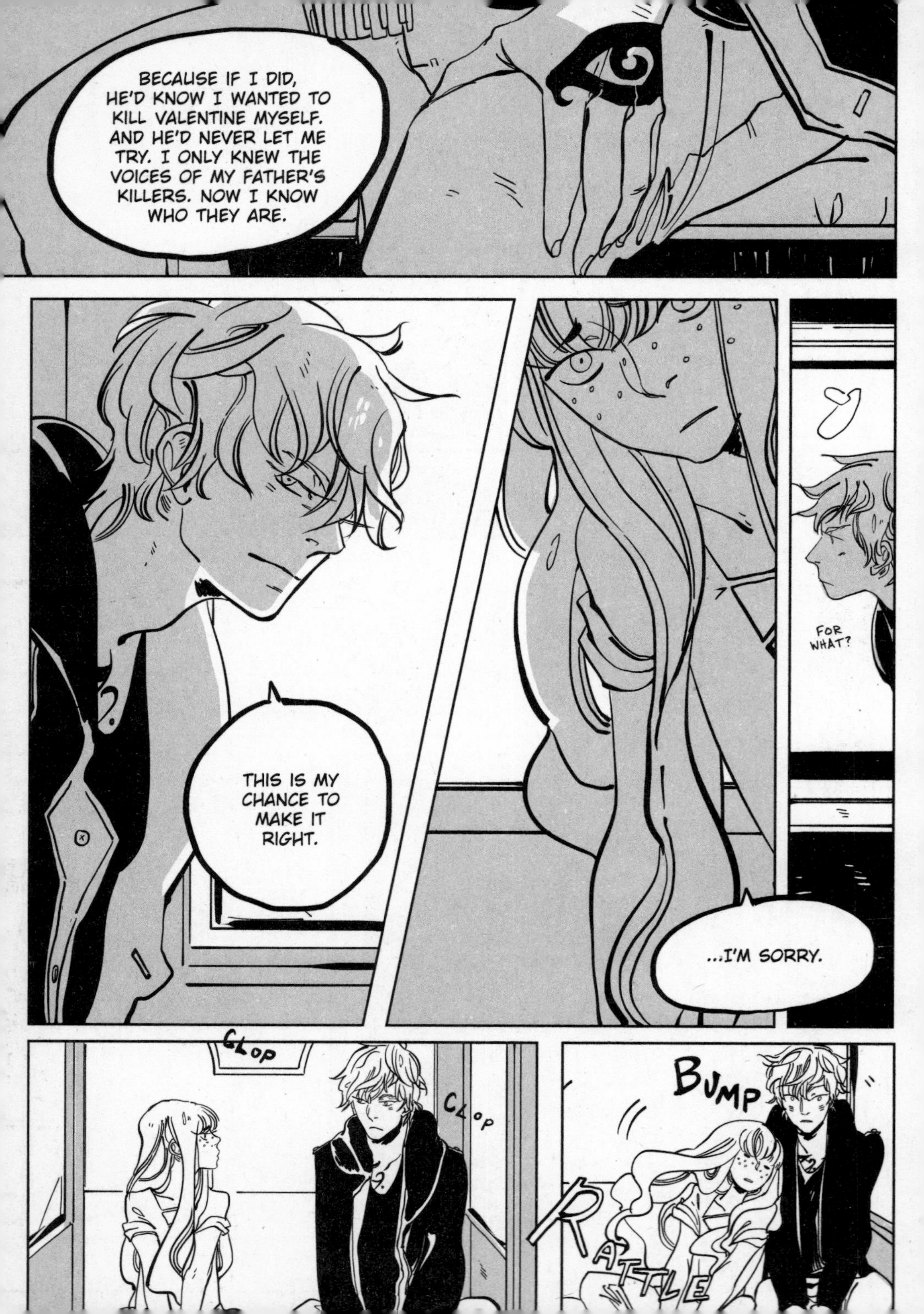
BECAUSE IF I DID, HE'D KNOW I WANTED TO KILL VALENTINE MYSELF. AND HE'D NEVER LET ME TRY. I ONLY KNEW THE VOICES OF MY FATHER'S KILLERS. NOW I KNOW WHO THEY ARE.
THIS IS MY CHANCE TO MAKE IT RIGHT.
...I'M SORRY.
FOR WHAT?
CLOP
CLOP
BUMP
RATTLE

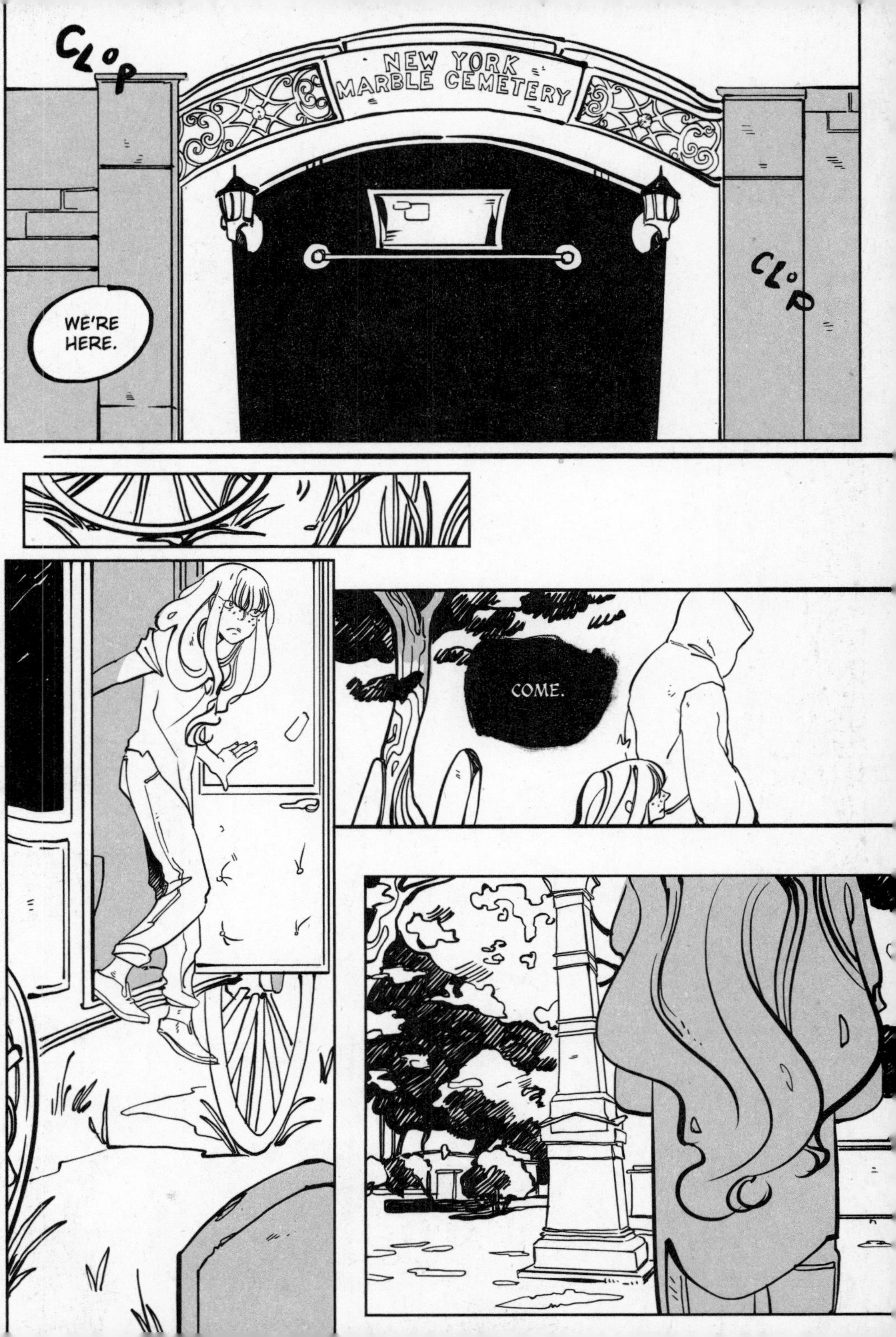
CLOP
NEW YORK MARBLE CEMETERY
WE'RE HERE.
CLOP
COME.

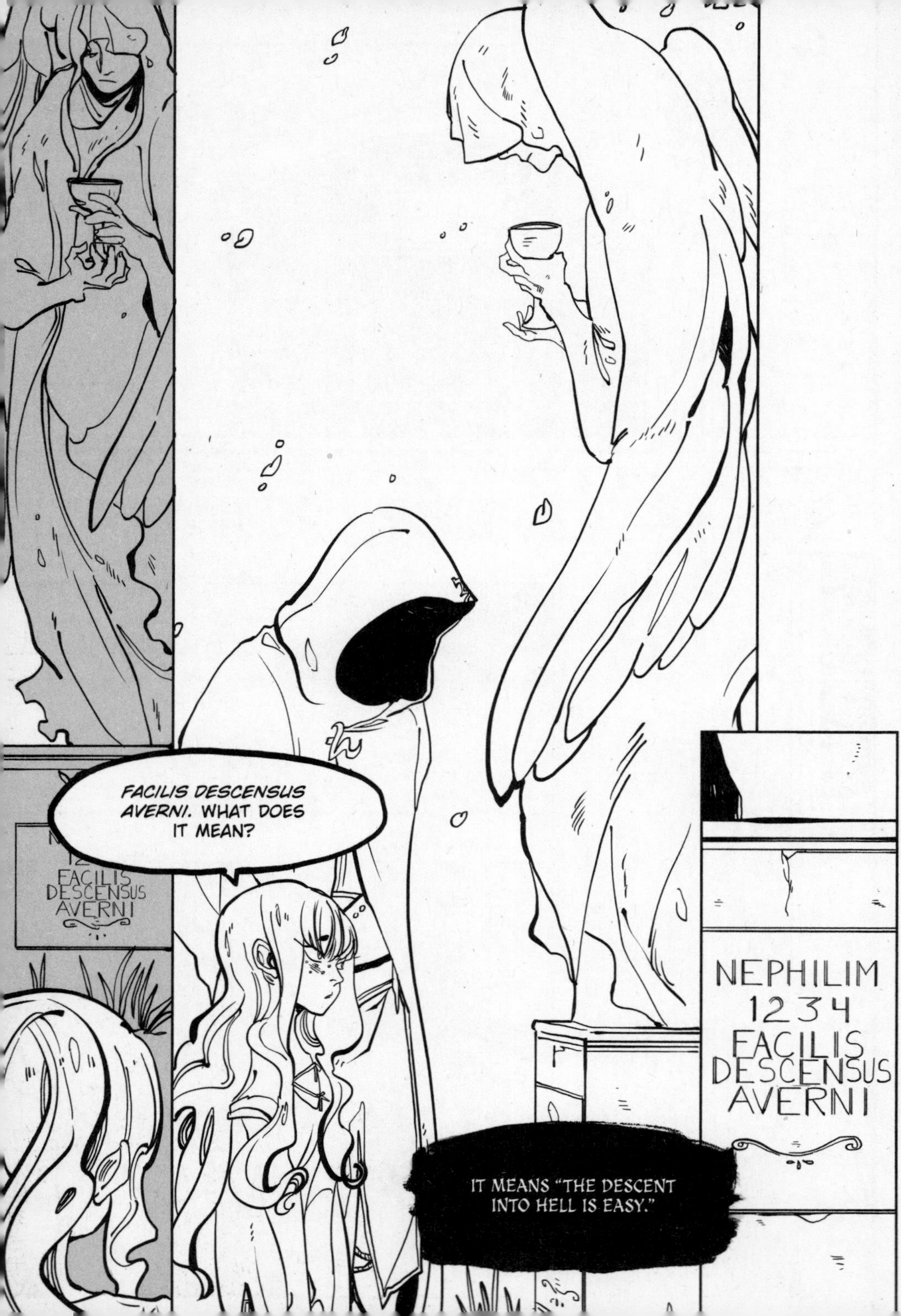
FACILIS DESCENSUS AVERNI
FACILIS DESCENSUS AVERNI. WHAT DOES IT MEAN?
NEPHILIM 1234 FACILIS DESCENSUS AVERNI
IT MEANS "THE DESCENT INTO HELL IS EASY."

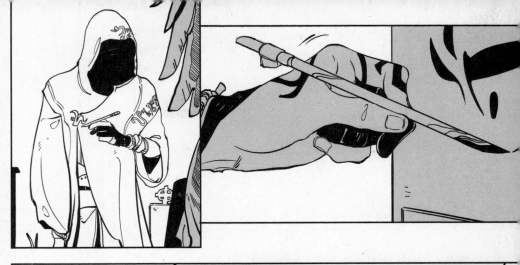

A SECRET ENTRANCE
IN A CEMETERY?
YOU'RE KIDDING!

YOU WANT
ME TO
HOLD YOUR
HAND?

STOP TALKING
DOWN TO ME.

YOU'RE
TOO
SHORT
TO TALK
UP TO.

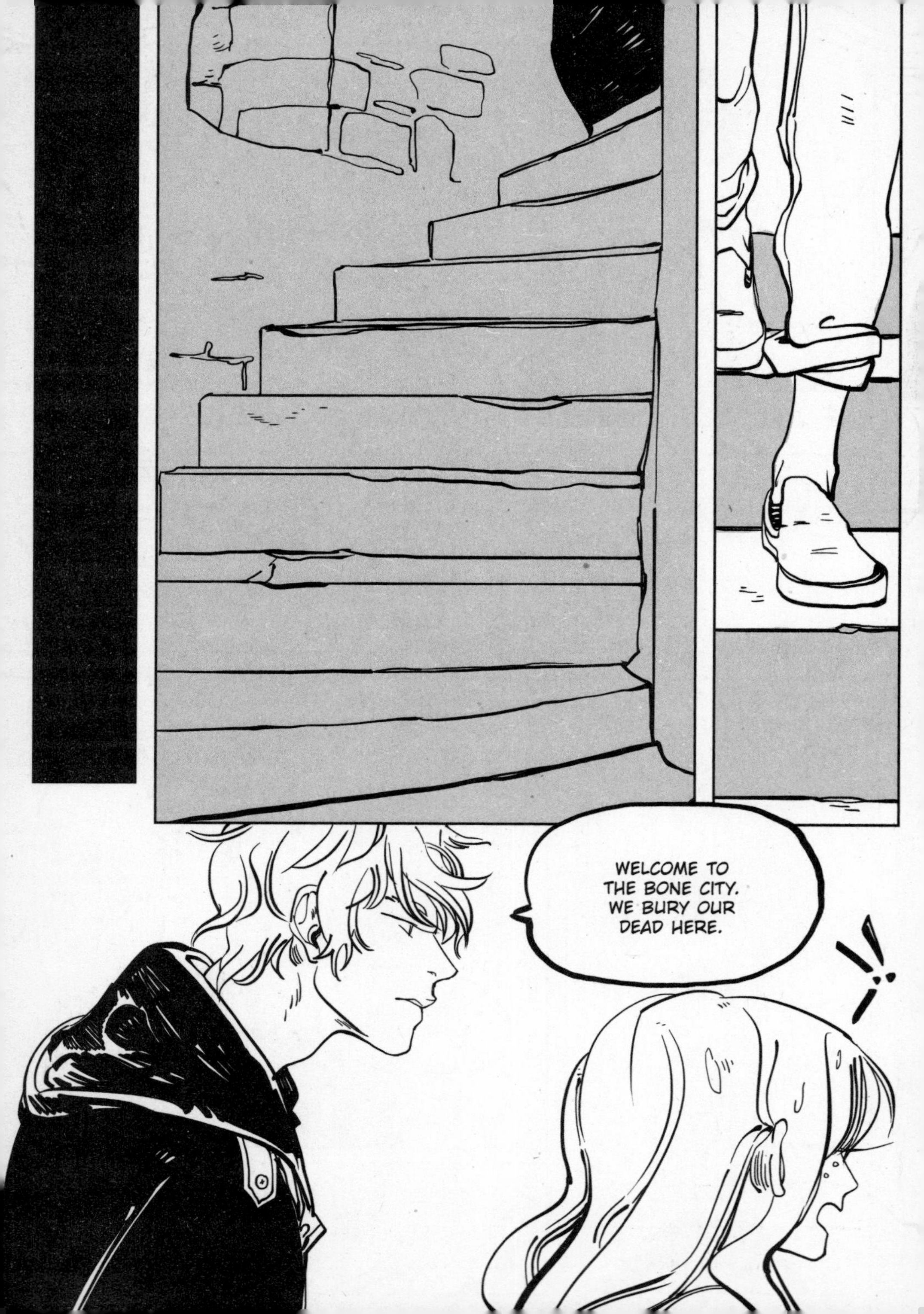
WELCOME TO THE BONE CITY. WE BURY OUR DEAD HERE.

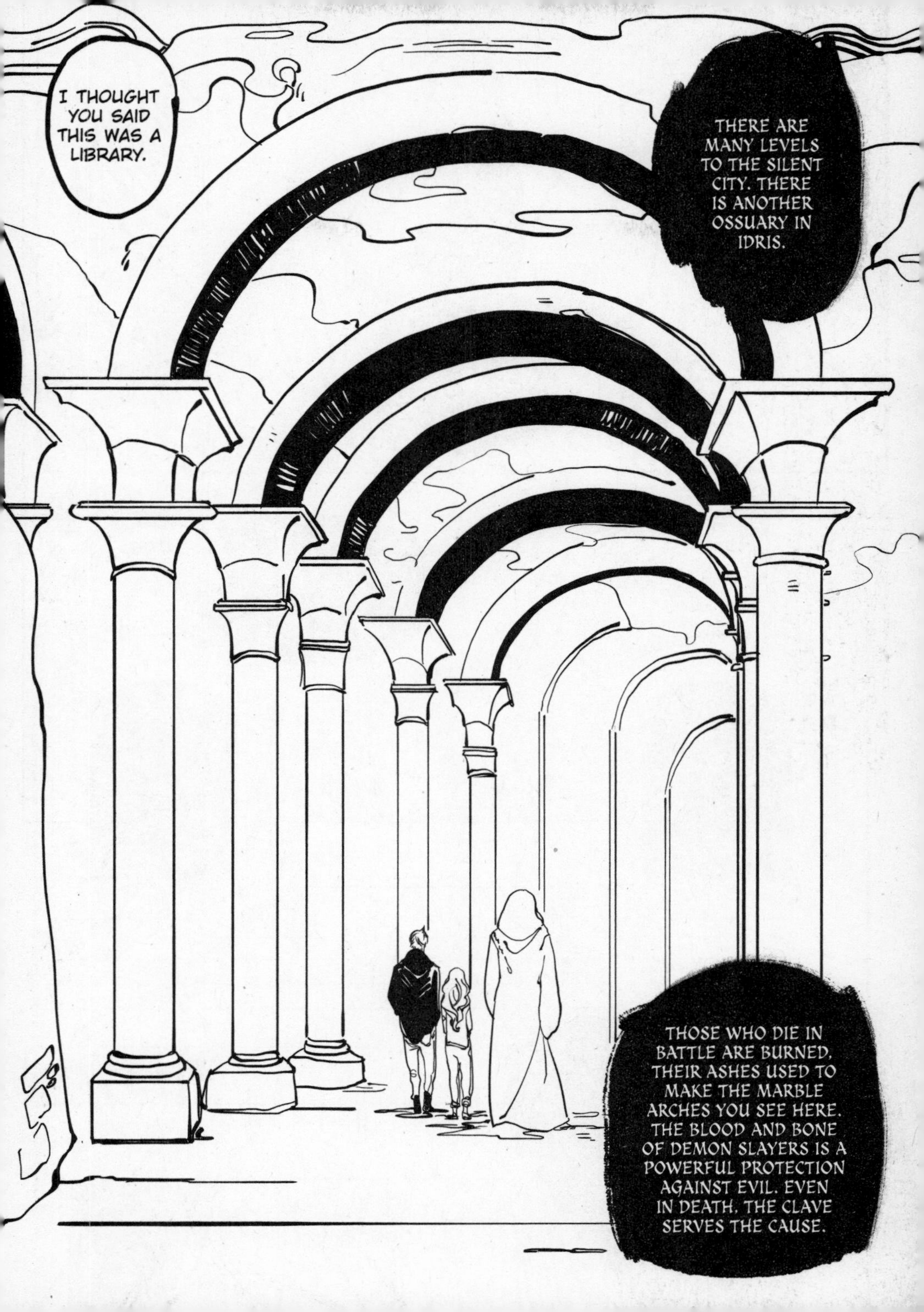
I THOUGHT YOU SAID THIS WAS A LIBRARY.
THERE ARE MANY LEVELS TO THE SILENT CITY. THERE IS ANOTHER OSSUARY IN IDRIS.
THOSE WHO DIE IN BATTLE ARE BURNED, THEIR ASHES USED TO MAKE THE MARBLE ARCHES YOU SEE HERE. THE BLOOD AND BONE OF DEMON SLAYERS IS A POWERFUL PROTECTION AGAINST EVIL. EVEN IN DEATH, THE CLAVE SERVES THE CAUSE.

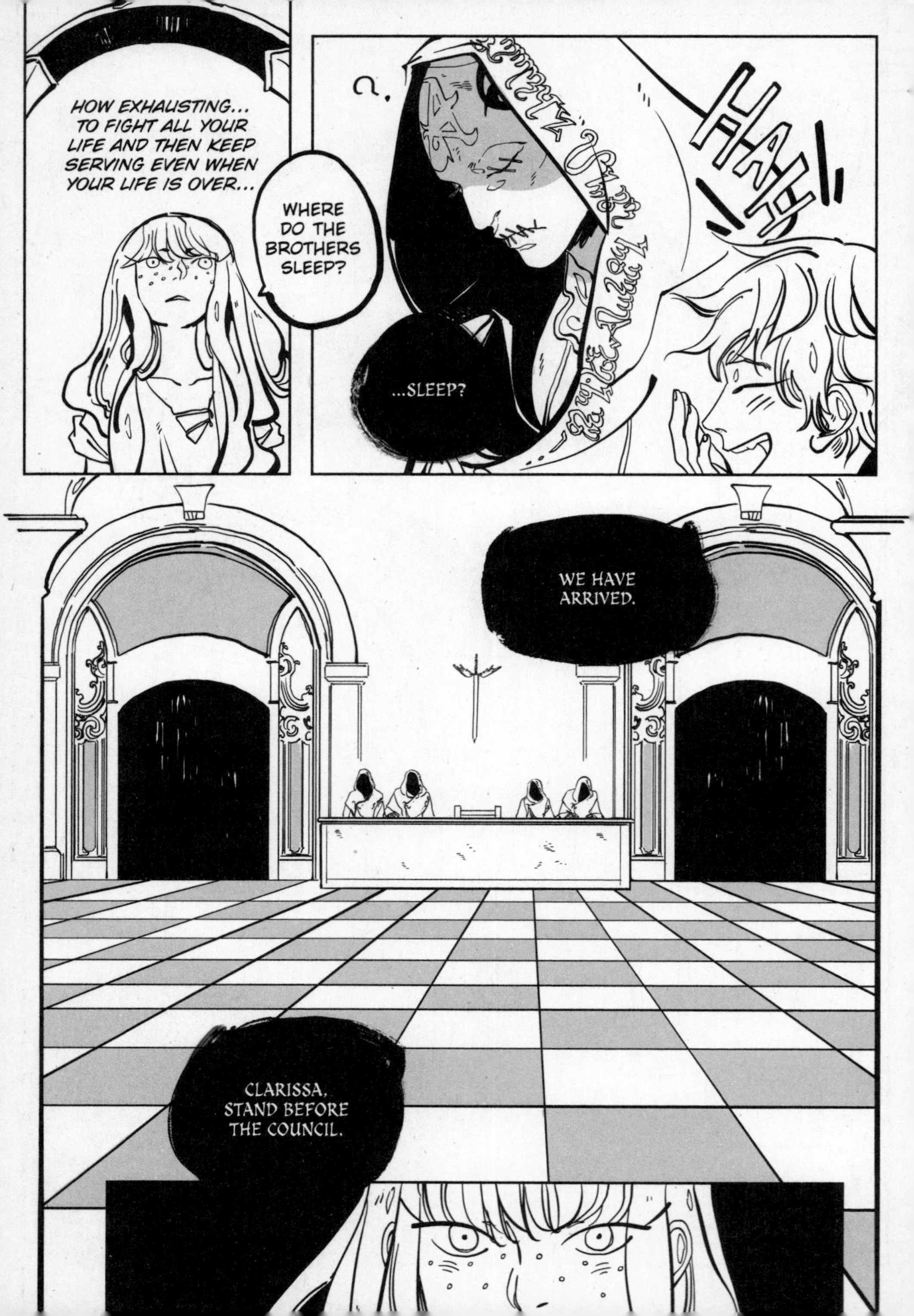
HOW EXHAUSTING... TO FIGHT ALL YOUR LIFE AND THEN KEEP SERVING EVEN WHEN YOUR LIFE IS OVER...
WHERE DO THE BROTHERS SLEEP?
...SLEEP?
WE HAVE ARRIVED.
CLARISSA, STAND BEFORE THE COUNCIL.

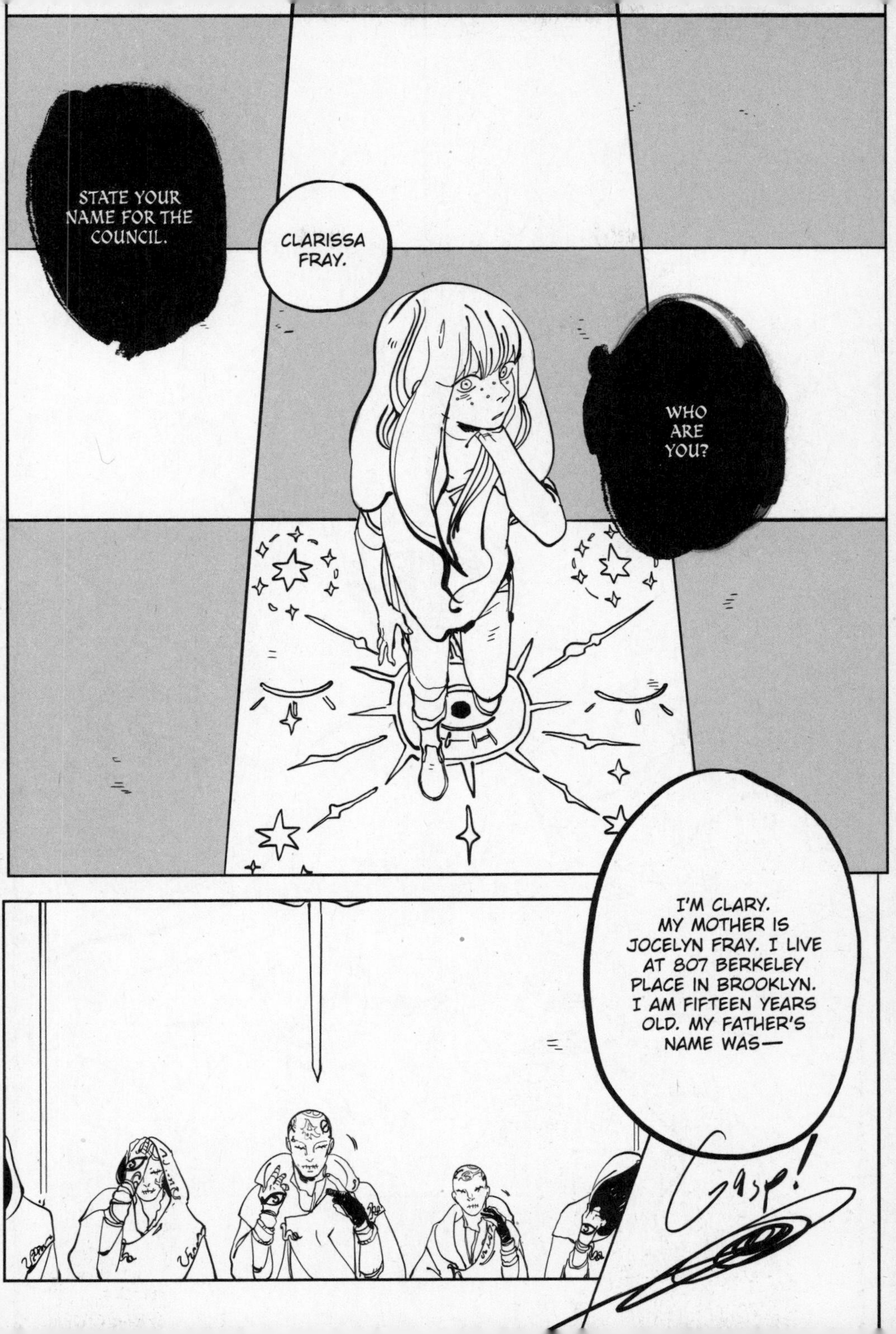
STATE YOUR NAME FOR THE COUNCIL.
CLARISSA FRAY.
WHO ARE YOU?
I'M CLARY. MY MOTHER IS JOCELYN FRAY. I LIVE AT 807 BERKELEY PLACE IN BROOKLYN. I AM FIFTEEN YEARS OLD. MY FATHER'S NAME WAS—
Gasp!

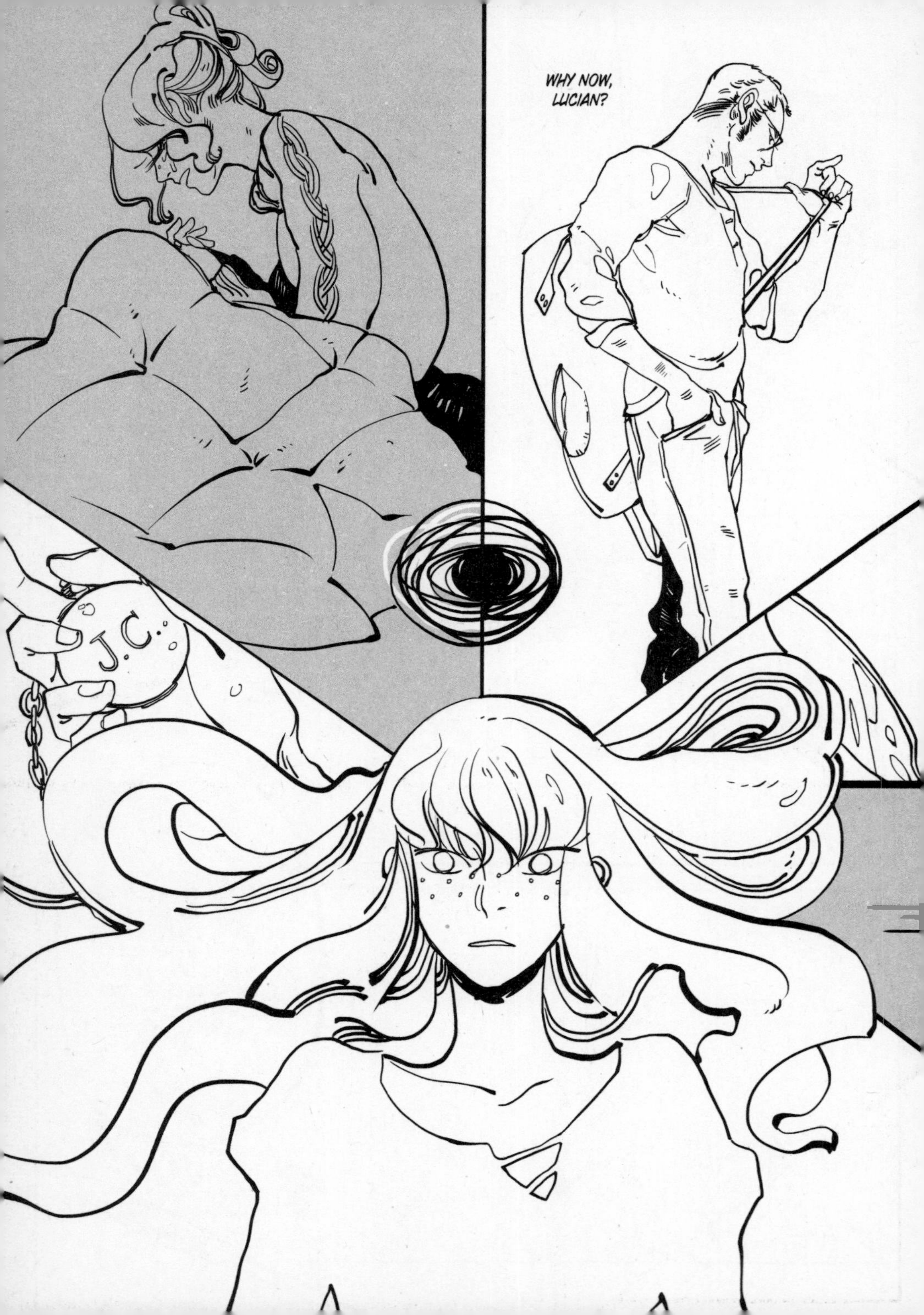
WHY NOW, LUCIAN?

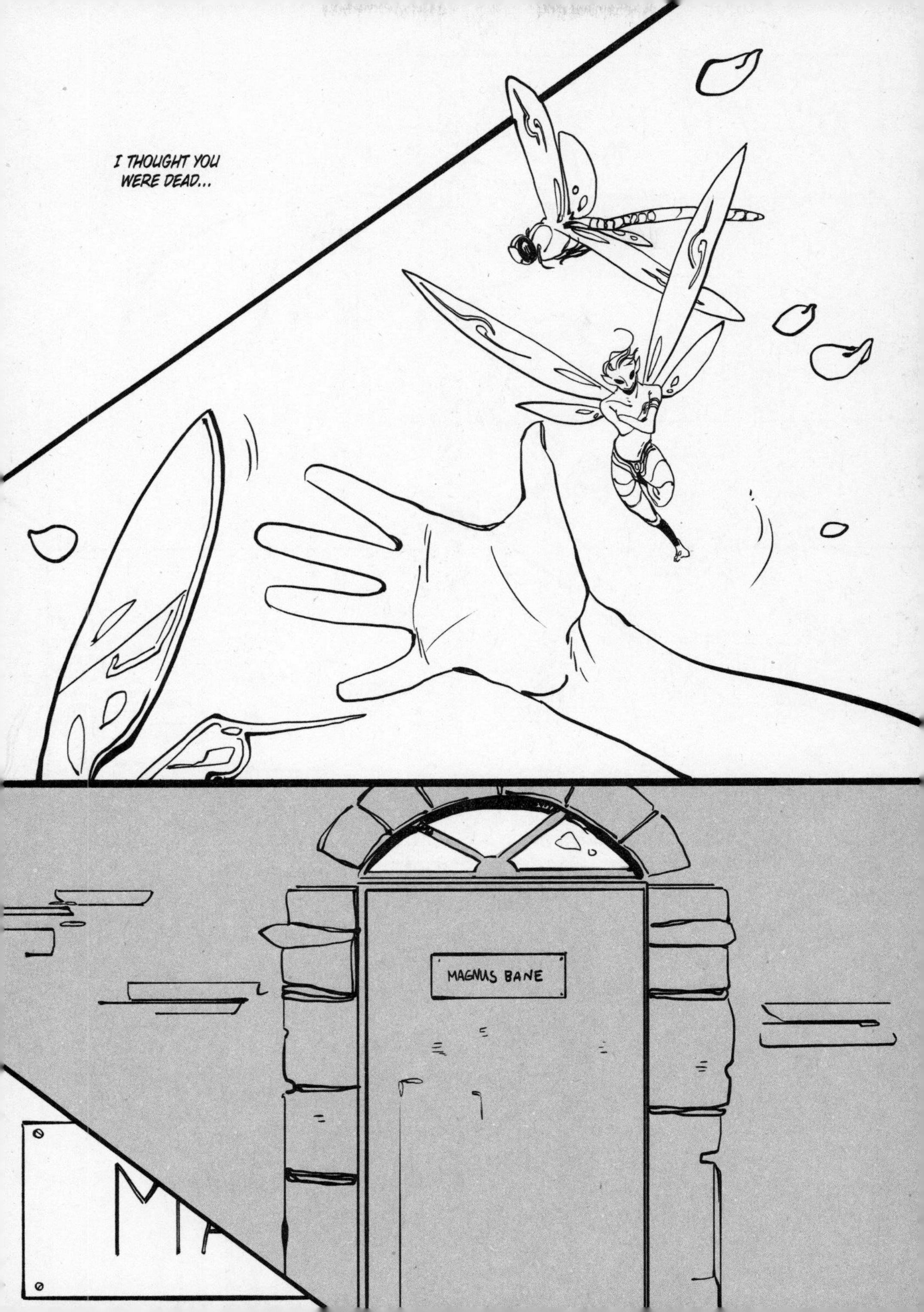
I THOUGHT YOU WERE DEAD...
MAGNUS BANE

MAGNUS BANE

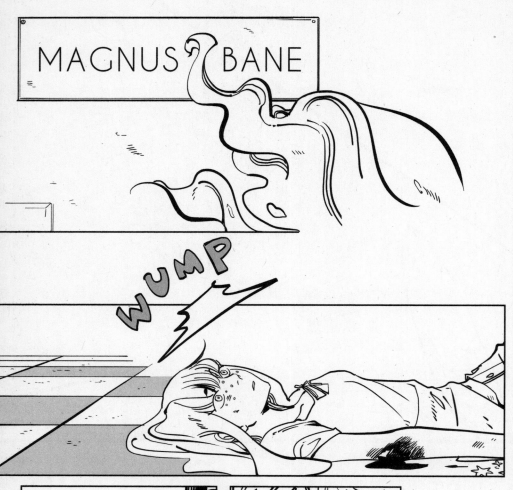

WUMP

MAGNUS
BANE?

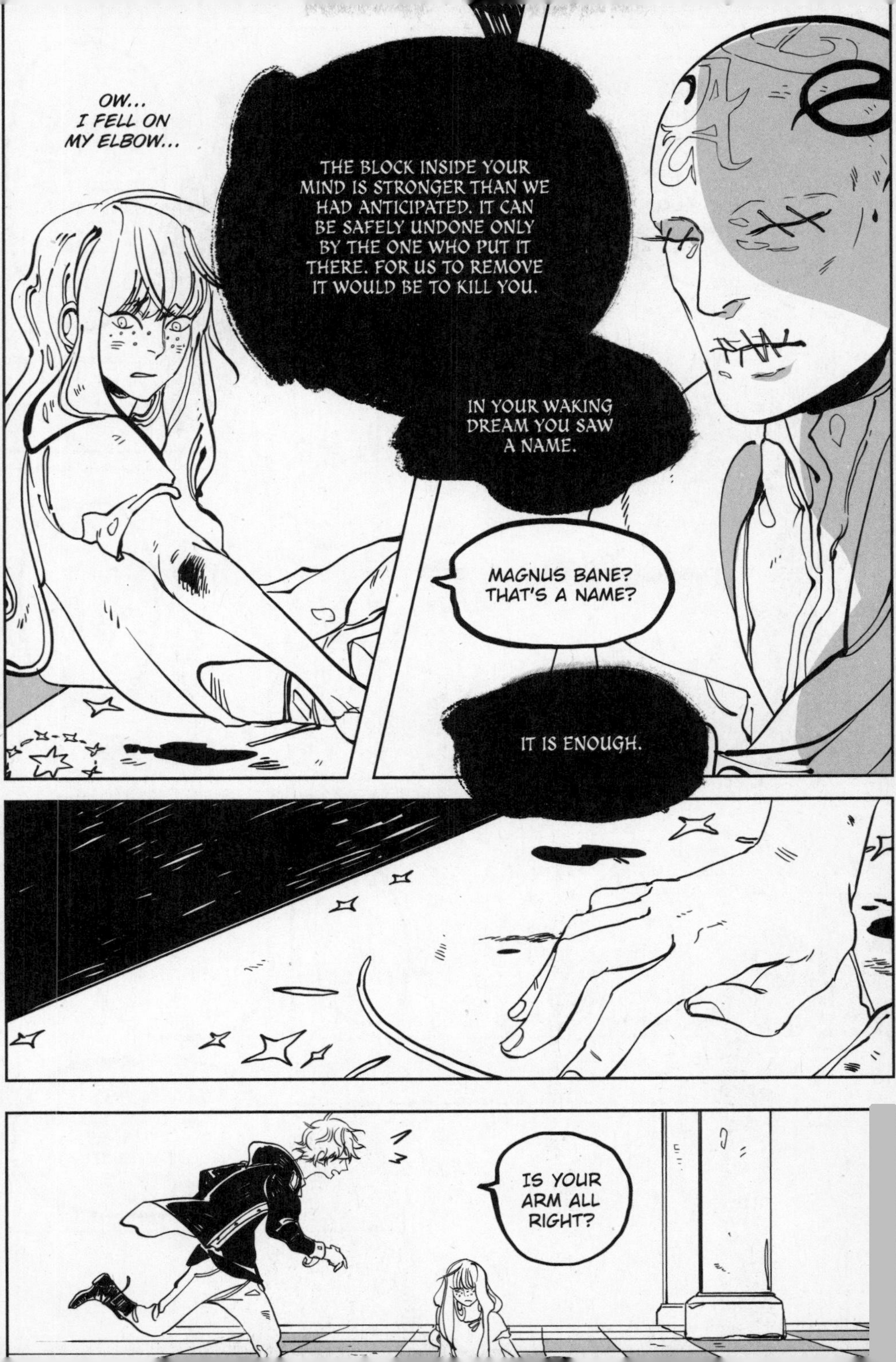
OW... I FELL ON MY ELBOW...
THE BLOCK INSIDE YOUR MIND IS STRONGER THAN WE HAD ANTICIPATED. IT CAN BE SAFELY UNDONE ONLY BY THE ONE WHO PUT IT THERE. FOR US TO REMOVE IT WOULD BE TO KILL YOU.
IN YOUR WAKING DREAM YOU SAW A NAME.
MAGNUS BANE? THAT'S A NAME?
IT IS ENOUGH.
IS YOUR ARM ALL RIGHT?

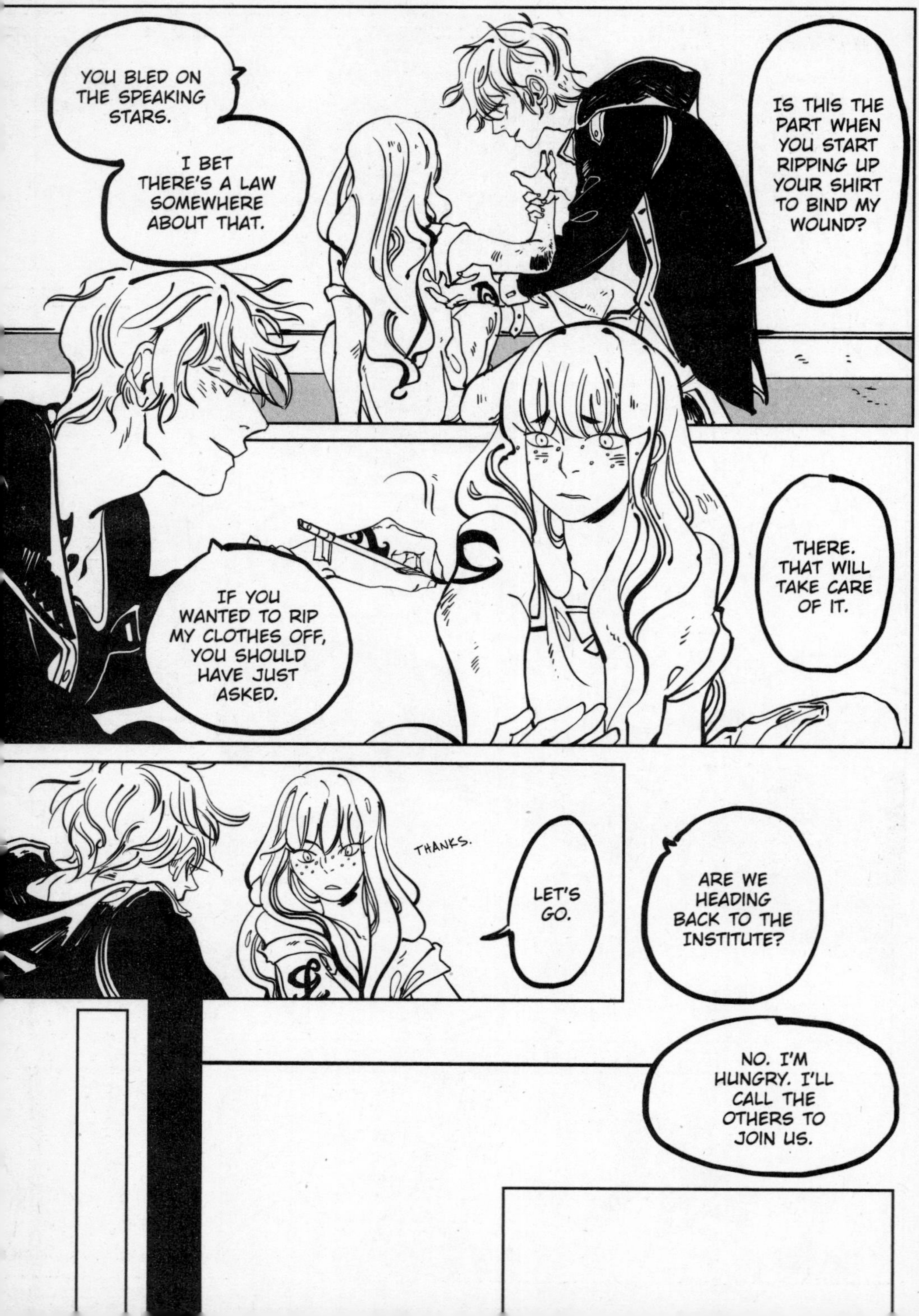
YOU BLED ON THE SPEAKING STARS.
I BET THERE'S A LAW SOMEWHERE ABOUT THAT.
IS THIS THE PART WHEN YOU START RIPPING UP YOUR SHIRT TO BIND MY WOUND?
IF YOU WANTED TO RIP MY CLOTHES OFF, YOU SHOULD HAVE JUST ASKED.
THERE. THAT WILL TAKE CARE OF IT.
THANKS.
LET'S GO.
ARE WE HEADING BACK TO THE INSTITUTE?
NO. I'M HUNGRY. I'LL CALL THE OTHERS TO JOIN US.

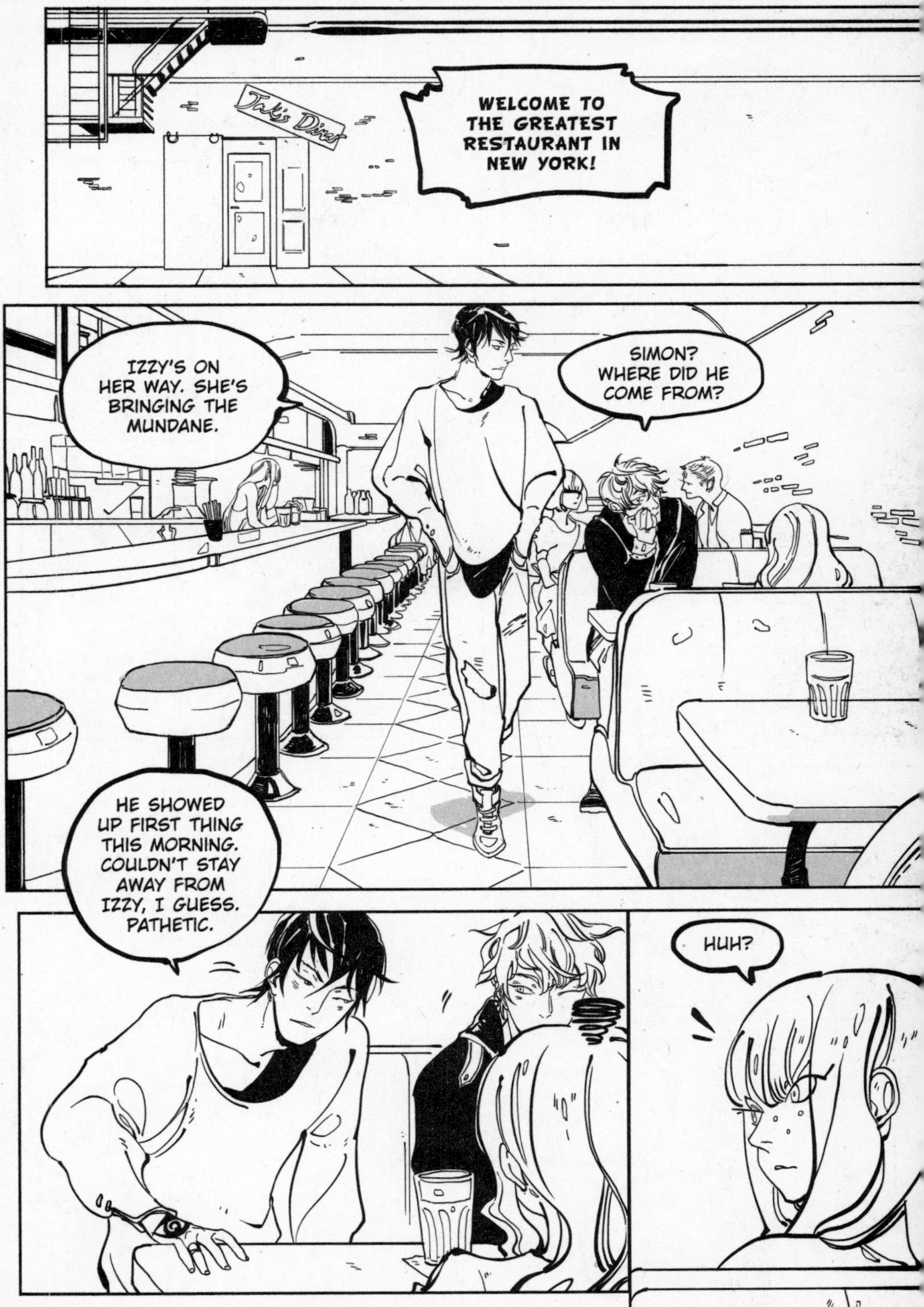
WELCOME TO THE GREATEST RESTAURANT IN NEW YORK!
IZZY'S ON HER WAY. SHE'S BRINGING THE MUNDANE.
SIMON? WHERE DID HE COME FROM?
HE SHOWED UP FIRST THING THIS MORNING. COULDN'T STAY AWAY FROM IZZY, I GUESS. PATHETIC.
HUH?

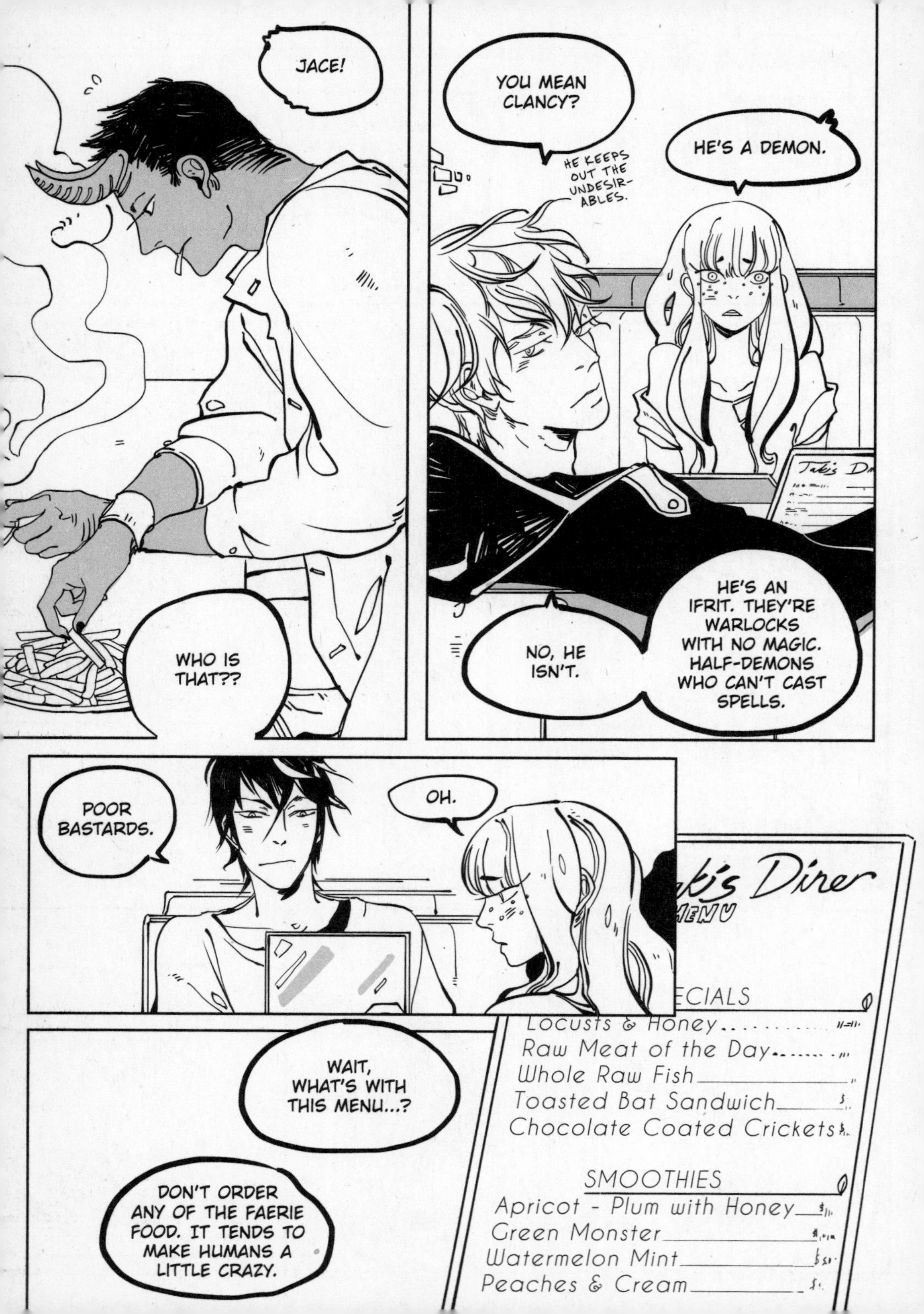

JACE!
WHO IS THAT??
YOU MEAN CLANCY?
HE KEEPS OUT THE UNDESIRABLES.
HE'S A DEMON.
NO, HE ISN'T.
HE'S AN IFRIT. THEY'RE WARLOCKS WITH NO MAGIC. HALF-DEMONS WHO CAN'T CAST SPELLS.
POOR BASTARDS.
OH.
WAIT, WHAT'S WITH THIS MENU...?
DON'T ORDER ANY OF THE FAERIE FOOD. IT TENDS TO MAKE HUMANS A LITTLE CRAZY.
Locusts & Honey
Raw Meat of the Day
Whole Raw Fish
Toasted Bat Sandwich
Chocolate Coated Crickets
SMOOTHIES
Apricot - Plum with Honey
Green Monster
Watermelon Mint
Peaches & Cream

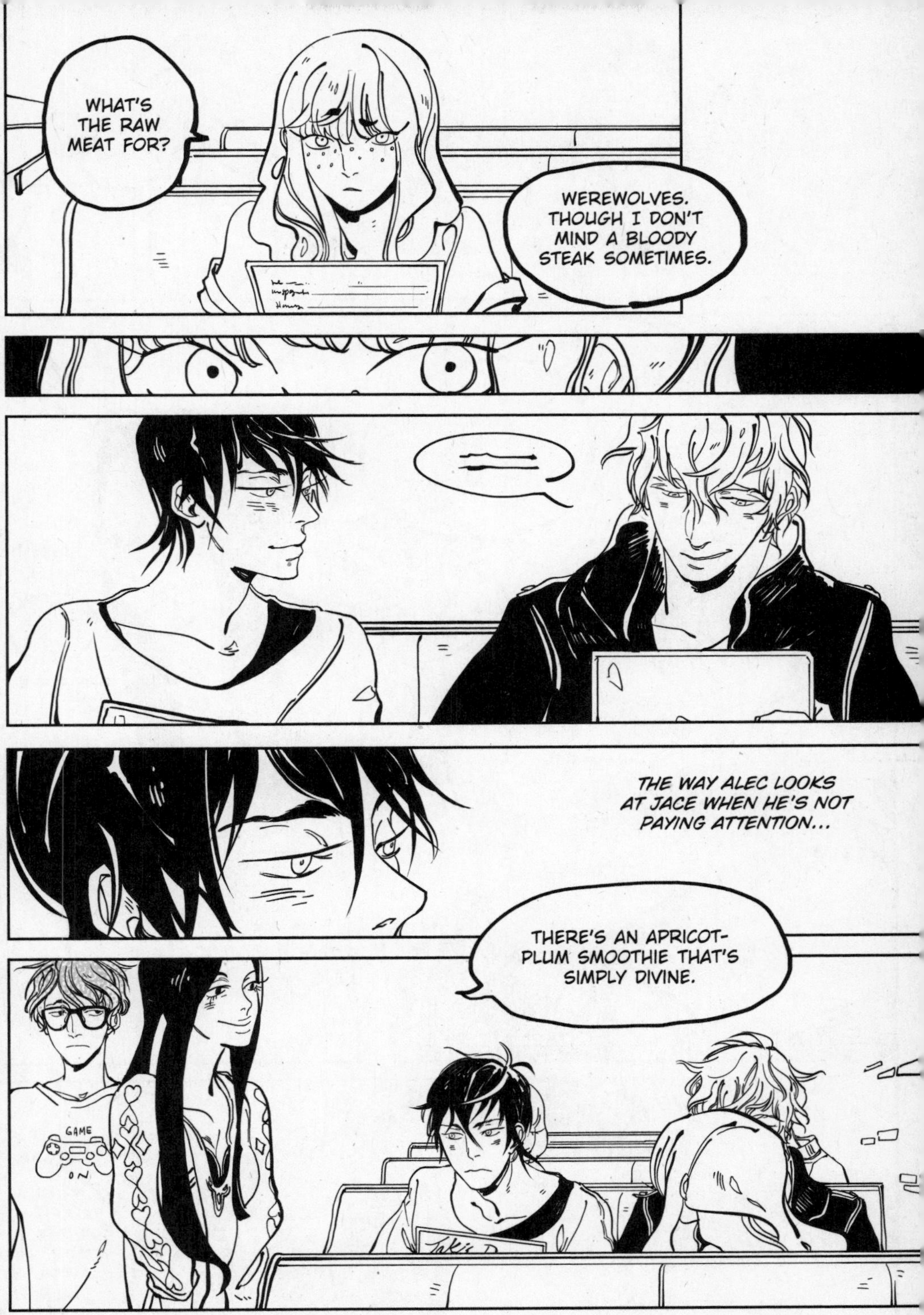
WHAT'S THE RAW MEAT FOR?
WEREWOLVES. THOUGH I DON'T MIND A BLOODY STEAK SOMETIMES.
THE WAY ALEC LOOKS AT JACE WHEN HE'S NOT PAYING ATTENTION...
THERE'S AN APRICOT-PLUM SMOOTHIE THAT'S SIMPLY DIVINE.
GAME ON

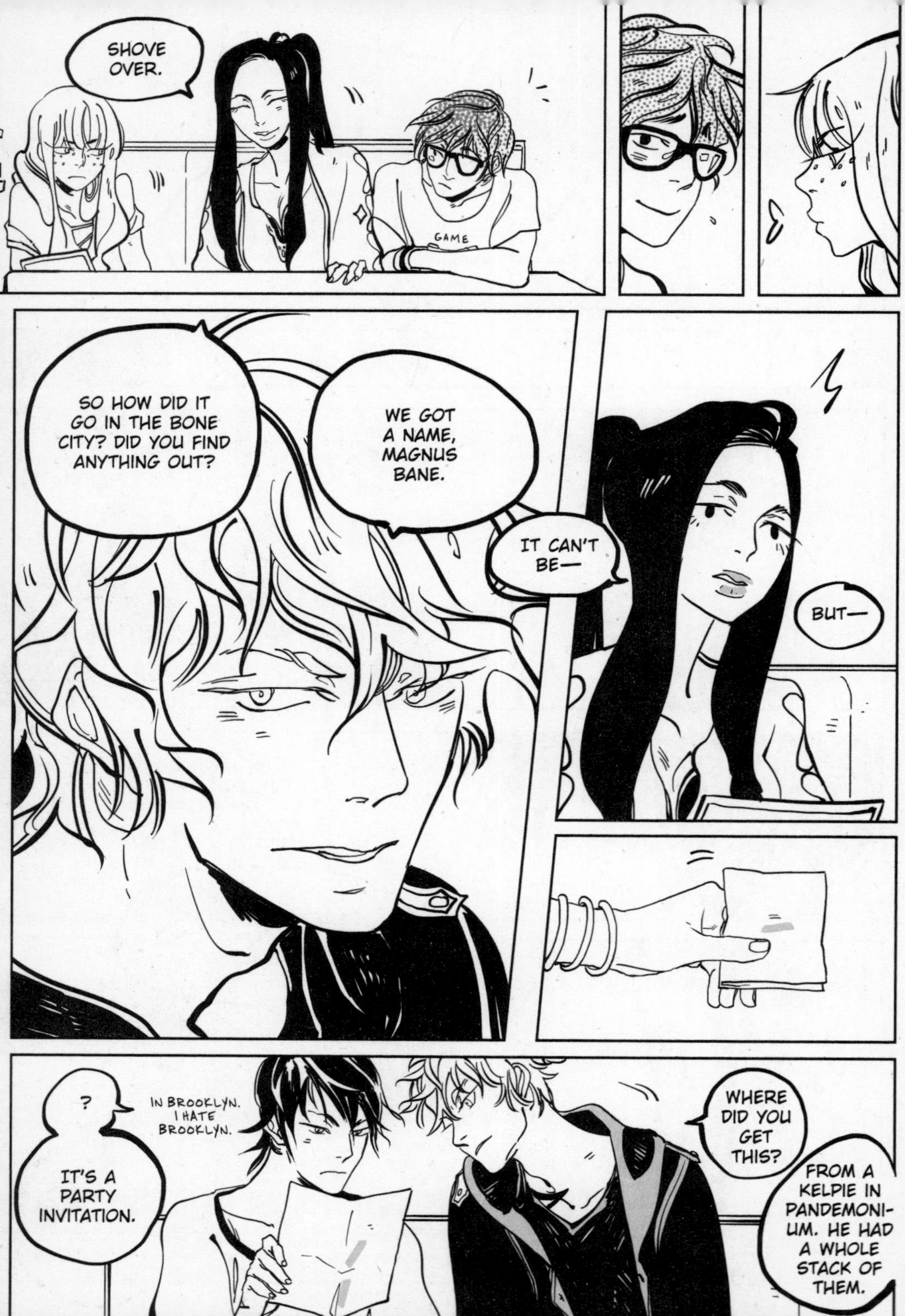
SHOVE OVER.
GAME
SO HOW DID IT GO IN THE BONE CITY? DID YOU FIND ANYTHING OUT?
WE GOT A NAME, MAGNUS BANE.
IT CAN'T BE—
BUT—
?
IN BROOKLYN. I HATE BROOKLYN.
IT'S A PARTY INVITATION.
WHERE DID YOU GET THIS?
FROM A KELPIE IN PANDEMONIUM. HE HAD A WHOLE STACK OF THEM.

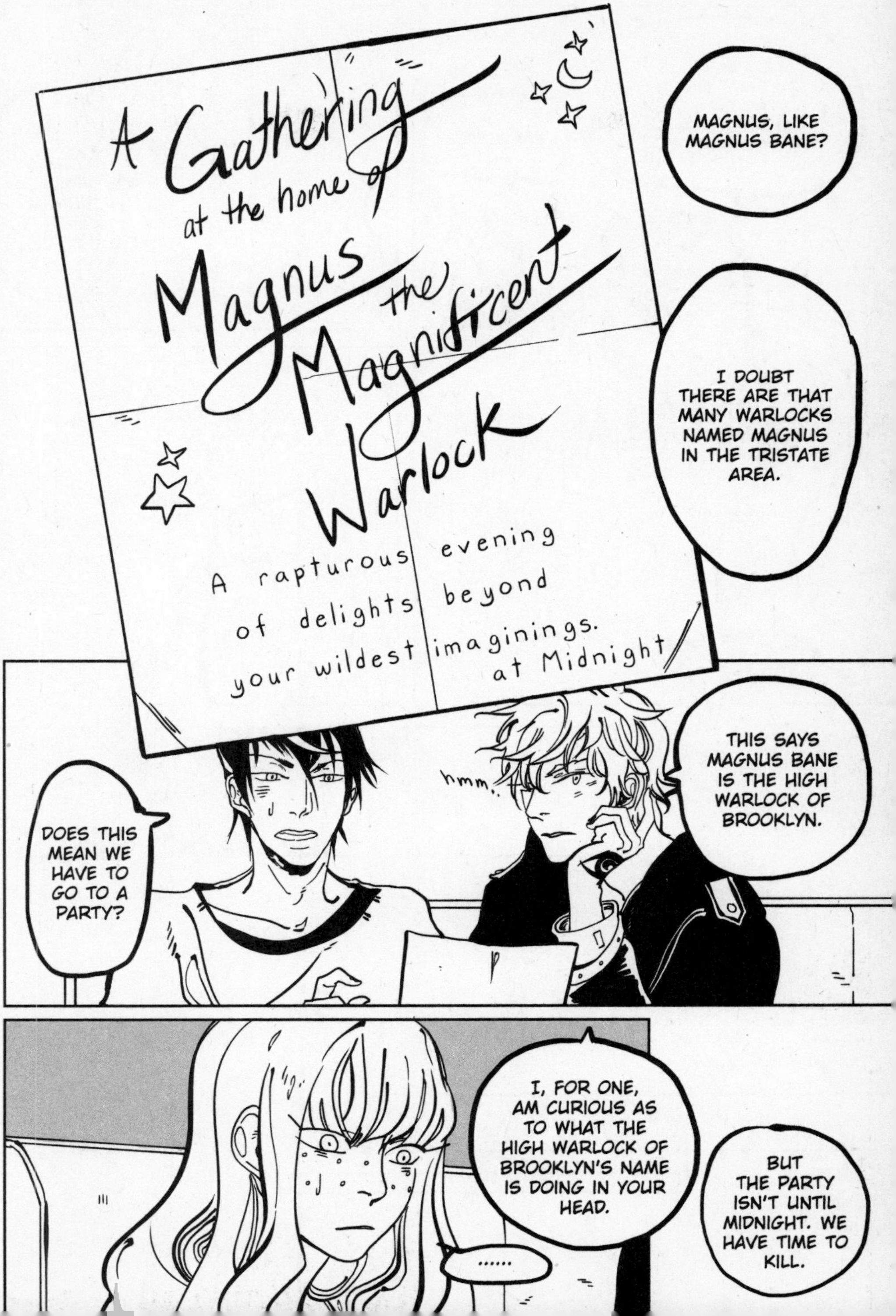
A Gathering at the home of Magnus the Magnificent Warlock
A rapturous evening of delights beyond your wildest imaginings.
at Midnight
MAGNUS, LIKE MAGNUS BANE?
I DOUBT THERE ARE THAT MANY WARLOCKS NAMED MAGNUS IN THE TRISTATE AREA.
DOES THIS MEAN WE HAVE TO GO TO A PARTY?
hmm..
THIS SAYS MAGNUS BANE IS THE HIGH WARLOCK OF BROOKLYN.
......
I, FOR ONE, AM CURIOUS AS TO WHAT THE HIGH WARLOCK OF BROOKLYN'S NAME IS DOING IN YOUR HEAD.
BUT THE PARTY ISN'T UNTIL MIDNIGHT. WE HAVE TIME TO KILL.

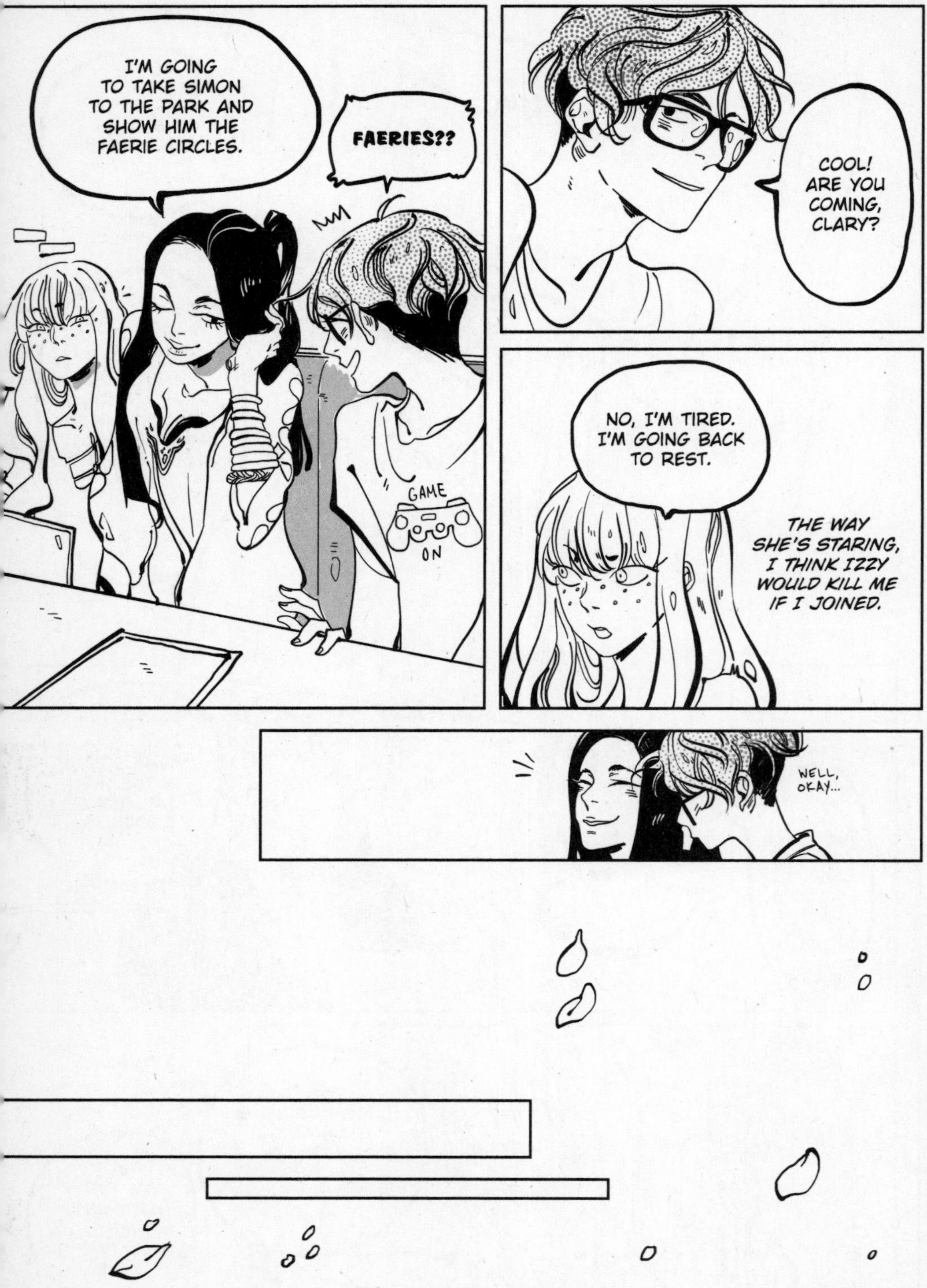
I'M GOING TO TAKE SIMON TO THE PARK AND SHOW HIM THE FAERIE CIRCLES.
FAERIES??
GAME ON
COOL! ARE YOU COMING, CLARY?
NO, I'M TIRED. I'M GOING BACK TO REST.
THE WAY SHE'S STARING, I THINK IZZY WOULD KILL ME IF I JOINED.
WELL, OKAY...

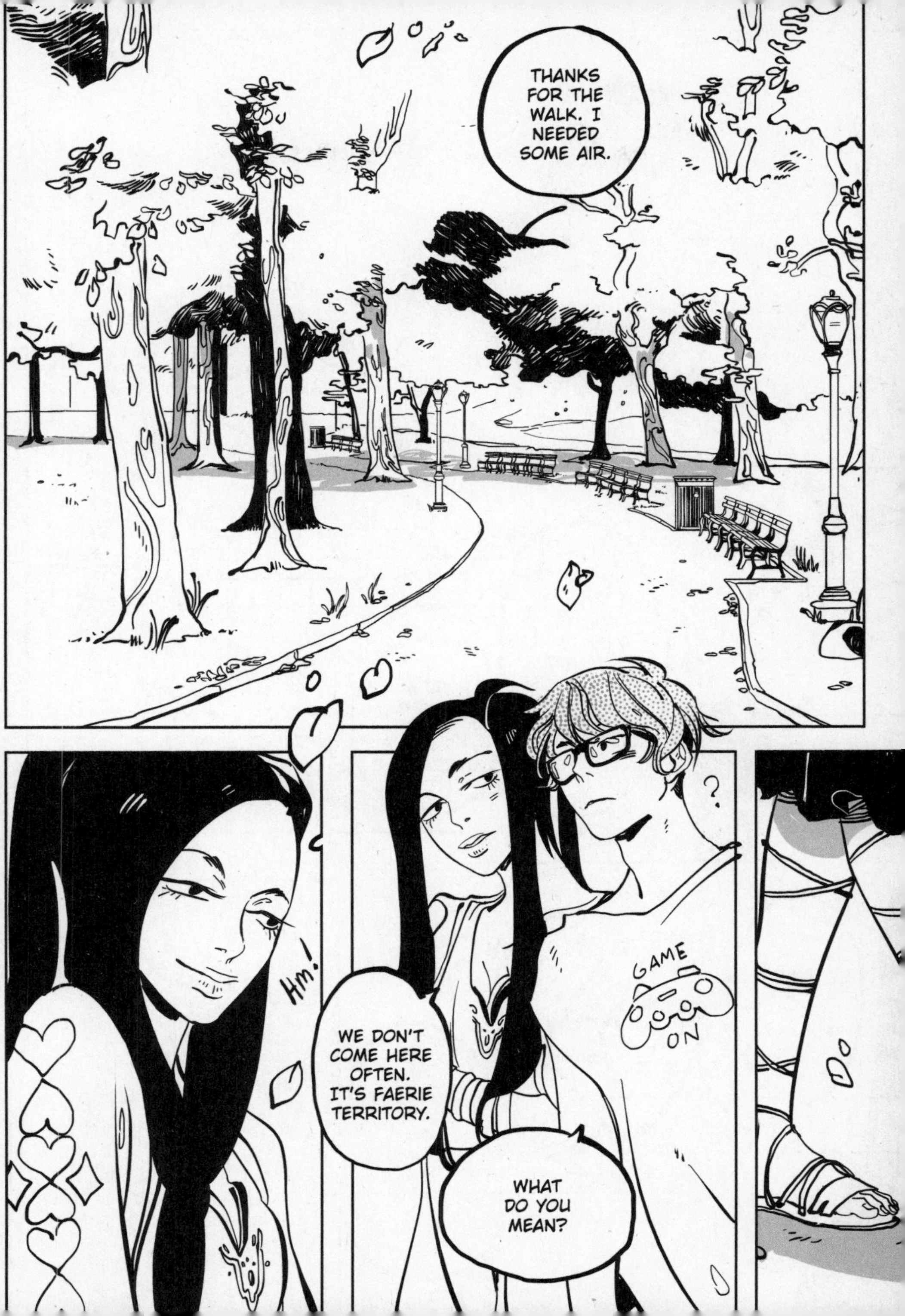
THANKS FOR THE WALK. I NEEDED SOME AIR.
Hm!
?
GAME ON
WE DON'T COME HERE OFTEN. IT'S FAERIE TERRITORY.
WHAT DO YOU MEAN?

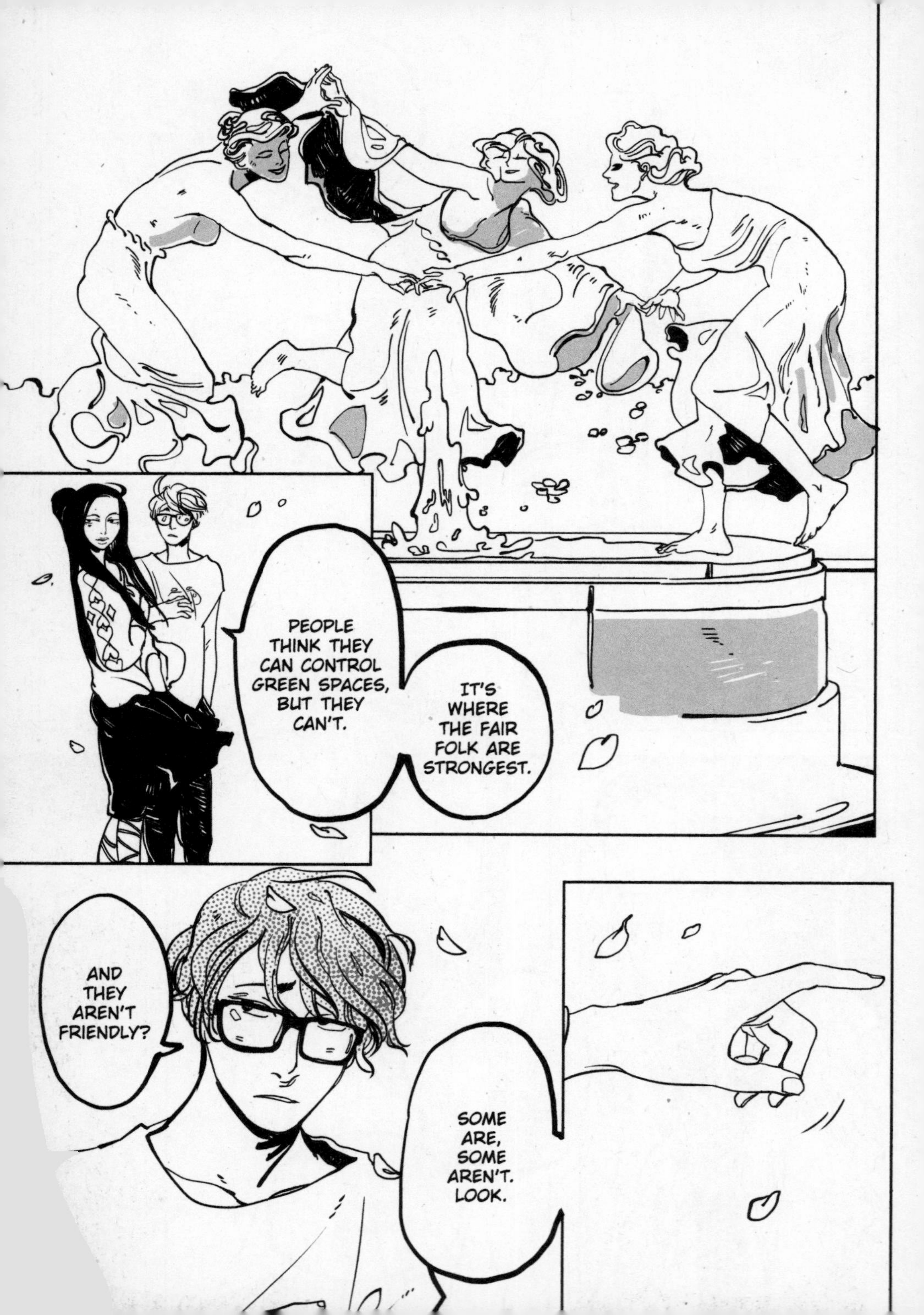
PEOPLE THINK THEY CAN CONTROL GREEN SPACES, BUT THEY CAN'T.
IT'S WHERE THE FAIR FOLK ARE STRONGEST.
AND THEY AREN'T FRIENDLY?
SOME ARE, SOME AREN'T. LOOK.

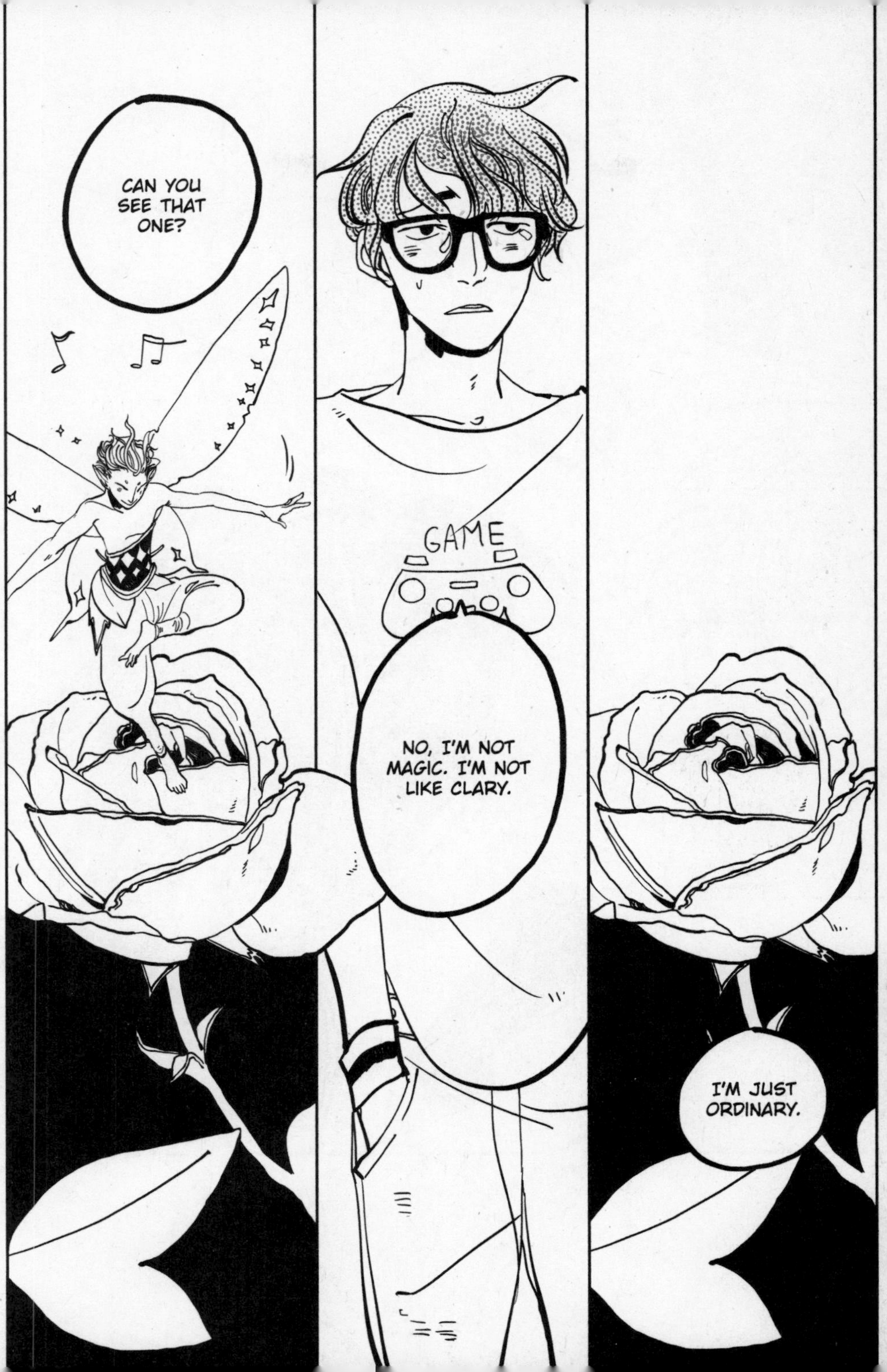
CAN YOU SEE THAT ONE?
GAME
NO, I'M NOT MAGIC. I'M NOT LIKE CLARY.
I'M JUST ORDINARY.

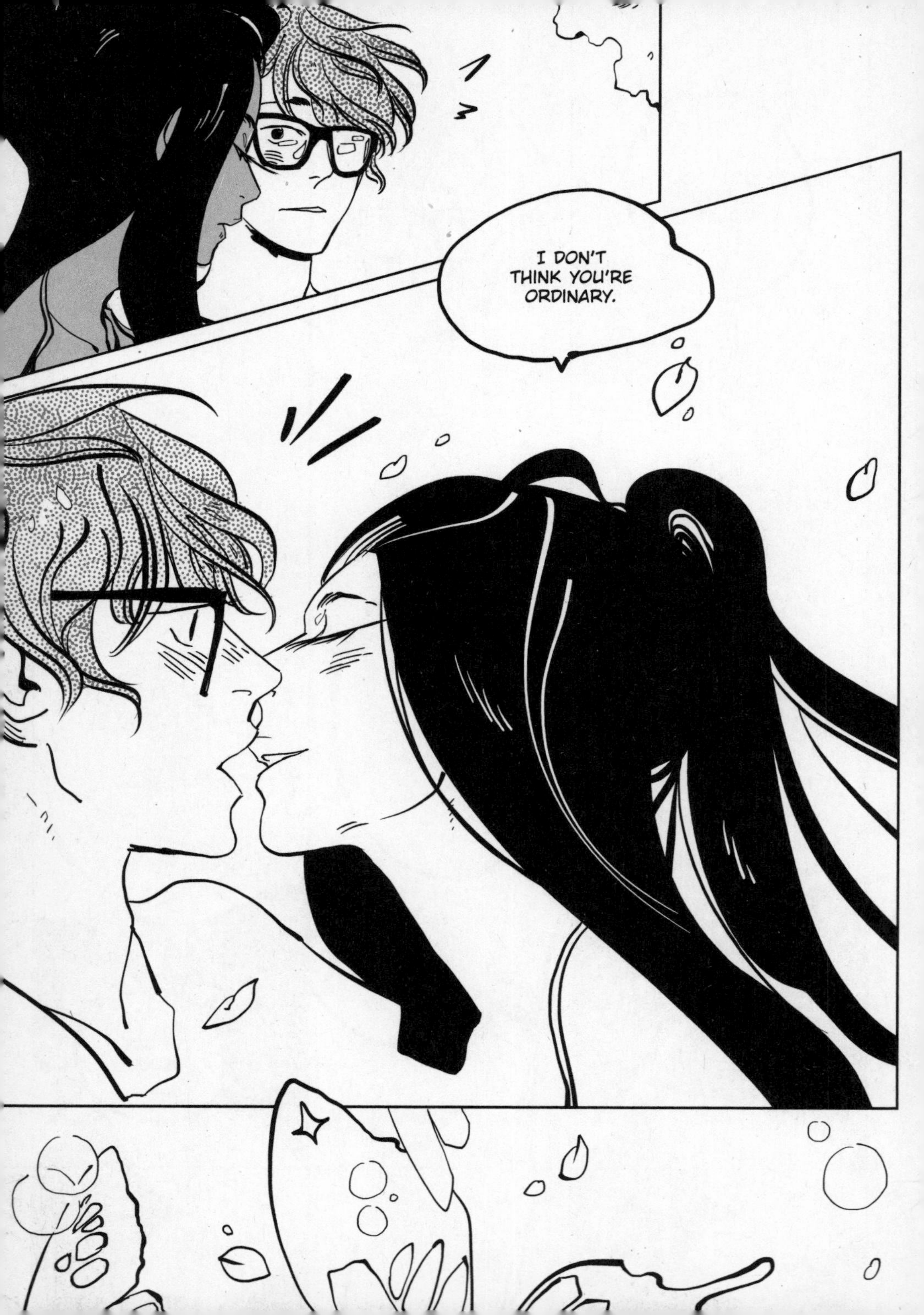
I DON'T THINK YOU'RE ORDINARY.

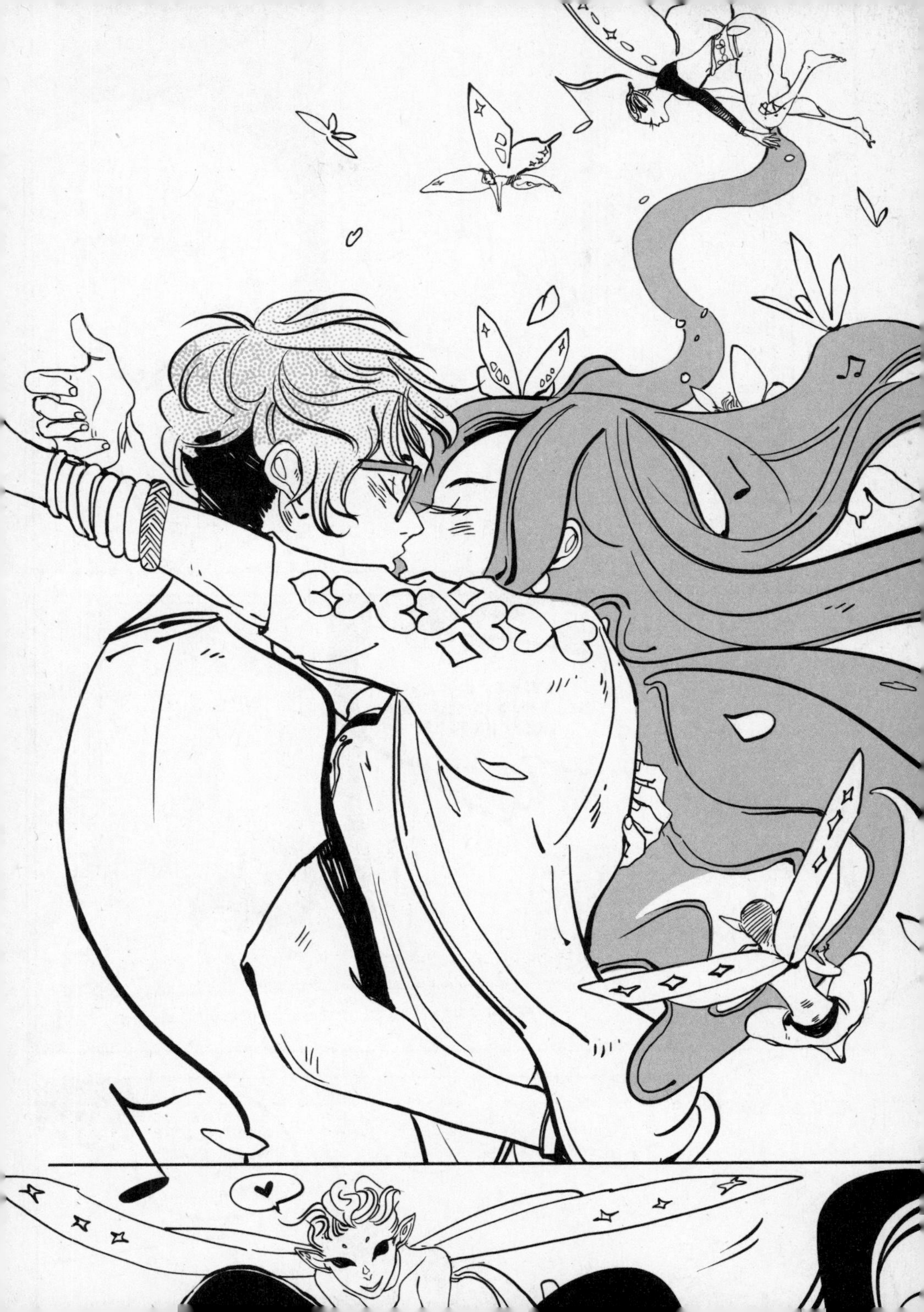

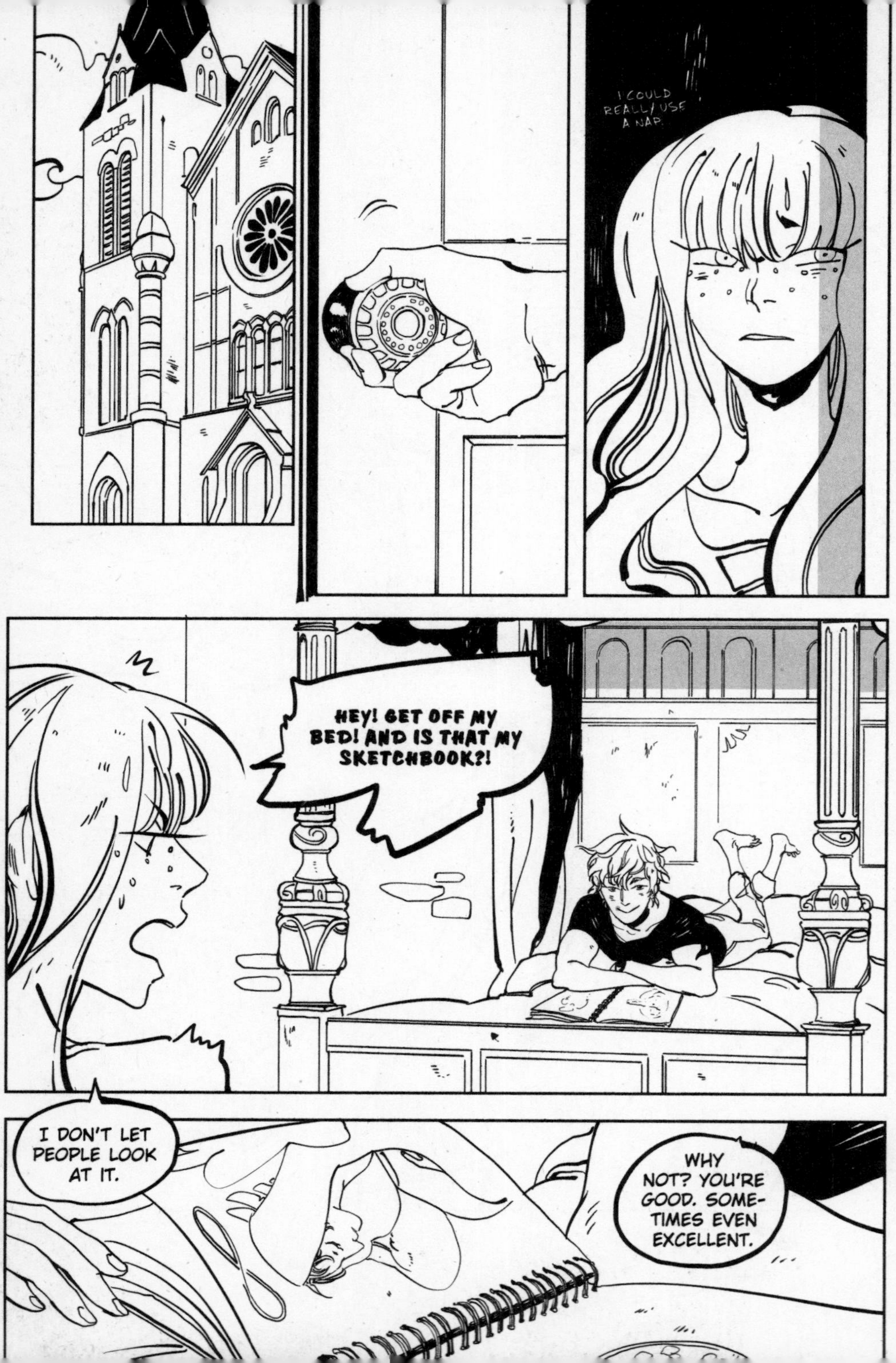
I COULD REALLY USE A NAP.
HEY! GET OFF MY BED! AND IS THAT MY SKETCHBOOK?!
I DON'T LET PEOPLE LOOK AT IT.
WHY NOT? YOU'RE GOOD. SOME-TIMES EVEN EXCELLENT.

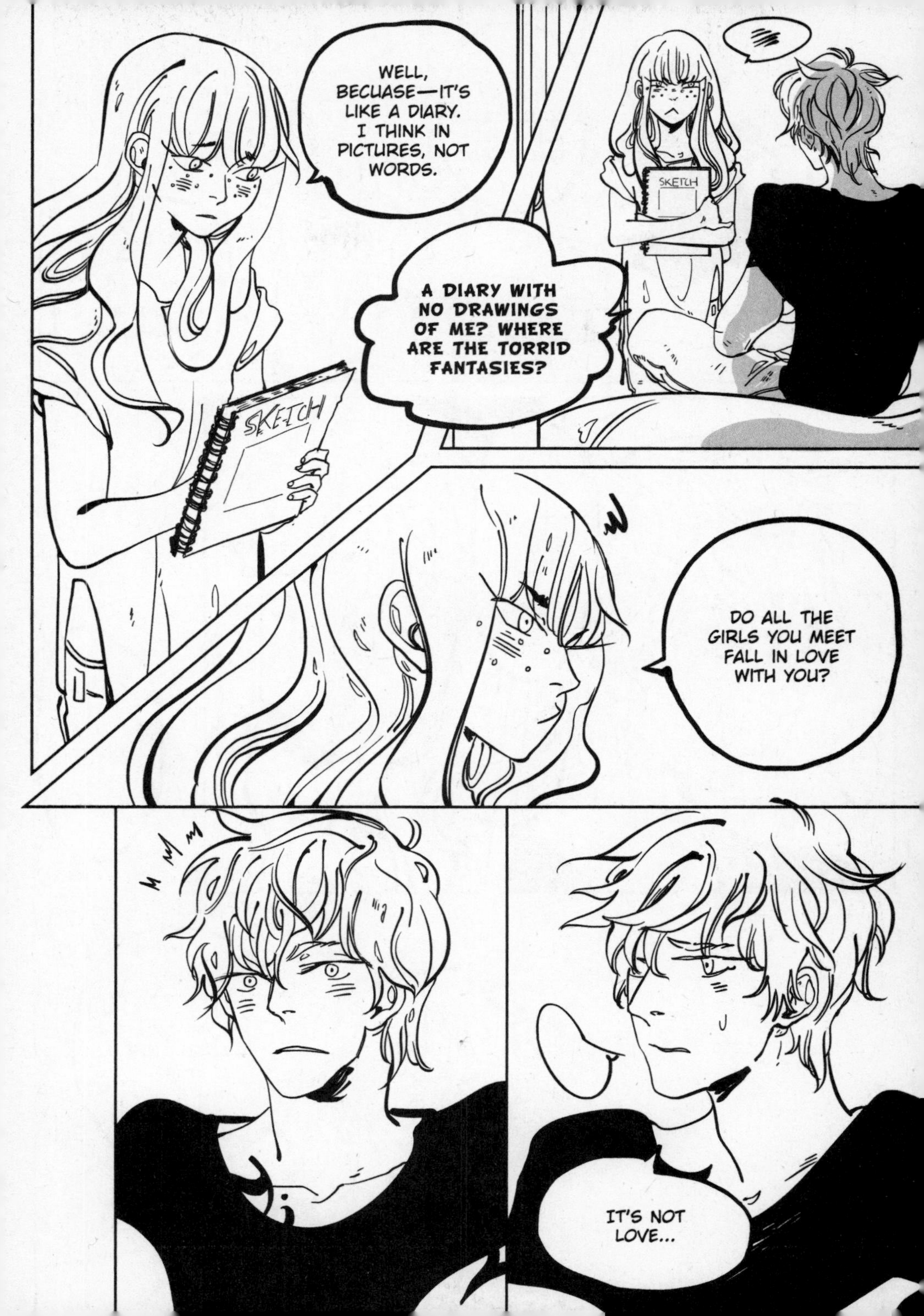
WELL, BECUASE—IT'S LIKE A DIARY. I THINK IN PICTURES, NOT WORDS.
SKETCH
SKETCH
A DIARY WITH NO DRAWINGS OF ME? WHERE ARE THE TORRID FANTASIES?
DO ALL THE GIRLS YOU MEET FALL IN LOVE WITH YOU?
IT'S NOT LOVE...

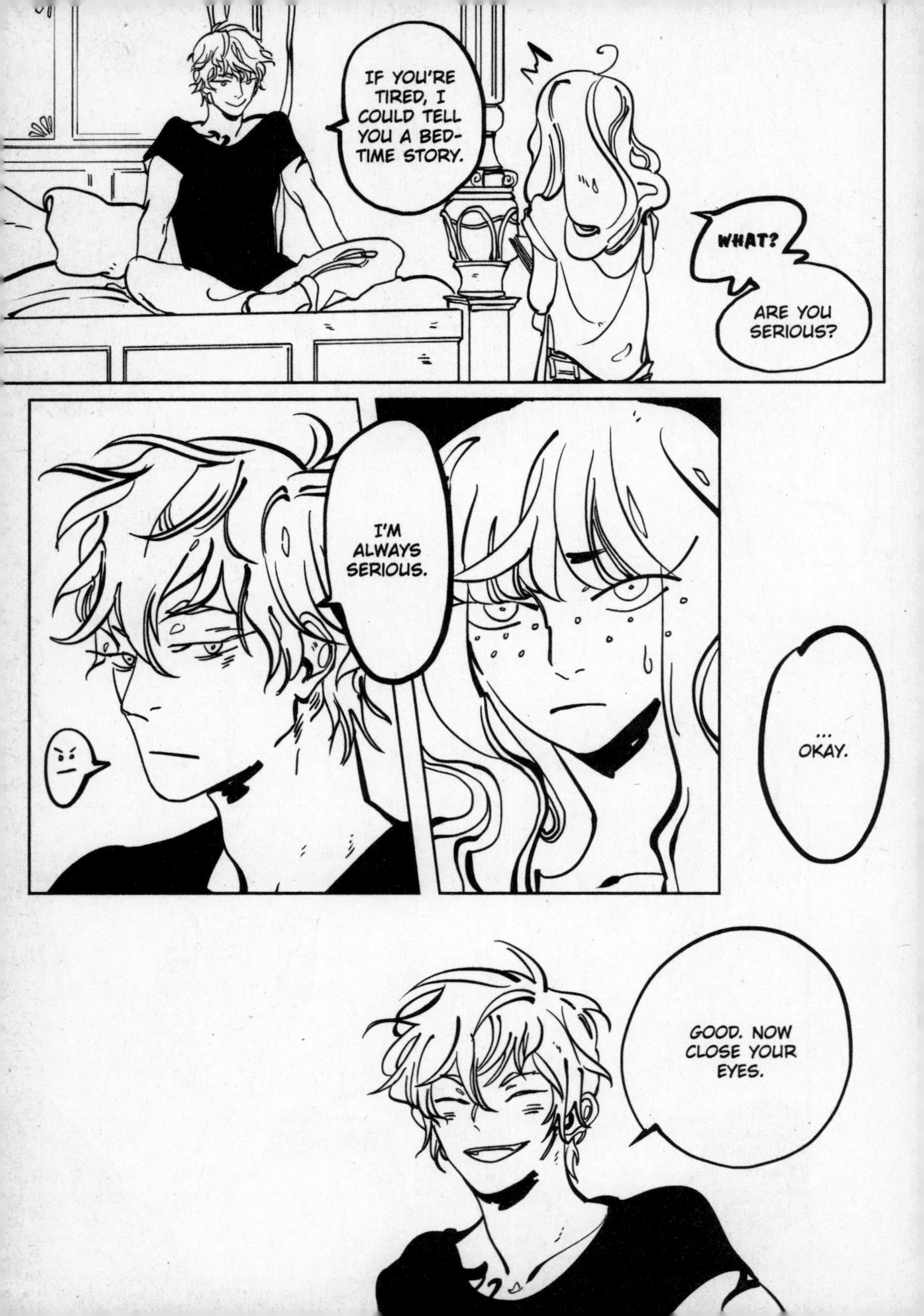
IF YOU'RE TIRED, I COULD TELL YOU A BED-TIME STORY.
WHAT?
ARE YOU SERIOUS?
I'M ALWAYS SERIOUS.
... OKAY.
GOOD. NOW CLOSE YOUR EYES.

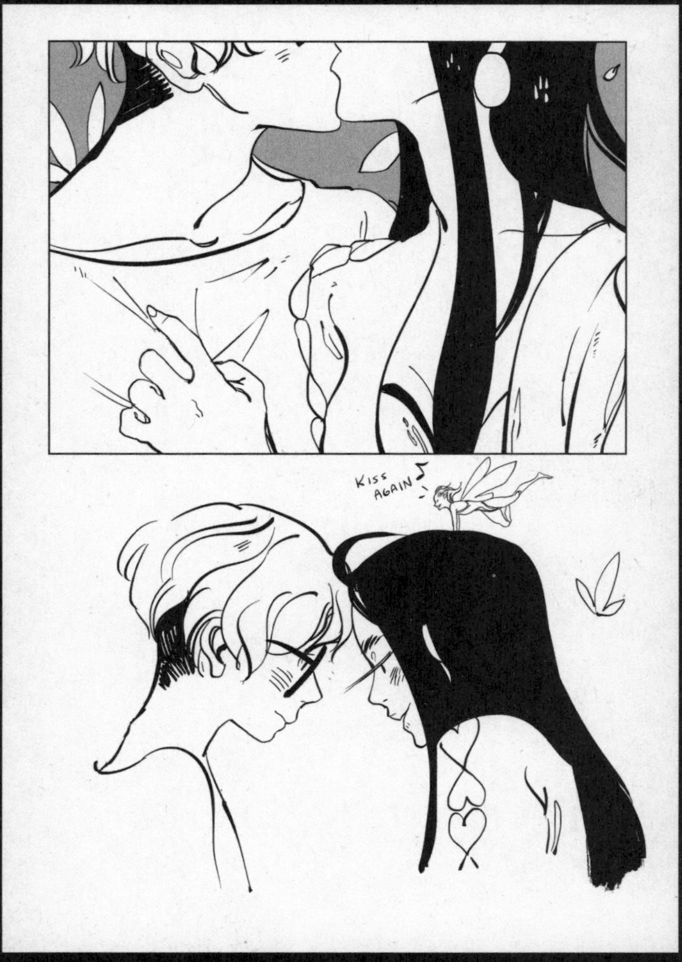
KISS AGAIN ♪

THE MORTAL INSTRUMENTS

THE GRAPHIC NOVEL

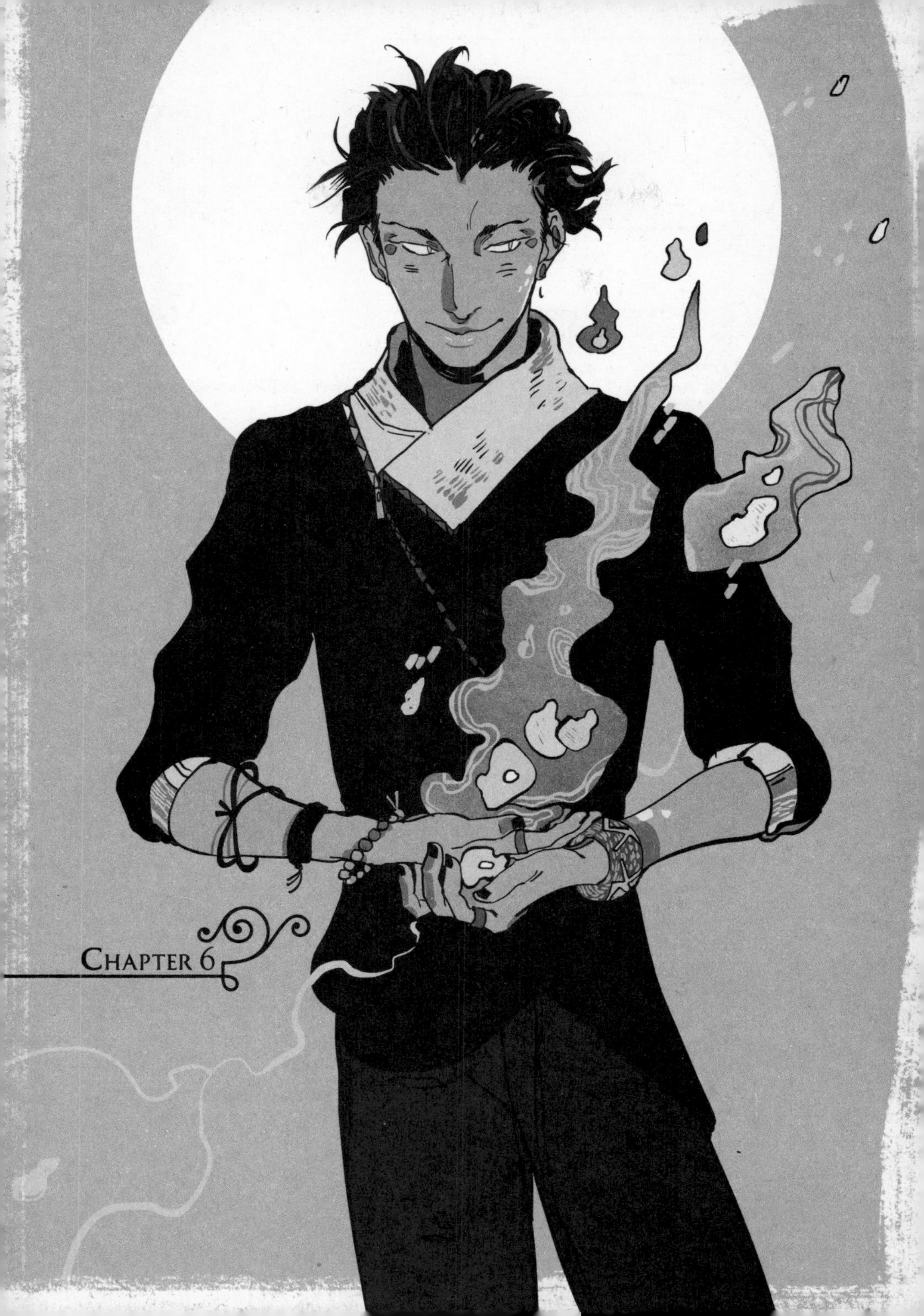

Chapter 6

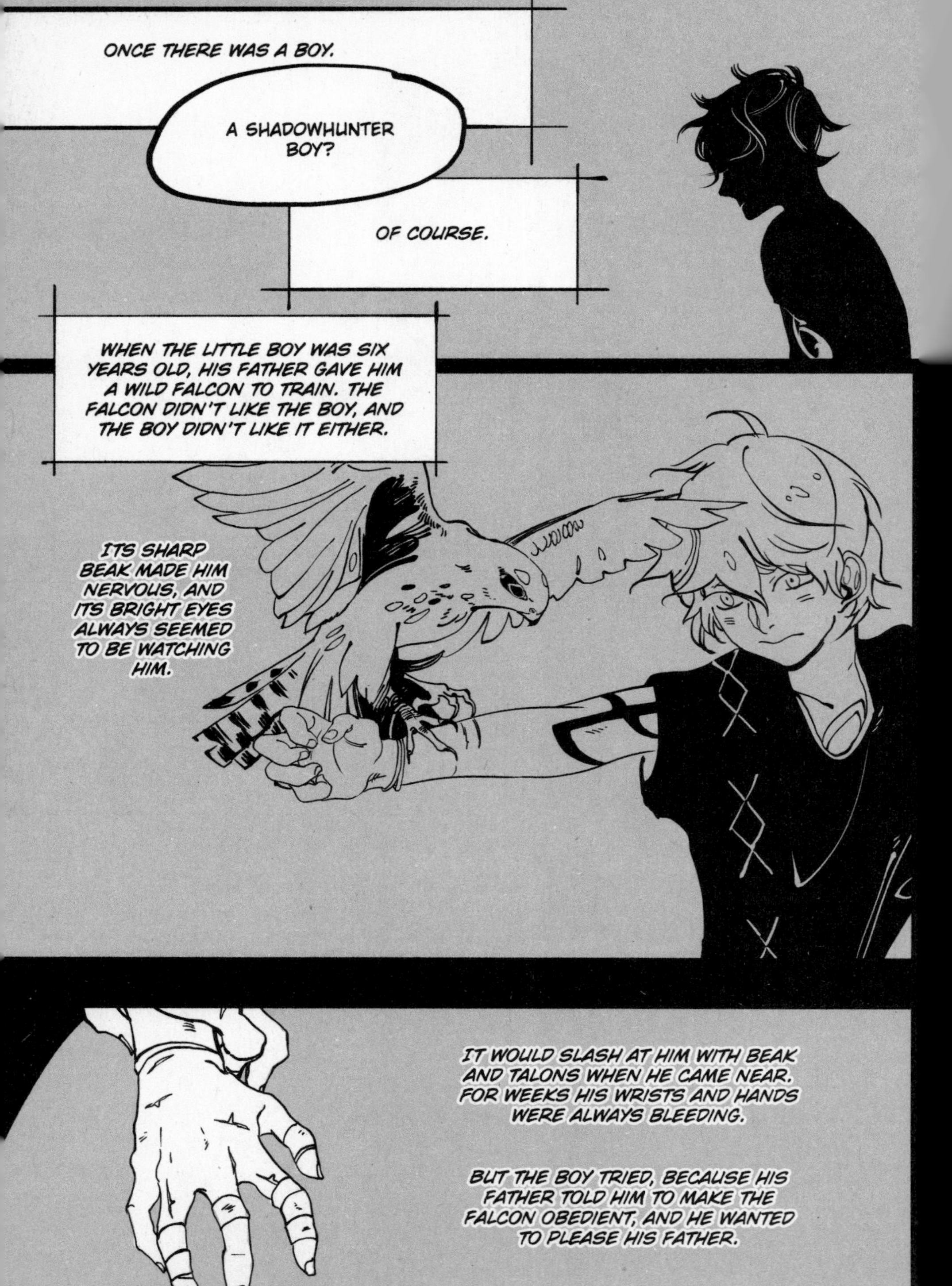
ONCE THERE WAS A BOY.
A SHADOWHUNTER BOY?
OF COURSE.
WHEN THE LITTLE BOY WAS SIX YEARS OLD, HIS FATHER GAVE HIM A WILD FALCON TO TRAIN. THE FALCON DIDN'T LIKE THE BOY, AND THE BOY DIDN'T LIKE IT EITHER.
ITS SHARP BEAK MADE HIM NERVOUS, AND ITS BRIGHT EYES ALWAYS SEEMED TO BE WATCHING HIM.
IT WOULD SLASH AT HIM WITH BEAK AND TALONS WHEN HE CAME NEAR. FOR WEEKS HIS WRISTS AND HANDS WERE ALWAYS BLEEDING.
BUT THE BOY TRIED, BECAUSE HIS FATHER TOLD HIM TO MAKE THE FALCON OBEDIENT, AND HE WANTED TO PLEASE HIS FATHER.

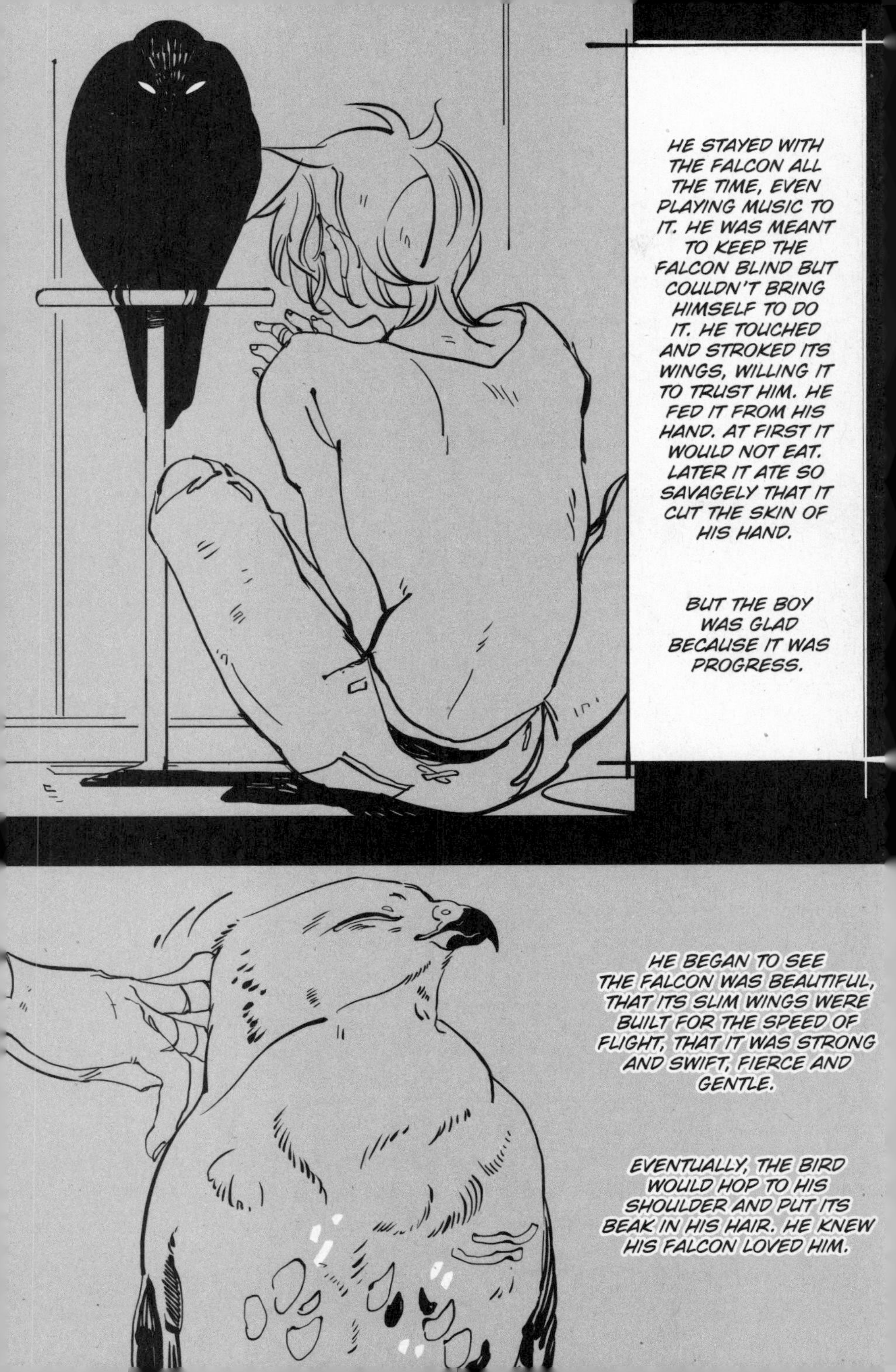
HE STAYED WITH THE FALCON ALL THE TIME, EVEN PLAYING MUSIC TO IT. HE WAS MEANT TO KEEP THE FALCON BLIND BUT COULDN'T BRING HIMSELF TO DO IT. HE TOUCHED AND STROKED ITS WINGS, WILLING IT TO TRUST HIM. HE FED IT FROM HIS HAND. AT FIRST IT WOULD NOT EAT. LATER IT ATE SO SAVAGELY THAT IT CUT THE SKIN OF HIS HAND.
BUT THE BOY WAS GLAD BECAUSE IT WAS PROGRESS.
HE BEGAN TO SEE THE FALCON WAS BEAUTIFUL, THAT ITS SLIM WINGS WERE BUILT FOR THE SPEED OF FLIGHT, THAT IT WAS STRONG AND SWIFT, FIERCE AND GENTLE.
EVENTUALLY, THE BIRD WOULD HOP TO HIS SHOULDER AND PUT ITS BEAK IN HIS HAIR. HE KNEW HIS FALCON LOVED HIM.

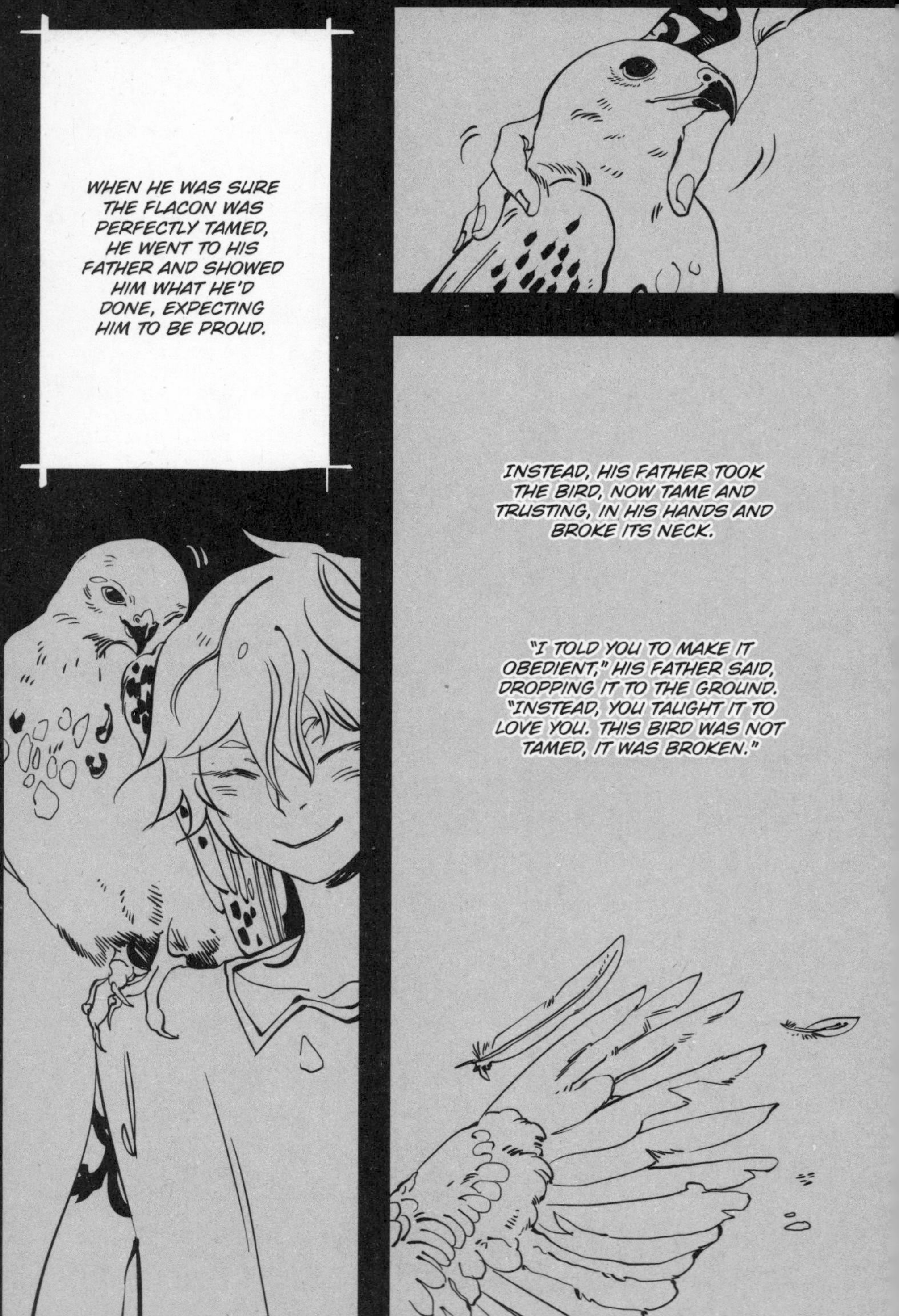
WHEN HE WAS SURE THE FLACON WAS PERFECTLY TAMED, HE WENT TO HIS FATHER AND SHOWED HIM WHAT HE'D DONE, EXPECTING HIM TO BE PROUD.
INSTEAD, HIS FATHER TOOK THE BIRD, NOW TAME AND TRUSTING, IN HIS HANDS AND BROKE ITS NECK.
"I TOLD YOU TO MAKE IT OBEDIENT," HIS FATHER SAID, DROPPING IT TO THE GROUND. "INSTEAD, YOU TAUGHT IT TO LOVE YOU. THIS BIRD WAS NOT TAMED, IT WAS BROKEN."

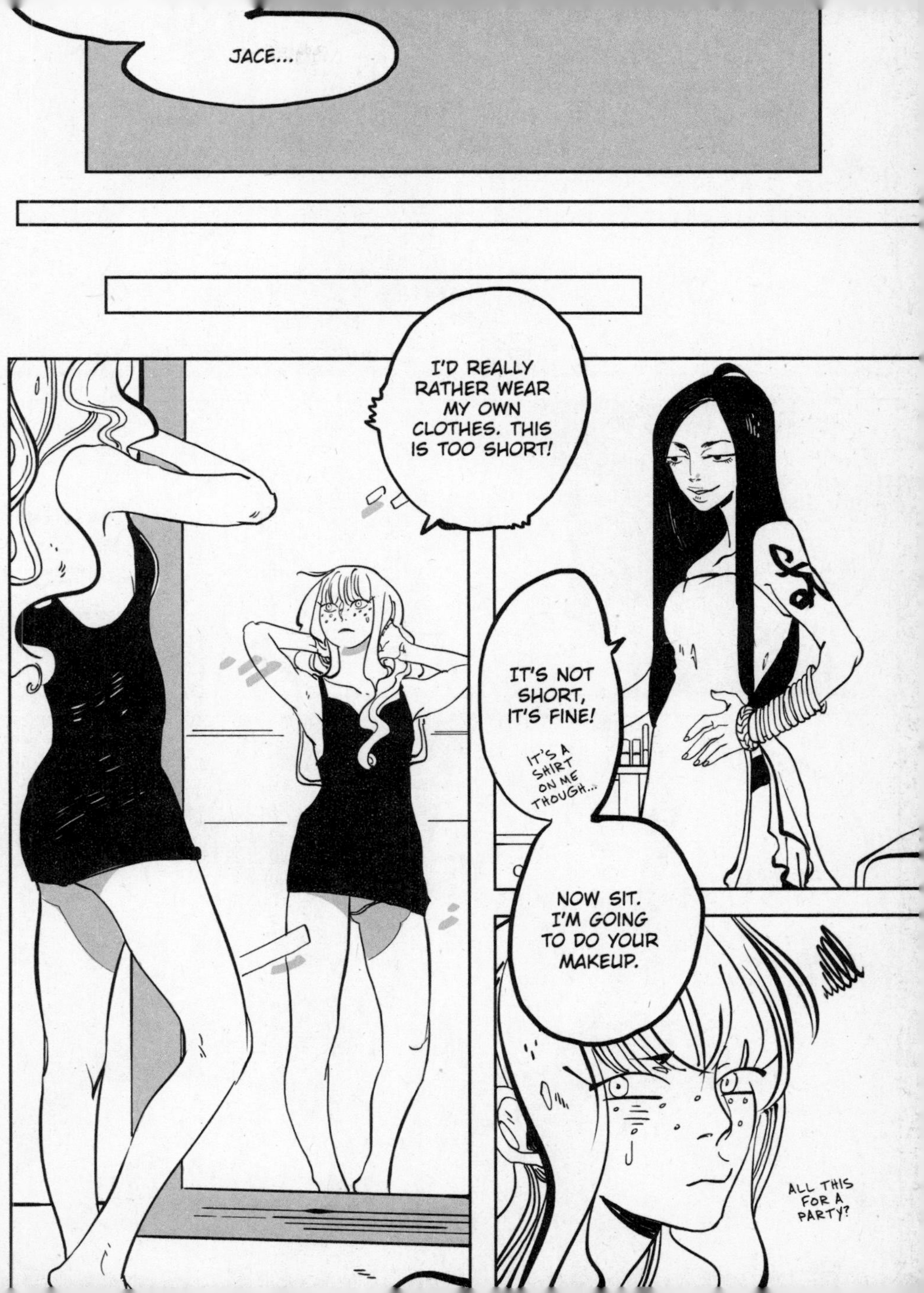
JACE...
I'D REALLY RATHER WEAR MY OWN CLOTHES. THIS IS TOO SHORT!
IT'S NOT SHORT, IT'S FINE!
IT'S A SHIRT ON ME THOUGH...
NOW SIT. I'M GOING TO DO YOUR MAKEUP.
ALL THIS FOR A PARTY?

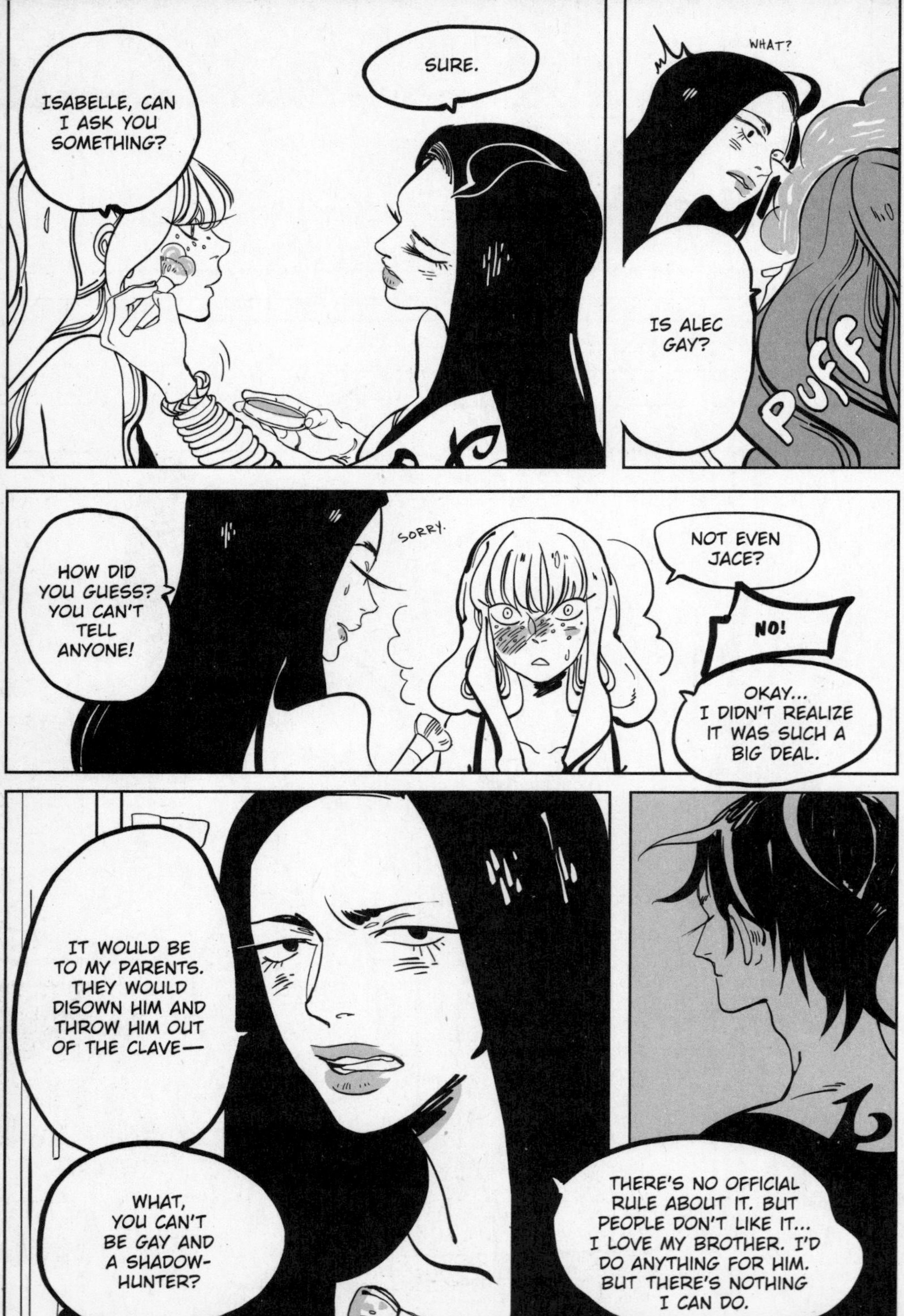
ISABELLE, CAN I ASK YOU SOMETHING?
SURE.
WHAT?
IS ALEC GAY?
PUFF
HOW DID YOU GUESS? YOU CAN'T TELL ANYONE!
SORRY.
NOT EVEN JACE?
NO!
OKAY... I DIDN'T REALIZE IT WAS SUCH A BIG DEAL.
IT WOULD BE TO MY PARENTS. THEY WOULD DISOWN HIM AND THROW HIM OUT OF THE CLAVE—
WHAT, YOU CAN'T BE GAY AND A SHADOW-HUNTER?
THERE'S NO OFFICIAL RULE ABOUT IT. BUT PEOPLE DON'T LIKE IT... I LOVE MY BROTHER. I'D DO ANYTHING FOR HIM. BUT THERE'S NOTHING I CAN DO.

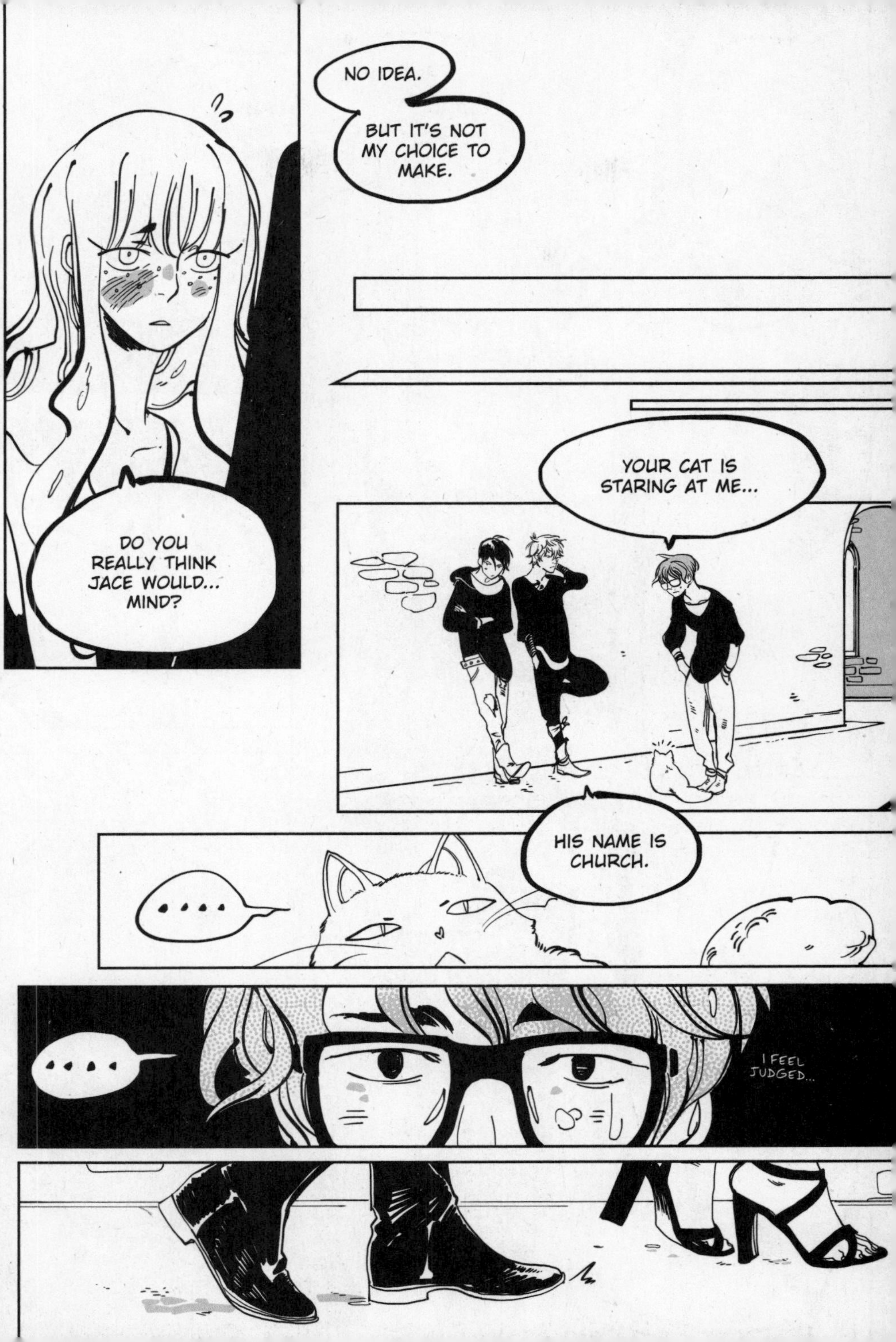
NO IDEA.
BUT IT'S NOT MY CHOICE TO MAKE.
DO YOU REALLY THINK JACE WOULD... MIND?
YOUR CAT IS STARING AT ME...
....
HIS NAME IS CHURCH.
....
I FEEL JUDGED...

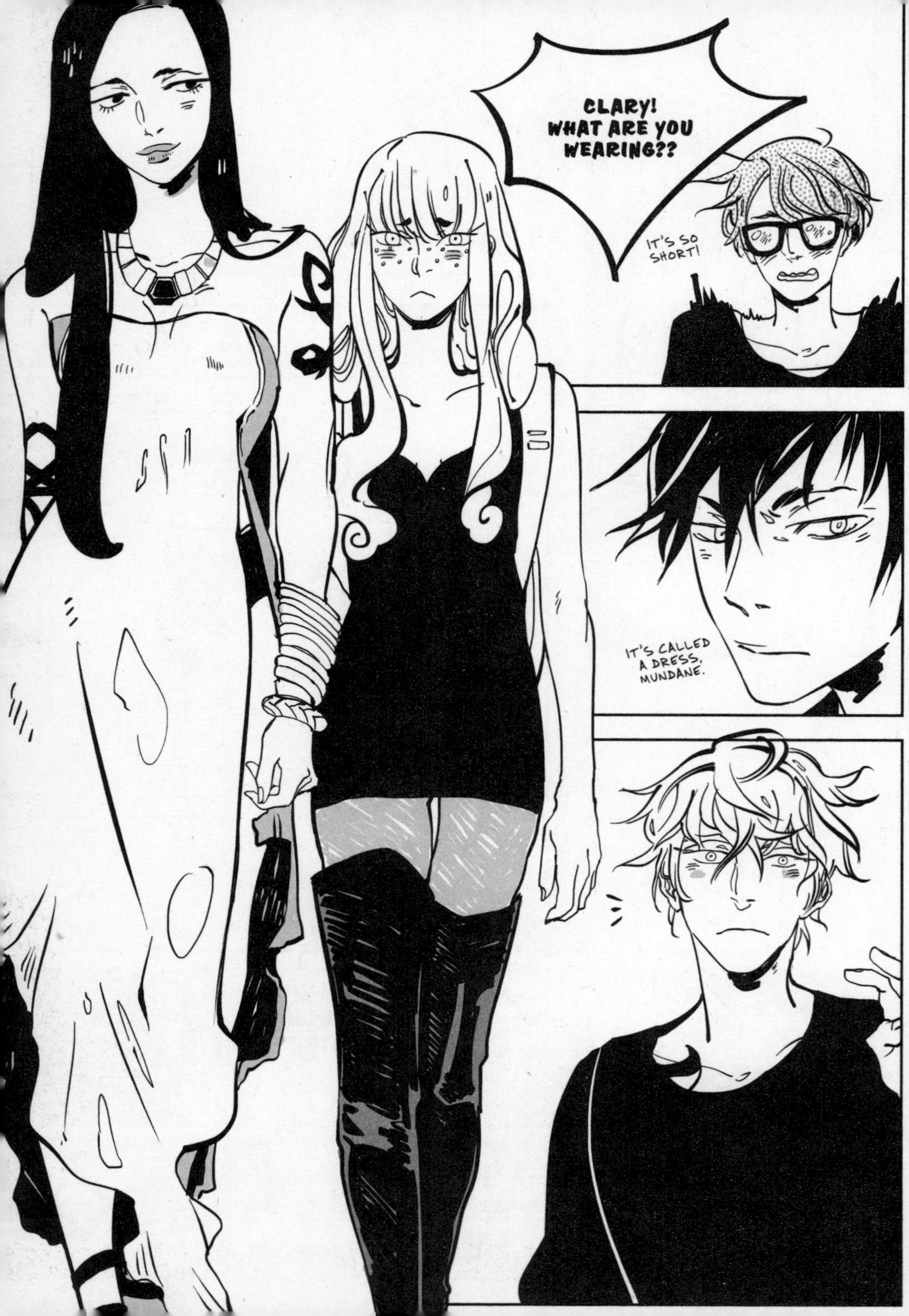
CLARY! WHAT ARE YOU WEARING??
IT'S SO SHORT!
IT'S CALLED A DRESS, MUNDANE.

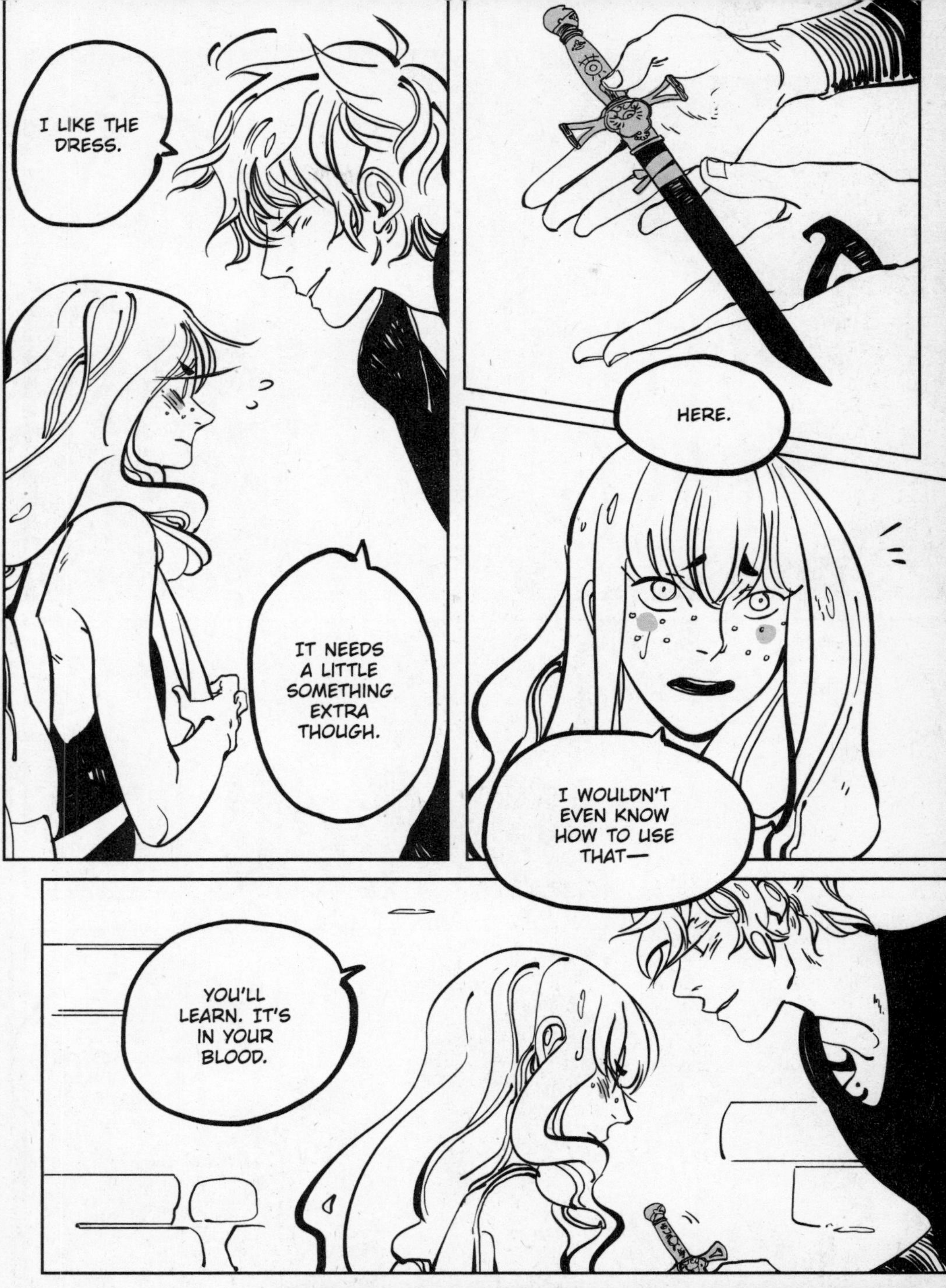
I LIKE THE DRESS.
IT NEEDS A LITTLE SOMETHING EXTRA THOUGH.
HERE.
I WOULDN'T EVEN KNOW HOW TO USE THAT—
YOU'LL LEARN. IT'S IN YOUR BLOOD.

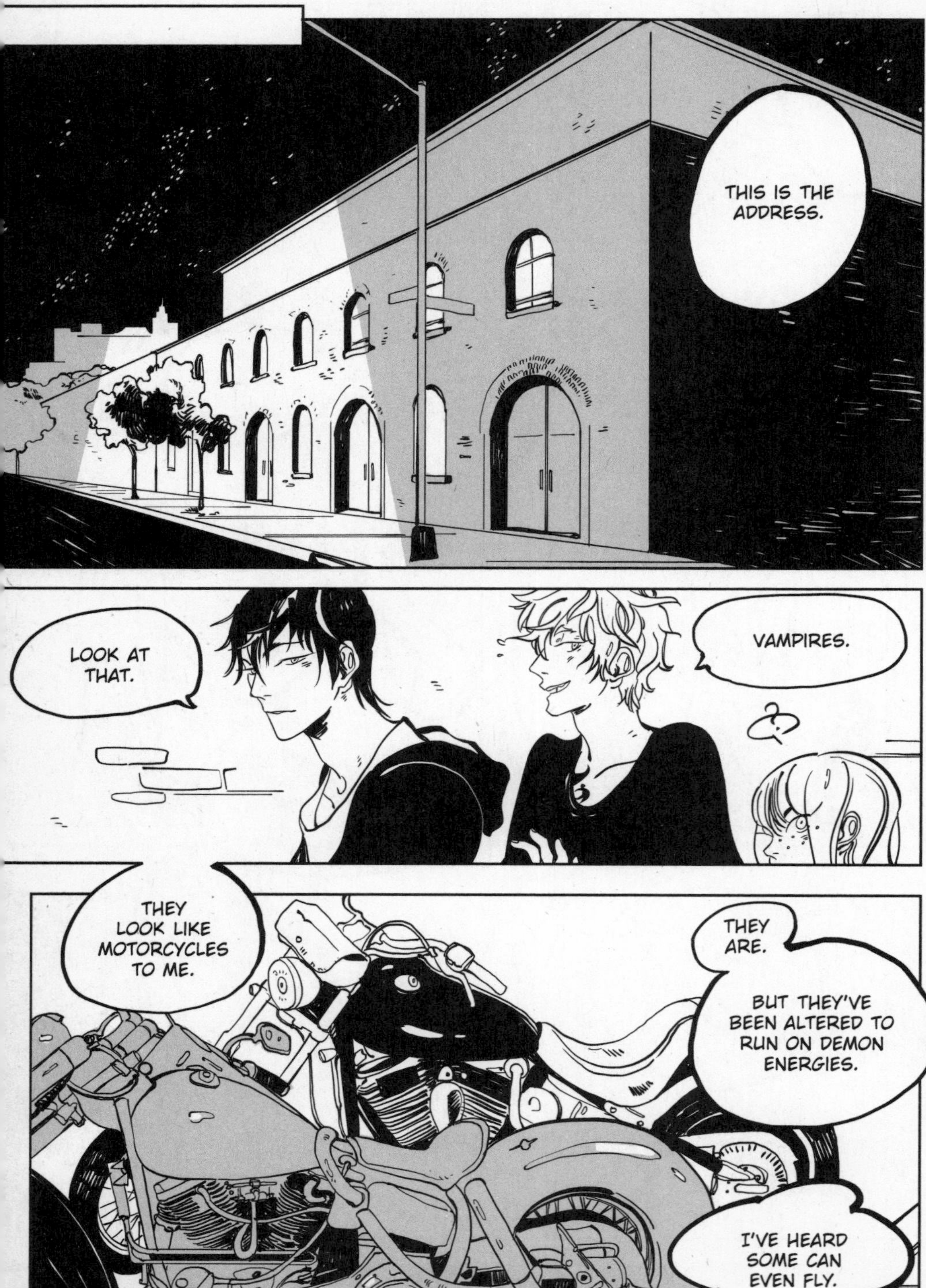
THIS IS THE ADDRESS.
LOOK AT THAT.
VAMPIRES.
THEY LOOK LIKE MOTORCYCLES TO ME.
THEY ARE.
BUT THEY'VE BEEN ALTERED TO RUN ON DEMON ENERGIES.
I'VE HEARD SOME CAN EVEN FLY.

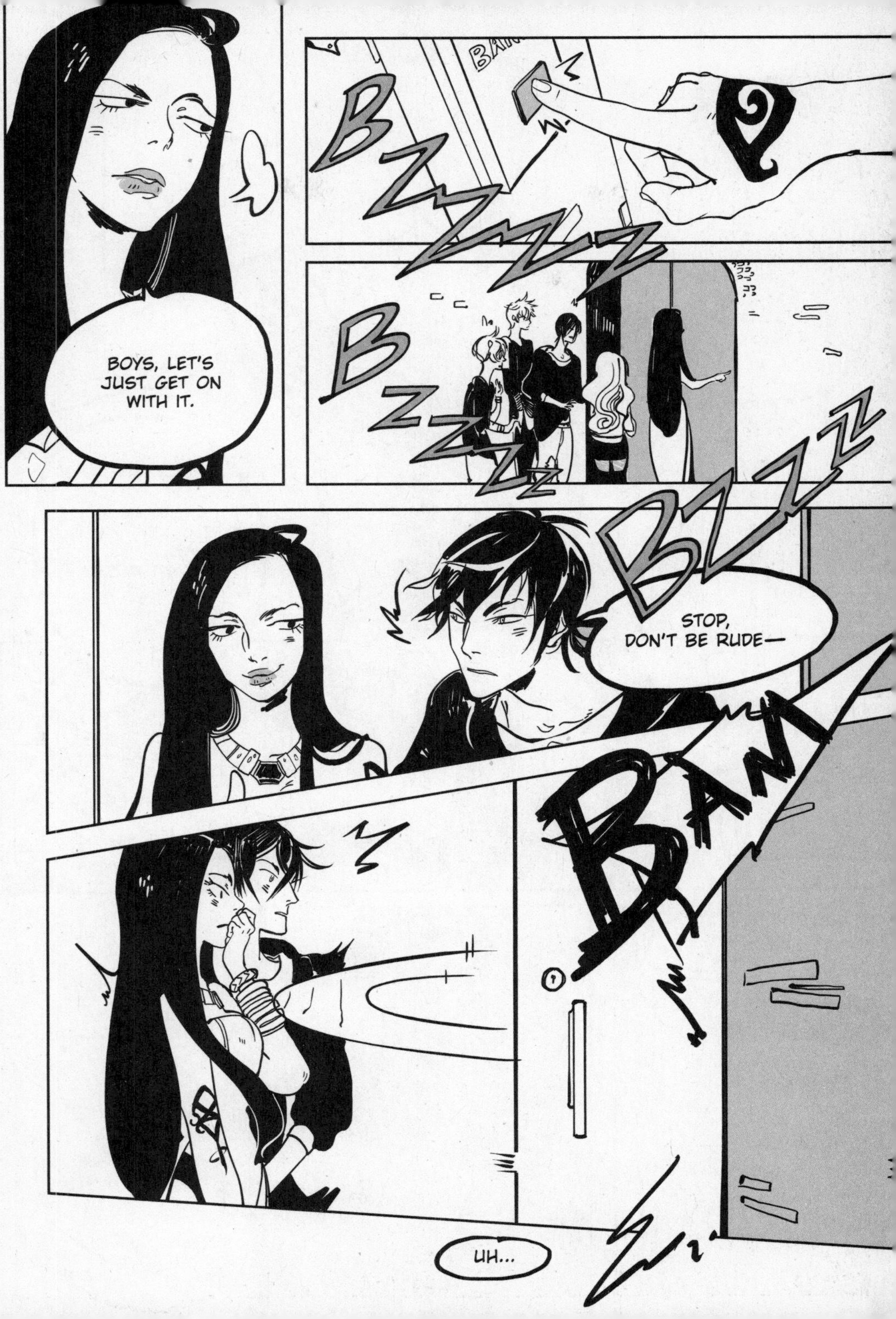
BOYS, LET'S JUST GET ON WITH IT.
BAN
BZZZZZZ
BZZZZZ
BZZZZ
STOP, DON'T BE RUDE—
BAM
UH...

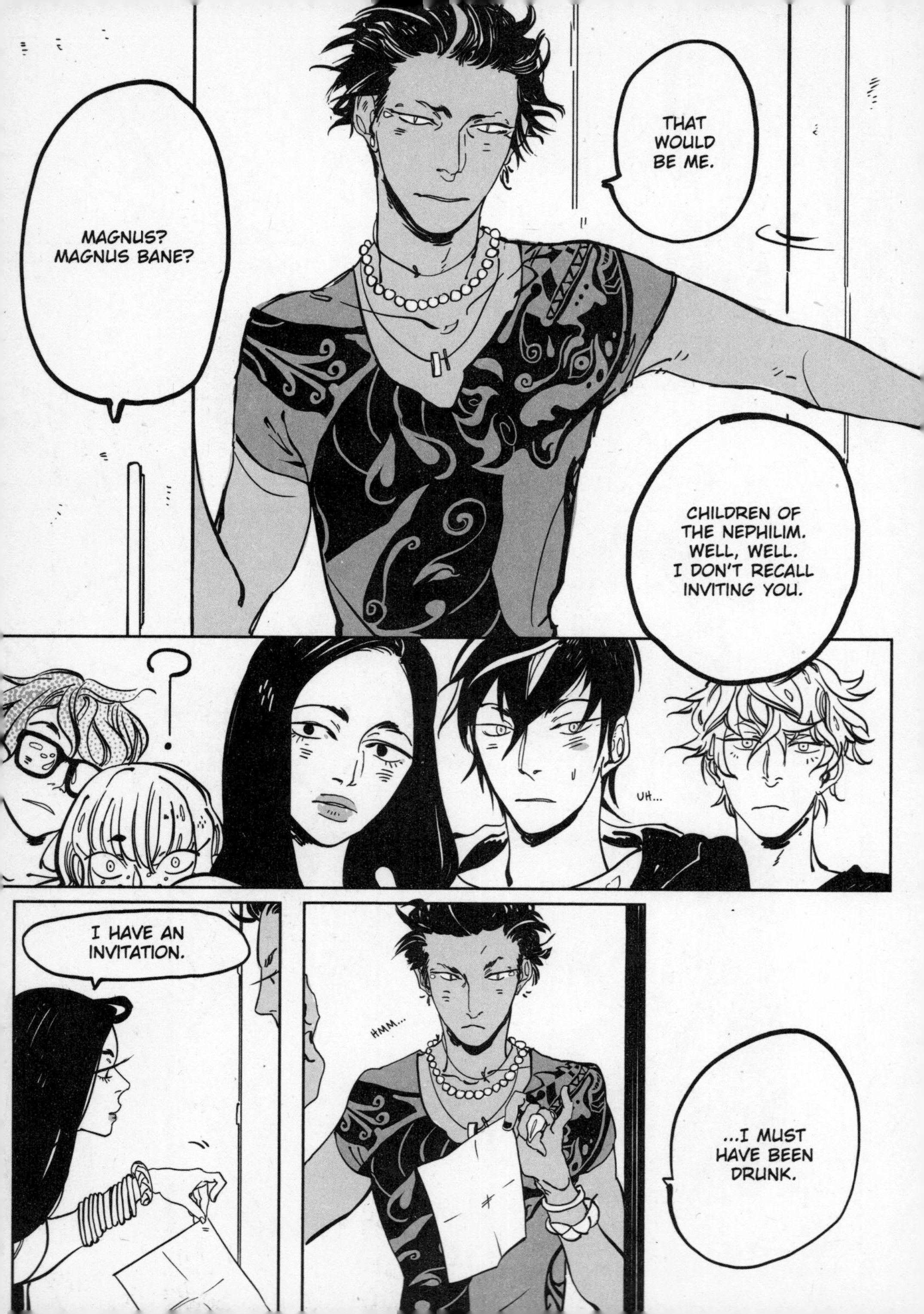
MAGNUS? MAGNUS BANE?
THAT WOULD BE ME.
CHILDREN OF THE NEPHILIM. WELL, WELL. I DON'T RECALL INVITING YOU.
?
!
UH...
I HAVE AN INVITATION.
HMM...
...I MUST HAVE BEEN DRUNK.

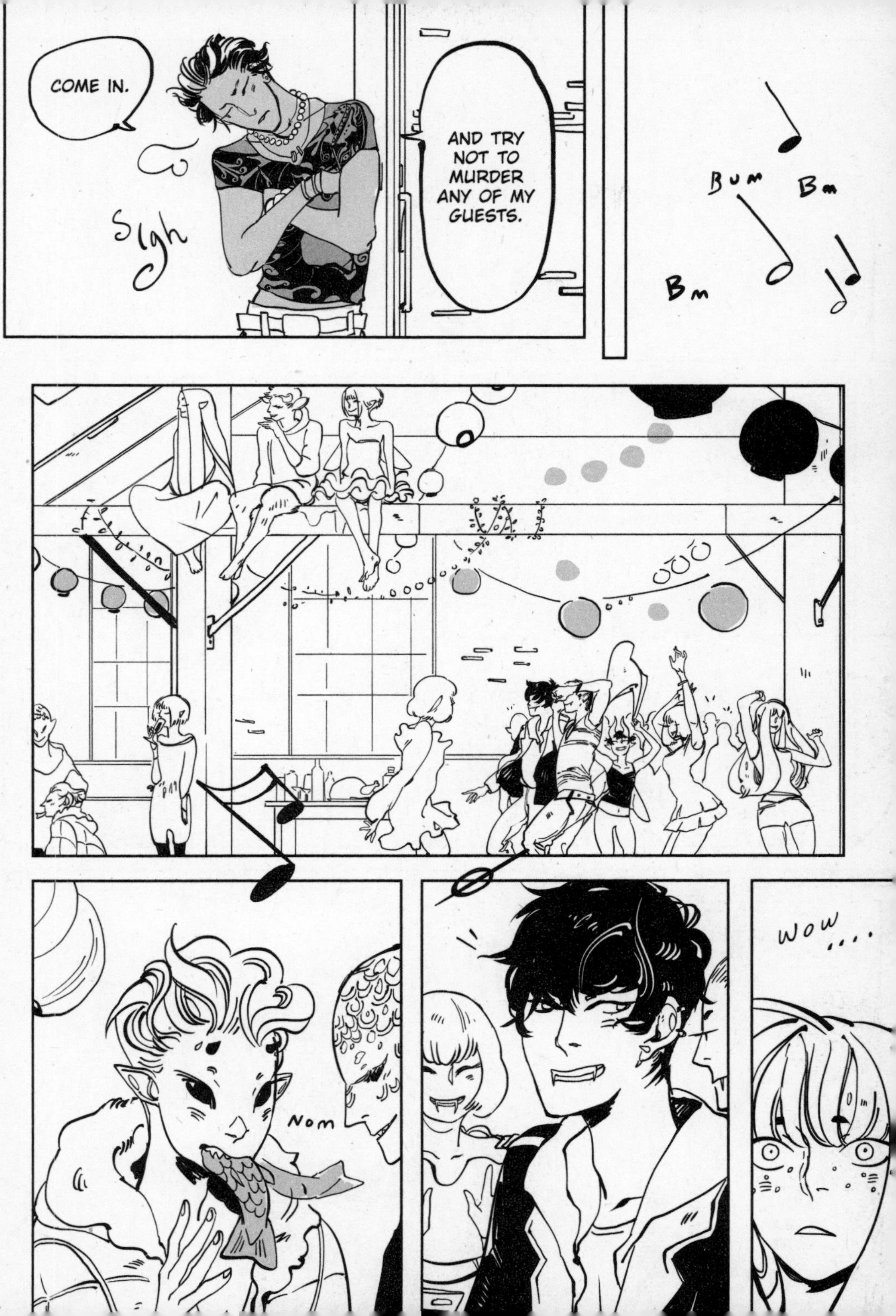
COME IN.
Sigh
AND TRY NOT TO MURDER ANY OF MY GUESTS.
Bum
Bm
Bm
Nom
WOW...

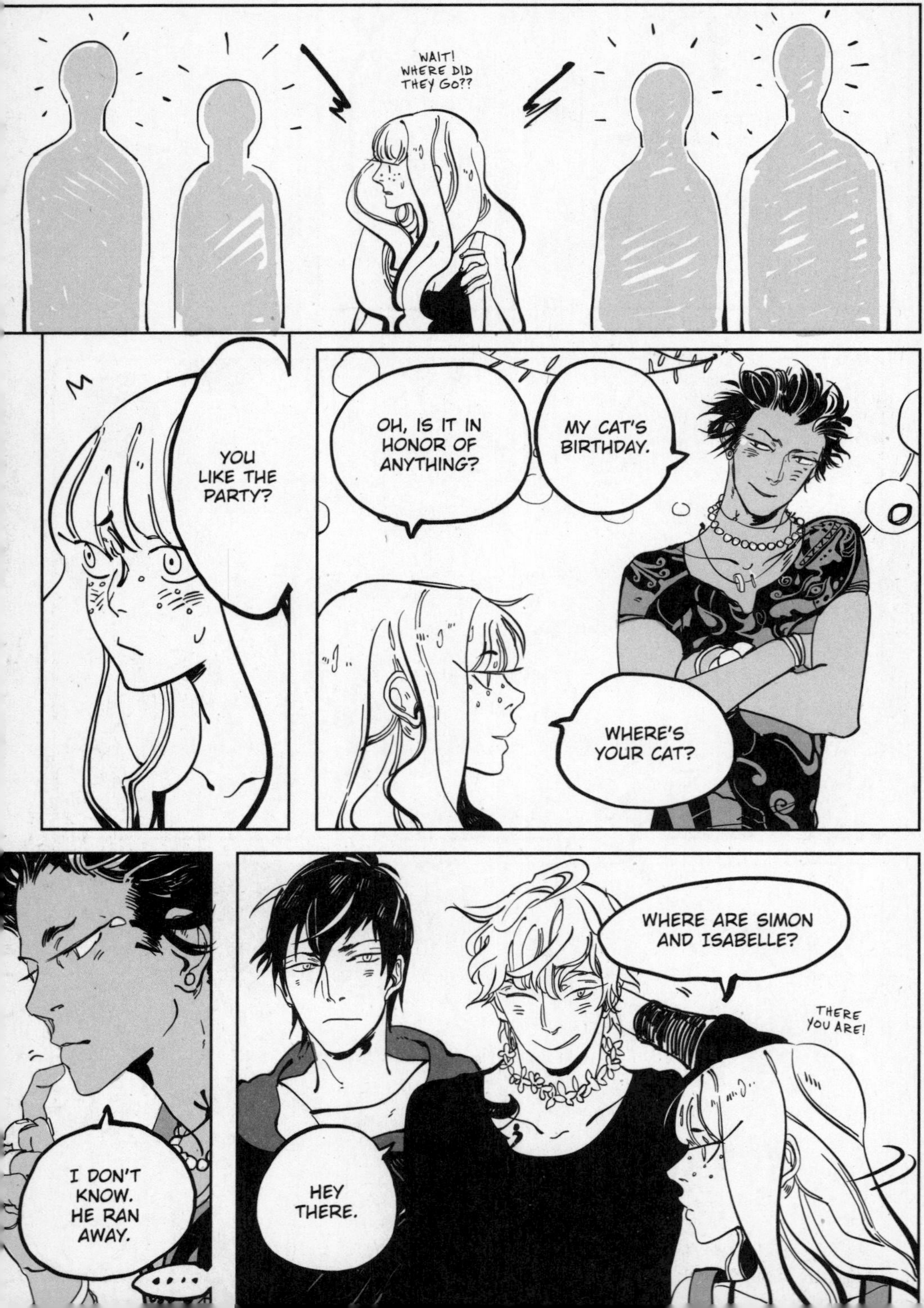
WAIT! WHERE DID THEY GO??
YOU LIKE THE PARTY?
OH, IS IT IN HONOR OF ANYTHING?
MY CAT'S BIRTHDAY.
WHERE'S YOUR CAT?
I DON'T KNOW. HE RAN AWAY.
HEY THERE.
WHERE ARE SIMON AND ISABELLE?
THERE YOU ARE!

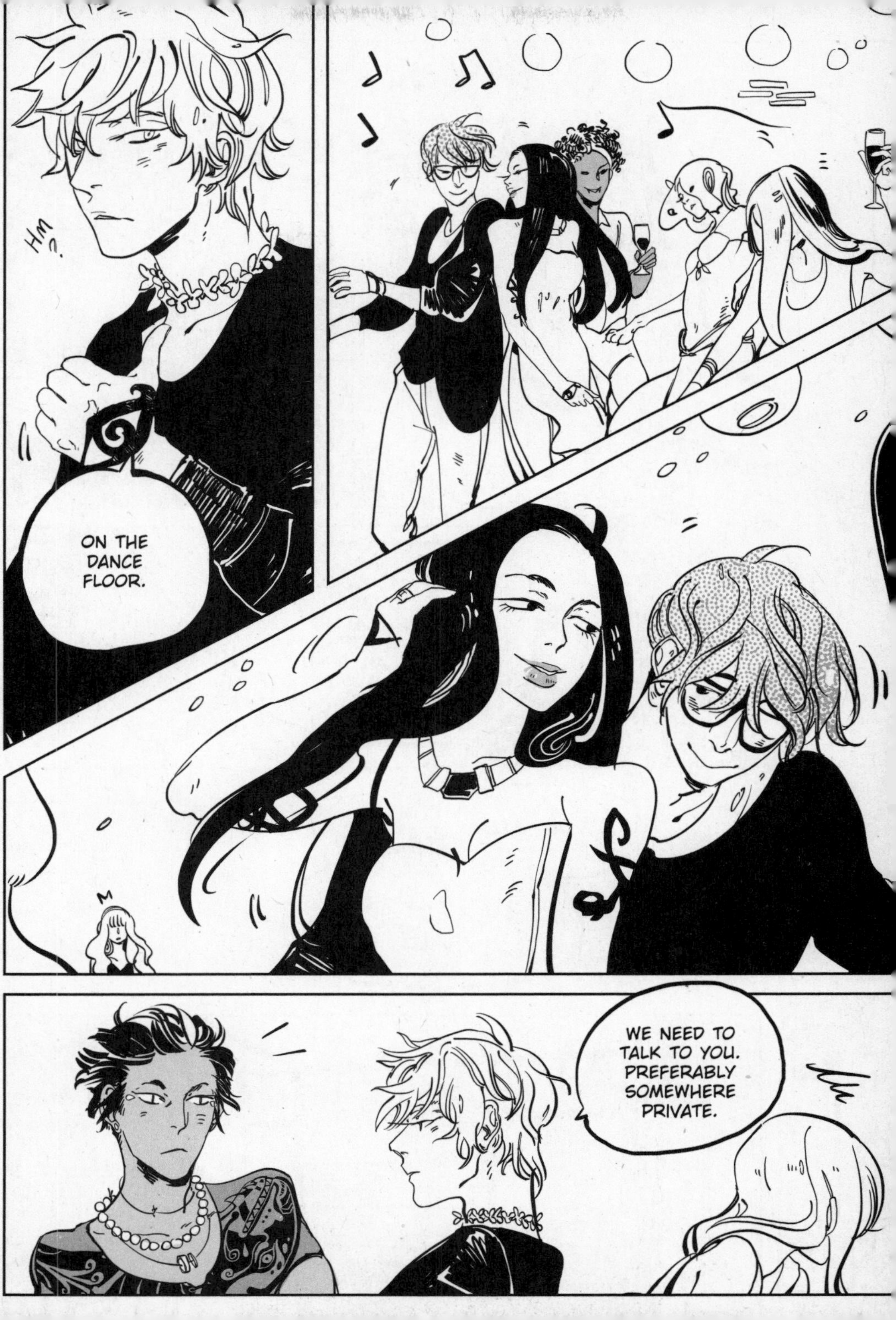
HM?
ON THE DANCE FLOOR.
WE NEED TO TALK TO YOU. PREFERABLY SOMEWHERE PRIVATE.

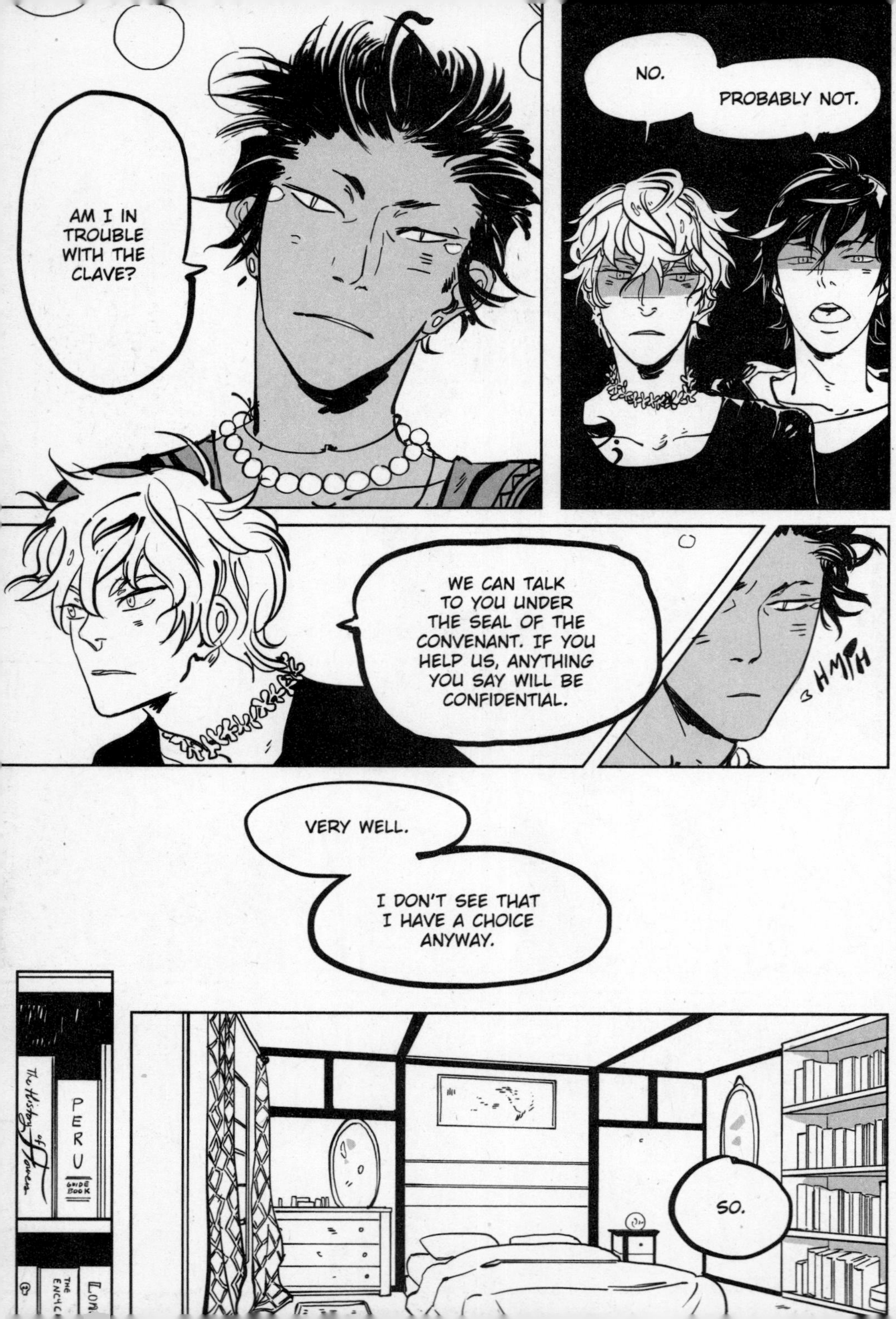
AM I IN TROUBLE WITH THE CLAVE?
NO.
PROBABLY NOT.
WE CAN TALK TO YOU UNDER THE SEAL OF THE CONVENANT. IF YOU HELP US, ANYTHING YOU SAY WILL BE CONFIDENTIAL.
HMPH
VERY WELL.
I DON'T SEE THAT I HAVE A CHOICE ANYWAY.
The History of Flowers
PERU
GUIDE BOOK
SO.

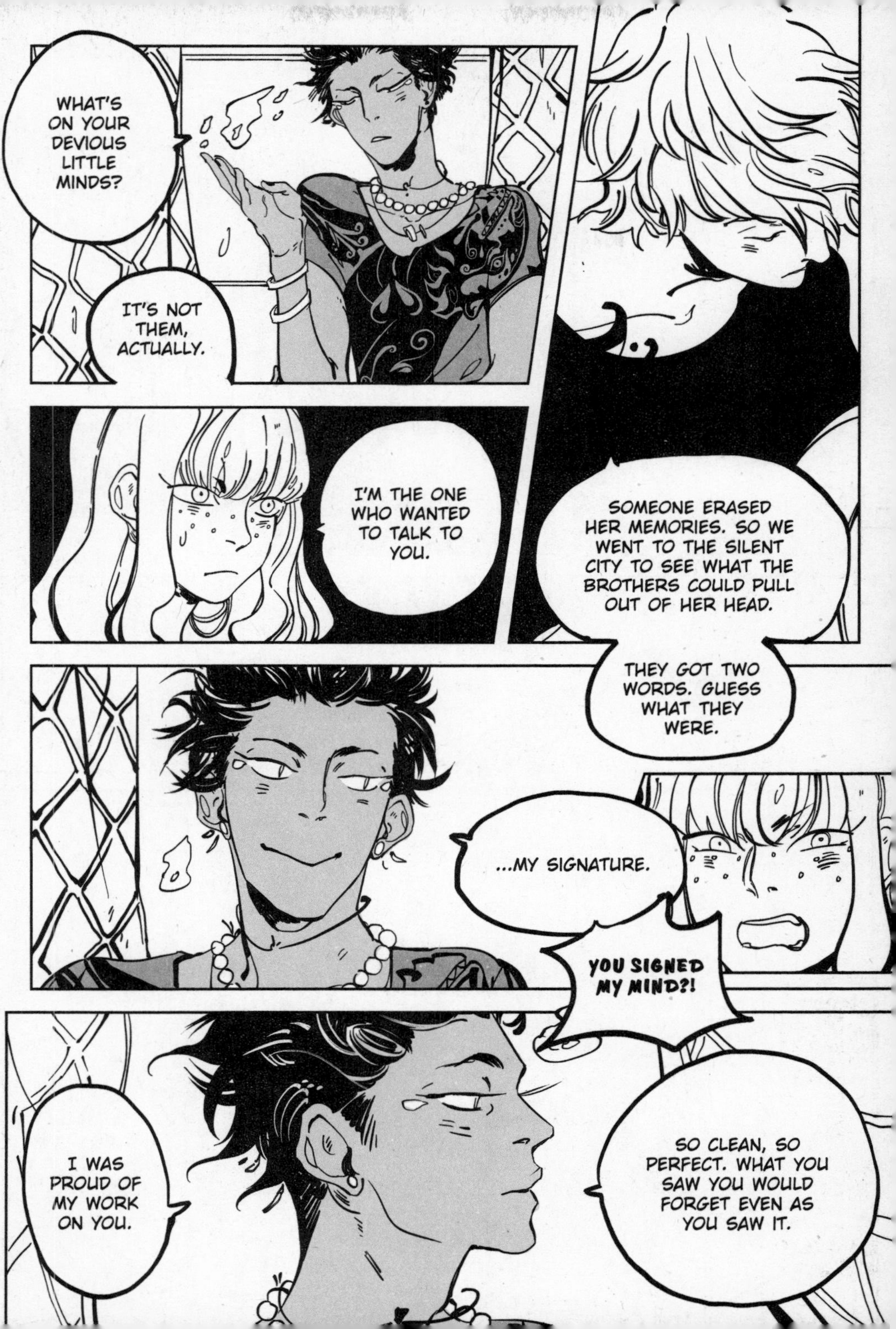
WHAT'S ON YOUR DEVIOUS LITTLE MINDS?
IT'S NOT THEM, ACTUALLY.
I'M THE ONE WHO WANTED TO TALK TO YOU.
SOMEONE ERASED HER MEMORIES. SO WE WENT TO THE SILENT CITY TO SEE WHAT THE BROTHERS COULD PULL OUT OF HER HEAD.
THEY GOT TWO WORDS. GUESS WHAT THEY WERE.
...MY SIGNATURE.
YOU SIGNED MY MIND?!
I WAS PROUD OF MY WORK ON YOU.
SO CLEAN, SO PERFECT. WHAT YOU SAW YOU WOULD FORGET EVEN AS YOU SAW IT.

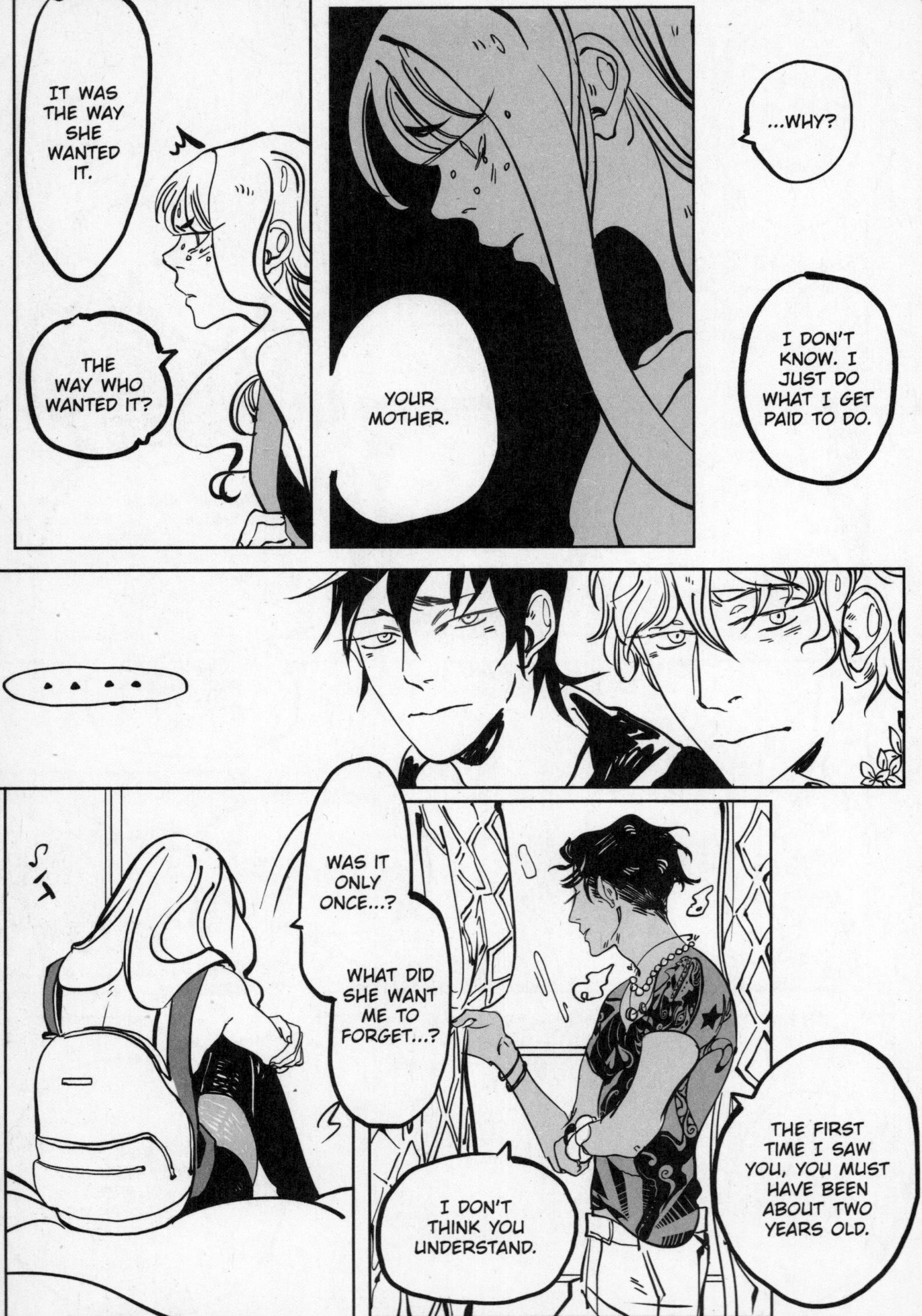
IT WAS THE WAY SHE WANTED IT.
THE WAY WHO WANTED IT?
YOUR MOTHER.
...WHY?
I DON'T KNOW. I JUST DO WHAT I GET PAID TO DO.
....
SIT
WAS IT ONLY ONCE...?
WHAT DID SHE WANT ME TO FORGET...?
I DON'T THINK YOU UNDERSTAND.
THE FIRST TIME I SAW YOU, YOU MUST HAVE BEEN ABOUT TWO YEARS OLD.

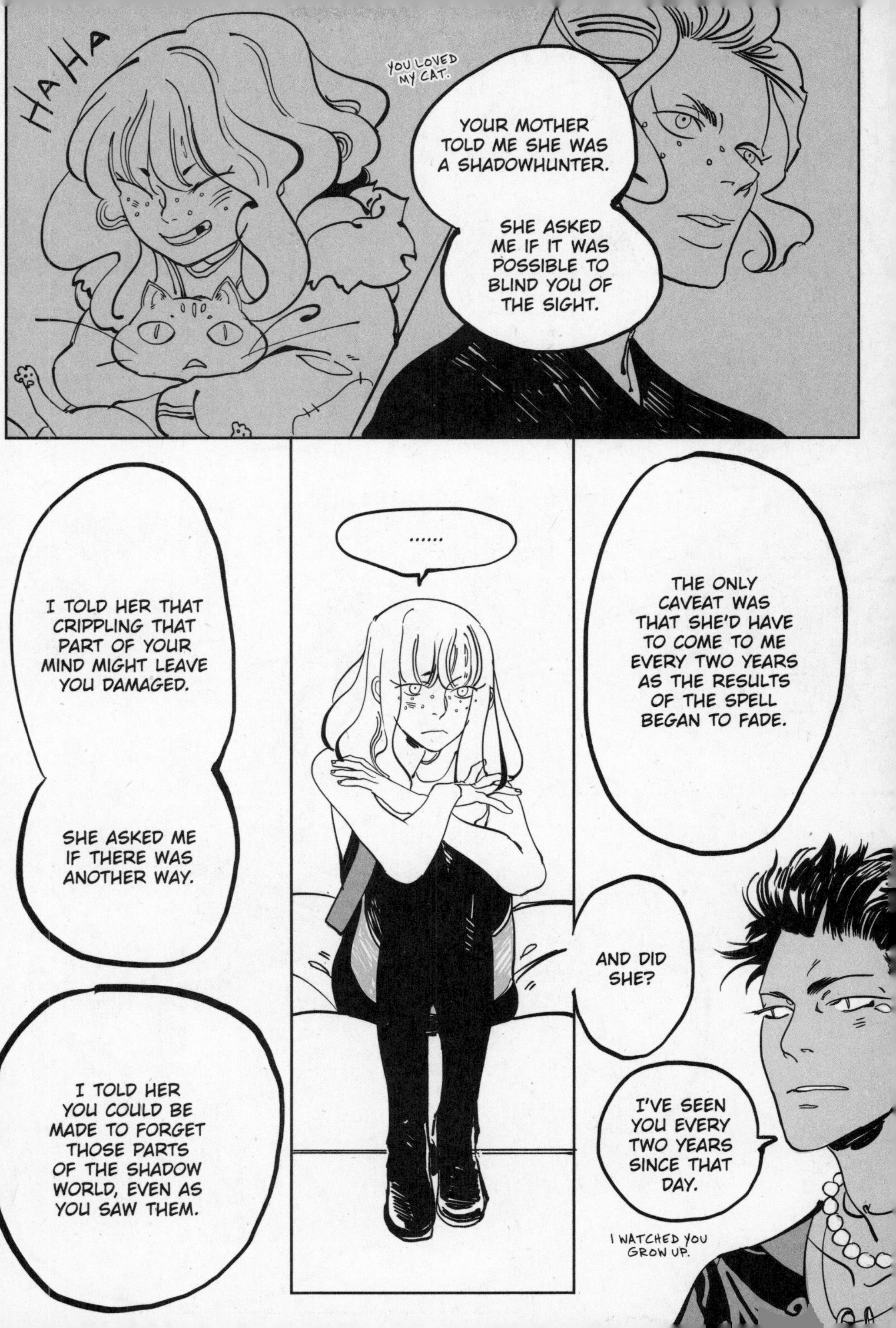
HAHA
YOU LOVED MY CAT.
YOUR MOTHER TOLD ME SHE WAS A SHADOWHUNTER.
SHE ASKED ME IF IT WAS POSSIBLE TO BLIND YOU OF THE SIGHT.
I TOLD HER THAT CRIPPLING THAT PART OF YOUR MIND MIGHT LEAVE YOU DAMAGED.
SHE ASKED ME IF THERE WAS ANOTHER WAY.
I TOLD HER YOU COULD BE MADE TO FORGET THOSE PARTS OF THE SHADOW WORLD, EVEN AS YOU SAW THEM.
......
THE ONLY CAVEAT WAS THAT SHE'D HAVE TO COME TO ME EVERY TWO YEARS AS THE RESULTS OF THE SPELL BEGAN TO FADE.
AND DID SHE?
I'VE SEEN YOU EVERY TWO YEARS SINCE THAT DAY.
I WATCHED YOU GROW UP.

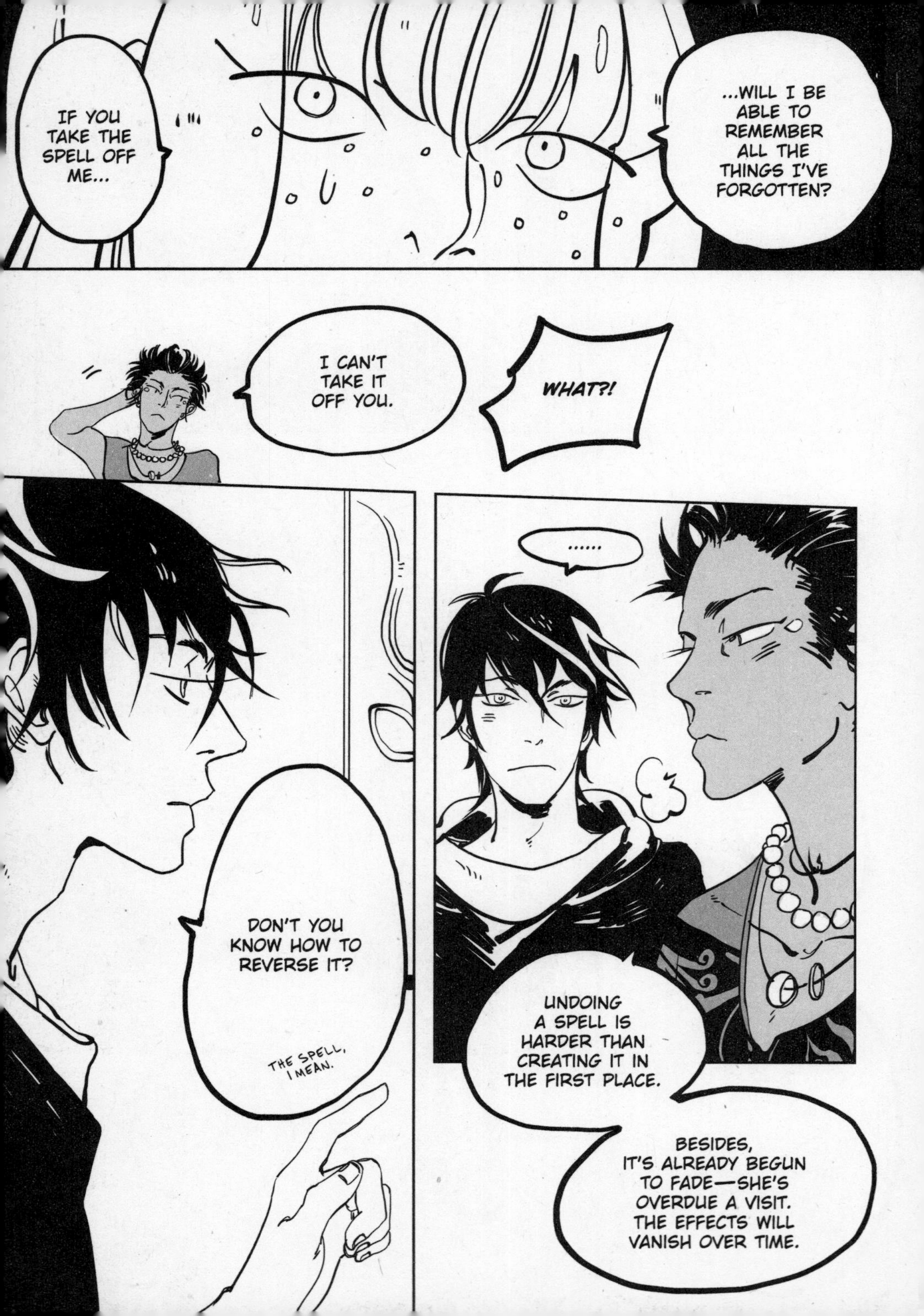
IF YOU TAKE THE SPELL OFF ME...
...WILL I BE ABLE TO REMEMBER ALL THE THINGS I'VE FORGOTTEN?
I CAN'T TAKE IT OFF YOU.
WHAT?!
DON'T YOU KNOW HOW TO REVERSE IT?
THE SPELL, I MEAN.
......
UNDOING A SPELL IS HARDER THAN CREATING IT IN THE FIRST PLACE.
BESIDES, IT'S ALREADY BEGUN TO FADE—SHE'S OVERDUE A VISIT. THE EFFECTS WILL VANISH OVER TIME.

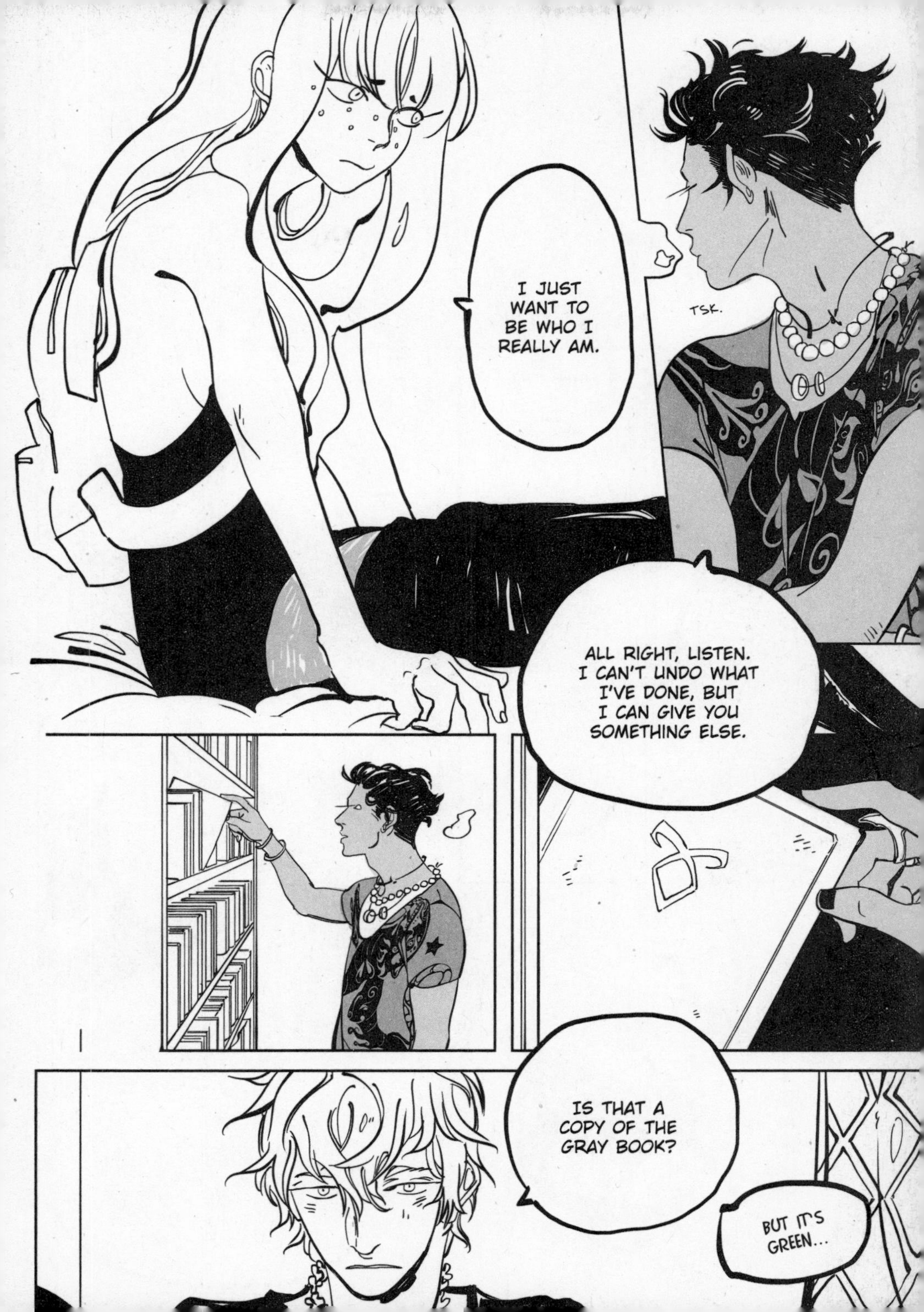
I JUST WANT TO BE WHO I REALLY AM.
TSK.
ALL RIGHT, LISTEN. I CAN'T UNDO WHAT I'VE DONE, BUT I CAN GIVE YOU SOMETHING ELSE.
IS THAT A COPY OF THE GRAY BOOK?
BUT IT'S GREEN...

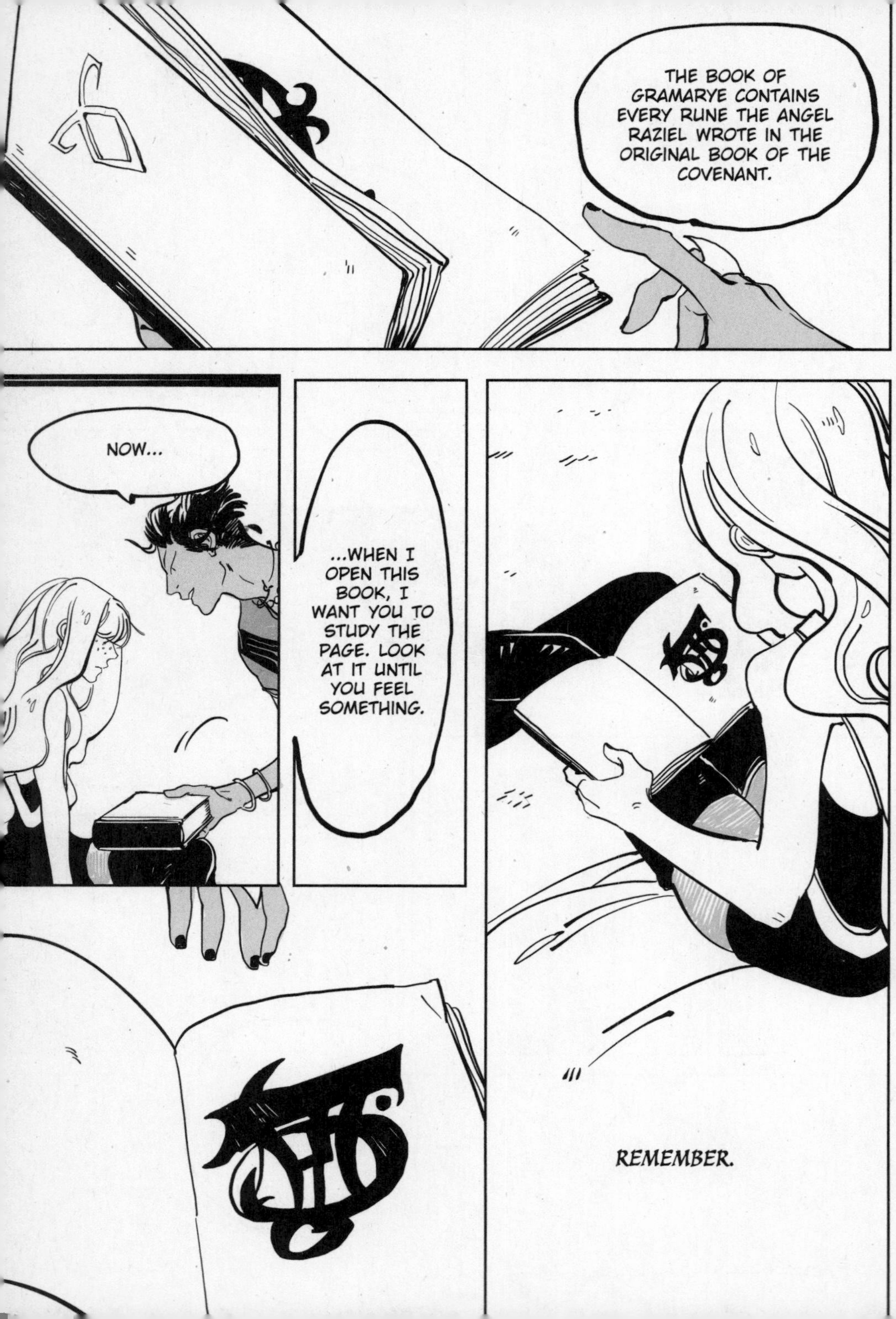
THE BOOK OF GRAMARYE CONTAINS EVERY RUNE THE ANGEL RAZIEL WROTE IN THE ORIGINAL BOOK OF THE COVENANT.
NOW...
...WHEN I OPEN THIS BOOK, I WANT YOU TO STUDY THE PAGE. LOOK AT IT UNTIL YOU FEEL SOMETHING.
REMEMBER.

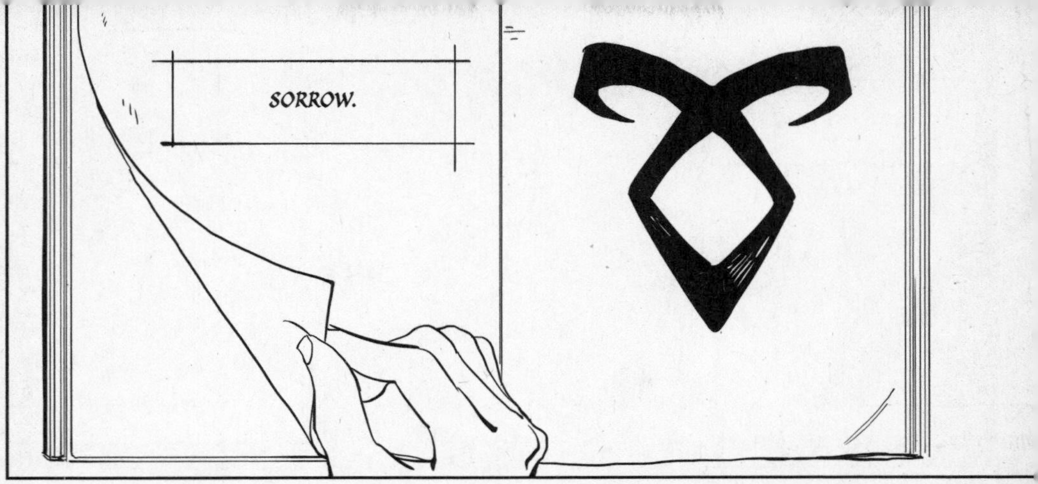
SORROW.

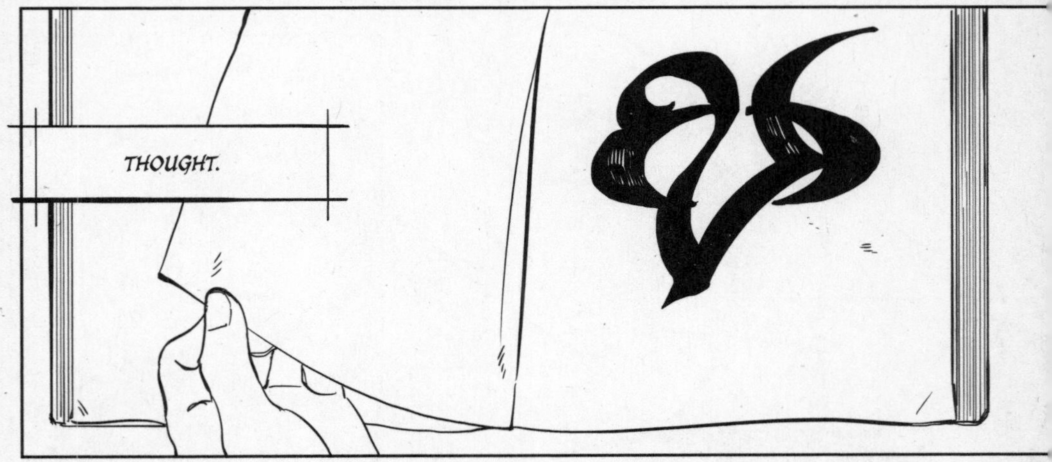
THOUGHT.

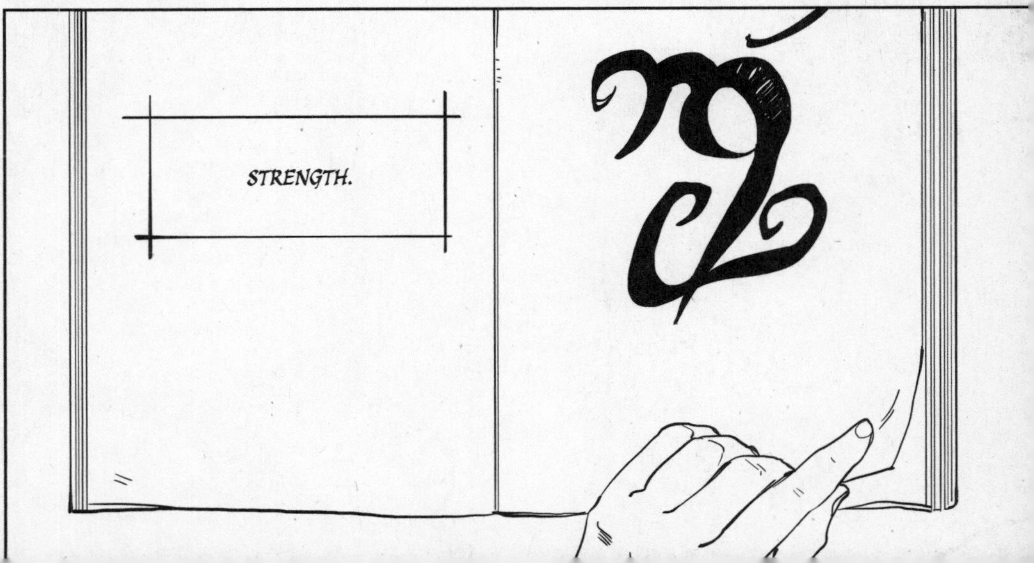
STRENGTH.

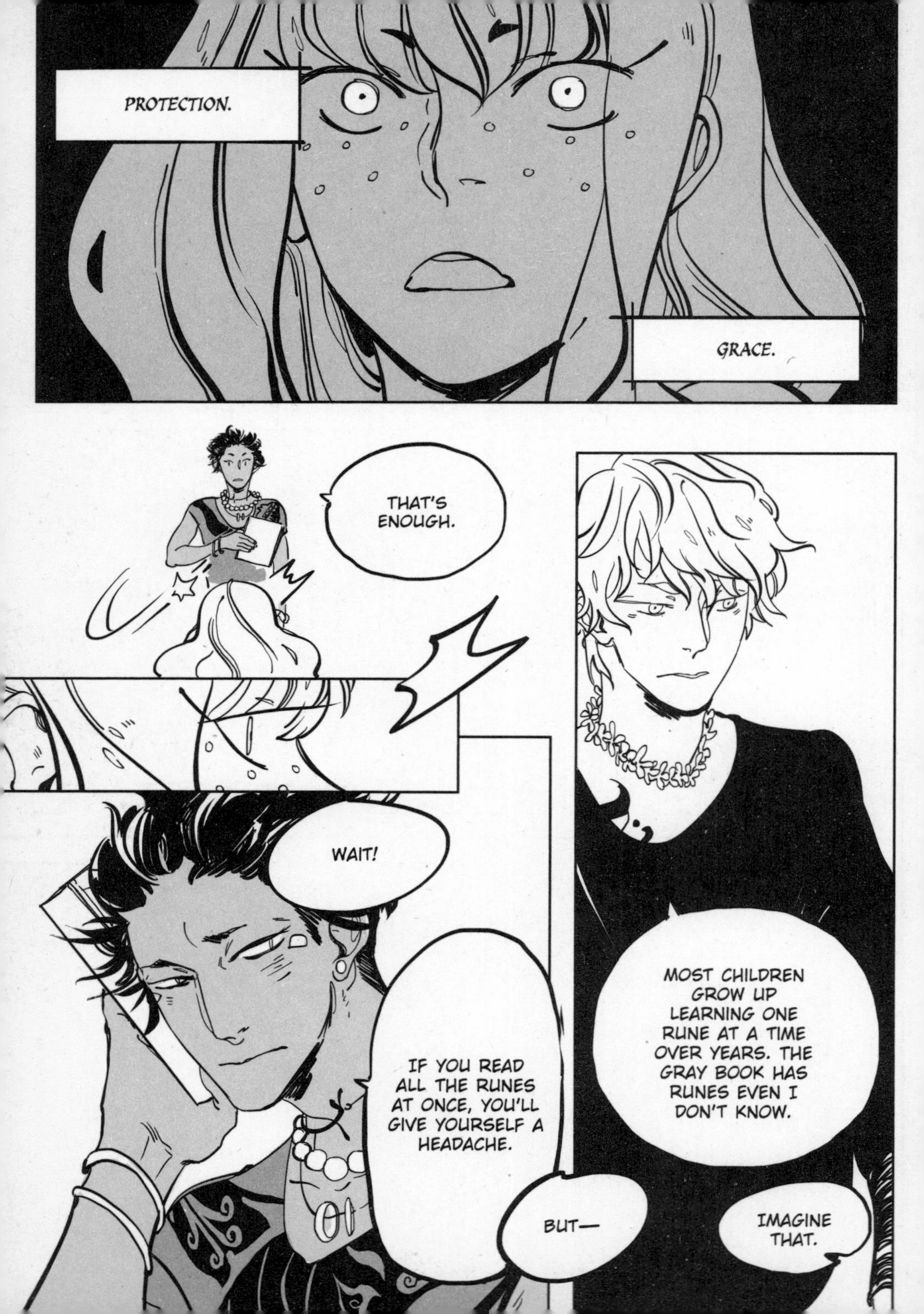
PROTECTION.
GRACE.
THAT'S ENOUGH.
WAIT!
IF YOU READ ALL THE RUNES AT ONCE, YOU'LL GIVE YOURSELF A HEADACHE.
BUT—
MOST CHILDREN GROW UP LEARNING ONE RUNE AT A TIME OVER YEARS. THE GRAY BOOK HAS RUNES EVEN I DON'T KNOW.
IMAGINE THAT.

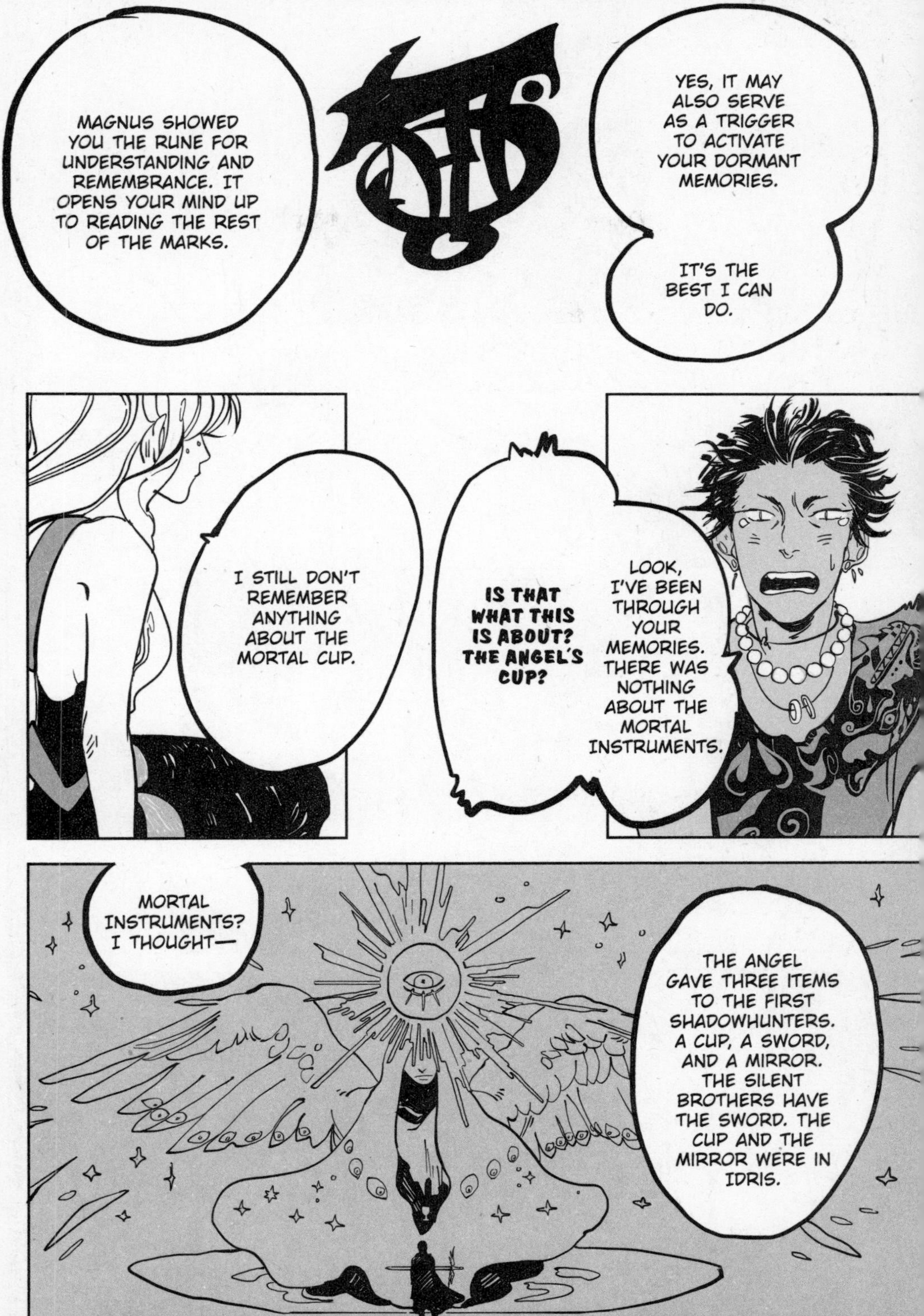
MAGNUS SHOWED YOU THE RUNE FOR UNDERSTANDING AND REMEMBRANCE. IT OPENS YOUR MIND UP TO READING THE REST OF THE MARKS.
YES, IT MAY ALSO SERVE AS A TRIGGER TO ACTIVATE YOUR DORMANT MEMORIES.
IT'S THE BEST I CAN DO.
I STILL DON'T REMEMBER ANYTHING ABOUT THE MORTAL CUP.
IS THAT WHAT THIS IS ABOUT? THE ANGEL'S CUP?
LOOK, I'VE BEEN THROUGH YOUR MEMORIES. THERE WAS NOTHING ABOUT THE MORTAL INSTRUMENTS.
MORTAL INSTRUMENTS? I THOUGHT—
THE ANGEL GAVE THREE ITEMS TO THE FIRST SHADOWHUNTERS. A CUP, A SWORD, AND A MIRROR. THE SILENT BROTHERS HAVE THE SWORD. THE CUP AND THE MIRROR WERE IN IDRIS.

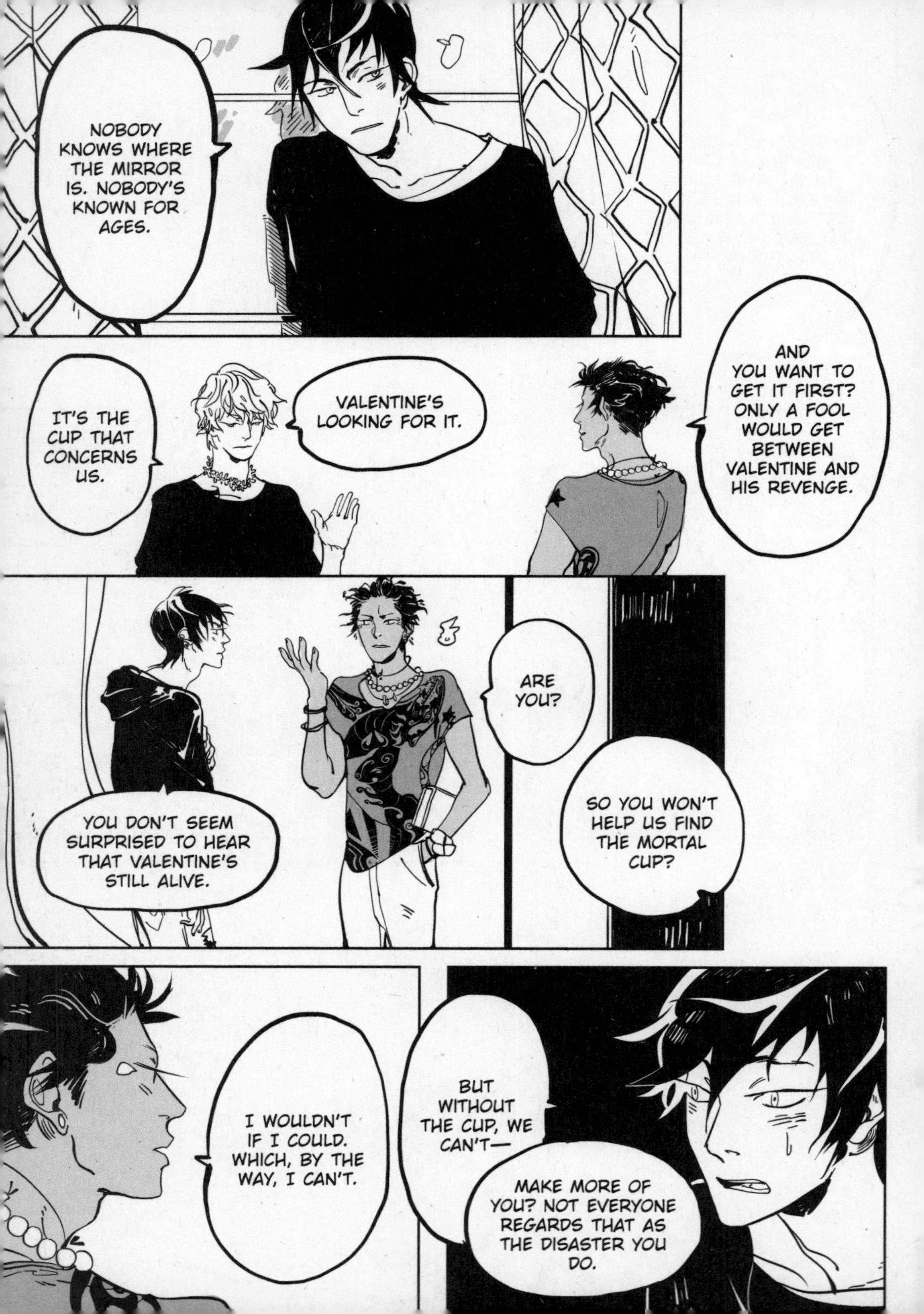
NOBODY KNOWS WHERE THE MIRROR IS. NOBODY'S KNOWN FOR AGES.
IT'S THE CUP THAT CONCERNS US.
VALENTINE'S LOOKING FOR IT.
AND YOU WANT TO GET IT FIRST? ONLY A FOOL WOULD GET BETWEEN VALENTINE AND HIS REVENGE.
YOU DON'T SEEM SURPRISED TO HEAR THAT VALENTINE'S STILL ALIVE.
ARE YOU?
SO YOU WON'T HELP US FIND THE MORTAL CUP?
I WOULDN'T IF I COULD. WHICH, BY THE WAY, I CAN'T.
BUT WITHOUT THE CUP, WE CAN'T—
MAKE MORE OF YOU? NOT EVERYONE REGARDS THAT AS THE DISASTER YOU DO.

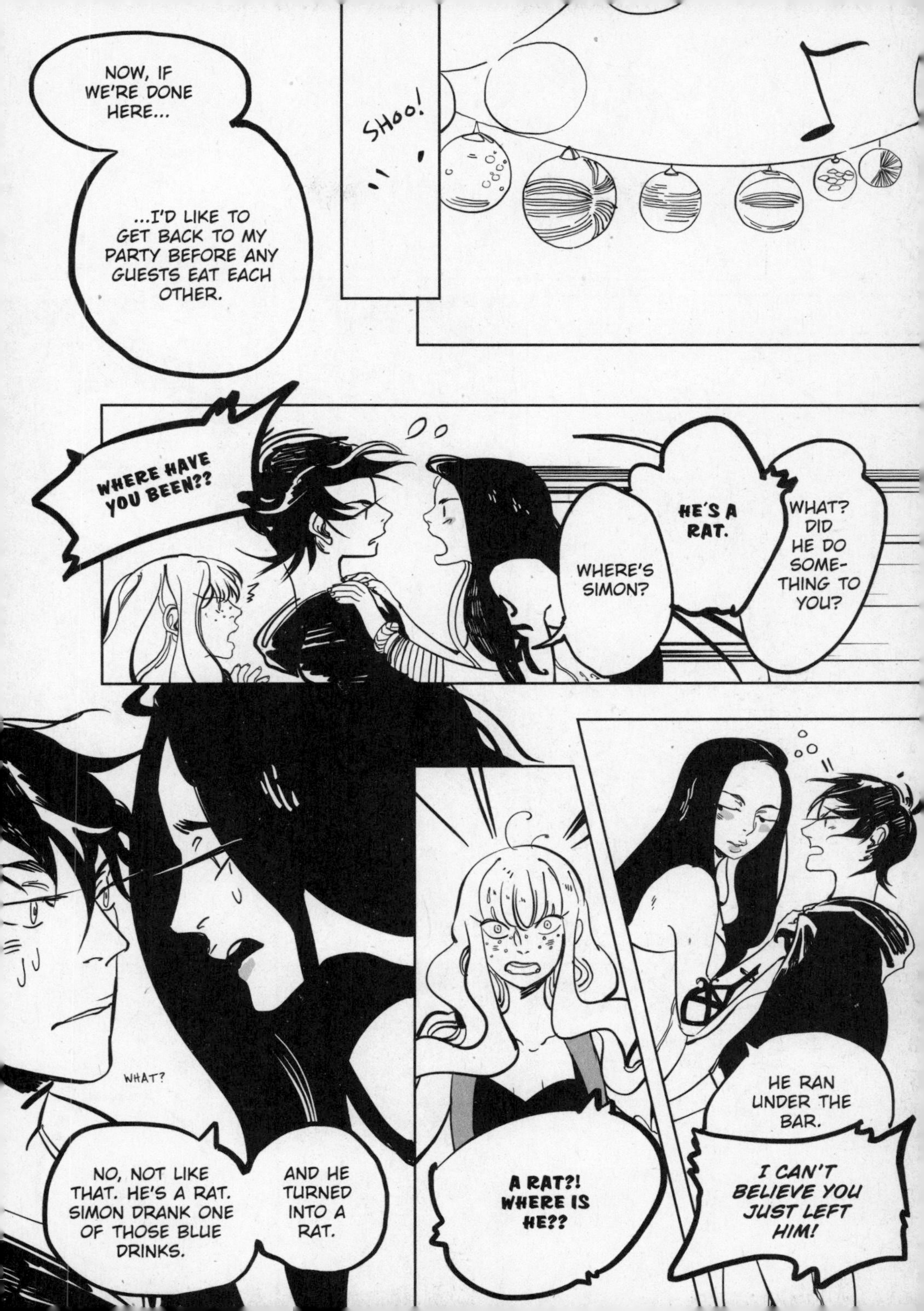
NOW, IF WE'RE DONE HERE...
...I'D LIKE TO GET BACK TO MY PARTY BEFORE ANY GUESTS EAT EACH OTHER.
SHOO!
WHERE HAVE YOU BEEN??
WHERE'S SIMON?
HE'S A RAT.
WHAT? DID HE DO SOME-THING TO YOU?
WHAT?
NO, NOT LIKE THAT. HE'S A RAT. SIMON DRANK ONE OF THOSE BLUE DRINKS.
AND HE TURNED INTO A RAT.
A RAT?! WHERE IS HE??
HE RAN UNDER THE BAR.
I CAN'T BELIEVE YOU JUST LEFT HIM!

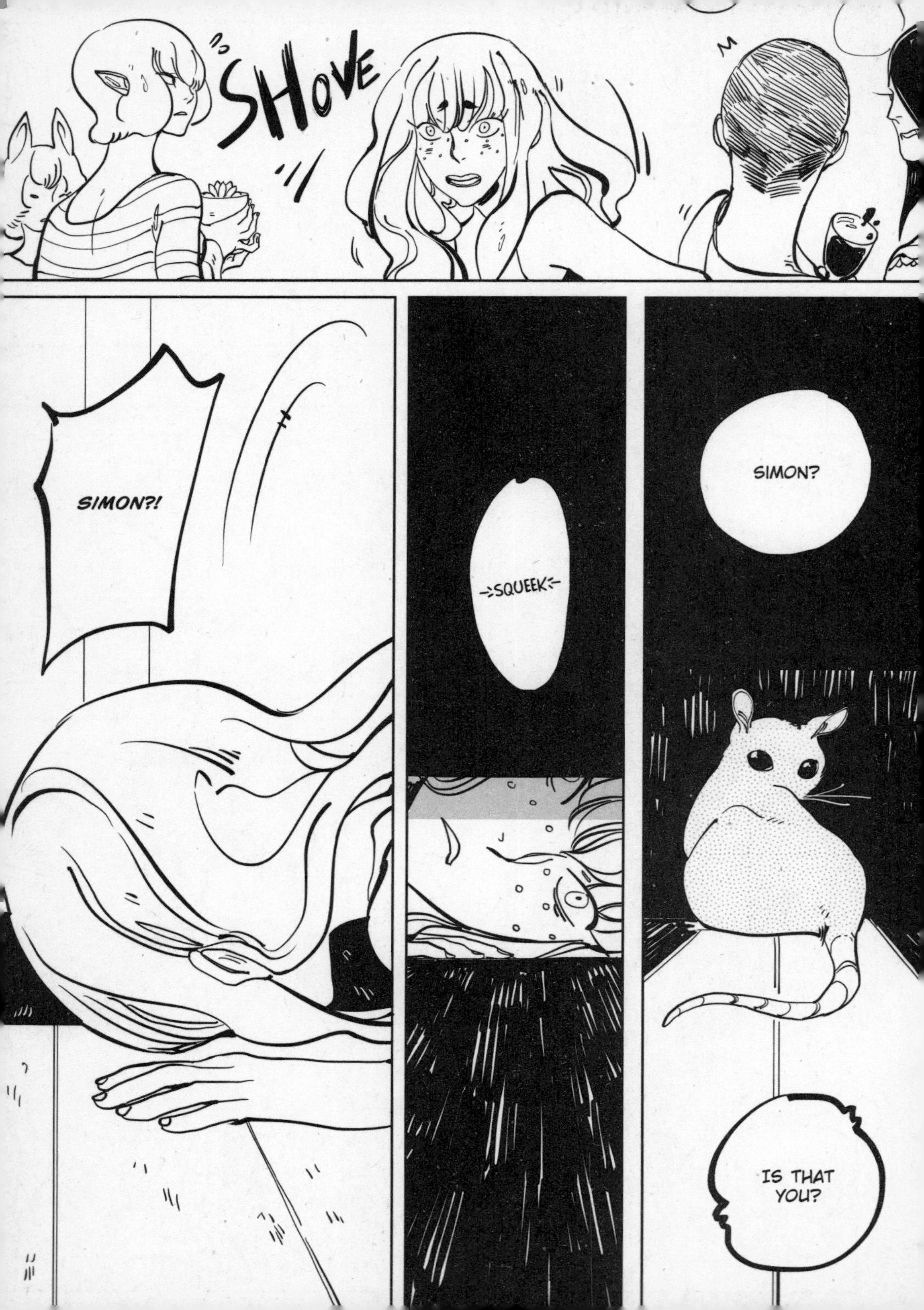
SHOVE
M
SIMON?!
SQUEEK
SIMON?
IS THAT YOU?

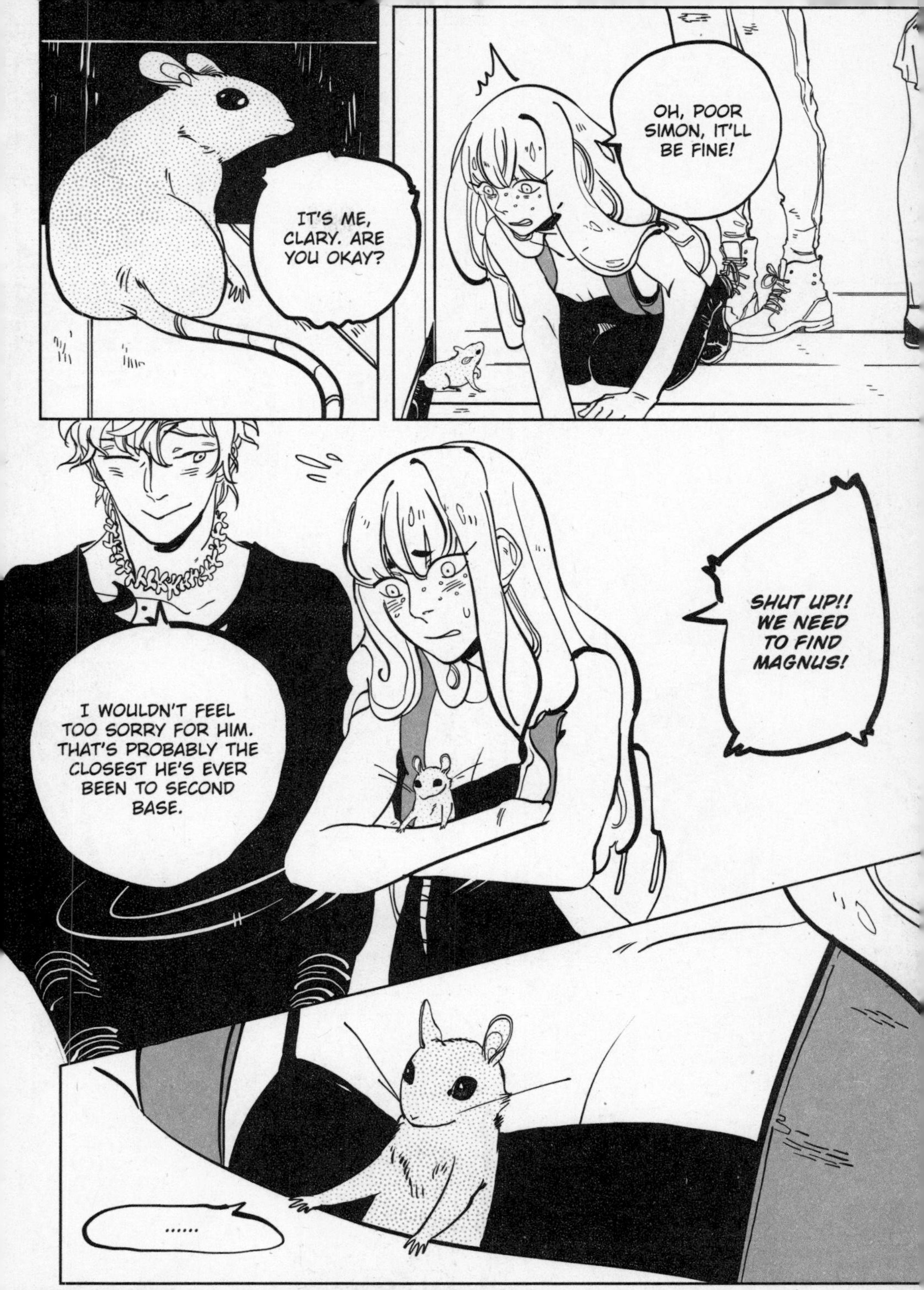
IT'S ME, CLARY. ARE YOU OKAY?
OH, POOR SIMON, IT'LL BE FINE!
I WOULDN'T FEEL TOO SORRY FOR HIM. THAT'S PROBABLY THE CLOSEST HE'S EVER BEEN TO SECOND BASE.
SHUT UP!! WE NEED TO FIND MAGNUS!
......

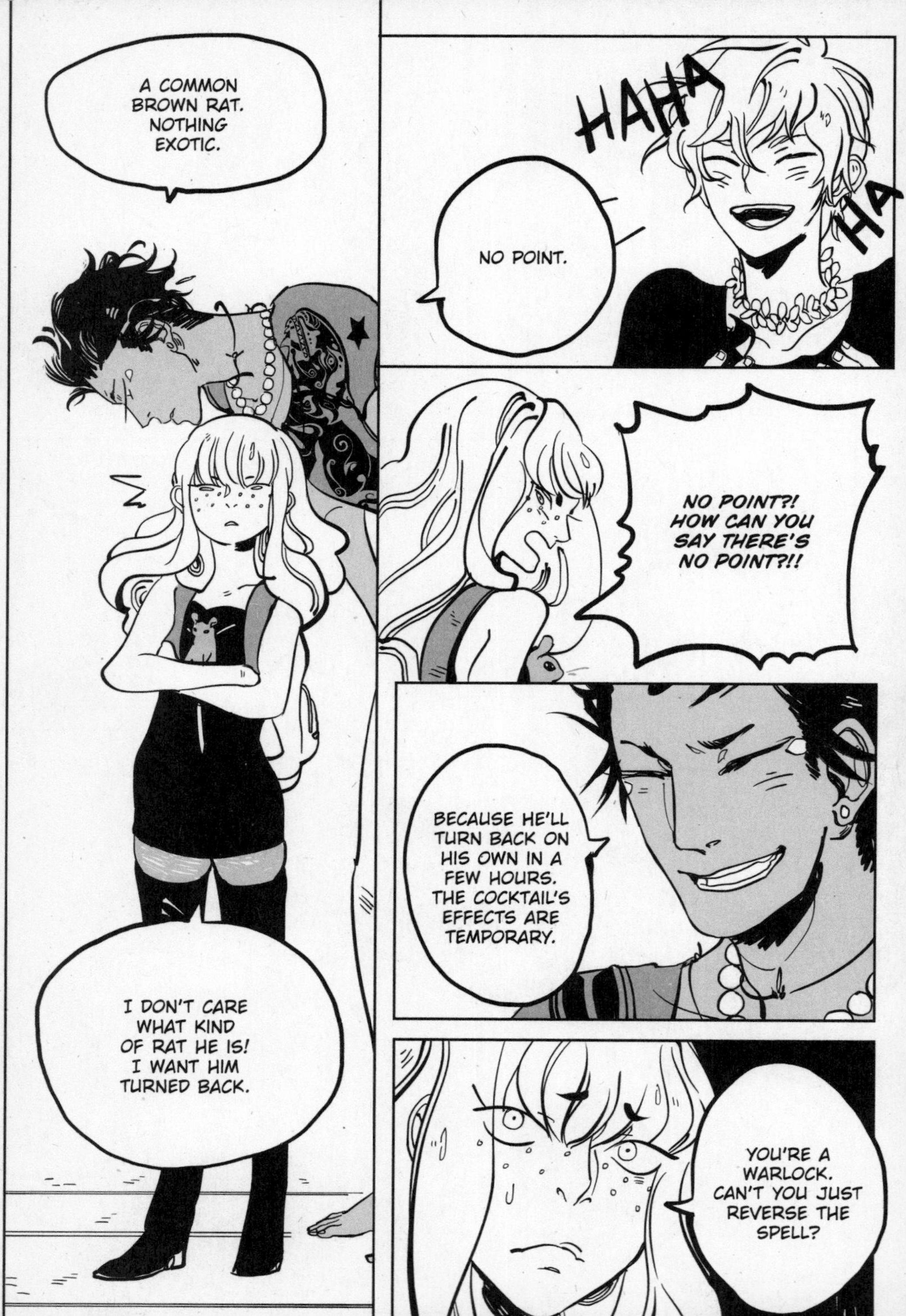
A COMMON BROWN RAT. NOTHING EXOTIC.
I DON'T CARE WHAT KIND OF RAT HE IS! I WANT HIM TURNED BACK.
HAHA
NO POINT.
HA
NO POINT?! HOW CAN YOU SAY THERE'S NO POINT?!!
BECAUSE HE'LL TURN BACK ON HIS OWN IN A FEW HOURS. THE COCKTAIL'S EFFECTS ARE TEMPORARY.
YOU'RE A WARLOCK. CAN'T YOU JUST REVERSE THE SPELL?

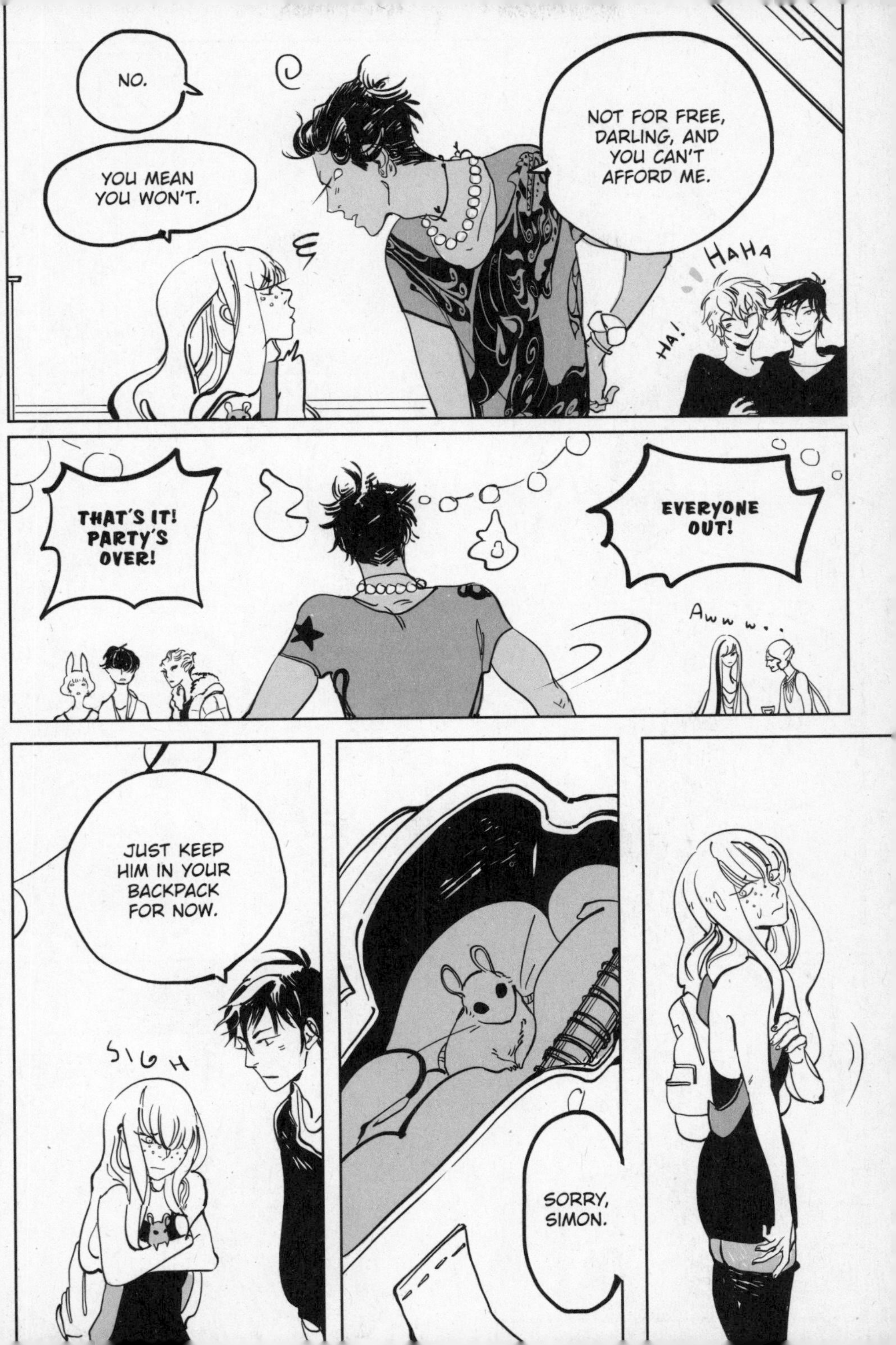
NO.
YOU MEAN YOU WON'T.
NOT FOR FREE, DARLING, AND YOU CAN'T AFFORD ME.
HaHa
HA!
THAT'S IT! PARTY'S OVER!
EVERYONE OUT!
Awww..
JUST KEEP HIM IN YOUR BACKPACK FOR NOW.
SIGH
SORRY, SIMON.

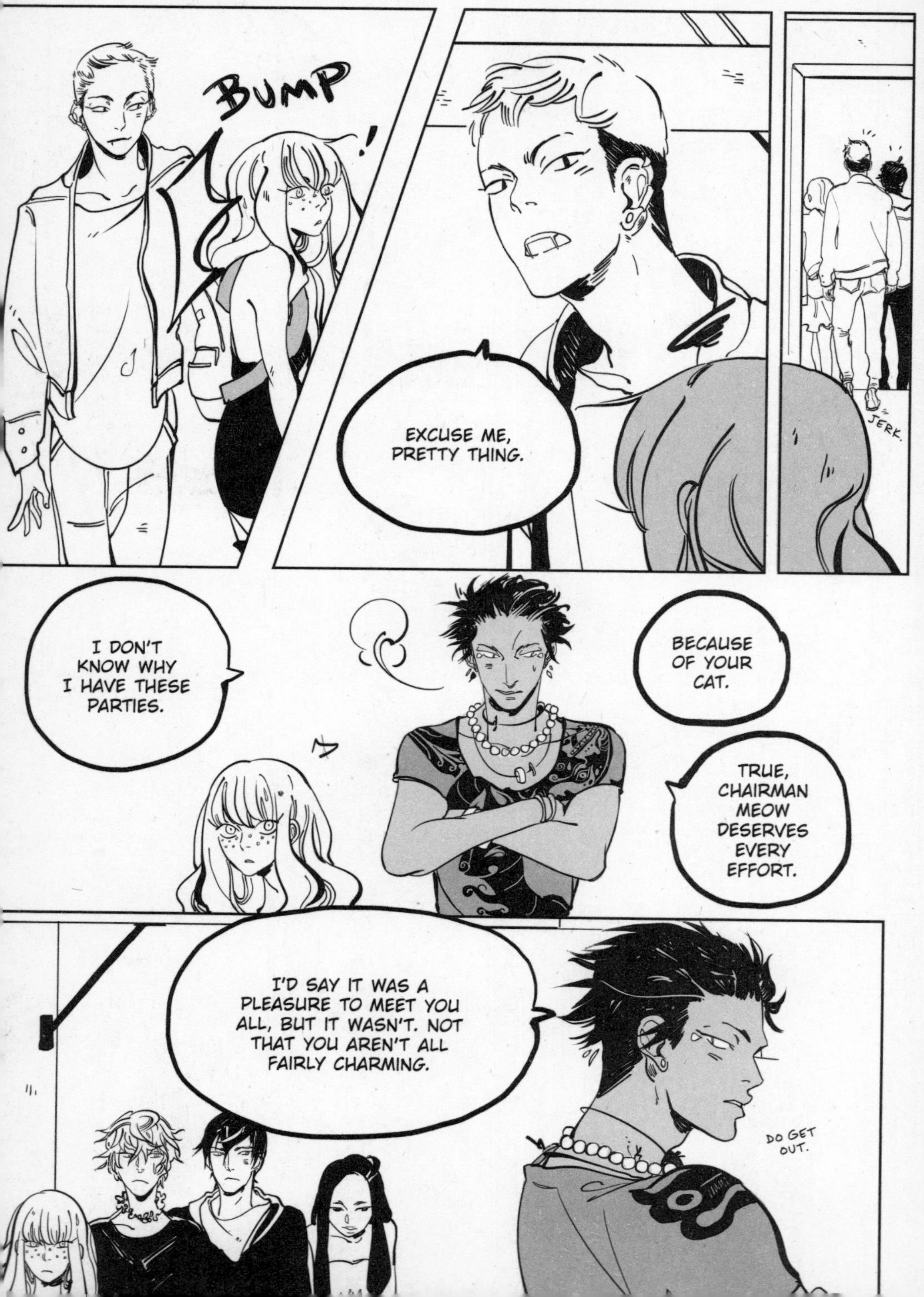
BUMP
!
EXCUSE ME, PRETTY THING.
JERK.
I DON'T KNOW WHY I HAVE THESE PARTIES.
BECAUSE OF YOUR CAT.
TRUE, CHAIRMAN MEOW DESERVES EVERY EFFORT.
I'D SAY IT WAS A PLEASURE TO MEET YOU ALL, BUT IT WASN'T. NOT THAT YOU AREN'T ALL FAIRLY CHARMING.
DO GET OUT.

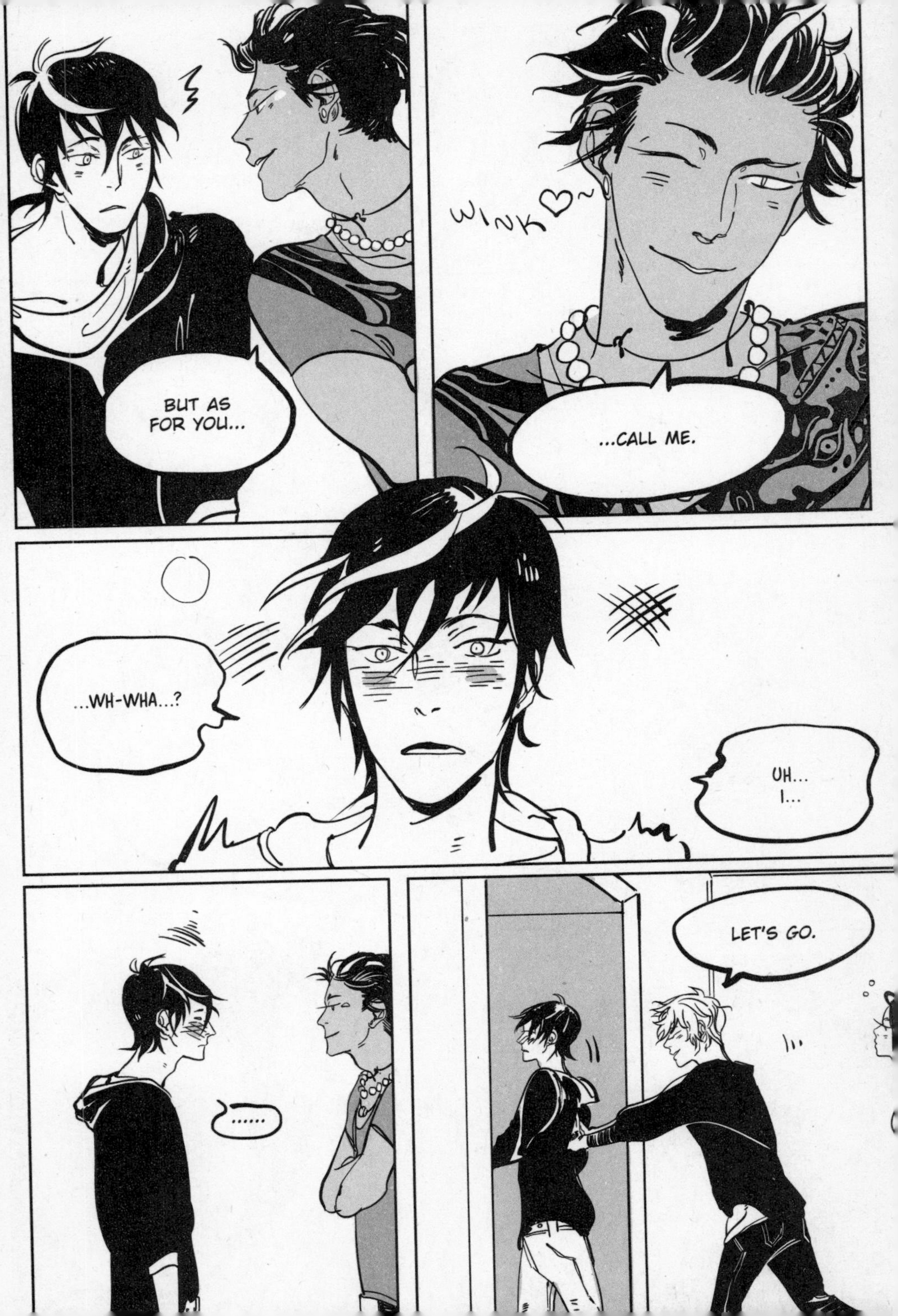
BUT AS FOR YOU...
WINK
...CALL ME.
...WH-WHA...?
UH... I...
......
LET'S GO.

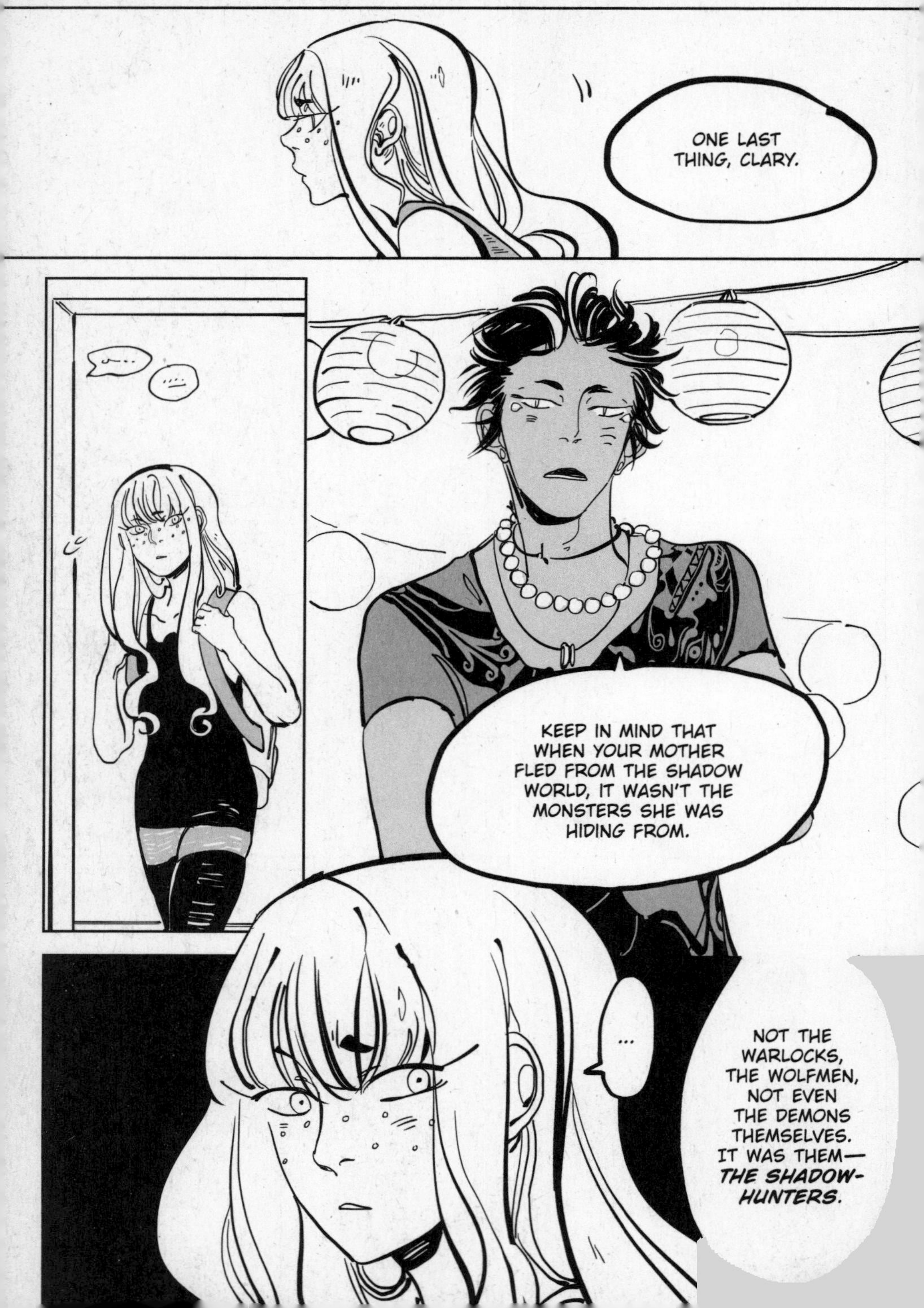
ONE LAST THING, CLARY.
KEEP IN MIND THAT WHEN YOUR MOTHER FLED FROM THE SHADOW WORLD, IT WASN'T THE MONSTERS SHE WAS HIDING FROM.
...
NOT THE WARLOCKS, THE WOLFMEN, NOT EVEN THE DEMONS THEMSELVES. IT WAS THEM—*THE SHADOW-HUNTERS.*

To be continued in the second volume of

THE MORTAL INSTRUMENTS
THE GRAPHIC NOVEL

Finally, I'm done!
Ready for volume 2?
EDITOR
!
YES
I am revived!

See you next time!!

-Cassandra Jean

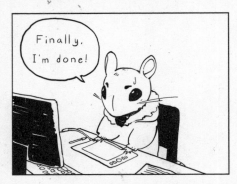

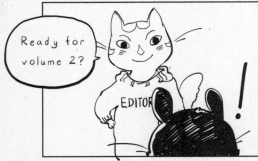

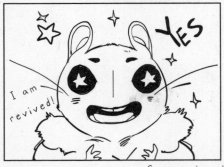